JUDICIAL INDEPENDENCE IN CHINA

This volume challenges the conventional wisdom about judicial independence in China and its relationship to economic growth, rule of law, human rights protection, and democracy.

The volume adopts an interdisciplinary approach that places China's judicial reforms and the struggle to enhance the professionalism, authority, and independence of the judiciary within a broader comparative and developmental framework.

Contributors debate the merits of international best practices and their applicability to China; provide new theoretical perspectives and empirical studies; and discuss civil, criminal, and administrative cases in urban and rural courts.

This volume contributes to several fields, including law and development; the promotion of rule of law and good governance; globalization studies; neoinstitutionalism and studies of the judiciary; the emerging literature on judicial reforms in authoritarian regimes; Asian legal studies; and comparative law more generally.

Randall Peerenboom, formerly a professor at UCLA Law School and Director of the Justice and Society Rule of Law in China Programme at the Oxford Foundation for Law, is currently Associate Fellow of the Oxford University Center for Socio-Legal Studies and a law professor at La Trobe University. He has been a consultant to the Asian Development Bank, Ford Foundation, UNDP, and other international organizations on legal reforms and rule of law in China and Asia. He is coeditor of *The Hague Journal of Rule of Law*. He is also a CIETAC arbitrator and frequently serves as an expert witness on Chinese legal issues. His recent books include *China Modernizes: Threat to the West or Model for the Rest?* (2007), *Regulation in Asia* (2009), *Human Rights in Asia* (2006), *Asian Discourses of Rule of Law* (2004), and *China's Long March toward Rule of Law* (2002).

Judicial Independence in China

LESSONS FOR GLOBAL RULE OF LAW PROMOTION

Edited by
RANDALL PEERENBOOM
La Trobe University

CAMBRIDGE
UNIVERSITY PRESS

CAMBRIDGE UNIVERSITY PRESS
Cambridge, New York, Melbourne, Madrid, Cape Town, Singapore,
São Paulo, Delhi, Dubai, Tokyo

Cambridge University Press
32 Avenue of the Americas, New York, NY 10013-2473, USA

www.cambridge.org
Information on this title: www.cambridge.org/9780521137348

First published 2010

Printed in the United States of America

A catalog record for this publication is available from the British Library.

Library of Congress Cataloging in Publication data

Judicial independence in China : lessons for global rule of law promotion / edited by Randall
Peerenboom.
    p.   cm.
Includes bibliographical references and index.
ISBN 978-0-521-19026-8 (hardback)
1. Judicial independence – China.   I. Peerenboom, R. P. (Randall P.), 1958–
KNQ1612.J83   2009
347.51′012–dc22   2009036866

ISBN 978-0-521-19026-8 Hardback
ISBN 978-0-521-13734-8 Paperback

Contents

Contributors

Randall Peerenboom was Professor at UCLA Law School from 1998 to 2007 and Director of the Justice and Society Rule of Law in China Programme at the Oxford Foundation for Law. He is Associate Fellow of the Oxford University Center for Socio-Legal Studies and a law professor at La Trobe University. He has been a consultant to the Asian Development Bank, Ford Foundation, EU–China, United Nations Development Program (UNDP), and other international organizations on legal reforms and rule of law in China and Asia. He is coeditor of *The Hague Journal of Rule of Law*. He is also a CIETAC arbitrator and frequently serves as an expert witness on Chinese legal issues. His recent books include *China Modernizes: Threat to the West or Model for the Rest?* (2007); *Regulation in Asia* (editor, with John Gillespie, 2009); *Human Rights in Asia* (editor, with Carole J. Petersen and Albert H. Y. Chen, 2006); *Asian Discourses of Rule of Law* (editor, 2004); and *China's Long March toward Rule of Law* (Cambridge University Press, 2002).

Stéphanie Balme is Senior Research Fellow at Sciences Po Paris (CERI) and a visiting professor at Tsinghua University Law School, where she heads the Justice, Law and Society in China Programme. Her teaching areas include comparative constitutional law, comparative politics, constitutional justice, judicial systems in Europe, and the sociology of law. She has worked as a consultant for various French and international organizations. Her most recent publications include *Building Constitutionalism in China* (editor, with Michael Dowdle, 2009); *What Do You Understand of Law and Justice?* (with Wang Yaqin, Nanjing Shifan, and Daxue Chubanshe, 2009) and *Chine, Les Idées Reçues* (2nd edition, 2008).

Chen Lixin is Associate Professor of Law at the Institute of Law of the Shanghai Academy of Social Sciences.

Fu Yulin is Associate Professor at the Peking University Law School. From 1987 to 1994, she served as a judge in the Wuhan Maritime Court. Her main fields of interest are civil procedure, arbitration, legal practice, and dispute resolution. Her publications include "Judicial Supervision, Independence and Justice," in *Supervision and Justice* (2005) and *Function and Construction of the Civil Judicial System* (2006).

Antoine Garapon is a former magistrate and Founder and Director of the Institut des Hautes Etudes sur la Justice and a member of the editorial board of the French magazine *Esprit*. He is the author of *Le Gardien des promesses* (1996), *Bien juger* (2001), *Des crimes qu'on ne peut ni punir ni pardonner* (2002), *Juger en Amérique et en France* (2003), and, most recently, *Peut-on réparer l'histoire* (2008).

Tom Ginsburg earned his BA, JD, and PhD (political science) degrees from the University of California, Berkeley. He is currently Professor of Law at the University of Chicago. He is the author of *Judicial Review in New Democracies* (Cambridge University Press, 2003), coeditor of *The Politics of Courts in Authoritarian Regimes* (with Tamir Moustafa, Cambridge University Press, 2008), and author or editor of several other books on law and politics in East Asia.

Carlo Guarnieri is Professor of Political Science at the University of Bologna. His research interests lie mainly in the field of the comparative analysis of judicial systems and their relationships with political systems. Among his publications in English are *The Power of Judges* (with Patrizia Pederzoli, 2002); "Courts and Marginalized Groups: Perspectives from Continental Europe," in *International Journal of Constitutional Law* (2007); and "Professional Qualifications of the Judiciary in Italy, France and Germany," in Transparency International's, *Global Corruption Report 2007: Corruption in Judicial Systems* (Cambridge University Press, 2007).

Xin He is Associate Professor at City University of Hong Kong Law School and a member of the NYU Global Faculty. He obtained his LLB and LLM degrees from Peking University and his JSM and JSD degrees from Stanford University. He has published many articles in leading journals on law and society, including "Why Do They Not Comply with the Law? Illegality and Semi-Legality among Rural–Urban Migrant Entrepreneurs in Beijing," *Law & Society Review* (2005) and "The Recent Decline of Economic Caseloads in China: Exploration of a Surprising Phenomenon," *The China Quarterly* (2007). His recent research interests focus on empirical research into the Chinese court system, including caseload change, litigants' confidence in the courts, access to justice, and the relationship between the courts and economic development.

Keith E. Henderson has BA and JD degrees and an LLM in international public law from Georgetown University. He was Senior Rule of Law and Anticorruption Adviser at the USAID and then at the IFES for more than eleven years. He led a rule of law assessment mission to China for UNDP in 2006. He has more than fifteen years' development experience on more than forty countries. Seven years ago at American University's Washington College of Law, he created and taught a course titled "Global Corruption and the Rule of Law." One of the world's leading rule of law and anticorruption specialists, he is the author of numerous reports and articles on judicial reforms, corruption, and independence.

Nicholas Calcina Howson is Assistant Professor at the University of Michigan Law School and a former partner of the New York–based international law firm Paul, Weiss, Rifkind, Wharton & Garrison LLP, practicing out of its New York, Paris, London, and Beijing offices. He writes and lectures widely on Chinese law, focusing on China's developing corporate and securities law and financial regulatory systems. He is a member of the Council on Foreign Relations in New York, a former Chair of the Asian Affairs Committee of the New York Bar Association, and a designated arbitrator of the CIETAC. He has consulted on Chinese law for the Ford Foundation, UNDP, Chinese Academy of Social Sciences, Asian Development Bank, and various Chinese ministries, administrative agencies, and law-drafting departments. He has served as an expert in China-related corporate and commercial litigation in the United States and internationally and has taught Chinese law at the Columbia, Cornell, and Harvard law schools.

Ling Li is a lecturer on international private law at the Northwest University of Political Science and Law in Xian, China, where she obtained her master of law degree. In 2002, she was awarded a scholarship from the EU–China Legal and Judicial Cooperation Program to pursue studies on European law. In 2005, she joined the Van Vollenhoven Institute of the University of Leiden in the Netherlands as a PhD researcher. Her current research is on corruption in China's courts.

Pei Fei is Assistant Professor of Law at the Institute of Law, Shanghai Academy of Social Sciences.

Minxin Pei is Senior Associate and Director of the China Program at the Carnegie Endowment for International Peace in Washington, DC. His research focuses on democratization of developing countries, economic reform and governance in China, and U.S.–China relations. He is the author of *From Reform to Revolution: The Demise of Communism in China and the Soviet Union* (1994) and *China's Trapped Transition: The Limits of Developmental Autocracy* (2006). Pei's research has been published in the journals *Foreign Policy, Foreign Affairs, National Interest, Modern China, China Quarterly*, and *Journal of Democracy*, and in many edited books. Pei is a frequent commentator on BBC World News, Voice of America, and National Public Radio. His op-eds have appeared in the *Financial Times, The New York Times, The Washington Post, Newsweek International, The International Herald Tribune*, and other major newspapers. He received his PhD in political science from Harvard University.

Zhu Suli is Dean of the Peking Law School. His research interests include judicial reforms in China, legal theory, sociology of law, and constitutional law. He is the author of many books and articles, including *Rule of Law and Local Resources* (1996), *Reading the Social Order* (1999), *Sending Laws to the Countryside* (2000), *Academia and Society in 20th Century China* (editor, 2001).

Zhang Guoyan is Professor of Law at the Institute of Law of the Shanghai Academy of Social Sciences.

1

Introduction

Randall Peerenboom

This is the first book in English on judicial independence in China.[1] This may not seem surprising given China remains an effectively single-party socialist authoritarian state, the widely reported prosecutions of political dissidents and the conventional wisdom that China has never had independent courts. On the other hand, this may seem surprising given that China has become a possible model for other developing countries – a model that challenges key assumptions of the multibillion-dollar rule of law promotion industry, including the central importance of judicial independence for all we hold near and dear. Although China's success in achieving economic growth and reducing poverty is well known, less well known is that China outscores the average country in its income class, including many democracies, on many rule of law and good governance indicators, as well as most major indicators of human rights and well-being, with the notable exception of civil and political rights.[2] How has China managed all this without independent courts?

WHY STUDY JUDICIAL INDEPENDENCE IN CHINA?

There are few ideas more cherished, and less critically scrutinized, than judicial independence. Judicial independence is regularly portrayed as essential to rule of law, good governance, economic growth, democracy, human rights, and geopolitical stability. Notwithstanding nearly universal support for the notion of judicial

---

[1] Other works provide an overview of the legal system and legal reforms, including the overall development of the judiciary. Randall Peerenboom, *China's Long March toward Rule of Law* (Cambridge: Cambridge University Press, 2002), Stanley Lubman, *Bird in a Cage* (Palo Alto: Stanford University Press, 1999), Albert Chen, *Introduction to the PRC Legal System* (Hong Kong: Butterworths, 2nd ed., 2004), Chen Jianfu, *Chinese Law: Context and Transformation* (Leiden and Boston: Nijhoff, 2008); Stéphanie Balme and Michael Dowdle eds., *Building Constitutionalism in China* (New York: Palgrave McMillan, 2009).

[2] Randall Peerenboom, *China Modernizes: Threat to the West or Model for the Rest?* (London and New York: Oxford University Press, 2008).

independence, the concept remains disturbingly contested and unclear even in economically advanced liberal democracies known for the rule of law, as pointed out
by two leading U.S. constitutional scholars:

> Consensus on broad values combined with discord over their application in par-
> ticular cases is hardly uncommon, in law or anything else. But the range of dis-
> agreement when it comes to judicial independence seems unusually wide. We
> expect controversy over how to draw the line between proper and improper judicial
> behavior in particular cases, but there is as much uncertainty in locating the line
> between proper and improper external influences. Indeed, we do not have anything
> approaching consensus even with respect to the normative conditions necessary to
> have a properly independent bench. There is disagreement about whether or how to
> criticize judges and their decisions, and about whether or how to discipline judges.
> There is disagreement about how to explain or justify our institutional arrange-
> ments . . . And, of course, there is pervasive disagreement about whether our judges
> exhibit too much or too little independence.[3]

The problems are magnified when we move beyond economically advanced
liberal democracies to developing countries and nonliberal authoritarian regimes.
As Tom Ginsburg observes in this volume: "Judicial independence has become
like freedom: everyone wants it but no one knows quite what it looks like, and it is
easiest to observe in its absence. We know when judges are dependent on politicians
or outside pressures, but have more difficulty saying definitively when judges are
independent."

One goal of this volume is to subject judicial independence and the claims made
on its behalf to critical scrutiny. China is useful for testing general theories in that
it represents a challenge to so much of the common wisdom about what judicial
independence means, its importance, its relation to other social objectives, and how
to achieve it. Most fundamentally, what *is* socialist rule of law? How does it differ
from rule of law in a liberal democracy? And what are the implications for judicial
independence?

China's rapid growth also challenges the prevailing wisdom. For many, China is
an exception to the rule in that it has grown allegedly without "the rule of law" and an
independent judiciary. But what role has the legal system played in economic growth
in China? Have the courts been able to handle commercial cases independently?
Are property rights protected in other ways? To the extent that there are external
influences on judges in commercial cases, including party and government policy
directives, do they promote or hinder economic development?

A second goal is to contribute to, and draw on, the emerging literature on the
development of legal systems in authoritarian regimes. Judicial independence is
often assumed to be impossible in authoritarian regimes, where law plays a limited

---

3   John A. Ferejohn and Larry D. Kramer, "Independent Judges, Dependent Judiciary: Institutionalizing
    Judicial Restraints," *New York University Law Review*, vol. 77 (2002).

role in governance and takes a back seat to government policies and ruling party diktats, legal institutions are unable to restrain political power, and judges are faithful servants of the ruling regime. Yet even a cursory glance at authoritarian regimes – whether historical or contemporary, whether in Europe or in East Asia, Latin America, Africa, or the Middle East – reveals that law plays a much larger role in authoritarian states than commonly believed.[4] Nor is that particularly surprising. Authoritarian regimes turn to courts for many reasons, including to facilitate economic growth, maintain social order, supervise and discipline local officials, define and enforce relationships between central and local governments, monitor boundaries between competing state organs, distance the ruling regime from unpopular decisions, and enhance regime legitimacy at home and abroad.[5]

Conversely, it is commonly assumed that democratic regimes favor judicial independence. Yet even the most cursory glance at democratic regimes – whether historical or contemporary, whether in Europe or in East Asia, Latin America, Africa, or the Middle East – demonstrates that democracy does not guarantee judicial independence.[6] Many legal systems in developing democracies are plagued by judicial corruption, incompetence, and inefficiency. The judiciary is often controlled by the executive, beholden to the political and economic elite, threatened by organized crime, and subject to social pressure from the public and media. Clearly, much depends on the particular regime, whether authoritarian or democratic. There is therefore a need to move beyond simplistic black and white portrayals based on regime type.

This is not to say that political structures are irrelevant. Courts in authoritarian states may enjoy considerable independence, although usually over a limited scope of issues. They often enjoy more autonomy in commercial law than with respect to protecting civil and political rights. One question is whether there will be spillover to other areas. More generally, what are the limits of law and judicial independence in authoritarian regimes? What mechanisms do authoritarian regimes use to limit judicial independence? Has China employed similar mechanisms? Has it developed alternative ways of controlling the judiciary?

A third related goal is to sort out sense from nonsense about judicial independence and the legal system in China. As with other authoritarian regimes, blanket

---

[4] See Tamir Moustafa and Tom Ginsburg, eds., *Rule by Law: The Politics of Courts in Authoritarian Regimes* (New York: Cambridge University Press, 2008); Lisa Hilbink, *Judges Beyond Politics in Democracy and Dictatorship* (Cambridge: Cambridge University Press, 2007); see also Chapters 12 and 13 in this volume and the cites therein.

[5] See Moustafa and Ginsburg, "Introduction: The Functions of Courts in Authoritarian Politics," in Moustafa and Ginsburg, *Rule by Law*.

[6] For problems in judicial independence, corruption, and incompetence in Bangladesh, Cambodia, Nepal, Indonesia, Pakistan, the Philippines, and Thailand, see Asian Development Bank, "Judicial Independence Overview and Country-level Summaries," (2003), p. 2, http://www.adb.org/Documents/Events/2003/RETA5987/Final_Overview_Report.pdf. See also Chapter 5 in this volume and the cites therein.

denunciations of the lack of meaningful independence in China fail to capture the more complex reality. The courts handle more than 8 million cases a year. Judicial independence is not an issue in many cases, nor is the source, likelihood, or impact of interference the same across cases.

There is therefore a pressing need to get beyond outdated stereotypes and broad generalizations, to examine a wider range of cases than just high-profile conflicts involving political dissidents so prominently featured in the reports of human rights groups and the Western media, and to overcome the knee-jerk reaction to blame all judicial shortcomings on the party and lack of U.S.-style separation of powers. In short, there is a need for more nuanced studies, new analytic frameworks, and thicker descriptions of the actual issues judges face in their daily lives, the reasons for existing policies, and the responses of the judiciary to such policies. The development of the legal system in China must also be situated within a broader comparative framework of other developing countries, many of which are experiencing similar issues.

Even assuming the conventional wisdom is correct and judicial independence is necessary or useful for many of the goals mentioned previously, there is still the all-important question of how to achieve it. Thus a fourth goal is to scrutinize the dominant approach of the rule of law industry to prescribing "international best practices." It is now clear in light of the historical development of legal systems in Euro-America, Asia, and some countries in Eastern Europe, Latin America, and the Middle East that there is no single path toward the rule of law and that rule of law principles are consistent with a wide variety of institutional arrangements, although implications for policy makers are far from clear. Moreover, the less than spectacular results of rule of law promotion efforts call into question the role and influence of foreign actors, as well as the assumption that the best way for developing states to achieve rule of law is to mimic or transplant Euro-American institutions, values, and practices.

China is an interesting test case in that it has pursued its own approach to reforms. China did not adopt the big bang approach to economic reforms or follow the neoliberal aspects of the Washington Consensus, including rapid privatization, deregulation, and opening of the domestic economy to international competition. Like other successful East Asian states, it has postponed democratization until it attains a higher level of economic and institutional development. Also, like other successful East Asian states, it has adopted a two-track approach to legal development that emphasizes commercial law while imposing limits on the exercise of civil and political rights. But what are the costs of this gradualist approach? Will China be able to maintain and deepen the reform agenda, or will the reform process stall, leaving China another example of a dysfunctional middle-income state that once showed great promise?

In addressing these issues, the authors in this volume adopt a variety of perspectives and approaches reflecting the interdisciplinary, holistic, and comparative nature of the development process. There are contributions from legal scholars, political scientists, and sociologists. Some authors take an institutional approach, whereas others opt for a historical–cultural approach. Several chapters address the debate over globalization and the need to adapt universal norms and practices to local contexts. Some chapters are comparative, with authors drawing on the experiences of countries in Europe, the Middle East, and East Asia. The authors also consider different levels of wealth and the diverse challenges faced by low-, middle-, and high-income countries, as well as differences in the nature of the political regime.

Theoretically, several chapters challenge conventional assumptions about judicial independence. Others develop new analytical frameworks that differentiate among types of cases, sources of interference, and levels of courts. Whereas some chapters focus on urban courts, others focus on rural courts. There are discussions of civil, criminal, and administrative cases. Several chapters present data from recent empirical studies, complementing and enriching new and existing theoretical perspectives.

CHAPTER SYNOPSES

The volume begins by situating the debate over judicial independence in China within the larger debate over the rule of law industry approach of promoting international best practices. In Chapter 2, Keith Henderson draws on his extensive experience in the industry to summarize international best practices, captured in 18 JIP (Judicial Integrity Principles). The JIP are modeled largely on the current institutions, values, and practices in economically advanced Western liberal democracies and reflect the experience of USAID, International Foundation for Electoral Systems (IFES), and others in promoting rule of law in developing countries. Henderson also summarizes the main principles of a pragmatic, context-specific methodology for judicial reforms developed more fully elsewhere.

Henderson draws on his personal experience in advising on judicial reforms in China to shed light on the applicability of international best practices to China. As he and others in this volume note, there is widespread support for more independent courts from the central government, from judges and other legal complex actors, from investors and business people, and from the broad public. However, notwithstanding general support for the JIP, he also found that some of the JIP were opposed by one group or another for a variety of political, institutional, historical, practical, and interest-based reasons. Many participants questioned the feasibility of some of the reforms, particularly those beyond the authority of the judiciary to implement on its own. As in other countries, including other successful East Asian countries during their phase of rapid growth under authoritarian regimes, the main emphasis was on politically safer reforms aimed at promoting judicial efficiency, legal predictability, and legal consistency in the economic sector.

In Chapter 3, although not disputing the normative desirability of the JIP, Antoine Garapon, a former judge and current director of the Institut des Hautes Etudes sur la Justice, raises serious doubts about the dominant approach of prescribing international best practices. Drawing on his own extensive comparative experiences,

Garapon argues that this approach ignores culture and politics and is inconsistent with the way legal systems actually develop. Legal reforms do not occur within a political vacuum. Powerful interests are at stake. For reforms to be successful, they must take into account opposing interests and existing conditions. In some cases, compromises are necessary, as in the "unholy alliance" between the Judges Club and Islamists in Egypt.

Garapon recommends more attention be paid to the process of reform and, in particular, to the historical process by which judicial independence has been achieved in developed countries, as well as the political battles being fought in countries now trying to establish independent judiciaries. Rather than beginning with a predetermined set of abstract principles for judicial independence, he suggests that we begin with a detailed study of the forms of interference and their impact in particular contexts. In that sense, the differences between Garapon and Henderson may not be as great as it first appears because Henderson advocates a similar methodology for judicial reforms in his chapter.

The debate between Henderson and Garapon reflects the different emphases of an institutional versus a cultural–historical approach,[7] which in turn reflects long-standing debates over the possibility and desirability of legal transplants.[8] In general, advocates of a cultural–historical approach place more emphasis on path dependencies and the often unpredictable nature of legal reforms. As such, they see legal development as nonlinear and the process as less teleological and more open-ended than one that focuses on achieving prescribed substantive standards or best practices.

In Chapter 4, Zhu Suli, Dean of Peking Law School and one of China's leading legal theorists, employs the cultural–historical approach in challenging the notion that judicial independence is the appropriate lens through which to view judicial reforms in China. Zhu provides a broad historical overview of the Kuomintang and Chinese Communist Party (CCP) regimes to situate the judiciary within the political context of an effectively single-party state. Echoing Garapon, he argues that "rather than searching for, or aspiring to, some decontextualized abstraction or ideal type of judicial independence, we should pay more attention to the actual role of the Party and its influence on the judiciary, the legal system, and China's efforts at modernization more generally." Although disagreeing with some party decisions, he concludes that, on balance, the CCP has played a positive role. Moreover, while some judicial problems may be attributable to party policies, he suggests

7 For the historical–cultural approach, see generally Paul Kahn, *The Cultural Study of Law* (Chicago: University of Chicago Press, 1999). In addition to the chapters by Garapon and Zhu in this volume, see also Jonathan Ocko and David Gilmartin, "State, Sovereignty, and the People: A Comparison of the 'Rule of Law' in China and India," *The Journal of Asian Studies*, vol. 68(1).

8 R.L. Abel, "Law as a Lag: Inertia as a Social Theory of Law," *Michigan L. Rev* vol. 80, pp. 775–809 (1982); Alan Watson, *Legal Transplants* (Athens: University of Georgia Press, 1983); William Twining, "Generalizing about Law: The Case of Legal Transplants" (2002), http://www.ucl.ac.uk/laws/jurisprudence/docs/twi_til_4.pdf.

that the more fundamental cause of shortcomings in the judiciary is the recent unprecedented social transformation of Chinese society.

In Chapter 5, Peerenboom also challenges many assumptions underlying common views about judicial independence in China, including that there is a single agreed upon model or generally accepted set of institutions and best practices articulated with sufficient specificity to guide reformers; that the main source of external interference is the party; and that if China were to suddenly democratize, judicial independence would no longer be a problem. He then breaks the concept of judicial independence down into different subcomponents and analyzes China's progress on each. Although progress has undoubtedly been made on each dimension, it has been uneven. He ends with policy recommendations for enhancing judicial independence and limiting judicial corruption.

Whereas Chapter 5 adopts an institutional approach, Fu Yulin and Peerenboom develop a new case-based analytical framework in Chapter 6. They distinguish between pure political cases, politically sensitive cases, and ordinary cases and highlight three types of politically sensitive cases: socio-economic, new crimes, and class actions. They then discuss the sources, nature, and impact of interference for each type of case and provide recommendations tailored to particular problems that arise. They emphasize, as do others, that judicial independence is not an end in itself but a means to other goals, and that there is substantive disagreement in China about how independent the courts should be and whether the courts are the appropriate forum for resolving certain types of disputes, notwithstanding the global trend toward judicialization. They also show that reforms to enhance judicial independence entail a wide range of changes that affect not just the judiciary as an institution but substantive and procedural law, the balance of power among state organs, party–state relations, and social attitudes and practices. An approach focused primarily on the judiciary, or even on state institutions, is therefore not sufficient.

In Chapter 7, Nicholas Howson illustrates the benefits of a case-based approach in his detailed study of more than 1000 corporate law cases in Shanghai courts. He notes that amendments to the Company Law in 2006 represent a radical shift from self-enforcement to a litigation-centered model for resolving corporate disputes. He finds that Shanghai courts are now more competent, autonomous, and independent, and have ruled against government entities, state-owned enterprises, and other politically and economically powerful, well-connected commercial actors and investors. The courts have also indirectly showed signs of autonomy in acting as guardians of the commercial order, seeking to protect a sphere for privately ordered economic activity from intrusion by mandatory business regulations.

On the other hand, the limits of judicial independence were evident in the courts' deference to national economic and social policies in contravention of the Company Law and in the courts' reluctance to hear cases involving companies limited by shares. In each case, the courts are animated by both explicit instruction from superior bureaucratic organs and voluntary self-restraint.

There are a number of reasons for these externally and internally imposed limitations. Some reflect the limited experience of the courts with new types of claims; others reflect plaintiff and judicial deference to the China Securities Regulatory Commission and public prosecutor; still others reflect concerns for market and social stability. Scholars and commentators may disagree about the wisdom of moving slowly or refusing to hear certain cases for these reasons, at least for the moment. More worrisome from the standpoint of judicial independence and justice is the refusal to hear cases because of the superior political power of one of the parties. This concern should not be overstated. As Howson points out, Shanghai courts decided against politically powerful parties in all of the more than 200 opinions reviewed in full where there was a discernable political interest.

Whatever the reasons for the court's reluctance to hear certain types of corporate cases, Howson argues that the failure to apply the new provisions to public companies is "tragic" because the Company Law was amended in part to address corporate governance in such firms. He concludes by suggesting that the current approach of Shanghai courts may not be sustainable in the long run given the rapid rise of group plaintiff cases and popular anger against politically and economically privileged insiders.

In Chapter 8, Stéphanie Balme provides the kind of thick description of the lived reality of judges in rural courts advocated by others in this volume as the proper basis for a successful reform agenda. Various studies cited in this volume have demonstrated significant differences between rural and urban courts in terms of the level of professionalism of judges, judicial salaries and benefits, judicial corruption, the nature of cases, enforcement of court judgments, and citizens' willingness to litigate and satisfaction levels when they do. On the whole, the quality of judges and justice is much higher in urban courts than in rural courts. Drawing on years of fieldwork in basic level courts in remote Shaanxi and Gansu provinces, two of the poorest provinces in China, Balme finds that local judges are better trained and more professional than in the past, although technical competence remains an issue, with only half of the judges in lower courts in these two provinces having obtained college degrees in law. She also finds that despite assurances of de jure independence, judges lack de facto independence. Until recently, local courts have been funded by the local government, although the State Council announced in 2008 that funding was to be centralized. Although centralized funding may lead to significantly less local protectionism and more independence vis-à-vis local governments, it remains to be seen whether the funding will be adequate and make its way to basic courts. Moreover, local people's congresses and party organs still play a role in the appointment and promotion of judges.

Lack of adequate funding is not the only issue, however. Judges in basic level courts, particularly in rural areas, lack prestige and social status. They are often treated like other civil servants and assigned nonjudicial or quasi-judicial tasks such as political mobilization and legal education for the public. Under Hu Jintao's leadership, the judiciary has been given the new roles of contributing to "social harmony" and, in light of the global economic crisis, of maintaining economic growth and social stability.

As Carlo Guarnieri points out in his chapter, judges are heavily influenced by their reference group. Yet rural judges in local courts are often isolated from professional networks and in some cases slighted by better trained and higher-paid judges in higher courts and urban areas. Thus, they may look to similarly situated judges or to local government and business elites. As Balme notes, like party and government officials, judges are somewhat more educated and better informed than the average villager. On the other hand, many judges are also similar in social background and economic status to the parties that appear before them in court. This close social proximity between judges and citizens may lead judges to be more sympathetic to the plight of weaker parties and thus to turn to alternative dispute resolution methods such as mediation, where judges enjoy greater discretion and exert greater control. Either way, the close relation to local elites or average citizens that characterizes the dense social network of local village life facilitates ex parte meetings and increases the likelihood of corruption. Nevertheless, Balme sees hope for the judiciary's future in the combination of top-down and bottom-up reform efforts aimed at enhancing the professionalism, financial security, and authority of judges in basic level courts, although fundamental changes that rely on forces beyond the judiciary's control will be necessary if China is to meet international standards for judicial independence.

In Chapter 9, Xin He focuses on a particular type of administrative case in rural areas involving "married out women" (MOW) – that is, women who leave their home village after they are married and are then denied economic benefits from their home village. He shows that lower courts in Guangdong province have effectively resisted pressure from party and government organs to solve these disputes, raising questions about the extent to which they are controlled by superior political powers. Citing legal barriers and enforcement difficulties, the courts resisted the global trend to judicialize these disputes, pushing them back to political and administrative channels. However, the courts then demonstrated their strategic sophistication by claiming the right to review the government's decisions in administrative litigation. In so doing, the courts retain an advantageous position in the power relationship with the governments. Moreover, as these cases inevitably leave some groups dissatisfied, the court can avoid public displeasure by forcing the government to make the decision. He concludes that Chinese courts are capable of deliberating about and transforming their situation by strategically interpreting the law and negotiating with superior powers. Consistent with findings in other chapters, he suggests that judicial independence in China is far more complicated than is often recognized and that judicial behavior cannot be adequately explained without thick descriptions of legal arguments, resource constraints, and strategic interpretations open to the courts in a particular context.

As Henderson points out, and empirical studies confirm, most judiciaries in developing countries, whether democratic or authoritarian, suffer from judicial corruption. Judicial corruption undermines judicial independence directly in particular cases and indirectly in support for long-term reforms that grant judges more independence. Simply put, giving more independence and authority to corrupt or incompetent judges will not lead to more just outcomes.[9] Thus, another lesson learned is the need to sequence reforms in a way that balances judicial independence and judicial accountability.

In Chapter 10, Ling Li draws on an extensive data set of confirmed cases of judges sanctioned for corruption over a ten-year period to develop a new analytical framework for judicial corruption. She distinguishes between corruption at different stages (case acceptance, adjudication phase, and enforcement); forms of corruption (physical abuse, theft and embezzlement, bribery or influence-peddling); levels of, and divisions within, courts; and rank of judges. Among her key findings are that corruption is most likely in civil (especially commercial) cases, followed by criminal cases, and rare in administrative cases. Corruption is most common during the adjudication phase, followed by enforcement, and relatively rare during the case acceptance phase. By far the most common type of corruption is bribery and influence-peddling. Physical abuse of parties is rare and largely confined to lower level courts. Although higher court judges did engage in corruption, there were few cases where the corruption resulted in a gross miscarriage of justice reflected in a judgment clearly at odds with the law. Rather, corrupt court presidents were most likely to be guilty of taking kickbacks on construction projects to build new courthouses or of accepting bribes from subordinates seeking promotions.

The next chapter, by Minxin Pei, Guoyan Zhang, Fei Pei, and Lixin Chen, fills in the picture presented by Ling Li by providing a detailed survey of commercial and property cases in Shanghai courts involving both private and corporate parties. The survey sheds light on when parties choose to litigate, the pretrial and trial processes, the extent and sources of outside influence on the courts, and people's attitudes and satisfaction levels, including their perceptions of corruption and the role of lawyers in resolving disputes. The study demonstrates that the judiciary has become more professional, at least in major urban areas, and that parties generally view the litigation process favorably. This confirms results found in several other surveys.[10]

Nevertheless, the courts are subject to considerable outside influence in civil cases, most notably from the parties themselves. Corporate parties are more likely than private parties to seek to influence judges, usually through gift-giving and dinners. This is not because private parties are loath to engage in such behavior, but because they do not know how to go about it. Corporate parties are more likely to hire lawyers

---

[9] Transparency International, "Global Corruption Report: Corruption and Judicial System," (2007) http://www.transparency.org/publications/gcr/download_gcr#download.

[10] See Chapter 6 and the cites therein.

or to be part of a social network that includes people on friendly terms with judges. In contrast, private parties rarely hire lawyers and, in urban areas, are generally not part of the same social and professional circles as judges. The importance of banquets and gift-giving in Chinese culture presents many opportunities for direct or indirect contact between company managers, lawyers, and judges. Much of the dining and gift-giving is part of longstanding social practices that occur among friends even when they have no cases pending rather than the explicit quid pro quo type where parties meet with a judge hearing a pending case to influence the outcome by offering gifts or other incentives.

Although the impact of such behavior is difficult to measure, the winning parties, whether corporate or private, generally believe that they won based on the merits of their case – the law and the facts – rather than because of corruption. On the other hand, a significant number of losing parties believe they lost because of outside influence. Interestingly, a much higher percentage of private parties thought they lost because of influence from the other side, even though in fact private parties were much less likely to engage in corrupt practices. Private parties may not have a good understanding of the law, and generally they do not hire lawyers. Accordingly, they may overestimate their chances of succeeding in court. Conversely, corporate clients are more likely to be repeat players and to have lawyers. Therefore, they are more likely to have a more accurate idea of their chances. In any event, the perception that judges are influenced by the other party, even if inaccurate, undermines public trust in the judiciary, particularly among private parties.

The volume ends by stepping back and situating China's progress within a broader comparative perspective. In Chapter 12, Carlo Guarnieri considers and applies the experiences of legal systems in authoritarian Europe to China. He emphasizes that judicial behavior depends on a judge's education and reference group(s). In democracies with a hierarchical civil law system, the reference group tends to lie within the judiciary, with judges looking to more senior judges, whereas in common law systems, judges tend to look outside the judiciary to the legal profession. In totalitarian regimes, judges mirror the views of the ruling regime. The situation is more complex in authoritarian regimes such as China where courts enjoy some independence and political power is less concentrated. Authoritarian regimes in Europe and elsewhere established separate military or national security courts or relied on police and security forces rather than the judiciary to deal with political challenges while permitting the regular courts to act autonomously in other areas, such as commercial law. As a result, judges could develop a professional identity, and the judiciary was poised to assume a larger role, including impartial resolution of politically sensitive cases, when political restraints were removed. This usually occurred after democratization.

Despite the different historical context, Guarnieri suggests that some lessons of legal system development in Europe also apply to China. He notes that political influence in the appointment process, together with external and internal restraints on judges, provide the necessary political assurance to the ruling regime that the courts may be trusted to handle certain cases and areas of law independently. He also notes a centralized judiciary that promotes judges largely based on merit would serve the central government's interest in controlling local officials. In the end, he believes it is possible for China to develop a professional judiciary with a reasonable degree of independence in some areas. The result would be a "thin" version of the rule of law and a situation similar to what prevailed in most European states before the middle of the twentieth century. He cites Singapore to show that the political–legal system need not evolve into a thick liberal democratic rule of law, although the experiences of Taiwan, South Korea, and Japan indicate that something similar is possible.

In the final chapter, Tom Ginsburg picks up where Guarnieri left off, locating China's legal development within the context of other Northeast Asian states. As he notes, Japan, Taiwan, and South Korea also featured a form of legal system that, by conventional measures, was fairly independent but not politicized. As in other authoritarian regimes, courts were able to act independently but within a limited range. In particular, the courts handled commercial cases in a fair and independent way but played a limited role in deciding politically sensitive issues. Based on the trajectory of these countries, Ginsburg suggests that Chinese courts could achieve a reasonable degree of independence if the judiciary were structured roughly along Japanese lines: the judiciary is reasonably independent but not politicized; judges do not regularly challenge political authorities; and the judiciary is hierarchically organized, with strong internal controls and a sense of corporate identity among the judges. Even this level of independence would require significant changes, including a higher status for judges; a rigorous meritocratic selection process and higher pay so that the best and brightest become judges rather than lawyers; and more independence from local government, including centralization of funding (as recently announced by the State Council).

KEY ISSUES AND FINDINGS

From Substance to Process

The lackluster results of efforts to promote rule of law based on the prescription of international best practices suggests that it is time to adopt a new approach that focuses less on substantive content and more on methodological issues and the processes of legal reform and development, including the historical and sociopolitical context. As several authors noted, there is a need for a more empirical, less ideological approach to assessing legal reforms in general and issues such as judicial independence or the role of the party in the judiciary in particular.

The many attempts to create independent judiciaries around the globe have demonstrated that the process is holistic, involving interrelated changes in the social, economic, political, and legal spheres and crossing academic disciplines and administrative jurisdictions. Given the lack of resources to solve all problems at once, legal reforms must be prioritized and sequenced. This is one of the most difficult challenges for developing countries.[11]

An IFES/USAID report highlights the many problems confronting judiciaries in developing countries: the citizenry has rising expectations; courts are often asked to handle controversial cases involving social and economic rights; there is generally a rise in crime, including complicated white collar and cross-border crime, as a country moves to a market economy and urbanizes; corruption is often a problem; and the relationship of the courts to other organs of state power is in flux. The report concludes: "It would be unrealistic to think that the judiciaries can carry the full burden for resolving these complex problems."[12]

China is confronting many of these issues. Yet China is relatively fortunate. Given its huge population and the strength of its tertiary schools, there are many extremely intelligent and qualified people in key institutions responsible for identifying problems and devising solutions. Moreover, China is a major economic force despite its low per capita income, and, as a member of the Security Council with nuclear weapons, a major geopolitical player. Accordingly, foreign governments and international development agencies have been eager to advise China. To its credit, China has followed the methodology recommended by IFES. Before undertaking any significant reform, the government conducts extensive comparative research, carries out empirical research, consults with a wide variety of stakeholders including academics and representatives from the main interest groups affected by reforms, increasingly invites public comment on major laws and pieces of public regulation, and establishes pilot programs to test results before scaling them up nationally.

To be sure, China's size also makes it difficult to implement reforms. Implementation requires qualified people at every level, in every position. In contrast, a small city-state such as Singapore will have a smaller talent pool to draw on to devise policies and reforms but will need fewer people to carry out state policies. In the end, each country must find its own way to success.

Judicial Independence and Its Limits

As Ginsburg notes, politicians have many tools with which they can send signals to the judiciary: they can influence the appointment and promotion processes to

---

[11] Sequencing, in particular prioritizing legal reforms aimed at strengthening rule of law before democratization, has recently come under attack. See, e.g., Thomas Carothers, "How Democracies Emerge: The 'Sequencing' Fallacy," (Jan. 2007). For a contrary view on that issue as well as a discussion of other sequencing issues, see Randall Peerenboom, "The East Asian Model and the Sequencing Debate: Lessons from China and Vietnam," in John Gillespie and Albert Chen eds., *Authoritarian Development: China and Vietnam Compared* (forthcoming Routledge).

[12] IFES/USAID, "Guidance for Promoting Judicial Independence and Impartiality," (2002), p. 6, http://www.usaid.gov/our_work/democracy_and_governance/publications/pdfs/pnacm007.pdf.

ensure loyalty; punish, terminate, or transfer to remote locations judges who do not decide cases as desired; overrule unfavorable decisions via subsequent legislation; and bypass regular courts by establishing military or security courts.

In China, the party retains veto power in the appointment and promotion process, although it rarely appears to use it. Judges are also not often sanctioned and dismissed, and when they are it is generally for legitimate reasons such as negligence or corruption. There are few reports of judges dismissed for political reasons. Interestingly, China has not followed other authoritarian regimes in establishing separate courts to handle politically charged cases. The ordinary courts hear all cases, although there is a separate system of administrative detention intended for "minor" offenses that do not rise to the level of a crime, which has been used against Falun Gong adherents among others, as well as some use and seeming abuse of psychiatric centers and "black prisons" to detain "troublemakers" such as people who repeatedly petition higher authorities for relief.

More important are various laws and regulations that constrain access to justice and incapacitate judicial support networks. For instance, parties are required to exhaust administrative remedies in certain cases, although the general rule allows parties to pursue their claims either administratively or in court. However, the Administrative Litigation Law does not allow citizens to challenge abstract acts (i.e., generally applicable rules). Rather, they may only challenge specific acts or government decisions, and even then not those that involve civil and political rights. Standing rules are also relatively stringent: parties need to be directly affected by the government decision, thus precluding the possibility of citizens or NGOs to act as private attorneys general. NGOs and civil society are also subject to various registration requirements and generally applicable time, place, and manner restrictions on public protests that give the authorities wide discretion to veto requests to demonstrate. Despite the recent passage of regulations to increase access to government information, the prevailing mindset of some government entities still appears to be to make information public on a need-to-know-only basis rather than the more common assumption in Western liberal democracies that all information should be readily available subject to specific limits. Although Chinese laws permit collective suits, and the number of such suits has increased dramatically in recent years, authorities have also noted with concern the tendency of some of these cases to lead to public demonstrations. Accordingly, local governments and the judiciary have taken steps to ensure that such cases do not undermine social stability. Perhaps most significantly, there is still no dedicated constitutional court or review body. Thus citizens' ability to raise constitutional challenges remains limited.

In light of these and other measures described in the chapters that follow, the ruling party has felt secure enough to turn to the courts for disposition of an increasingly wide range of controversial cases, in keeping with other studies that have found that entrenched regimes with long time horizons are more likely to turn over core governance functions to courts. For various reasons, the range of cases has waxed and waned over time. The years immediately following the Tiananmen incident in 1989 represented the nadir. However, as China grew economically and the ruling party gained in confidence, the courts enjoyed greater independence and authority over a wider range of issues. More recently, the rapid rise in mass demonstrations, coupled with severe social disruptions resulting from the global economic crisis, have led to greater political influence over cases deemed threatening to economic and social stability.

To be sure, judges have not been passive actors in the unfolding drama. The judiciary, like any other political actor, has responded strategically to pursue its institutional interests, gain a greater share of scare resources, and increase the status, authority, and independence of judges.

In so doing, they have adopted strategies employed by courts in other countries. Courts in authoritarian states in particular must take care not to challenge the regime on key issues that threaten the regime's authority to rule. Thus one strategy is to exercise self-restraint, as evident in certain types of corporate cases and even more clearly in high-profile cases involving political dissidents.

Courts in China have also adopted the time-tested strategy of deferring to other branches on the substantive issue while enhancing their authority by claiming jurisdiction to decide such cases. Similarly courts have deferred on the substantive issue while imposing procedural restrictions. For instance, courts have quashed government decisions where the agency has failed to provide an adequate record for the decision. This is a far cry from the allegedly "hard look" review of U.S. courts, as government agencies can readily rectify the error by providing the grounds on which their decision was based. Nevertheless, it shows a more aggressive judiciary willing to push administrative agencies.

Still another strategy is to seek public support. Again, the Married Out Women (MOW) cases are illustrative in that the courts shifted many of the hardest decisions to others. More generally, the courts have resisted the pressure to judicialize what are at bottom socioeconomic disputes arising out of the lack of an adequate welfare system, including unemployment insurance for employees laid off in the wake of company closings resulting from the global recession. The move to mediate disputes is also in part an attempt of the judiciary to enhance its legitimacy by responding to the needs of citizens, many of whom, particularly in rural areas, want decisions that reflect local customs and norms rather than the formal central laws promulgated by national legislators in far off Beijing. The increasingly popular practice of senior judges meeting with parties in potentially incendiary large collective suits to explain legal issues is another example.

It is true that courts may go too far in courting public opinion. In the Philippines, for instance, the desire of the courts to please the public has led to an outcome-oriented jurisprudence, "as if the courts were in a perpetual popularity contest refereed by polling groups and single-interest lobbies, all of them oblivious to the professional demands of the legal craftsman."[13] Although Guarnieri's chapter suggests that judges in China are more likely to look to the party and government as their main referent group, some studies have suggested that courts are increasingly influenced by public opinion.[14]

As the experiences of other authoritarian regimes in Europe and particularly East Asia show, there is considerable scope for a further expansion and deepening of judicial independence and authority in China within the current political structure. However, as those countries also demonstrate, there are likely to be limits to what the ruling party will tolerate. Ultimately, judicial independence in its most robust form seems possible only within democracies, and even then it is difficult to achieve and maintain.

The poor performance of third-wave democracies combined with the success of China has led to hyperbolic portrayals of a new Cold War between democratic and authoritarian regimes.[15] China leaders have been abundantly clear that they want to develop their own variant of rule of law. More fundamentally, China's experience of markets without democracy merits attention. But portraying differences over the best path for development as a geopolitical struggle over ideology is fundamentally inaccurate. The end goal of the development process for most people in China, as in Russia, Vietnam, and around the world, remains democracy, albeit not necessarily the particular forms of liberal democracy found in Euro-America.

Economic Growth

China is often considered an exception to the general rule that economic growth requires rule of law and an independent judiciary capable of enforcing property rights. However, the general rule appears to be more dogma than fact. First, judicial independence is hard to measure, and the correlations with economic growth, human rights protection, and other social goods are weaker than assumed (see Chapter 5). Second, investors face many risks; legal risk is only one of them and not always high on the list. Some studies show that foreign investors either ignore or place little weight on legal risks.[16] Third, the emphasis on judicial enforcement of property rights

---

[13] Raul Pangalangan, *The Philippine "People Power" Constitution, Rule of Law, and the Limits of Liberal Constitutionalism*, in Randall Peerenboom ed., *Asian Discourses of Rule of Law* (London: Routledge, 2006), p. 379.

[14] Benjamin Liebman, "A Populist Threat to Chinese Courts," in Mary Gallagher et al. eds. *Chinese Justice: Civil Dispute Resolution in Contemporary China* (forthcoming Harvard University Press).

[15] See Robert Kagan, *The Return of History and the End of Dreams* (New York: Alfred A. Knopf, 2008). On the problems of third-wave democracies, see Thomas Carothers, *Critical Mission: Essays on Democracy Promotion* (Washington D.C.: Carnegie Endowment for International Peace, 2004); Larry Diamond, *The Spirit of Democracy* (New York: Henry Hold and Company, 2008).

[16] Amanda Perry, "An Ideal System for Attracting Foreign Direct Investment? Some Theory and Reality," *American University International Law Review* vol. 15, p. 1627 (2000).

is much too narrow. Much more important to investors is quality of the business environment. For instance, since 1999, foreign investors in China have cited as the four biggest challenges for doing business in China lack of transparency (major challenge for 41 percent of respondents), inconsistent regulatory interpretation (37 percent), unclear regulations (34 percent), and excessive bureaucracy (31 percent), followed by human resource constraints (29 percent) and intellectual property infringements (26 percent). Notable for their absence are lack of judicial independence, inability to enforce property rights, and corruption, judicial or otherwise.[17] Perhaps even more significant, for all of the complaints, 83 percent of respondents in a U.S.–China Business Council survey were profitable, with two-thirds enjoying profitability rates that meet or exceeded their company's global rate, and over 90 percent of respondents from both surveys are bullish about their companies' future in China.[18]

In fact, China has made significant progress in building institutions and improving the business environment. China ranked 34th of 131 countries in the 2007–2008 World Economic Forum's Global Competitiveness Index, and 57th of 127 countries on the Business Competitiveness Index.[19] In 2008, the World Bank ranked China 92nd of 178 countries for doing business overall.[20] Reflecting the considerable investment in institutions, China now outperforms the average in its income class on World Bank's indexes for government effectiveness, regulatory quality, and rule of law.

In any event, the view that Chinese courts do not adequately protect property rights is overstated and in need of qualification. The surveys of courts reported in this volume demonstrate that judges are more competent and professional than in the past, and that parties are reasonably happy with the courts, with most parties obtaining results in line with their expectations despite problems in particular types of cases and attempts by the parties to influence the outcome in some cases.

More fundamentally, the government has adopted an approach that seeks to promote economic development while protecting social stability by issuing policy guidance to the courts, restricting some types of commercial lawsuits while encouraging others, and providing administrative and political remedies and nonjudicial

---

[17] See American Chamber of Commerce, "The Business Climate for US Firms in China" (2007), at http://www.amcham-china.org.cn/amcham/show/content.php?Id=2361&menuid=&submid=&PHPSESSID=11eade809492f6ad040c37af69cec8af.

[18] U.S.–China Business Council, "'US Companies' China Outlook: Continuing Optimism Tempered by Operating Challenges, Protectionist Threats," October 4, 2007, http://www.uschina.org/public/documents/2007/10/uscbc-member-survey-20.

[19] The index is based on twelve pillars: institutions, infrastructure, macro economy, health and primary education, higher education and training, goods market efficiency, technological readiness, labor market efficiency, financial market sophistication, market size, business sophistication, and innovation.

[20] China fared better on some indicators than others, including enforcing contracts (20), registering property (28), trading across borders (31), closing a business (76), and protecting investors (86). Problem areas include the time and difficulty to start a business (128), dealing with licenses (175), and the amount and administrative burden of paying taxes (173).

relief to parties in bankruptcy cases, mass tort cases like the melamine milk scandal, and other politically sensitive cases with a major economic impact. Whether the overall impact of this approach on economic growth and GDP is positive is simply not clear. It is possible that more efficient, impartial, and independent courts might lead to higher growth rates, perhaps at a cost to social stability and equity. But at this point, the government clearly has decided that how to balance these objectives is a political decision to be made by political organs rather than judges.

Judicial Independence, Corruption, and Good Governance

If judicial corruption is difficult to measure, the impact of corruption on the outcome of cases is often even more difficult to determine. Generally, the public overestimates the amount of judicial corruption and the impact on the outcome of cases. Overall, China appears to do somewhat better than the average in its income class in restraining judicial corruption.[21] However, reliability of the data is suspect, particularly given the discrepancies between local and national data pointed out by Ling Li in this volume.

Courts themselves are not likely to emerge as significant institutions in the battle against government corruption. Most cases are handled through party discipline committees and the nonjudicial party detention system (*shuanggui*). It is unlikely in an effectively single-party authoritarian state that courts would be able to independently handle cases against senior government officials who are ultimately appointed by and responsible to the ruling party. Within East Asia, Hong Kong and Singapore are famous for their reliance on anticorruption commissions that were granted wide powers and effectively insulated from judicial challenges. Yet a recent Organisation for Economic Co-operation and Development (OECD) study found that although the number of anticorruption institutions worldwide is growing, there is no strong evidence that they help reduce corruption, and there are more failures than successes.[22]

WHITHER CHINA? RECENT DEBATES OVER THE ROLE OF THE JUDICIARY AND THE WAY FORWARD

There has been considerable debate in recent years over the proper role of the judiciary in China, especially since the appointment of Wang Shengjun to replace Xiao Yang as head of the Supreme People's Court (SPC). Taking note of the Color Revolutions in the former Soviet republics where foreign governments supported

---

[21] See Dali Yang, *Remaking the Chinese Leviathan: Market Transition and the Politics of Governance in China* (Stanford: Stanford University Press, 2004), pp. 254–257.
[22] Organisation for Economic Co-operation and Development, "Specialised anti-corruption institutions – review of models," (2007), http://www.eldis.org/cf/rdr/?doc=38569&em=061108&sub=gov.

international and domestic NGOs that used the courts to push for democratization and political reforms, party leaders have expressed concern that foreign parties may use legal institutions to undermine party power. As a result, they have insisted that Chinese courts not simply mimic courts in Western liberal democracies. These announcements have been coupled with an ongoing effort to shore up loyalty in the courts, procuracy, and public security institutions.

At the same time, the Politburo has reconfirmed its commitment to rule of law, Hu Jintao emphasized in a major speech to mark the thirtieth anniversary of opening and reforms that the only way forward is to deepen reforms, and senior leaders within and outside the judiciary have repeatedly called for changes that would increase the competence, independence, and authority of the courts.

The appointments of Wang Shengjun and Cao Jianmin as head of the Supreme People's Procuracy reflect these seemingly inconsistent trends. Critics have noted that in comparison to the more extensive legal and academically qualified background of Xiao Yang, Wang's background is much more that of a "political–legal cadre." Many commentators have interpreted this as a conservative appointment likely to lead to more party control of the judiciary and more restraints on judicial independence.

But what is needed from the SPC president varies over time. Xiao Yang was arguably better for the previous decade because China was still a low-income country and the judiciary was weak and being rebuilt. The basic task was institution building to increase the overall capacity of judges and courts and to increase efficiency.

As countries enter the middle-income stage, political economy issues become more important. What will the role of the judiciary be in policy making? Over what types of cases will courts exercise jurisdiction? On what basis will judges decide them? What will the judiciary's relations be with other political organs? Will the procuracy and people's congress continue to review final court decisions? Will the court be able to determine its own budget? How much say will the judiciary have in promotions and appointments? What will the role of the court be vis-à-vis party organs and the Political–legal committee? These are the issues the courts are confronting now. They require someone who understands how the various organs relate and who has the trust of the various players and the stature to get something done – to negotiate an agreement, a modus vivendi, acceptable to all the stakeholders. In fact, many judges have called for a politically strong head of the court. Given his background, Wang understands the concerns of the party leadership and how party organs operate. He is thus well placed to suggest feasible reforms acceptable to other stakeholders and yet make the judiciary more effective in responding to rising demands and the changing circumstances.

Of course, whether Wang will prove to be an effective advocate for greater professionalism and judicial authority remains to be seen. Early into his tenure, the jury is still out. Many judges and legal scholars are concerned that he has in his public speeches given a prominent role to ideas perceived as conservative or reflecting a more political role for the courts, including the importance of the "three supremes": the supremacy of the party, of the people, and of the constitution and laws. But a more careful reading shows that his speeches offer something for everyone. He calls for both judicial independence and judicial accountability; more emphasis on professionalism and expertise but also a more democratic judiciary that responds to the needs of citizens; deciding cases based on law and yet promoting mediation and settlement; learning from international best practices and foreign experiences but adapting global experience to Chinese conditions.

As spokesperson for the judiciary, Wang has to represent all viewpoints, which range from liberal to moderate to conservative. In that sense, his public speeches are political speeches and thus filled with contradictions. For instance, Wang emphasizes that the courts, law, and legal system are a means to economic growth, and thus judges need to consider the consequences for development when deciding cases. And yet he also emphasizes the important role of the courts in promoting social harmony. Both of these ideas have some merit, but they are also in tension. What is a judge supposed to do if promoting social harmony requires redistributing wealth to the most vulnerable and least productive members of society, or if strictly enforcing labor rights pushes companies out of business, or if protecting the environment slows development?[23]

On the other hand, the challenges facing the procuracy (and even more so the police and public security) are precisely the opposite. The procuracy needs more professionalization and less politics from its leadership. Accordingly, the appointment of Cao, a law professor with years of experience at the SPC, in theory bodes well for the procuracy and for the courts. He is likely to emphasize the kinds of internal reforms emphasized by Xiao Yang in the SPC reform agenda, which have increased the professionalism of the judiciary. Given his background in the courts, Cao is also likely to appreciate the way procuracy review undermines judicial independence and thus be more willing to work out a mutually acceptable solution that acknowledges that the transition to a market economy, criminal law reforms, and long-term global trends toward judicialization and rule of law will inevitably increase the role of the judiciary and its stature within the political structure of China. But again, it remains to be seen whether this will be the case. The SPC and National People's Congress (NPC) both resisted recent attempts to revise the civil procedure law to limit review of individual case supervision.

There will be various ways to measure progress. Centralization of funding is an important step in the right direction, but the funding must be adequate and reach the basic level courts. A complementary step would be to centralize appointments and to take further measures to ensure that appointments and promotions are based on

---

[23] Wang Shengjun, *Shenru guanche luoshi dang de shiqi da jingshen – zhashi zuohao renmin fayuan gexiang gongzuo* [Thoroughly Implement the Spirit of the 17th Party Congress – Resolutely Carry Out Each of the Courts' Tasks], *Qiushi* vol. 485 (Aug 16, 2008), available at http://www.qsjournal.com.cn/qs/20080816/GB/qs%5E485%5E0%5E1.htm.

merit, with a greater role for judges, the legal profession, and perhaps civil society in the process. Other possible indicators of a more ascendant judiciary would include amendment of the Criminal Procedure Law and passage of criminal evidence rules, both currently bogged down in disputes between the public security, procuracy, and those pushing for reforms, including defense lawyers and human rights activists; revisions to, if not elimination of, a form of administrative detention known as Re-education through Labor; ratification of the International Covenant on Civil and Political Rights, which China signed in 1998; enhancement of the powers of the courts to review abstract acts; elimination of the adjudicative committee at least in higher level courts; elimination of the right of the procuracy and people's congress to review final court decisions; greater clarification of the legal role of the political–legal committee and party organs, and the incorporation of these organs and their role into the formal legal system; the creation of a dedicated constitutional review body; greater public participation in the law-making and governance processes, including more access to information, more channels to participate, and more robust or deliberative participation beyond just commenting on laws, along with a general requirement that the government respond to public comments and give reasons both for adopting laws and regulations and rejecting alternatives; and increased monitoring and supervision by civil society after laws are promulgated, including through various forms of litigation. Most if not all of these issues are currently being debated and "in play."

The Supreme People's Court's Third Five-Year Agenda for Judicial Reforms, the first under Wang, emphasized the courts must operate consistent with China's political structure, level of development, and national conditions and not mimic courts in Western liberal democracies while at the same time setting out an ambitious program of technical reforms. Unlike previous agendas, however, the new agenda acknowledges the structural nature of many problems confronting the judiciary and much more explicitly invokes the need to cooperate with other state organs. The agenda does not address some of the more fundamental institutional reforms such as expanded powers of judicial review or the creation of a constitutional court. Such changes may require legislative action or even an amendment to the constitution. But more importantly they would put the judiciary at odds with other organs at a time when the judiciary needs their support on other pressing issues.

The new agenda reflects a pragmatic political compromise. The court accepts some limits on its powers and refrains from challenging other organs in exchange for cooperation on certain issues that enhance the power and authority of the judiciary. Whether increased cooperation with state and party organs will meet citizen expectations and ultimately lead to a more authoritative and independent judiciary remains to be seen.

This volume is one of the publications emerging from the "Rule of Law in China" program run by the Foundation for Law, Justice and Society, an independent institution affiliated with the Centre for Socio-Legal Studies, Oxford University. The main objective of this program is to study the ways in which Chinese law and legal institutions encounter and interact with the social environment, including economic and political factors at local, regional, national, and international levels. Other publications in this program can be downloaded from www.fljs.org/Chinapublications.

This volume is the product of a workshop in Paris in December 2007 organized by the Foundation for Law, Justice and Society in collaboration with Sciences Po Paris, Sciences Po's research program in China "Law, Justice and Society," and the Institut des Hautes Etudes sur la Justice. The generous support of these organizations is gratefully acknowledged.

2

Halfway Home and a Long Way to Go

China's Rule of Law Evolution and the Global Road to Judicial Independence, Judicial Impartiality, and Judicial Integrity

Keith E. Henderson

This chapter focuses on an important issue under intense debate within many circles in China – the independence, impartiality, and integrity of the judiciary. The outcome of this debate has significant implications for China's future, for international judicial cooperation on a range of fronts, and for globalizing the rule of law in the developing world, where China has an ever-growing interest and influence.

China will not likely make the historic cultural, social, and legal transformation from the rule of man to the rule of law or realize her full economic and political potential over the long term without enhancing the independence, impartiality, integrity, and capacity of the judiciary. Global experience demonstrates that an independent judiciary is central to rule of law, and that it serves a number of important mutually supportive purposes, including: (i) safeguarding and enforcing people's property rights and human rights; (ii) resolving economic and political disputes; (iii) promoting international judicial cooperation fairly and predictably; (iv) addressing, mitigating, and preventing judicial and governmental corruption; (v) promoting social justice and social harmony; and (vi) promoting national and international political legitimacy. Because there are other institutional mechanisms in some countries that perform some of these essential tasks, particularly at the local and informal levels, most developing countries today are trying to create an independent judiciary with integrity as one of their long-term objectives. China is no exception.

Global experience shows that the fair implementation of myriad new laws, regulations, and policies passed in China during the last thirty years, adoption of the emerging global best practice of judicial review, and increased trade and investment are all more likely if there is a strong, independent judiciary capable of promoting justice and a rule of law culture. China's emerging new generation of leaders have sent clear political and legal signals that they intend to build a rules-based legal system and the institutions necessary to make it work over time. This is seen in the sea of new laws and regulations as well as in economic, political, and judicial five-year plans. The growing number of political statements from both Beijing and key power centers such as Shanghai supports the notion that the rule of law is necessary for the government to gain the trust of the general public, the growing middle class, investors, businesses, and the global community in the twenty-first century. Whether the Chinese Communist Party leadership will allow this legal and cultural development to happen in time to avoid an economic or political crisis is one of the most important issues confronting the international community and the Chinese people today.

Part I sets out the current consensus regarding international best practices and, equally as important, a methodology for identifying problems, devising solutions, and monitoring results to guide and structure the judicial reform process. Part II discusses China's efforts to enhance the independence, competence, and integrity of the judiciary in light of the principles and methodology described in the first part, including projects in which the author was personally involved. Part III takes a brief look at judicial corruption. Part IV provides key policy recommendations for future reforms. Part V concludes.

GLOBAL JUDICIAL INTEGRITY PRINCIPLES AND BEST PRACTICES

There is an emerging global consensus that there are minimal judicial independence, impartiality, and integrity principles that countries of various political stripes should adhere to, including what these principles mean in both legal theory and actual practice in different regional contexts.[1] These principles or best practices are articulated in numerous international treaties, constitutions, court cases, human rights commission reports, and governmental and nongovernmental protocols. They

---

[1] Curtis J. Milhaupt and Katharina Pistor, *Law and Capitalism* (Chicago: University of Chicago Press, 2008). This book provides an excellent overview of these issues, including country case studies. The www.ifes.org Web site includes a series of white papers and country State of the Judiciary Reports. IFES is one of the largest and oldest international democracy and governance nongovernmental organizations in the world. These publications, either written or edited by myself, explain the full rationale for and actual experience of promoting minimal judicial independence and integrity principles globally and in various countries, including Haiti, Honduras, Malawi, Egypt, Jordan, Morocco, and Lebanon. See, e.g., "Global Best Practices: A Model State of the Judiciary Report," (2004); "A Strategic Tool for Promoting, Monitoring and Reporting on Judicial Integrity Reforms," (2004); "Global Lessons and Best Practices: Corruption and Judicial Independence," (2004). Other relevant white papers include those that relate to best practices for judicial councils, judicial income and asset disclosure, and the enforcement of court judgments. A number of these reports have been translated into Chinese and are being used in judicial training programs across China. They are available in many Chinese law school book stores and can be accessed in Chinese on the following official judicial web site www.chinacourt.org. A summary of these white papers and in-country experience is captured, in part, in a recent chapter I authored entitled: "A Framework for an Annual State of the Judiciary Report," Canivet, Andenas, and Fairgreive eds. *Independence, Accountability and the Judiciary* (United Kingdom: British Institute of International and Comparative Law, 2006).

reflect lessons learned from global legal development experience.[2] The main task ahead for countries and other stakeholders is to embrace, adapt, prioritize, and implement them in a holistic manner through systematic monitoring and reporting.

Some of the more prominent statements of these principles include the Universal Declaration of Human Rights, the 1985 United Nations Basic Principles on the Independence of the Judiciary, the United Nations Convention Against Corruption, The Universal Charter of the Judge, and the 1995 Beijing Statement of Principles of the Independence of the Judiciary, codeveloped and endorsed by the president of the Supreme People's Court in China and more than two-thirds of the chief justices representing the Asia-Pacific region.[3]

The following eighteen Global Judicial Integrity Principles (JIP) reflect the emerging global consensus. The JIP are based on both exhaustive global research and practical in-country experience captured in a series of IFES (International Foundation for Electronic Systems) white papers and country-specific State of the Judiciary Reports.

1. Guarantee of judicial independence, the right to a fair trial, equality under the law, and access to justice.
2. Institutional and personal/decisional independence of judges.
3. Clear and effective jurisdiction of ordinary courts and judicial review powers.
4. Adequate judicial resources and salaries.
5. Adequate training and continuing legal education.
6. Security of tenure.
7. Fair and effective enforcement of judgments.
8. Judicial freedom of expression and association.
9. Adequate qualification and objective and transparent selection and appointment process.
10. Objective and transparent processes of the judicial career.
11. Objective, transparent, fair, and effective disciplinary process.
12. Limited judicial immunity from civil and criminal suit.
13. Conflict of interest rules.
14. Income and asset disclosure.
15. High standards of judicial conduct and rules of judicial ethics.
16. Objective and transparent court administration and judicial processes.
17. Judicial access to legal and judicial information.
18. Public access to legal and judicial information.

---

[2] Samuel Paul, *Holding the State to Account – Citizen Monitoring in Action* (Bangalore: Books for Change, 2002), providing compelling case studies from Bangalore and elsewhere that citizen monitoring and reporting is key to promoting the rule of law and to holding the state accountable.

[3] For full citations to many of the documents referenced in this section, see United States Agency for International Development, Lecce, Colliver, and Henderson, "Guidance for Promoting Judicial Independence and Impartiality, Appendix A" (2002), http://www.usaid.gov and http://www.ifes.org, and Luu Tien Dung, "Judicial Independence in Transitional Countries," (2003), http://www.undp.org.

Although one could debate which of the eighteen judicial integrity principles or global best practices are most important and which ones are politically implementable within different country contexts, an analysis of the global research and country experience by governmental and nongovernmental reformers in different countries leads one to the general conclusion that they are soundly grounded in both legal theory and real-world development experience. This does not mean the principles are static, that they are worded perfectly for every country, or that some will not be further clarified or refined over time. Indeed, just like the rolling or dynamic relationship between the law and the economy, the terminology and scope of these principles are constantly evolving, and the manner in which they are sequenced will necessarily vary from country to country. In essence, these principles represent the current state of "thin and thick" international law and current consensus among various country experts and international development practitioners.

Key Implementation Challenges: A Methodology for Judicial Reforms

The challenge for most developing countries, such as China, is to firmly embrace the minimal judicial independence principles that virtually all countries have officially and legally committed themselves to implement through international conventions and their own constitutions and laws. This challenge, to a large extent, is a question of political will, although resource constraints, cultural practices and beliefs, interest group politics, and endemic governmental corruption also affect the ability of many countries to implement these principles.

Moreover, even assuming necessary support for reforms, implementing these principles requires a short- and long-term holistic institution-building rule of law strategy and a prioritized action plan grounded, both culturally and politically, to a country-specific context. We know from experience with other international conventions that a participatory monitoring and reporting methodology for promoting and implementing complex politically sensitive reforms is the most effective path to success. This type of approach requires intensive public discussion and debate and thus presents a special challenge for China and other developing countries where political and technocratic elite have driven the reform process and civil society is weak and subject to political and legal restrictions.

Over the years, IFES has developed and tested, to varying degrees, a methodological framework in different country contexts around the world, including China, for purposes of debating, promoting, adopting, adapting, sequencing, linking-up, monitoring, and reporting key reforms and problems. This methodology is based on the principles of broad stakeholder country engagement and buy-in, participation and consensus building, thorough cross-disciplinary research and analysis, and focused but flexible implementation in light of the legal, political, socioeconomic, and cultural context of a particular country. The process involves carefully planned academic and applied research, including strategic surveys, and a series of workshops with key stakeholders over an extended period of time, usually one to two years. Ideally, this methodology includes four key steps:

(i)   reviewing, analyzing, and debating major issues and challenges among key governmental and nongovernmental stakeholders;

(ii) adapting, prioritizing, and adopting the principles, key issues, and indicators of progress within a particular country context;

(iii) adopting recommendations and a strategic systematic framework for purposes of promoting, monitoring, and reporting reforms and the resolution of key issues on an annual basis; and

(iv) developing an annual state of the judiciary report for monitoring and reporting purposes through collaboration or cooperation between the courts, the prosecutors, the police, the legal profession, relevant ministries, and nongovernmental organizations, such as human rights groups and country scholars.

Both the principles and methodology can be used by multiple stakeholders for multiple purposes, including the development of the Annual State of the Judiciary Report. This report, if adopted by judiciaries, donors, and civil society groups on a country-by-country basis, would systematically document and analyze progress made in implementing each principle and key reforms, thus enabling reformers in any given country to follow the progress and lessons learned from other countries on similar issues. This annual report would also include sections related to current problems and reform recommendations, as well as planned actions for the year ahead.[4] Of course, in some countries it may not be possible for the judiciary and nongovernmental organizations to prepare a collaborative report. In these cases, as well as in countries where collaboration is possible, best monitoring and reporting practices call for two reports that follow a similar reporting framework, one governmental and the other nongovernmental. In this way, comparative information can be developed on high-priority issues as well as a more complete overall objective picture of the state of the judiciary, including the status of key reforms and the resolution of specific problems over time.

The JIP principles and reform methodology have now been utilized and tested, to varying degrees, in a number of developing countries, including China and several countries in the Middle East and Latin America. Generally speaking, they have yet to be seriously challenged in either theory or practice. Although there is

[4] This report and the research and ideas behind it can be found in several of the IFES white papers referenced above, as well as in a regional report prepared by the author and several IFES colleagues who hailed from Europe and Latin America for the Inter-American Development Bank, "A Model Framework for Promoting Judicial Independence and Impartiality in the Americas," (2004), http://www.ifes.org and http://www.idb.org.

no doubt room for refinement and need for country adaptation and prioritization, this kind of systematic monitoring and reporting approach to reform has generally been an effective framework and reform tool for various purposes, including: (i) engaging a broader range of stakeholders in more concrete and focused strategic discussions; (ii) enhancing coalition building and informed advocacy; (iii) prioritizing and sequencing judicial and interrelated reforms; (iv) raising public awareness; (v) promoting more judicial transparency, accountability, and openness; and (vi) highlighting recurrent problems and institution-building issues.

IMPLEMENTATION OF THE JIP IN CHINA

The legal concept of judicial independence is embedded in China's last three Chinese constitutions (1912, 1954, and 1982). However, a review of twentieth-century Chinese history reveals that the full meaning of this concept has long been debated and that conflicting provisions of these constitutions, as well as actual political practice, have meant that judicial independence has usually been interpreted to only apply to the judicial decision-making process related to individual cases – not the institutional independence of the judiciary.[5] Throughout Chinese history, the judiciary has always been subservient in practice to the emperor, the National People's Congress, or party officials at the central or local levels.

Nevertheless, more government officials, policy makers, judges, academics, and nongovernmental organizations in China are coalescing around the notion that a reliable legal system and a more independent judiciary would help them work more effectively in addressing daily governance and various socioeconomic development problems. At the same time, there appears to be virtual unanimity among the ruling elite that it needs to create a rule of law society to seal its own political legitimacy.

IFES's recent experience with China's Supreme People's Court, as well as China's own experience with myriad judicial reforms, demonstrates that many minimal judicial independence and integrity principles may not be as controversial in China as the casual observer might think. This is particularly true for those directly or indirectly related to China's own self-interest, such as those who touch upon China's ability to address certain high-priority socioeconomic and social justice issues, including land and property disputes, economic integration, environmental degradation,

---

[5] Jerome Cohen, "The Chinese Communist Party and Judicial Independence," *Harvard Law Review*, vol. 5, p. 966 (1969). Cohen shows that in the early 1950s party records and leading academics took the position that judicial independence unquestionably applied to the decision-making process with regard to individual cases, not the institution of the judiciary. Perhaps this old-line party position should be the focal point for making the judiciary more independent today. Some leading Chinese academics and constitutional scholars argue that judicial independence should also apply to China's powerful public security organs, which often try to control or intervene in politically sensitive cases. See Xin Chunying, "Judicial Independence," in Yuwen Li ed., *Chinese Courts History and Transition* (Beijing: Law Press China, 2001).

legal harmonization in judicial enforcement, social stability, and national and inter-national political legitimacy. There also appears to be an opportunity to promote the personal independence of individual judges because many judges and scholars are receptive to adapting international best practices related to both substantive law and internal decision-making procedures to the evolving Chinese context. These reforms are generally seen as more realistic than more broad-based institutional and highly political reforms to achieve complete (or at least a high degree of) institutional independence.

The IFES project in China, unlike other more traditional judicial reform projects in other countries, focused mainly on two crosscutting judicial reform themes. After intensive discussions with representatives from the Supreme People's Court during several months, agreement was reached that the primary focal point of the IFES project should be on the interrelated issues of judicial enforcement (JIP 7) and judicial transparency (JIP 2, 9, 10, 11, 13, 14, 16, 17, and 18). Whereas the Chinese organizers acknowledged they were also grappling with the full range of judicial independence principles, they noted that a number of them were already being addressed in the 2004–2008 Five Year Judicial Reform Plan and other initiatives of the Supreme People's Court. In any event, as expected, these themes promoted open, frank debate on virtually the full range of judicial independence and integrity principles, including the sensitive topic of judicial corruption.

From 2004 to 2006, approximately 200 judges from the Supreme People's Court and the Yunnan and Sichuan High Courts, along with a number of leading Chinese academics and international experts representing several regions of the world and disciplines, carefully reviewed and openly debated the judicial transparency and enforcement themes and many judicial integrity principles within the evolving China context.

By all accounts, the China project was seen as a positive and eye-opening experi-ence by both Chinese participants and the IFES global experts from Latin America, Europe, and the United States. Generally speaking, the participating judges as well as participants from the broader legal and academic communities embraced the international best practices principles and participatory methodological approach to judicial reform. Chinese participants emphasized that they appreciated the fact that seasoned judges and judicial reform experts with unique regional and global exper-tise helped guide the workshop discussions on many technical issues, and that they benefited from the global experiences and best practices/lessons learned/coalition-building approach to judicial reform.

The debate among Chinese project participants was mainly about the sequencing and implementation of the JIP – not their substance or importance. IFES found par-ticipants to be receptive to debate and discussion on almost all of the JIP, although there was intense debate about how and when to implement them. Chinese partici-pants acknowledged that implementing some of the principles would require strong political support from party officials and the National People's Congress, and that it was virtually pointless, if not impossible, to implement some of the more political ones from a purely technical perspective.

Among those seen as the most long-term, political, and problematic were those related to:

(i)   judicial independence and access to justice (JIP1);
(ii) the institutional and decisional independence of judges (JIP 2);
(iii) judicial review (JIP3);
(iv) judicial freedom of expression and association (JIP 8);[6] and
(v)   structural and local government issues related to judicial enforcement (JIP 7).

Some of these principles – particularly those regarding access to justice, judicial enforcement, and judicial budget issues – involve resource allocation decisions that the judiciary cannot alone decide. Some also raise issues that are fundamentally economic in nature and generally problematic in lower- and middle-income countries like China. Others, such as the decisional independence of individual judges, reflect the way the Chinese judiciary and the decision-making process are structured internally. For example, most cases are heard by a panel of three judges, not an individual judge. Moreover, major and complex cases are by law reviewed by an adjudicative committee consisting of senior judges within the court. Other principles, such as judicial review, involve the relation of the judiciary to other political organs, including party organs, and were likewise seen as beyond the legal reach of the courts. As with resource allocation issues, reforms that alter the fundamental balance of power between the judiciary and other political actors were also seen as issues beyond the reach of the judiciary.

Most other principles were seen as relevant and related to reforms both politically and technically implementable in the short term once adapted to either the provincial or national context.

In sum, not unlike their counterparts in many other countries, China's leaders have chosen to limit the scope of judicial reforms and the application of judicial independence, impartiality, and integrity principles mainly to those related to promoting judicial efficiency, legal predictability, and legal harmony in the economic sector. Whether and when China or other countries will extend these minimalist principles to those related to criminal justice and universal human rights remains to be seen.

---

[6] There are two different types of concerns here. The first is a more general concern about the proper role for judges in engaging in political activities or commenting on public issues. See Garapon's chapter in this volume for a discussion of the very different way this issue is treated in the United States and France. The second issue involves the limits of freedom of expression and association in China, regardless of whether one is a judge or not. For an excellent discussion, see Randall Peerenboom, *China Modernizes: Threat to the West or Model for the Rest?* (London and New York: Oxford University Press, 2007).

However, as policy makers and donors contemplate their role and next reform steps in China, it is worth remembering that sustained growth, social stability, and domestic and international political legitimacy are all central party objectives. As a result, the incentives for fundamental judicial reform are strong and growing. The need for economic growth, as well as the government's global and social objectives, make the rule of law and judicial independence possible for perhaps the first time in China's long and rich history. This evolution can be most easily seen in modern urban centers of commerce like Shanghai, where the professionalism and independence of the judiciary seems to be growing.[7]

Given these objectives, a rule of law development strategy promoting judicial transparency and openness, including the personal independence of judges, seems to be the best way to enhance judicial independence and integrity in China.

From a methodological perspective, IFES found the basic Chinese approach to judicial reform was systematic and prioritized, not unlike the IFES approach. Indeed, the Chinese judicial reform approach is basically the same as the methodology through which Chinese economic reformers had successfully passed and implemented, at least in part, numerous laws, regulations, and policies to promote a market-based economy. In the economic arena, and now in the judicial reform arena, Chinese policy makers and economic and judicial reformers have scoured the world for international best practices and lessons learned, and then adapted and incorporated some of the most relevant or politically palatable of these to national or local context through pilot projects.[8] Their almost unparalleled success, so far, seems beyond doubt.

China's reform efforts on the broader legal, economic, and political fronts demonstrate that the law's interaction with social life is not monolithic and that the methodological approach and reform pace sets China apart from most developing countries. Pilot programming, academic and applied research, as well as extensive planning and political consultation and accountability, are all hallmarks of the Chinese reform process when the authorities are really serious about implementing reforms. The question now is how serious are they about creating the key institution necessary to create the rule of law and to implementing China's own officially approved judicial reform plans?

---

7   V.M. Hung, "Judicial Reform in China: Lessons Learned from Shanghai," Carnegie Endowment for International Peace Working Paper 58 (April 2005), http://www.ceip.org; Xin He, "The Enforcement of Commercial Judgments in China," in Randall Peerenboom ed. *Dispute Resolution in China* (Oxford: Foundation for Law, Justice and Society, 2008), noting improvements in enforcement of court judgments in urban areas with ongoing problems in rural areas. Randall Peerenboom, "Development of the Legal Profession in China," (2009), http://papers.ssrn.com/sol3/results.cfm?RequestTimeout= 50000000, demonstrating how development of a legal system and the legal profession have closely tracked patterns of economic development in China.

8   For a more detailed and comprehensive discussion of China's reform methodology, see Peerenboom, *China Modernizes*; Michael Dowdle, "Of Parliaments, Pragmatism, and the Dynamics of Constitutional Development: The Curious Case of China," *New York University Journal of International Law and Politics*, vol. 35, 1 (2002).

JUDICIAL CORRUPTION

Only recently has serious empirical research and debate been undertaken on the issue of endemic judicial corruption in most developing countries. Although there are a number of reasons for this phenomenon and the causes vary somewhat from country to country, we now know that corruption within judiciaries is often well-organized and intentionally perpetuated by the powers that be, usually as a form of overall political control and self-protection. Recent research on judicial corruption in a number of countries, including China, reveals that a combination of forces, including corrupt judges and lawyers, corrupt government officials, corrupt businesses, and corrupt political party networks collude to perpetuate judicial corruption as the best form of protection from criminal investigations.[9]

The Supreme People's Court's Second Five Year Judicial Reform Plan and the Chinese Communist Party's (CCP) multipronged National Anti-Corruption Strategy are revealing for what they include and exclude.[10] Although the former expressly highlights judicial independence, the latter hardly references the role of an independent and impartial judiciary in fighting corruption and laying the foundation for rule of law.

The dichotomy between these two intensely debated official documents helps illuminate the party's views of the judiciary and shows that the party's anticorruption and rule of law priorities have not risen to their rightful place on the policy table yet. To be sure, many other countries have similar rule of law and judicial deficiencies, particularly when it comes to reining in corruption and the political and economic influence of powerful actors.[11] However, because of China's growing economic and financial influence around the world and the need for more international cooperation with China on a range of fronts, becoming a rule of law state is all the more important to the global community.

China appears to be doing about as much as most countries to address the fundamental crosscutting institutional problem of endemic judicial corruption. However, China's efforts, as in other countries, will have to be dramatically stepped-up before

---

[9] Keith Henderson, "The Rule of Law and Judicial Corruption: Half-Way Over the Great Wall," in Transparency International, *Global Corruption Report* (2007); Minxin Pei, "Corruption Threatens China's Future," Carnegie Endowment for International Peace Policy Brief No. 55 (2007), http://carnegieendowment.org/publications/index.cfm?fa-=view&id=18110; Transparency International, "Combating Corruption in Judicial Systems: Advocacy Toolkit," (2007), http://www.transparency.org.

[10] APEC, "Summary of the Anti-Corruption Efforts in China," APEC Workshop on Denial of Safe Haven, Asset Recovery and Extradition, Shanghai, China (2006), http://www.apec.org; Congressional Executive Commission on China, "SPC's Five-Year Judicial Reform Agenda (2004–2008)" http://cecc.gov/pages/virtualAcad/index.phpd?showsingle=38564.

[11] Keith Henderson, "Half-Way Home and a Long Way to Go: Challenges of Corruption and Reform Implementation Facing the Post-Communist States – 10 Years Later," Background Paper, The World Bank Annual Meeting (2000), http://www.worldbank.org/rol; see also the IFES white papers referenced in footnote 1.

the rule of law and an independent and impartial judiciary with integrity can take root. This could and should be a high-priority reform, and it is an area where China could set an example for other developing countries, not unlike what Singapore did several decades ago. Of course, an independent judiciary is only one formal mechanism of addressing corruption and promoting accountability, as the Singaporean example shows. Other formal and informal mechanisms will have to be strengthened, particularly at the local level. Again, much depends on political will at the national and local levels, public engagement and access to information, and whether there are incentives in place to prevent corruption before it occurs and to punish those engaged in it when it does.

KEY POLICY RECOMMENDATIONS

Other chapters in this volume provide detailed, context-specific recommendations for how to enhance judicial independence, judicial impartiality, and judicial integrity. General recommendations that follow, which are based on an updated analysis of international law, global best practices, and lessons learned from in-country judicial reform experience around the world, take a more macrolevel holistic perspective. The foregoing analysis suggests that such reforms should be based on at least five mutually supportive principles.

First, give high priority to reforms that promote transparency in judicial appointments and promotions, in judicial decision making and enforcement processes, and in the personal independence and integrity of judges. These recommendations mirror the key recommendation made by more than twenty-six country and global experts in Global Guidance for Promoting Judicial Independence and Impartiality, and represent the views of many of the judges and scholars IFES interacted with in China and other countries. Fortunately, there appears to be a growing consensus among Chinese reformers that promoting the personal independence of judges through various transparency and accountability reform initiatives is both politically and technically feasible.

Second, centralize and adequately fund judicial budgets at all levels. The way judiciaries are funded is problematic in many countries, but in a huge, complex transition country like China, judicial funding has special institutional, business, and party characteristics that cry out for immediate attention. Indeed, 73 percent of those surveyed in Shanghai in 2003 and 2004 believed this reform would promote judicial independence more than any other.[12] The central authorities have recently announced that funding for the judiciary will be centralized.[13] This policy

---

[12] Hung, "Judicial Reform in China."
[13] Opinion of the Central Political–Legal Commission on Several Issues in the Deepening of Reform in the Judicial System and the Work Mechanism, November 29, 2008.

pronouncement emanates from the Second Five Year Reform Program of the People's Courts (2004–2008). It is worth noting that this issue has been studied and debated for years, which means it was supported by the former president of the Supreme People's Court, Xiao Yang, and blessed by President Hu Jintao.

Many China scholars, China watchers, and reformers see it as a move in the right direction. However, there is reason to wait and see whether this new policy will be fully implemented and fully funded by the central powers. Indeed, this policy may present the new president of the Supreme People's Court, Wang Shengjun, seen as less of a reformer than his predecessor, with his first true judicial reform test. It will also test President Hu's commitment to deeper structural and political reforms.

On the one hand, if the new policy is implemented in practice, it will likely help insulate the local judiciary in rural China from being totally subservient to local party officials. On the other hand, some China scholars and watchers also believe this policy could be used by the central legal–political committee, in collaboration with the Supreme People's Court and the National People's Congress, to gain more control over the decision-making and personnel processes of local judiciaries. The reality is that party officials still decide major economic and political issues at the end of the day, at all levels, and they effectively control all key personnel decisions, because the judiciary must still depend on party support for related operational services as well as public legitimacy. Moreover, because local judiciaries are always receptive to receiving more money and resources from local officials, the opportunity for interference remains.

Even if more supervisory central party control is the real intent of the current leadership, managing this process will be problematic given China's size and multiple competing institutions and decision makers that exist at all levels in China's complex society. Given the range and weight of other related judicial reforms under way, this reform ultimately opens the judicial door more widely to independence. Thus, although addressing and preventing systemic judicial corruption will require a broader structural approach, adequate centralized funding represents one important element of a true reform package.

Third, target reforms centered on strengthening civil society, the legal profession, and an independent media to engage and promote reforms. This includes greater political and legal support for a more independent legal profession and a more independent media. Until the public and the media can openly but responsibly critique government action, and until defense lawyers can defend those charged with exposing corruption without fear of career or financial retribution if not jail or loss of life, it is unlikely that endemic corruption can be seriously addressed or prevented. The IFES program revealed that like many other developing countries, the code of silence with regard to judicial independence, judicial corruption, and access to judicial information still prevails in China. Self-censorship is still the norm. The media and the Internet are also kept under tight legal and political control, and laws that criminalize people for defaming or insulting public officials are still on the books and appear to be arbitrarily enforced.[14] Moreover, criminal defense and rights lawyers are often harassed and punished in various ways.[15]

Nevertheless, the IFES project revealed that Chinese reformers, as well as many judges, prosecutors, parliamentarians, scholars, and defense lawyers, are actively seeking ways to engage these sensitive but all-important issues, both among themselves as well as with the public and the international community. However, there are political limits as to what they can do and what information they have access to without due support from the international community. A review of the second Five Year Judicial Reform Plan and the passage of recent open government and access to information regulations suggest that judicial reforms related to transparency, open courts, and access to information are finally being given higher priority – at least on paper. Now these reforms need to be implemented in practice.

Fourth, and related, support reforms designed to promote open government and public access to information. Specifically, fully implement the State Council's new access to information ordinance.[16] The actual implementation and enforcement of the Disclosure of Government Information Provisions has the potential to be a catalyst for many other interrelated economic, political, and legal good governance reforms, including promoting judicial independence and integrity.[17] Indeed, if global experience tells us anything, opening the doors of the courthouses and institutions of justice to more sunlight will do more to root out judicial corruption and promote social justice and a rule of law culture than any other single initiative. Although the new information ordinance primarily applies to administrative agencies, it expressly gives Chinese citizens the right to appeal administrative decisions denying them information to the judiciary. No doubt over time the courts will be deluged with such appeals and this will be where many legal issues will be played out. Because this newfound right will likely be popular among the Chinese, it will place greater public demands and expectations upon the evolving Chinese judiciary.

Fifth, enhancing judicial independence is only one aspect of social justice and a harmonious society. China's reformers should look beyond the traditional rule of law orthodoxy, with a heavy focus on formal law and the courts, to nontraditional legal

---

[14] Benjamin Liebman, "Watchdog or Demagogue? The Media in the Chinese Legal System," *Columbia Law Review*, vol. 105, p. 1 (2005).

[15] Fu Hualing, "When Lawyers Are Prosecuted: The Struggle of a Profession in Transition," (2006), http://ssrn.com/abstract=956500, and Fu Hualing and Richard Cullen, "*Weiquan* (Rights Protection) Lawyering in an Authoritarian State: Toward Critical Lawyering," http://ssrn.com/abstract=1083925 (March 2008).

[16] State Council, Provisions of the People's Republic of China on the Disclosure of Government Information (2007), http://www.freedominfo.cn/blog.

[17] Keith Henderson, "Breaking the Culture of Secrecy: Strong Support for an Independent Judiciary, Human Rights and an Independent Media," (2000), http://www.oas.org. This paper was prepared to complement a model whistleblower statute written for purposes of implementing the United Nations Convention Against Corruption in Latin America.

empowerment alternatives that make civil society an effective reform partner.[18] More fundamentally, there is a need to shift from a focus on aggregate growth to a focus on higher quality, more equitable, more environmentally friendly, sustainable growth. The Chinese government grasped this more quickly than many other developing countries, evidenced in a host of recent policy pronouncements aimed at creating a harmonious society. Nevertheless, much remains to be done if these policies are to be implemented fairly and effectively, particularly at the provincial and local levels.

CONCLUSION

A number of significant developments in China during the last three decades demonstrate that the judiciary is moving toward becoming more independent, impartial, and ethical and that the rule of law is slowly but begrudgingly emerging, law by law, province by province, case by case, and judicial interpretation by judicial interpretation. A wide-ranging transparency-oriented judicial reform plan, a modern-day judicial ethics code, a law stipulating judicial qualifications, specialized training of judges, progressive judicial interpretations, and uniform guidance with nationwide application are now all in place. The challenge of the day is to implement them, including addressing a number of institutional issues needed to enhance the professionalism, authority, and independence of the judiciary.

Global lessons learned in implementing international best practices; new and sometimes contradictory international legal developments related to the independence, impartiality, and integrity of the judiciary; the need to balance independence with accountability; and an increased demand for more effective international judicial cooperation, good governance, and treaty enforcement, all highlight opportunities and challenges for promoting judicial independence, impartiality, and integrity in China and around the world. China's own heavy global footsteps, particularly in the developing world, where the rule of law and the institution of the judiciary are often weak, increase the importance of seizing the opportunities and overcoming the challenges for China in the judicial reform arena.

Now is the time for the Chinese and the international community to make judicial independence, impartiality, and integrity a higher priority agenda item on the Chinese and global stage.

---

[18] Stephen Golub, "Beyond Rule of Law Orthodoxy, The Legal Empowerment Alternative," Carnegie Working Paper 41 (October 2003), http://www.ceip.org.

3

A New Approach for Promoting Judicial Independence

Antoine Garapon

Suggesting a new approach for promoting judicial independence is an ambitious but necessary project. This chapter begins with a critique of the current dominant approach based on global best practices and then considers alternatives. Examples are used throughout to illustrate both criticisms of the best-practices approach and the potential benefits of alternative approaches. These alternatives emphasize the need to pay more attention to context, to culture and politics, to bad local processes, and to actual results of particular reforms. Real-life examples are essential because so-called international best-practice standards are often too abstract and too far removed from reality in many countries to be effectively implemented. Although international best practices may serve a useful heuristic purpose for legal reformers in some circumstances, they can easily become intolerant one-size-fits-all dogmas that hinder progress.

WHAT IS WRONG WITH GLOBAL STANDARDS? THE DENIAL OF CULTURE AND POLITICS

In *Global best practises: a model state of the judiciary report, a strategic tool for promoting, monitoring and reporting on judicial integrity reforms*, IFES (International Foundation for Electoral Systems), one of the most experienced and influential actors in the rule of law promotion business, states:

> One of the best ways to promote the implementation of key, priority judicial reforms, particularly those that relate to transparency and accountability in the judiciary, is to democratize the judiciary by providing the public with quality information on the state of the judiciary through annual, systematic, prioritized monitoring and reporting tools. . . . The Judicial Integrity Principles represent high priority consensus principles and emerging best practises found in virtually all global and

regional governmental and non-governmental instruments and key international case law related to the independence and impartiality of the judiciary.[1]

This approach of promoting judicial independence and judicial integrity through global standards ignores culture and downplays local politics and the competing interests that often undermine reform efforts. It is guilty of what Peter Evans calls "institutional monocropping" – the imposition of "blueprints based on idealized versions of Anglo-American institutions, the applicability of which is presumed to transcend national circumstances and cultures."[2]

The global-standards approach defines substantive principles, rules, and practices in a broad way that nobody would disagree with. It then adopts a problem-solving approach to realize the prescribed substantive standards through a set of reform processes and procedures. The problem, however, is that it avoids politics (considered a bad thing in American culture), cultural differences, and difficult theoretical problems intrinsic to the pursuit of judicial integrity. It recommends standards (and the institutions and practices to implement them) as if they were uncontroversial rather than the site for intense political struggles between different interest groups, including state organs with competing agendas.

One cannot understand how a system works without taking culture into consideration. I mainly work on comparisons between French and American judicial cultures, that is, between two economically developed Western liberal democratic countries. Yet there are still significant differences. Let us take the example of the idea of procedure. French and American civil trials seem to perform a similar role, but they belong to different cultures. A civil trial in France is considered a public service (*service public*) as part of the civil administration. In the United States, a civil action serves the political myth that every injustice should be remedied through a civil trial. From there flows the idea of a "fishing expedition" (i.e., to discover, after the complaint has been filed, evidence and legal grounds missing at the beginning) and the idea of settlement (a high percentage of civil actions settle before trial).

No matter how universal and based on reason it purports to be, every system – even the American – is founded on a set of beliefs. To take another example, in the United States, dissenting opinions are considered necessary to ensure public confidence in the trial process. If the judges disagree, it is after the issues have been discussed and arguments fully presented, so the decision is really theirs. In contrast, in France the myth is that the court's decision is the solution. It is difficult if not impossible to say which culture is best or more rational; it depends on the society it belongs to. It has to do with the nature of authority in each culture and the specific way each society gives form and meaning to social interactions.[3]

---

[1] *IFES Rule of Law White Paper Series*, April 2004, www.ifes.org.
[2] Peter Evans, "Developments as Institutional Change: The Pitfalls of Monocropping and Potential of Deliberation," *Studies in Comparative International Development*, vol. 38 (winter 2004), p. 30.
[3] See generally Paul Kahn, *The Cultural Study of Law* (Chicago: University of Chicago Press, 1999).

Global standards purport to be suitable for every situation, which is impossible. Their extension comes at the expense of a deeper comprehension of reality.

FROM AN INDIVIDUAL LEGAL APPROACH TO A COLLECTIVE POLITICAL APPROACH

What is needed is an approach that emphasizes collective politics rather than a narrow legal approach centered on individuals, as if the problems were due to corrupt, incompetent, or insufficiently independent judges. Justice is often not a problem of individuals. The allocation of power in society makes it difficult for individual judges to resist the pressure of corruption. The question must therefore also be seen in terms of political battles: who opposes whom, who struggles for more independence, and what means do they have and employ?

In emphasizing politics, we must take politics as it is, not as we wish it might be, as in some of the more idealistic accounts of deliberative democracy. I fully agree with the view that deliberative institutions founded on the "thick democracy" of public discussion improve developmental performance. However, there are two problems with this view when applied to courts. The first has to do with the confusion of politics with deliberation. Deliberation is still too procedural: it's a very Habermasian, soft, liberal way of speaking of politics. Unfortunately, politics also consists of threats, coercion, violence, and power relations.

It is naïve to claim, as Evans does, that "deliberative institutions must, under some set of empirically plausible conditions, be able to overcome the 'political economy problem': the opposition of power holders who have vested interests in existing decision-making structures."[4] Of course there is a problem; it is called power, which is the ability to make other people do what they would not have done spontaneously.

Deliberative processes are closely linked to the dynamics of party competition, interest group competition, and alliances among competing economic, political, religious, and social factions. How then can political struggle and power be reconciled with judicial independence and the image of courts as above the political fray?

Conceptualizing the Independence of the Judiciary as a Political Struggle

The best-practices approach relies on processes and procedures because they are neutral and universal, whereas politics and culture seem too particular. Politics send us back to history, to political forces. Since 1989, the credo of European politics of democratization has encouraged constitutions and procedures to promote good governance in general terms without taking into account the specificity of each country.

---

[4]   Evans, "Pitfalls of Mono-cropping," p. 38.

Let us consider a concrete example to illustrate the politics of judicial reforms and judicial independence: Egyptian judges. In 1968, the Judges Club took advantage of the general political crisis following the Six-Day War with Israel to issue a statement calling for greater freedom and to elect a new board, with a group of reformers winning the elections for the board in 1969. President Nasser reacted with harsh measures known as the "massacre of the judiciary," including the dismissal of over more than a hundred sitting judges. Today, the Judges Club, with a membership of 8000 judges, is a symbol of the struggle for democratic reforms. As Hassan Nafaa has noted, the current role of the Judges Club has much in common with that played by the Officers Club on the eve of the 1952 Revolution.[5]

What can be learned from the Egyptian laboratory? First, the experience of the Judges Club illustrates how in authoritarian regimes doctor or lawyer associations can perform the role of political parties. The more general lesson is that we have to deal with history, with politics, with relations of power. There have been demonstrations and even confrontations with the Egyptian police in what has been called a "judicial intifada." In 1991, the Judges Club developed a comprehensive draft law for the judiciary. "These reforms are not aimed at comprehensive liberalization but instead stem from a sense of violated status: Egyptian judges tend to take the separation of powers quite seriously and resent any infringement on their autonomy."[6]

Another point to be underscored is that judges in their struggle for more independence have made a deal with Islamists. This development has worried many NGOs. The judges claim there is no danger because there is a consensus among judges and Islamists in favor of the rule of law. However, there are crucial differences in thick conceptions of rule of law between judges and Islamists, for example, with respect to key issues such as the role of Sharia and the proper interpretation of international human rights. In any event, the crucial point is that there are no politics without political deals. The making of such deals, and the compromises involved, are far removed from global best-practice standards for the rule of law and IFES' eighteen judicial integrity principles.

Another issue raised by the Egyptian case is foreign funding and the nature of support for rule of law reforms. Reform-minded Egyptian judges do not need money. They need political support from Western countries; they need to be backed up by their judicial colleagues in Egypt and globally. Money from the World Bank or from Christian charities does not have the same meaning as support from other judges. Support from colleagues is crucial because we are witnessing the building of a global community of judges. This is a big shift even for French judges: some are now more interested in fighting terrorism and the mafia and feel closer to their Italian or German colleagues than to the chief judge or other judges in their court dealing with commercial cases.

---

5   *Al-Haram* weekly on line, May 18–24, 2006.
6   Nathan J. Brown and Hesham Nasr, "Egypt's Judges Step Forward: The Judicial Election Boycott and Egyptian Reform," *Carnegie Endowment for International Peace* (May 2005).

There is no substantive contradiction between the goals of reformist judges in Egypt and global standards with respect to the call for more judicial independence. But it is not necessarily a good starting point for these standards to come from abroad. They must be owned by local actors and be promoted as a matter of national pride. The rule of law must rely on a national feeling.

Paying Attention to Power Relations within the Judiciary

We should avoid a naïve analysis that juxtaposes good judges with bad politicians. In Egypt, reformist judges found that their adversaries were located within the judiciary as well as the executive branch. The political struggle and activism of Egyptian judges is familiar to French judges. In France, there are also politically active judges' unions. This may surprise common law judges. But we have to acknowledge that judges do not unite around the same causes in all countries. For example, the president of a worldwide women judges' association complained that there was no such group in France. But this is meaningless to French judges: in France, the distinction between men and women is not the most relevant criterion on which to organize. It would make more sense to form groups around sensitive themes such as children's rights, environmental law, human rights, and so on. An association like Magistrats Européens pour la Démocratie et les Libertés (MEDEL)[7] would be impossible from an American perspective because the group's activities would be seen as undermining judicial impartiality.

A RESULTS-ORIENTED APPROACH RATHER THAN A FORMALISTIC APPROACH

Thomas Carothers laments the lack of knowledge regarding the real impact of programs designed to promote the rule of law and identifies five reasons for this lack of knowledge:[8]

(i). "The unavoidable fact that the 'rule of law' is an area of great conceptual and practical complexity." I fully agree and would add that it is very difficult – if not impossible – to translate the concept of rule of law into French. I am not speaking of a very remote tribe on the border of Nepal, nor of Islam or socialism, but of another tradition which encompasses all civil law countries that are more numerous than the countries of Anglo-American tradition.

---

[7] Magistrats Européens pour la Démocratie et les Libertés, http://www.medelnet.org/pages/89_1.html. MEDEL is an association with more than 15,000 members from national judges and prosecutors associations from eleven European Union countries. MEDEL seeks to promote judicial independence, rule of law, democracy, and the protection of human rights and campaigns for democratization of the judiciary, including freedom of expression for the judiciary.

[8] Thomas Carothers, "Promoting the Rule of Law Abroad: The Problem of Knowledge," *Carnegie Endowment Series* vol. 34 (2003), p. 12.

(ii). The tremendous diversity of legal systems, "or perhaps, better stated, the functioning of law." We face the "daunting challenge of understanding the realities of law in that particular society."

(iii). Aid organizations are not prepared to devote sufficient resources to research or implementation of training programs and other reforms necessary to achieve the capacity-building and institution-building required for the realization of a rule of law compliant legal system.

(iv). These matters are not a high-priority interest in political science and law departments. They require a wide range of knowledge, not only about substantive law, but also about sociology and culture. This is exactly the mission of the Institut des Hautes Etudes sur la Justice:[9] to bridge the gap between substantive law, judges' concerns, and academic research, and overcome the divide between judicial cultures.

(v). Lawyers involved in this field of judicial development often have formalistic views of legal change. There is confusion between descriptive and prescriptive studies.

To improve judicial integrity, we must first enhance judicial studies, which are insufficiently developed. The following are areas that require further study.

The Idea of Separation of Powers

All international action needs a common language for the participants to understand each other and to be able to organize collective action. Building a common vocabulary is necessary but takes for granted what is problematic. It assumes what should be the aim of the project. For instance, before talking about separation of power, let us first attend to what we mean by power; before thinking about formal institutional arrangements, let us first focus on what roles the different branches actually play. The global-standards approach regarding separation of powers is too closely linked to the American perception of politics and obviously grounded in American history. There are different conceptions in the United States and France, and in other countries.

In China, the PRC, the hierarchical structure of the state power flows downward from the top. On the top there is only one entity, the National People's Congress, not three separate branches as in the United States. The Chinese way of resolving the contradiction between one source of power and the independence of the judiciary is not so strange for a continental lawyer. It "tries to ameliorate the conflict between the leadership of the Chinese Communist Party (CCP) and promotion of judicial professionalism by making a distinction between a general leading role and specific interference...The CCP leads in a general and abstract way, not on

9   See www.ihej.org.

specific issues."[10] Just think of *la Loi* (which is again very difficult to translate into English) instead of the CCP and you have French republican positivism. So the difference between judicial independence in France and in China does not come from the formal system but from something deeper.

The idea of a divisible power is related to a specific form of society, namely democracy. Democracy should not be reduced to a political system: it is also a form of society, as Tocqueville stated. That is why I use the idea of forms of power rather than culture, referring here to a tradition of French political philosophy that characterizes a society by its form of political organization: feudalism, monarchy, totalitarianism, and democracy, that is, the way the power, as a symbolic place, gives form and meaning to social and political interactions.[11]

In democracies, there is a separation between the exercise of power and the idea in the name of which it is exercised. We do not know a lot about this. And it is very particular to every country. For example, the election of judges in some American states contains an idea of separation of powers that is difficult to extend to the rest of the world. It is crucial to our topic, because power is not only a strength found in a society (e.g., in a political party, in a tribe, in a single-party system, in communities) but a specific form of organization.

If we adopt this perspective, it is not enough to just change the rules or to understand the competing political forces. We also need to consider where the authority lies and how this kind of authority shapes relations among society. As a system, democracy is built by procedures and standards; as a society, democracy is built on abstract principles, like equality, the shared perception that every man or woman is an equal and that all differences based on caste, class, gender, sexual orientation, or even nationality are artificial and must be abolished. But these abstract principles must be linked to public expectations within the society. To be efficient, formal rules must fit with deep representations. We do not pay enough attention to this reality. If judges accept a same-sex marriage on behalf of equality in a traditional Muslim country, they can trigger public outrage. Law will not be accepted as a legitimate power, a force legitimate enough to overrule a fundamental religious principle. On the other hand, we should also be careful about the Sharia. Although it has a very negative image in Western countries, it has been adopted as a common reference by liberals, including feminists, in various Arab countries to advance a more progressive agenda, thus depriving radical Islamists of a monopoly on religious authority.[12]

---

[10] Yu Xingzhong, "Judicial Professionalism in China: From Discourse to Reality," conference paper, Professions in China, Harvard University, January 28–30, 2005.

[11] This tradition traces back to Marcel Mauss, Louis Dumont, Cornelius Castoriadis, Claude Lefort, and Marcel Gauchet.

[12] See, e.g., "Jean-Philippe Bras, La réforme du Code de la famille au Maroc et en Algérie: quelles avancées pour la démocratie?" *Critique internationale* vol. 37 (2007), p. 112.

Enhancing judicial independence in a holistic society requires certain precautions. We must be aware of these deep obstacles to find the best remedy, the most suitable solution.

Let us take another example: judges in Palestinian society, and the difficulties they meet in being independent (although the same concerns arise in many countries). As one Palestinian commentator has noted:

> In Palestinian society, people spontaneously prefer to resort to traditional mechanisms of conflict resolution than to the state court. Whereas traditional mechanisms of conflict resolution involve 'middlemen' who appear to represent societal values and whose task is to facilitate the resolution of disputes, the 'modern' judge appears to represent the more idealized values of the centralized state rather than the values of the society itself. Insofar as this is the case, the judge becomes the civil servant of the state. Finding no social force to rely upon, the judge will face enormous difficulties in keeping his/her independence from the state apparatus, and especially from the executive. From a social analysis point of view, the independence of the judge in the Palestinian context is an act of faith.[13]

The main challenge for a Palestinian judge is to maintain a proper distance from both traditional society and the executive branch, a balancing act made all the more difficult by the inability of the judge to draw on a tradition of respect for formal law.

Again, the nature of the polity will also matter. As Carlo Guarnieri points out in Chapter 12, judges in nondemocratic societies see government officials rather than fellow judges or citizens as their referent group, making it more difficult to maintain proper distance from the executive. Conversely, in some transition states, the judiciary, in an effort to stake out its turf vis-à-vis other state organs in the new political order, may become too dependent on popular support to decide cases consistently in accordance with law as required by the rule of law.

Judicial Independence Grows with Individualism

If judicial independence is closely related to the kind of society in which one lives (and human rights are closely related to individualism), then there may very well be a direct link between individualism and judicial independence. In comparing attitudes on ethics in France, the United States, and other countries, I have found significant differences. Liberal cultures show a greater regard for individual identities.[14] My impression is that the more individualistic a society, the more attention paid to each person, the more the idea of human rights makes sense, and the more the idea of a judge, standing alone against state and social power, can be encouraged. Such a

---

[13] Camille Mansour, "Rule of law and reestablishment of the judiciary in Palestine," Feb. 21, 2000, available at http://www.lcps-lebanon.org/conf/oo/mdf3/papers/mansour.pdf.

[14] This leads to categorizing people, which is not the way the French have sought (at least until the recent challenge to this idea) to create a homogenous society, "la République," where everyone is alike treated the same, enjoys benefits from the same services, and shares one national identity.

claim should be tested in particular situations such as the tensions between former President Musharraf and the judiciary in Pakistan, and in African societies, where there is considerable pressure on the individual from the group.

The global standards approach takes for granted that the judge is a personality. This is a very American idea because in most countries a judge is a kind of civil servant, a member of a larger body of people. For example, it would be impossible for me, a French judge, to draft a judgment speaking as "I." It would be unthinkable because I consider myself a civil servant. This comes from the Latin idea of an office (*officium*). I would say that a judge is a "clerc," a concept that is almost impossible to translate into English. This just does not exist in the American culture.

Yu Xingzhong makes a similar point when he notes how in an administrative judiciary controlled by the party judges tend to become lazy and irresponsible. They consider themselves a cog in a wheel. In response, since 2000 the Guangzhou Maritime Court has required judges to write opinions in their own name, including dissenting opinions (and no longer in the name of the court as an abstract and collective entity). "This seemingly insignificant change is intended to make judicial opinions more specific and judges more responsible.... In so doing, judgments would reflect the true opinion of judges, who actually hear the cases, and clarify the responsibility of their judges. It is a positive move toward broader transparency and observable justice. It places responsibilities on individual judges who will have to brush up on their professional and language skills in order to compose a good judgment. This is also seen as a way of bringing up reputable judges."[15] In other words, judges are no longer anonymous members of a collective body but individual personalities.

This reform may signal a change in the prevailing emphasis on the judiciary's independence as the whole or the court as an entity rather than the particular judge who hears the case, and in the administrative and hierarchical nature of Chinese courts. Nevertheless, we should not assume that this particular "international best practice" will function as expected or necessarily have the desired effect.

The impact of this change on the Guangzhou Maritime Court and on the Chinese judiciary remains to be seen. The impact may be limited given that other institutional factors have not changed. The courts continue to function within a single-party authoritarian structure. As in other civil law systems, judges continue to be seen as civil servants. The internal incentive structure for judges, along with the appointment and promotion processes, continues to reinforce the administrative and hierarchical nature of the courts.[16] Once again this calls attention to the holistic nature of reform and demonstrates the need to situate reform measures within the broader context.

---

[15] Yu Xingzhong, "Judicial Professionalism in China."

[16] On the internal incentive structure, see Carl Minzner, "Judicial Disciplinary Systems for Incorrectly Decided Cases" in Mary Gallagher et al. eds., *Chinese Justice: Civil Dispute Resolution in Contemporary China* (Cambridge: Harvard University Press, forthcoming).

Why Are Judges Willing to Be Independent?

The maritime court example reframes the debate and leads to another question: Why are judges willing to be independent? It is not enough to be formally independent: a judge must feel that he is independent. It would be interesting to compare the situation in the United States, the United Kingdom, France, and China, for example, using general criteria like attitudes toward money, power, fellow judges, and society. We would find different attitudes in each country. For example, American and French cultures do not place the same value on someone who remains in public service without earning a lot of money.

Or, to return to an earlier example, what motivates Egyptian judges to get involved in the political struggle for the rule of law and judicial independence? Universal values, like human rights or human dignity, are surely part of the story. But Egyptian judges are also eager to promote the international image of Egypt. There is a tradition of law that they can rely on and an element of national pride in the legal system and the role of law and judges.

Some of these factors, such as motivations and the effects of history, can be analyzed only qualitatively, not quantitatively. This reflects another problem with the global-standards approach, which assumes that what is relevant is only what can be measured. In downplaying or ignoring what cannot be measured, this approach chooses a way of representation that seems more neutral and more scientific and is obviously needed (and here it should be noted that French legal scholars do not do enough quantitative research). Yet this methodology, this form of representation, must be supplemented and completed by other methodologies and forms of representations. Much of the complexity of reality is lost in the process of producing quantitative indicators.

Judges as Political Actors

Although the rule of law is not the privilege of a closed club of Western countries, we should appreciate that implementing the rule of law entails deep changes in a country. Establishing the rule of law is not like bringing water to a village or building a bridge: it is closely tied to conceptions and perceptions of legitimacy. Separation of powers, for instance, is taken for granted as if it were the consensual, never questioned solution of all democratic countries. This assumption leaps over centuries of struggle to achieve this separation, which has been conceived and implemented to different degrees through diverse institutional arrangements, even in Western countries known for the rule of law.

Judicial integrity principles are a useful heuristic tool for analyzing the basic criteria for judicial independence and the rule of law. These principles are easily understood all over the world and in all societies. No country will disagree with rules demanding diligent and hard-working judges and punishing those who sentenced the wrong man. Consensus on these basic rules is easily achieved. But another part of the story is to admit that judges perform a political role, censuring acts voted by national parliaments or deciding controversial issues like same-sex marriage. It has nothing to do with independence or with integrity but with the political role expected in longstanding democracies. Very few countries will follow the American example, including France.

Even in authoritarian regimes, the global trend toward judicialization of controversial economic, social, and political disputes has led to debates about whether the courts are the proper forum for resolving such disputes (see, e.g., Fu and Peerenboom's chapter in this volume). Indeed, as He Xin points out in his chapter, in some cases the judiciary itself prefers to limit access to the courts, shifting responsibility for resolving the controversial issues to political and administrative entities.

The Ambiguity of Rule of Law and the Implications for Judging: Which Ends Do Independent Judges Serve?

The idea of rule of law is double-edged, encompassing both fairness and congruency with some core values (substantive or thick conceptions of rule of law), and regularity, predictability, and visibility (procedural or thin conceptions of rule of law). Realization of a procedural rule of law will not lead to just outcomes if the rules being enforced are themselves unfair.

More attention needs to be paid to what substantive purposes legal reforms that seek to promote rule of law and judicial independence will serve and whether the reforms achieve those substantive goals. In some cases, increased judicial independence may have negative side effects, including increased corruption. In other cases, the emphasis on global best practices may contribute to political hypocrisy, with some countries paying lip service to rule of law and the enhancement of judicial independence while the real battle lines are drawn elsewhere. Zhu Suli's chapter in this volume, for instance, presents an extreme form of this argument in claiming that Western conceptions of judicial independence are of little practical value for understanding the legal system in China and in particular the role of the party with respect to the judiciary.

ANALYZING LOCAL BAD HABITS RATHER THAN PRAISING GLOBAL BEST PRACTICES

The worst enemy of judicial integrity is global gibberish. Yet rather than providing an incentive for judicial independence and integrity, global best practices can sometimes provide a powerful incentive to conceal deep differences in political systems or major deficiencies in domestic legal systems, and in particular the influence of particular groups.

I remember acting as a human rights activist in former communist countries. We were first treated to a presentation of formal laws, which were even better than in France, followed by a learned speech about socialist rule of law. It was unimpeachable ... until we got to a specific case, assuming we were even allowed to discuss the actual operation of the legal system.

There is the famous difference between law on the books, or law as it should be, and law in action, or the reality of law. International aid for the rule of law should look at what is happening in reality. Let us describe real practices in a proper way and understand them, in both developing and developed countries.

There is a risk of fragmentation between the reality of the judiciary and public speeches about modernization and best practices. All too often the reality of the legal system and the judiciary in developing countries is compared to an idealized version of how the legal system should operate in developed countries. Promoting international best practices therefore risks widening the gap between globalized and international lawyers and judges, who have it right, and the others, who have it wrong. The danger is that local bad practices will become even more invisible as local actors seek to hide real problems or deviations from global standards.

Take corruption. Corruption as a single universal phenomenon doesn't exist: there are as many types of corruption as there are countries. Each country generates a specific kind of corruption, and there are different forms of corruption within a country. A judge being bribed by one of the parties is different from a judge under pressure because of family ties or a judge threatened by the local mafia or under government pressure. In China, local protectionism, the nature of the judicial hierarchy, and the internal incentive system for judges, budgetary problems, and populism (which doesn't have the same meaning as in France) are all specific causes of corruption.[17]

So, I suggest starting from the opposite point: not what best practices should be, but what is wrong? Today it seems more important to have a good study on judicial corruption, in let's say, commercial cases in basic level courts in Shanghai, as provided by Minxin Pei et al. in their chapter, rather than to have another tirade of the international gospel about good governance and judicial independence. This shift in approaching rule of law policies throughout the world would lead us toward particular situations not only in countries but in various parts of a country. It would lead to the specific and idiosyncratic, because the good inclines toward the universal, and the bad leads us toward the particular, and it is the particular that is significant.

Visibility as a Political Task

All too often we speak about a general problem without first fully understanding the nature of the problem in a particular country. For example, we need to know

---

[17] Yu Xingzhong, "Judicial Professionalism in China." See also Benjamin Liebman, "A Populist Threat to Chinese Courts," in Mary Gallagher et al. eds., *Chinese Justice: Civil Dispute Resolution in Contemporary China* (forthcoming Harvard University Press).

more about the specific forms of judicial corruption and interference in judicial independence in China, and indeed the specific forms in different types of cases, different level courts, and different regions in China. This task would benefit from both a thick (in the Geertzian sense) social science description of what happens and an emotional perception of the lived reality through films and other narrative forms.

Howard Whitton for instance makes films on situations involving corruption. His films are subtle, and they show several possible endings to the same situation. The same should be done for judicial corruption. Stéphanie Balme's work highlights the value of such an approach. Her field research on a remote local court in Shaanxi consists of both a classical written analysis of the situation of these rural courts and photos showing their poor conditions and the daily lived reality of the judges and citizens who use the courts.[18] Corruption draws its strength from its invisibility. Like Dracula, it fears the light; the best disinfecting tool is to put it on stage.

The global-standards approach relies on both transparency and accountability. Visibility, however, is not just transparency; visibility has to do with representation, which is different from transparency. Representation is not only "let them see": it is a work in itself that involves how to make arrangements to mobilize people around a theme or cause. Politics can be quickly defined as the art of putting internal divisions on stage peacefully.[19] Building parties and support for a position is the very essence of the political process. Emphasizing visibility, therefore, means taking seriously the possibility that forging an alliance between judges and prosecutors, or between judges and Islamists, is much more crucial than transparency.

This process of putting on stage divisions about the meaning to give to judicial independence is not possible without a previous representation of the problems that limit or undermine judicial independence. Yet there are relatively few studies describing judicial independence and the obstacles to it in particular countries compared to the vast normative literature extolling its virtues. It is as if the medical profession would write books and books about the importance of good health and good practices ("mind your eyes," "wash your hands") while ignoring diseases and their symptoms and causes! If we want to cure the disease, we should start describing the symptoms and causes rather than avoiding them in favor of generalizations about international best practices for a healthy life.

This is a methodological point: when learning a foreign language it is much more efficient to stress and work on mistakes rather than focus on the perfect usage of words. It is easier to become aware of the imperfections of something that is not smooth, not perfect. Observing imperfections allows people to acquire criteria about good practices. This is thus a more pedagogical approach.

---

[18] See Balme's chapter in this volume.
[19] Claude Lefort states: "C'est la mise en scène, mise en forme et mise en sens des divisions." See Bernard Flynn, *The Philosophy of Claude Lefort: Interpreting the Political* (Evanston, IN: Northwestern University Press, 2005).

A PROBLEM-SHARING APPROACH RATHER THAN A MODEL APPROACH

The best-practices approach is a largely closed one.[20] It is appalling to tell other countries that there is one model. This is not true. This approach idealizes the reality of courts in Western countries. The problem with the model approach is that it presents itself as something simple and obvious. Judicial independence (and democracy) must be taken both as an aspiration and a problem. Judicial independence is complicated in all countries, even democracies, recently and vividly demonstrated by the tension between the Bush administration and judges on issues of national security and the war on terrorism. The model approach, emphasizing democracy and judicial independence, sends the wrong message: democracy is the freedom to choose global standards, that is, what we want (for you)![21] The value of the democracy is its openness, its indeterminacy.[22] Because of this indeterminacy, open societies, as Friedrich Hayek puts it, are always in an unstable balance.

Remove Shame about the Miscarriage of Justice

As mentioned previously, there is nothing worse than international waffle. To avoid this risk, it is better to remove the shame associated with judicial corruption (just as it is better for a physician to create an atmosphere that encourages the patient to tell the truth about his bad health habits). Eliminating shame and guilt is the first step to finding out what is wrong. The best way to create such an atmosphere is for international promoters of judicial independence to discuss the problems they face in their own legal systems.

When I was in China, I decided not to speak about the rule of law and judicial independence as noble goals or a set of best practices, but rather to talk about a serious miscarriage of justice in France: the *Outreau* case.[23] The idea was to talk to Chinese judges as colleagues, not as a minister preaching the gospel of how the West got it right and has worked out all of the problems. In *Outreau*, a bipartisan parliamentary commission was formed, which is unusual. I was surprised to learn that in the United States, some similar miscarriages of justice had occurred, but they did not result in major scandals. In the *Admirault* case, for instance, a man stayed in jail for eighteen years before being released because he was innocent. Yet there was

---

[20] "L'idée d'un universalisme fermé du modèle doit ainsi céder le pas à un universalisme ouvert de la confrontation des expériences." Pierre Rosanvallon, "L'universalisme démocratique: histoire et problèmes," *ESPRIT*, Dec. 17, 2007.

[21] This is not to deny, of course, that there is often strong local demand and support for some form of democracy, rule of law, judicial independence, and human rights.

[22] Claude Lefort insists on this specific trend of democracy as compared to other forms of regimes.

[23] The Outreau Case is one of alleged massive sexual abuse on children in a small town of Northern France. The criminal trial, in July 2004, put under light the disfunctioning of the media, the judicial institutions, and the social workers.

no scandal. Why? Most Americans think the system works, that it is the best system in the world.[24] Overconfidence is not always an advantage.

There Is Not One Model but Several Ways to Translate Common Principles into Reality

I advocate judicial diversity as a matter of necessity. It is not possible to get free of cultural biases or historical legacies: the only possibility is to offer various solutions to a common problem.

The model approach is presented as a "take it or leave it" choice. There is no way to find one's own way because the value itself and its cultural translation and institutional manifestation are presented as one and the same. The IFES report contains both a defense of judicial independence and another message: to reach it, you have to share the American way.

The challenge for all of us today is to move from a universalism by extension (the United States and to a certain extent the European Union) to an open universalism by problem-sharing and the representation of conflicts. We must find the resources within each culture and country to address the problems in that country. The starting point must be from each country toward universal standards.

CONCLUSION

Judicial integrity is a serious matter that requires more than singing an international gospel with very few results. I do not want to give the impression that we should abandon global standards entirely. They are obviously necessary, although insufficient. I stressed the importance of understanding local politics and of appreciating the tension between local politics and global principles of judicial integrity. I am acutely aware that this argument can be used by those within a country to oppose reforms that would be welfare-enhancing for the public. In response, I advocate a nonculturalist use of culture. Culture must be taken as a starting point but not an excuse: there is no culture plea as there is an insanity plea. As Montesquieu observed, culture cannot be separated from politics.

---

[24] But American citizens become worried when defendants are denied access to the judicial system, as in the case of detainees in Guantanamo Bay, in part for the same reason – their faith in the judicial system to uphold what is right, which requires access to the courts.

4

The Party and the Courts

Zhu Suli

The dominant view among Western legal scholars, human rights activists, and pundits is that the Chinese judiciary lacks meaningful independence in large part because China is a single-party authoritarian state. According to this view, the Chinese Communist Party (CCP) is the main source of interference with the courts and the biggest obstacle to judicial independence. This chapter challenges the prevailing wisdom about the party and its role with respect to judicial independence, legal reforms, and China's efforts to modernize more generally.

The dominant view is the result of analytical and methodological errors typical of Western China watchers' efforts to understand China's legal system and the legal systems in other developing states, authoritarian ones in particular. It is based on four unwarranted assumptions. First, there exists some pure state of reality that deserves to be called judicial autonomy. Second, it is possible to construct a set of standards for, or an objective model of, this judicial autonomy, either as a political structure or as a set of social conventions. Third, this model can show that the CCP exercises political influence on judges and the courts in a way that is inimical to and undermines judicial autonomy. Fourth, it is possible to identify and examine the actual social effect of such influence, and the overall effect of party influence is negative. Rationally considered, however, these suppositions are simply unrealistic.

The dominant view also reflects a deep ideological bias central to the West's proclaimed moral authority (a shaky proclamation evaporating rapidly in the aftermath of 9/11) of the Western (or at least American) notion of legal autonomy and rule of law.

These analytical and methodological errors, together with this ideological bias, have prevented scholars from understanding China, its legal system, and its development.

Contrary to the dominant view, I argue that the CCP is still the most important political and developmental force for contemporary China. No comparable alternative institutions or political forces exist. The CCP constitutes the most important component of the constitutional and governmental structure of modern China. It is still the major force mobilizing, promoting, and implementing reform within the judiciary, even though some of the reform measures promoted by the party have been clear mistakes, and even though party leaders and policies have hindered the development of an independent judiciary. Nevertheless, on balance, the CCP's oversight has discouraged at least to some extent judicial corruption and judicial arrogance, two common by-products of the judiciary's ongoing transformation and the global trend toward judicialization of all disputes.

A closer examination of the party's role suggests the importance of keeping an open mind and understanding the development of the Chinese judiciary in its own historical and social context. Visions of judicial independence drawn from distinctly Western experience are not particularly meaningful for modern China, and evaluations and judgments based on these experiences or from their underlying ideology (an ideology that emerged out of the strategic consideration of Western politicians) have limited academic value and practical use for China. From the perspective of evolutionary economics, any institutional innovation that survives in competition with other social forces is a valid institution. Social development has no predetermined path or institutional model. The same is true with regard to China's judiciary.

Part I questions the suitability of Western conceptions of judicial independence in a political system where the party's influence is so far-reaching, beginning with a historical comparison of the Kuomintang (KMT) and the CCP. Part II challenges the notion that there is an accepted universal standard for how independent the judiciary should be or a universal consensus regarding the proper relationship between law and politics. I argue that rather than searching for, or aspiring to, some decontextualized abstraction or ideal type of judicial independence, we should pay more attention to the actual role of the party and its influence on the judiciary, the legal system, and China's efforts at modernization more generally. As suggested by Antoine Garapon in the previous chapter, we should examine how the legal system actually operates, what the problems are, and what can be done to address them, without presupposing a particular solution based on how Western countries now address similar problems (although they may not have addressed them in the same way at earlier stages of the development process). In particular, we need first to better understand the actual influence of the party and party institutions on the courts and then assess both the positive and negative aspects of the party's role in how the legal system operates now and in supporting or facilitating reforms that could improve the situation.

Part III addresses some of the methodological issues and the ideological bias of many Western studies of the Chinese legal system, cautioning against the assumption that China must follow the same institutional development path as Western countries.

Part IV concludes with a response to some criticisms and objections to my view.

LOCATING THE PARTY

It is hard to identify a distinct party interference in the everyday operation of the judiciary and daily life more generally. Such efforts would only exacerbate ideological misinterpretations of both the CCP's and the courts' contributions to China's constitutional structure. They would not help further our understanding of the actual operation or problems of courts in China.

Both Chinese and foreign scholars – inside and outside of the legal studies field – have correctly pointed out the CCP's influence throughout Chinese political society. Although the CCP has never formally accepted the earlier KMT notion of a party-state, it has nevertheless inherited from its former political enemy the legacy of having to construct and rule a nation-state through the leadership of a single political party – a party that, as proposed early in the twentieth century by Sun Yat-sen, had to be above the nation-state.[1]

In fact, the CCP's post-1949 leadership over the nation-state has been far more extensive and effective than that of the earlier KMT. During the KMT's rule, different parts of the country were controlled by various provincial strongmen, making national unification during 1927–1949 purely symbolic.[2] In addition, the CCP itself represented a strong and alternative political force able to control substantial areas of the country with the help of its own loyal and strong army. Although the KMT included many independent and socially influential technocrats and bureaucrats, its internal incompetence caused it to remain highly dependent on a historical pattern of power-sharing with an urban gentry class. The KMT government had very little influence in rural China.[3] For this reason, the KMT was unable to exert complete control over China, and as such was unable to implement its political program throughout society.[4]

In contrast, the CCP has been much more effective at constructing a strong and centralized unitary state. Although China officially sports a number of other political parties, they all operate under the authority of the CCP. In fact, some of

---

[1] Sun Yat-sen, *Sun Yat-sen Quanji* [Complete Works of Sun Yah-sen], (Beijing: Zhonghua Shuju, 1986), vol. 8, pp. 267–268; vol. 9, pp. 103–104.

[2] *Deng Xiaoping Xuanji* [Selected Readings of Deng Xiao Ping], 3 vols. 2nd ed., (Beijing: Renmin Chubanshe, 1994), vol. 2, p. 299.

[3] Fei Xiaotong, *Huangquan he Shenquan* [Emperor's Power and the Power of Gentry Class], (Beijing: Tianji Renmin Chubanshe, 1988).

[4] Historical research demonstrates that conflicts between KMT local branches and local governments always ended with the victory of local governments. Cf. Wang Xianzhi, "*Kangzhan Shiqi Guomindang Zuzhi Jianshe yu Zuzhi Fazhan de Jige Wenti*" [Issues on KMT's Organizational Construction and Development During the Anti-Japanese War], *Jindaishi Yanjiu*, 1990/2, pp. 230–250; Zhongshen and Tang Sengshu, "*Shilun Nanjing Guomin Zhengfu Xunzheng Qianqi (1928–1937) de Difang Dangzheng Jiufeng*" [The Local Party-Government Conflicts in Early Tutelary Period (1928–1937) of Nanjing National Government], *Shixue Yuekan*, 1999/2, pp. 53–58.

these other parties' leaders are themselves also CCP members.[5] Others are loyal communists.[6] Since 1978, these parties have been given some space for autonomous policy formation, and the CCP has developed various formal and informal institutions for gathering and selectively adopting their policy advice. But the overall system operates under the ultimate control of the CCP.

The majority of China's social elites, either including those serving in universities or in commercial circles, are CCP members. The CCP membership even includes people sometimes regarded by Western observers as political dissidents. Other social elites in China accept the political leadership of CCP even when they themselves are not CCP members. In this sense, although the CCP has long proclaimed itself a dictatorship specifically of China's proletarian working classes, and although its final goal continues to be the realization of a working-class communism,[7] it ultimately evolved (long before Jiang Zemin's declaration of "the three represents"[8]) into a national party seeking to advance the fundamental interests of the Chinese people as a whole, not simply those of a particular class.[9] And its basic goals are widely accepted by the public.

Because of its strict organizational structure and the influence of its political programs, the CCP's political influence is far-reaching in today's China. For this reason, distinguishing between CCP policy and governmental policy – although there are sometimes differences in terms of ideas, ideals, and conflicts of interests – is often difficult. For example, all of China's provincial governors are also CCP members who are politically subordinate to the provincial CCP party secretary. Party and governmental officials often rotate among both party and governmental positions. Many provincial governors move on to become provincial party secretaries. Many provincial CCP party secretaries become governors of other provinces or assume other governmental positions. This system of party–state cross-fertilization includes within its ambit every significant party and state position at the national and local levels. A similar intermingling can be found in almost all of China's social, trade, and educational organizations.

---

[5] The former or current leaders of such political parties as Democratic League, China National Democratic Consultation Association, Zi Gong Party, and Taiwan Democratic Self-government League were or are CCP members.

[6] Two late non-CCP vice presidents of China are examples. One is Song Qinqlin, wife of Dr. Sun Yat-sen, who applied for and was approved to join the CCP before her death; the other is Rong Yiren, the number one commercial entrepreneur, who was called a loyal communist in the official obituary.

[7] "General Principles," CCP Constitution, adopted in the sixteenth CCP national conference on November 14, 2002.

[8] It is emphasized that CCP represents the fundamental interests of the overwhelming majority of the Chinese people, the development trend of China's advanced productive forces, and the orientation of China's advanced culture. It is widely considered an important change of CCP in terms of its organizational constitution and political ideology.

[9] Cf. CCP Constitutions of seventh and eighth CCP National Conferences.

Insofar as China's judiciary is concerned, since 1954 every president of the Supreme People's Court (SPC) has also been in charge of the CCP's oversight of judicial operations. The presidents of lower courts have invariably occupied similar positions within their respective regional CCP organizations. Although one of a court's several vice president positions will usually be held by someone who is not a CCP member, these persons will nevertheless be carefully selected by the relevant branch of the CCP and will be people the party trusts. Also, that person will frequently participate in CCP meetings relevant to judicial operations.

Within such a system, it can difficult to distinguish whether particular interferences or influences issue from the CCP or from the government, people's congress, or even from some element of China's emerging private society. Not all judicial interference, even that which formally issues from particular party organizations or party officials, is consistent with CCP policies (see Fu and Peerenboom's chapter in this volume). On the contrary, some of this interference is aimed at outcomes that directly contravene CCP policies. CCP officials may use their position within the CCP to interfere with the performance of a court in pursuit of their own selfish and perhaps even illegal personal or local interests. Courts and procuratorates are supposed to resist this kind of interference, according to both the law and rules of party discipline, although it is often hard for them to do so. It is mistaken to call interference that operates in direct contravention of the CCP's own policies, even when it comes from persons with party affiliation, party interference.

From within the judiciary, it becomes even more difficult to distinguish CCP influence from other factors affecting court decisions. A decision formally issuing from the SPC, even from its adjudication committee – perhaps the most professionalized judicial organ within China – may simply reiterate a position previously arrived at by the Central Committee of CCP. On the other hand, a higher court's reversal of some lower court judgment may in fact have been made autonomously but will nevertheless be presented as the product of CCP direction to enhance its weight in the affected lower court. Similarly, CCP interference often takes the form of generalized instructions. Sometimes, these instructions simply interpret particular provisions in the black letter law. Such abstract interpretations are essentially legislative in character. And although they may implicate possible CCP interference in or usurpation of the legislative powers of the people's government or people's congress, they would not seem to indicate interference in the courts (which in China lack formal powers of abstract interpretation). Also, such generalized instructions themselves can be subject to interpretation by the presiding judge in the process of applying them to a particular case (or by the SPC through various forms of judicial interpretation). The judge's decision or SPC interpretation may claim the authority of party backing even though they represent the judge's or SPC's own position.

Clearly, party officials and party organs influence the functioning of the judiciary because of the party's overall influence on society and politics. And in many cases, party interventions have been unjust and unfair to the point of contributing to various political disasters in Chinese history. Yet even during the party's most radical movements, such as the Cultural Revolution (1966–1976), there also were CCP officials and organizations – including those in judiciary – who, within the scope of their ability and influence, reduced and even prevented some of the unfairness and injustice that stemmed from that radicalism. Although today it is popular to attribute all China's problems to the CCP, it is difficult to imagine how the current state of Chinese society and judiciary would have been better off without the modern revolution led by the CCP. Of course, only history will have the final word on this, but the striking success of China's recent development forces one to acknowledge that the revolution led by the CCP has had some positive influence on China. And with that, one also has to accept that the CCP's interference could also, at least occasionally, have a similarly positive influence upon China's judiciary.

For example, sometimes CCP interference represents and promotes a local population's particular understandings of what justice and fairness demand in the handling of a particular case. Such interference certainly does not respect the U.S. model of separation of power, and as such it is often criticized by many legal scholars whose appreciation for Western practices leads them to think that the CCP should keep quiet regarding cases pending trial. Yet this kind of interference might actually be beneficial for a majority of Chinese who do not care about foreign experience but seek justice and social solidarity. From a Western constitutional perspective, such interference seems to be improper. But from a political perspective, it is hard to see why legal control over a case is always and necessarily more morally just or reasonable than political control. Why should a technocratic judicial determination always be superior to a political one? In practice, this kind of interference can be a legitimate and beneficial exercise of the CCP's core political function of social integration and representation.

Along these lines, the CCP is a kind of alternative source of Chinese constitutionalism. The CCP has long been aware that national modernization cannot be accomplished by the party's political elite alone. The task of social integration required that the party enjoy some degree of voluntary support from other social forces in China. This requires, in turn, that it be able to comprehend and appreciate the different interests underlying these different social forces. The CCP has responded to this by adopting a certain degree of democracy within the party. In this sense, the party itself becomes a quasi-constitutional structure – whose own internal democracy can supplement or even compete with (and through such competition improve) the more formal constitutional apparatus of the state.

THE PROBLEM OF REFERENCE: FROM ABSTRACT IDEALS
TO PRAGMATIC ASSESSMENT OF ACTUAL CONSEQUENCES

Simply put, there is no universal framework of reference for evaluating when judicial independence exists or for evaluating whether and when such independence is beneficial or costly insofar as the larger constitutional order is concerned. Even where the CCP's interference is possible to identify, it is difficult to evaluate its actual consequences. There are many flaws in the judiciary today. Although some of these can be attributed to the governance of the CCP, I would argue that overall, the judiciary's problems are more meaningfully attributed to the recent, unprecedented social transformation of Chinese society. One reason I wrote *Sending Law to the Countryside* was to move us beyond our uncritical reference to simplistic Western notions of judicial independence so that we could more meaningfully identify and situate these problems and thereby search more effectively for solutions.[10]

For one thing, we might first note that all modern constitutional countries have mass-based political parties like the CCP. And although some principle of judicial independence is commonly acknowledged in these countries, these political parties invariably enjoy significant influence over the judiciary and sometimes interfere with the courts' activities.

For example, according to America's famous Supreme Court Justice Oliver Wendell Holmes Jr., the United States Supreme Court's famous power of judicial review was itself the product in significant part of the party loyalties of its Chief Justice, John Marshall. According to Holmes, Marshall saw this new power as a way to help his Federalist Party resist the Republic–Democratic Party of President Thomas Jefferson.[11] Paradoxically, this new power would subsequently be regarded as a core component of judicial independence in the United States.

One may object that this development occurred long ago during the early stages of the evolution of the U.S. judiciary. But even now, party politics are still deeply embedded in the functioning of the American judiciary. For example, the U.S. Constitution requires that federal judges be nominated by the president and confirmed by the Senate. Both of these institutions are centers of party policy formation, and party politics clearly influence decisions regarding judicial appointments.

The Democrats' successful effort to thwart President Ronald Reagan's nomination of Judge Robert Bork in 1987 was a dramatic example of this. Judge Bork himself referred to this as an unconscionable "political seduction" of the judiciary.[12] But, one might ask, isn't this simply an overstatement reflecting Judge Bork's anger and disappointment? Let us imagine instead then that the nomination had been confirmed by a Republican-dominated Senate. Would not this affirmation, against the

[10] Zhu Suli, *Song fa xiaxiang: Zhongguo jiceng sifazhidu yanjiu* [Sending Law to the Countryside: Research on China's Basic-Level Judicial System], (Beijing: The Chinese University of Law and Politics Press, 2000), p. 466. For an extended review, see Frank K. Upham, "Who Will Find the Defendant if He Stays with His Sheep? Justice in Rural China," *The Yale Law Journal*, vol. 114: 1675 et seq.

[11] Oliver Wendell Holmes, "John Marshall," in *The Essential Holmes: Selections from the Letters, Speeches, Judicial Opinions, and Other Writings of Oliver Wendell Holmes, Jr.* Richard A. Posner ed., (Chicago: University of Chicago Press, 1992), pp. 206–209.

[12] Robert H. Bork, *The Tempting of America: The Political Seduction of the Law* (New York: Simon & Schuster, 1990).

opposition of a large number of Democratic lawmakers, have itself been the product of party politics? And although the politics surrounding Judge Bork's nomination were exceptionally dramatic, they were not exceptional per se.

One recent study suggests that a growing number of even noncontroversial nominations to the federal judiciary are being subject to similar party-based political dynamics. It found that:

> [T]he more important the court, the greater the difficulty of having the [judicial nominee] confirmed. Although the confirmation rates have fallen and the length of the confirmation process has lengthened dramatically, the ex-post measures of judicial quality of circuit court nominees... [and] judicial independence have been decreasing over time.... The most troubling results strongly indicate that circuit court judges who turn out to be the most successful judges... faced the most difficult confirmation battles.[13]

As to the cause of this, the author of the study speculates that perhaps "senators of the party opposite the president only really care about preventing the best judges from being on the circuit court because they will have the most impact."[14] This implies that even in the United States, political parties themselves see judges, at least in part, as party actors.

Politics and political party interferences are evident not only with regard to the nomination and confirmation of judges, but also in the handling of particular cases. One example of this already mentioned is the role that party loyalty played in the famous U.S. Supreme Court case of Marbury v. Madison.[15] But many American judges, justices, and the courts they oversee evince patterns of decision making that closely track, sometimes uncomfortably so, the political platforms of the Democratic or Republican parties. Studies have found some degree of party interpenetration in the Warren Court, Burger Court, and Rehnquist Court.[16] More recently, the dramatic case of Bush v. Gore[17] caused Americans to again remember the uncomfortably close correspondence between political parties and court decisions in the United States.[18] At the state level, in some states, political party capacity to influence

---

[13] See John R. Lott, Jr., "The Judicial Confirmation Process: The Difficulty with Being Smart," *Journal of Empirical Legal Studies*, vol. 2/3 (2005), pp. 443–444.

[14] Id at 444.

[15] Marbury v. Madison, 1 Cranch 137 (1803).

[16] Lucas A. Powe Jr., *The Warren Court and American Politics*, (Cambridge: Harvard University Press, 2000); Earl M. Maltz, *The Chief Justiceship of Warren Burger, 1969–1986* (Chapel Hill: University of South Carolina Press, 2000); Tinsley E. Yarbrough, *The Rehnquist Court and the Constitution* (London: Oxford University Press, 2001); and Earl M. Maltz ed., *Rehnquist Justice: Understanding the Court Dynamic* (Lawrence: University of Kansas Press, 2003).

[17] 531 U.S. 98 (2000).

[18] Cf. Richard A. Posner, *Breaking the Deadlock: The 2000 Election, the Constitution, and the Courts*, (Princeton: Princeton University Press, 2001); and Cass R. Sunstein and Richard A. Epstein ed., *The Vote: Bush, Gore, and the Supreme Court* (Chicago: University of Chicago Press, 2001).

judicial decision making is further enhanced by a constant threat of the distinctively political – and essentially party-driven – process of judicial recall.[19]

Without a doubt, party-based influence over the activities of courts in China is a different order of magnitude than in U.S. courts. In America, the political inclination of the judiciary may result from the personal convictions of individual judges consistent with a particular party's vision of law and society. At the same time, lifetime tenure and a high salary make it possible for judges to oppose both government and political party pressure when so inclined.[20] In China, by contrast, judges enjoy no such protections and are further subject to political party influence through the party's disciplinary oversight of the judiciary and individual judges. Chinese judges thus tend to see themselves more as civil servants rather than independent professionals. They are more likely to defer to rather than confront existing political and administrative hierarchies in which they themselves are embedded. They leave the articulation of dissenting opinions and interpretations to legal scholars. To be sure, judges in civil law systems generally see themselves as civil servants. Moreover, the degree of judicial activism varies widely and is dependent on many factors besides the nature of the polity. Japanese judges, for example, are known for being independent and yet restrained in their exercise of judicial review.

What then are we to make of the party's influence in China? The fact that party influence in China differs, either quantitatively or qualitatively, from political influence on judiciaries in other countries is not itself a meaningful basis for critique. To develop a useful understanding of the problems of courts in China and of their prospects for reform we have to examine in detail not only the existence, degree, and process of CCP influences on judicial behavior but also their actual effect. It is on this basis, rather than some abstract notion of judicial independence, that a study of party–judiciary relations in contemporary China should proceed. Regarding China's current, overall sociopolitical context, CCP–judiciary relations are representative of CCP relations with other constitutional institutions. The CCP perceives itself as, and to a great extent is, the principal driver of a necessary social transformation in China – and that includes a necessary social transformation of the judiciary.

The relationship between China's political parties and the Chinese judiciary evolved within the ongoing historical process of China's modernization. Since 1840, the most important task for China has been to transform itself: economically, from an agricultural economy into an industrial and commercial economy; politically, from a premodern community based on personal relationships into a modern nation-state; and culturally, from one dominated by extrapolations from Confucian humanities into one dominated by hard and soft scientific investigation.[21]

---

[19] Henry J. Abraham, *The Judicial Process, An Introductory Analysis of the Courts of the United States, England, and France,* 7th ed. (Oxford: Oxford University Press, 1998), pp. 37–42.

[20] Cf. Laurence H. Tribe, *Constitutional Choices* (Cambridge: Harvard University Press, 1985).

[21] Suli, *Daolu Tongxiang Chengshi – Zhuanxing Zhongguo de Fazhi* [All Roads Lead to Cities – Rule of Law in China's Transformation], (Beijing: Falu Chubanshe, 2004), esp. Introduction.

It is unrealistic to expect a localized, premodern agricultural society like that of traditional China to evolve naturally or spontaneously in such a direction. China's recent history confirms this. On both the Mainland and in Taiwan, China's effective modernization only commenced with the development of an effective party leadership over the state.

As political parties, both the CCP and the KMT evolved under conditions and in a way that differed markedly from the development path of political parties found in the contemporary Western world. Political parties in the West were established and operated within nation-states that had already modernized and were already effectively constituted. Both the CCP and the KMT, by contrast, have had to be much more active and aggressive in mobilizing and rationalizing China's fragmented and premodern political and social forces into a unified modern nation – and through this attain the national independence and related capacities for social and economic development that political parties in the West were generally able to take for granted.[22]

For this reason, both the CCP and KMT evolved as revolutionary parties that opposed not simply other political factions but the constitutional status quo as a whole. Even after their respective revolutions they had to retain their revolutionary character to direct the ongoing and comprehensive social revolution – that is, the economic, political, and social transformations outlined above – necessary to bring about China's modernization.

This dictated that both the KMT and the CCP be elitist parties – capable of mobilizing and leading the masses effectively from above. Social transformation is necessarily a top-down process[23] because ordinary people tend to be more socially conservative than the political elite. The elite nature of the CCP and KMT was reflected in their emphasis on "organized democracy," "disciplined freedom," and "democratic centralism"; in the strength of their political ideologies; and in the powerful internal institutions designed to instill strict party discipline.[24]

Although the KMT and CCP share a common origin as elite revolutionary parties, in this aspect at least there have been significant differences in their subsequent evolution that affect their relationships with their respective judiciaries. Contrary to what most people think, these differences were determined more by the different social context in which these parties had to operate and in the different social resources they had at their disposal than by ideological differences. For a variety of reasons, the KMT inherited most of China's technocrats, professionals, and other educated elite. By contrast, it was harder for the CCP to attract such elite to join

---

[22] Sun Yat-sen proposed three stages to China's constitutionalism: the military government, the tutelary government, and the constitutional government. Cf. "*Guomin Zhengfu Jianguo Dagang*" [A Constitutional Program of the National Government], *Sun Zhongshan Quanji* [Complete Works of Sun Yat-sen], vol. 9, (Beijing: Zhonghua Shuju, 1986), pp. 126–129.

[23] William C. Kirby, "*Renshi 20 Shiji Zhongguo*" [Understanding China of 20th Century], *21st Century*, 2001/10, p. 114–24 and also in http://www.usc.cuhk.edu.hk/wk_wzdetails.asp?id=1523.

[24] CCP Constitution, General Principles; KMT Constitution, arts. 3, 4, 5, and ch. 12.

their riskier and basically more militarily oriented adventure, even though the CCP has consistently pursued a united front. Poor farmers or people from lower social and economic classes were the main sources for CCP members. They were less open, less exposed to the outside world, and often lacked the kind of professionalized discipline and working habits that contributed to effective collective action.[25]

The CCP could not transform from a revolutionary party into a governing party because it lacked the necessary educated elite, the technocrats, and professionals, such as judges, lawyers, and civil servants. The CCP thus continued to rely on its stronger party organization and stronger party leadership, including stricter discipline and a stronger ideological basis, to facilitate collective action in the absence of an effective administrative bureaucracy.

But this, in turn, also impeded the subsequent development of such bureaucracies. For a long time, the CCP did not feel pressure to rationalize and professionalize the administration of governance or society. It remained revolutionary in character. In all aspects of governance, the CCP played a decisive role and dominated the scene. Even after assuming control of the state, political loyalty and ideological purity continued to be the most important criteria for selecting government employees, including the judiciary.[26]

This began to change in the 1980s, when the CCP began to pay attention to professional training and higher education, leading to an increase in the number of university graduates. During the middle of the 1980s, the CCP also proposed the separation of party from government, but this reform was formally suspended after 1989. Nevertheless, there was a fundamental change in the CCP's understanding of its relationship with modern government in the early 1990s, as evidenced in the passage of the Provisional Civil Servant Act in 1993.[27] Not coincidentally, academic criticism of appointing discharged military officers as judges also started at this time.[28] The call for judicial reforms was in part the result of the rise and growing influence within the judiciary of the first generation of trained legal professionals (who were generally around forty years old) following the Cultural Revolution. They challenged the courts' party-centric institutional structure, leading to a series of judicial reforms.[29]

Today the CCP is increasingly aware that national modernization cannot be accomplished by the party's political elite alone. The CCP needs some degree of voluntary support from other social forces in China to achieve social integration. As

---

[25] Cf. Mao Tse-Tung, "On Correcting Mistaken Ideas in the Party," *Selected Works of Mao Tse-Tung*, vol. 1 (Peking: Foreign Language Press, 1975).

[26] Cf. Dong Biwu, *Dong Biwu Faxue Wenji* [Legal Works of Dong Biwu], (Beijing: Falu Chubanshe, 2001).

[27] Issued on August 14, 1993, effective on October 1, 1993.

[28] He Weifang, "*Fuzhuan Junren Jin Fayuan*" [Discharged Military Officers Come to the Courts], *Nanfang Zhoumo*, Jan. 2, 1998.

[29] Renmin Fayue Wunian Gaige Gangyao [A 5 Year Programme for the Reform of People's Courts], *Zhonghua Renmin Gongheguo Zuigao Renmin Fayuan Gongbao*, 1999/6.

a consequence, the party has had to learn to better understand and appreciate the different interests that underlie these different social forces. The CCP has responded accordingly. It has promoted greater democracy within the party. It has adjusted its policies, relying increasingly on laws and conventional organs of governance, such as the National People's Congress and Supreme People's Court, rather than on revolutionary fervor or party diktats. It has aggressively recruited qualified civil servants and set up bureaucracies. And finally, it has set about transforming the judiciary and improving its function. But the historical task of China's revolutionary social and political modernization cannot be accomplished all at once. The transformation of state, society, and now even the CCP itself is an ongoing process in China.

All in all, China faces many complicated problems. The reform process is long and difficult. The CCP's performance is often subject to withering scrutiny and harsh criticism from Western governments and scholars in line with their own political opinions. Some of these criticisms are justified and deserve the CCP's attention. However, we must also acknowledge that the CCP's leadership has been successful on many fronts, including reducing poverty, improving the living standards of most Chinese citizens, and improving governance. These achievements are all the more remarkable when compared against the performance of other developing countries, whether democratic or not.[30] The CCP found a way to modernize a country in the absence of a preexisting modern administrative state or a modern constitutional structure. Today, China's inherited political and constitutional institutions may not be as effective as one would like them to be, or as they are in some other countries, but the real question is whether abolishing the CCP, or radically altering its role and influence, would make China better off and help it develop faster in the future.

Put differently, without the CCP can China continue to develop in the way that it has? This is a difficult and emotionally charged question, one for which I have no definitive answer. But at least for the present and foreseeable future, the CCP remains the most important political and developmental force for contemporary China. There are no other institutions or political forces capable of overseeing China's drive to modernization and overcoming conflicts of interests and other political economy obstacles that cause so many developing countries to falter once they reach the middle-income stage.[31]

This is equally true with legal reforms. The motivations for continued reforms and improvement of the judiciary and the legal system more generally are many, including the needs of a market-based economy and the desire for social justice,

---

[30] See Randall Peerenboom, *China Modernizes: Threat to the West or Model for the Rest?* (Oxford: Oxford University Press, 2007).

[31] Ronald Daniels and Michael Trebilcock, "The Political Economy of Rule of Law Reforms in Developing Countries," available at http://www.wdi.bus.umich.edu/global_conf/papers/revised/Trebilcock_Michael.pdf (grouping obstacles to rule of law into three general categories – resource and institutional capacity shortcomings; social–cultural–historical problems; and political–economy barriers – and arguing that political–economy obstacles, including opposition by key interest groups, have been the biggest barriers in Latin America and Central and Eastern Europe).

which is the cornerstone of the CCP's stated goal of a harmonious society. The demands for further reforms therefore come from many sources, including businesses and the commercial sector, as well as citizens and the private sector. The demand for further reforms is also strong among government officials and members of the legal complex (judges, lawyers, prosecutors, police, notaries, etc.) who face obstacles every day in carrying out their responsibilities. Nevertheless, the CCP is still the major force mobilizing, promoting, and implementing reform within the judiciary and the legal system more broadly.

I do not support many of the reform measures it has promoted – some are clear mistakes.[32] The CCP leadership has been an obstacle to the development of a sufficiently independent judiciary. However, on balance, the CCP's oversight has also discouraged to some extent judicial corruption and judicial arrogance, though this claim is controversial among lawyers and legal scholars, and promoted the professionalism of the judiciary.

CCP leadership will also be required to overcome institutional conflicts between the courts and the people's congress, procuracy, and the police, which are now inhibiting the development of an independent judiciary and at least in some cases contributing to inefficiency and injustice. CCP leadership will also be necessary to enhance the role of civil society, including the media, in supervising the courts and thus promoting justice while at the same time ensuring that the courts are not subject to undue populist pressure from the public, stirred up by a media that is itself subject to corruption and in need of further professionalization and higher ethical standards.

The continuing leadership and control of the party is simply inescapable as a historical process. For this reason alone, visions of judicial independence drawn from distinctly Western experience or international best practices based on the particular institutional configurations found in economically advanced Western countries are not the best lens for understanding or predicting the development of the Chinese judiciary.

What is needed is a new approach to studying China's legal system and to studying development more generally that begins with a detailed understanding and analysis of the current situation and then proposes feasible solutions within that context, rather than simply insisting that China and other developing countries mimic the institutions and practices found in certain other countries whose history and current circumstances are very different.

A NEW MODEL FOR STUDYING CHINA

Once we understand the CCP's function of social mobilization and representation, its role in the constitution of the nation-state and the institutional construction, we

---

[32] Cf. Suli, *Daolu Tongxiang Chengshi – Zhuanxing Zhongguo de Fazhi* [All Roads Lead to Cities – Rule of Law in China's Transformation] (Beijing: Falu Chubanshe, 2004).

must be academically vigilant regarding the relevance of successful experiences of the West with rule of law and judicial practices. Such vigilance does not imply hostility. The point is that we should not take a model deeply embedded in the historical, institutional, theoretical, and discursive contexts of the West, decontextualize it, and accept it uncritically as the standard of reference for China's experience. Otherwise, China's progress becomes solely defined by the standards and interests of the West.

Of course, many people who use Western judicial ideology and experiences to understand China also make conscientious efforts to understand China. But the social context and experiences they know still sometimes prevent them from placing themselves in the position of Chinese citizens. Their experience limits the world of their imagination. This is not a problem unique to them, it is common to all of us.

But there are problems that may be more particular to American scholars in their efforts to understand China. For example, during the Cold War, American scholars contributed much to our understanding of the judiciaries and governmental structures of the Soviet Union and Eastern European countries. But this may also have prevented them from realizing the uniqueness of China's experience. In the Soviet Union and Eastern European countries, the major function of the communist party was to control a preexisting bureaucracy, including that of judicial professionals. They therefore assume that bureaucracy and government are innately prior to the party, and those conflicts and problems in governance are a result of the party imposing its control over an innately and properly autonomous bureaucracy.

This presupposition is reasonable, and possibly right, in considering the context of these particular countries. Many Red Army generals in the Soviet Union's early years were formerly military officers of the tsar, such as Marshal Mikhail Nikolaevieh Tukhachevski, and the hero of the Second World War, Marshal Georgy Konstantinovich Zhukov. To secure the leadership and control of the Communist Party over the military, the party sent political commissars to ensure the implementation of the party's policies within the Red Army. It was the same with regard to many other organizations, enterprises, and governmental agencies in the early Soviet Union, and with regard to the expansion of Soviet communism into Eastern European countries following the end of the war.

However, this presumption of a bureaucratic state innately preceding the party is not applicable to modern China. As noted, in modern China the party preceded the bureaucratic state.[33] It is noteworthy that long before the CCP gained control of the Chinese state, CCP leaders clearly recognized the importance of this difference between their own developmental trajectory and that of the Soviet Union. In 1936, when a presidium political commissar, Yang Chengwu, was reappointed as the military commander, Mao Zedong explained that the Chinese Red Army was different

---

[33] The first national conference of KMT was convened in 1924, and the first military college, which became the major force of the national army under KMT, opened in 1925, and the national government of KMT actually came into being in 1927. The first national conference of CCP was convened in 1921, the Chinese Red Army was founded in 1927, and the CCP national government in 1949.

from that of the Soviet Union. He noted that in the latter, most military officers were former White Army officers. In the Chinese Red Army, both military officers and political–military officers were trained by CCP.[34] Yang Chengwu became one of the most famous generals of the People's Liberation Army (PLA), but before that he was a political commissar of the CCP and not a military professional. Yang's history was not unique in this regard. Similar persons could be found throughout the PLA leadership, as well as in the leadership of other professions.

This is not to say that the Chinese model of the party preceding the state is good or right as a value judgment. I am simply making an empirical point of great importance not only in understanding the history of modern China but also in developing effective and practical suggestions for China's further social, political, and judicial reform. Scholars, both abroad and in China, must be aware that such historical path dependencies channel the options available for social and legal development in China.

China may develop institutions that function well within the Chinese context. Institutions such as adjudicative committees, or the political–legal committee, for instance, were developed to respond to particular needs. Of course, whether they will survive the process of modernization remains to be seen. Some of the conditions that gave rise to them are already disappearing or weakening as judges are increasingly well-trained and capable of handling important decisions responsibly and in accordance with law. At the same time, there may still be a need for adjudicative committees in courts where the level of competence remains low, or for political–legal committees to ensure that judicial decisions keep with macro-level development goals and that the court has the resources and competence to provide an effective remedy in cases that are often the result of systemic shortcomings in the economy or social welfare system, as illustrated by the "Married Out Women" cases discussed by Xin He in chapter 9 of this volume. The point is not to prejudge results based on idealized versions of how legal systems operate in other countries.

CONCLUSION

I expect to be, and at times have been, criticized or even condemned by some scholars from both the left and the right – both for my largely similar treatment of the CCP and KMT as well as for my argument that the CCP represents a possible constitutional alternative for China's social transformation. These general objections do not bother me. I would, however, like to respond to certain criticisms and objections to prevent misunderstanding and to clarify what I am claiming and not claiming.

First, I have argued that given the party's far-reaching influence, it is often difficult to distinguish between party influence on the courts and influence by the

---

[34] Yang Chengwu, *Yang Chengwu Huiyilu* [Memoirs of Yang Chengwu], (Beijing: Jiefangjun Chubanshe, 1987), p. 334.

government, people's congress, or other state actors. Difficult, of course, does not mean impossible in all cases. Nor does it mean that it is not necessary or useful to distinguish between influence from party organs and other state organs. Some forms of state intervention are legitimate in the sense of permitted within China's constitutional structure and grounded in law. Other forms of intervention by state organs or individual government officials are not legitimate in that sense.

Second, and related as noted previously, not all influence by party members is consistent with party policies; thus legitimate party influence should be distinguished from illegitimate party influence by individual party members pursuing their own interests. In addition, particular forms or instances of party influence should be assessed on their merits with an open mind. This, too, will require more detailed study of the various channels and methods of party influence and the impact of that influence. For instance, there is still a need for a systematic empirical study of the role of the political–legal committee that distinguishes between the various roles of the committee in setting policy and intervening in specific cases. Given the wide variation in China, the study should be conducted in different regions and distinguish between different levels of courts and types of cases. A similar study that examines the role of the court president and the adjudicative committee is also needed. The dominant view simply dismisses these institutional innovations as inconsistent with international best practices, Western institutions, and the prevailing conception of judicial independence in the West. Yet they may serve a useful purpose. Of course, a detailed study might also demonstrate that they should be eliminated or reformed in significant ways.

Third, although I have focused on the influence of the party on the courts, the party is not the only source of influence on the courts. In addition to influence from various state organs, individual parties, the media, civil society, and others also exert direct or indirect influence on the court. Again, others in this volume and elsewhere have examined these nonparty, nonstate influences in detail.

Although I have suggested that absolute judicial independence vis-à-vis the party is not useful for viewing the role of the party in relation to the courts, judicial independence has many aspects and includes independence from other sources of interference. Each has its own characteristics. Some are more prevalent in certain types of cases; some vary by level of court or region of the country; some are more serious than others. Much can be done to improve the performance of the courts and to enhance judicial independence by attending to these other sources of interference and proposing reforms targeted at the specific problems that take into consideration regional differences and differences in the type of case, level of court, and so on. The dominant view's emphasis on intervention by the party, particularly in a limited number of (albeit significant) politically sensitive cases detracts from the broader project of building a professional, autonomous, and functional judiciary.

Fourth, although I have described the party's influence as far-reaching, that does not mean that party control extends to every nook and cranny of society or everyday life. Even under Mao, the party could not extend control to all aspects of life and society. During the reform era, the party's influence has diminished in many ways in virtually all sectors, and its role has changed toward macro-management and policy setting. As noted, there has been considerable de facto separation of party and state since the early 1990s, with state organs assuming greater responsibilities and acting more autonomously. There is a need therefore for a more detailed study of party–state relations and the different incentives and behavioral patterns of officials depending on whether they are serving as government or party officials. A mayor of a city has a different role and will be promoted based on different criteria than the party secretary for the same city. Similarly, a court president may respond differently to the same set of facts when he is the head of the court than he would were he head of the political–legal committee.

Most importantly, nothing I said should be construed as supporting the simple-minded view common in certain quarters that the only thing one needs to know about China is that it is a single-party authoritarian state and that the courts are therefore incapable of handling any case independently and fairly. Such a conclusion overstates the degree and nature of party influence on the courts and fails to take into consideration the party's own goals for sustained economic growth and social justice and stability, goals that require a fair and efficient resolution of commercial and noncommercial disputes.

5

Judicial Independence in China

Common Myths and Unfounded Assumptions

Randall Peerenboom

The Chinese judiciary is regularly criticized for the lack of (meaningful) independence.[1] The lack of "genuine progress" in establishing an independent judiciary is then cited as evidence that China's reform process is trapped in transition.[2] In response, international donor agencies and bilateral legal cooperation programs have encouraged China to adopt the institutions and practices found in advanced Western states known for the rule of law.

Surrounding these views is a set of common myths and unfounded assumptions. The first assumption is substantive: the concept of judicial independence is clear, and there is a single agreed upon model or generally accepted set of institutions and best practices articulated with sufficient specificity to guide reformers.[3] The second

---

[1] See, e.g., Kenneth Dam, *The Law-Growth Nexus* (Washington D.C., Brookings Institute: 2006), p. 250 (discussing puzzle of high growth rates despite "the lack of judicial independence"); see also Ethan Michelson, "Lawyers, Political Embeddedness, and Institutional Continuity in China's Transition from Socialism," *American Journal of Sociology*, vol. 113, no. 2, p. 353 (2007) ("the judiciary remains fused to the state, embedded in and subordinated to the rest of the government bureaucracy (i.e., there is no meaningful separation of powers or judicial autonomy," and citing in support the works of seven scholars). Claims that China lacks meaningful independence entail that courts are independent to some degree or in some cases, and thus are at odds with blanket claims about the "lack of independence." Presumably, they are also not meant literally, that is, to suggest that judicial independence is not meaningful to parties in those cases that are decided independently on the merits. Thus, such claims would seem to mean that judicial independence is extremely limited in general or that there is no or extremely limited independence in particular types of cases, or that although judges do enjoy de facto independence in some cases, interference could occur if the authorities desired to intervene.

[2] Minxin Pei, "Is China's Transition Trapped?" in Randall Peerenboom ed., *Is China Trapped in Transition?* (Oxford: Foundation for Law, Justice and Society, 2007), http://www.fljs.org/section .aspx?id=1939.

[3] To this could be added three other assumptions. The first is political: foreign actors will be able to play a significant role in domestic reforms within the target country, and foreign states and international donor agencies have the political will and financial resources adequate to the task and are willing to spend them notwithstanding national security and other realpolitik concerns. The second is epistemological: international donor agencies and other foreign actors have sufficient local knowledge of existing

assumption is methodological: there are clear standards for measuring judicial independence. The third assumption is normative: we know how independent courts should be (at each stage of development). The fourth assumption is the more independence the better. The fifth assumption is that the lack of judicial independence is a serious problem in all types of cases in China. The sixth is that China's courts lack independence because independence is impossible within a single-party state. The seventh, and a corollary, is that the party is the main source of interference with the courts. The eighth – and perhaps the granddaddy of them all – is that were China to suddenly democratize, judicial independence would no longer be a problem.

This chapter advances three main theses. First, each assumption is either wrong or needs to be qualified. Second, general statements about the lack of judicial independence or impossibility of achieving judicial independence in a single-party state fail to capture the complex reality of China or other authoritarian regimes. Third, legal reforms that assign a high priority to judicial independence will be unsuccessful or limited in their effectiveness until there is a deeper understanding of these issues as they apply to China and to developing countries. Moreover, to the extent they are successful in pushing toward greater independence and an expanded role for the courts in resolving certain types of controversial issues, they may in some circumstances do more harm than good.

Part I distinguishes between various aspects or subcomponents of judicial independence. Disaggregating judicial independence allows for a more nuanced discussion of judicial independence in China. Part II then takes each subcomponent of judicial independence in turn, reserving a discussion of the main external constraints on judicial independence for Part III. Parts II and III demonstrate that judicial independence has increased in China. Judges are allowed – indeed required – to decide most cases independently. Further, the party is not the main source of interference. Even when party organs do intervene, such "interference" may be justified. I do not mean to suggest that judicial independence is not an issue in some cases or that further improvements are not needed in some areas. But it is incorrect to conclude that parties cannot obtain a fair trial in all cases, especially commercial cases, because the judiciary lacks independence or because China is a single-party socialist state. Part IV discusses the implications of China's efforts to increase judicial independence

institutions, citizen demands, and the competing interests of various interest groups affected by reforms to intervene successfully in the legal reform process within the target country. The third is institutional: international donor agencies are clear about their purposes in promoting rule of law and judicial independence and have the incentive to acquire knowledge about the process and sequencing of legal reforms, to test the impact of such reforms, and to share the knowledge acquired and adapt their advice accordingly. For serious doubts about all of these assumptions, see the essays in Thomas Carothers ed., *Promoting the Rule of Law Abroad: In Search of Knowledge* (Washington D.C., Carnegie Endowment for International Peace, 2006). See also Alvaro Santos, "The World Bank's Uses of the 'Rule of Law' Promise in Economic Development," in David Trubek and Alvaro Santos eds., *The New Law and Economic Development: A Critical Appraisal* (New York: Cambridge University Press, 2006).

for the law and development movement, including observations about methodology and the relationship between regime type and judicial independence. Part V concludes with recommendations on how to address the related problems of judicial corruption and judicial independence.

JUDICIAL INDEPENDENCE

Judicial independence is a multifaceted concept.[4] The most basic form of judicial independence, decisional independence, refers to the ability of judges to decide cases independently in accordance with law and without (undue, inappropriate, or illegal) interference from other parties or entities. One prerequisite for decisional independence is that judges enjoy personal independence, which requires that their terms of office be reasonably secure; appointments and promotions should be relatively depoliticized; judges should be provided an adequate salary and should not be dismissed or have their salaries reduced as long as they are performing adequately; transfers and promotions should be fair and according to preestablished rules; and judges should be assigned cases in an impartial manner.

Internal independence refers to the ability of judges to decide cases without regard to administrative hierarchies within the court and in particular without interference from senior judges. External independence refers to judges being able to decide cases without interference from external sources such as the Chinese Communist Party (CCP), people's congresses, the government, administrative agencies, the procuracy, the military, or members of society. External independence, and ultimately decisional independence, requires the collective independence of the judiciary, which is the judiciary's ability as a whole and any individual court as a collective entity to function free from undue influence by other entities. Collective independence requires that the courts be adequately funded and that they have sufficient powers vis-à-vis other political organs for the legal system to function as a system of laws. Courts must not only be strong enough to resist pressure from outside forces in deciding cases; they must also have the authority and power to ensure that their judgments are enforced and that other political actors comply with their orders.

Contrary to common (mis)understanding, there is no single model of judicial independence or generally accepted set of institutions or best practices, at least none articulated with sufficient specificity to be useful for reformers.[5] To be sure,

---

4 Shimon Shetreet and Jules Deschenes, *Judicial Independence: The Contemporary Debate* (Boston: Martinus Nijhoff Publishers, 1985).

5 See Asian Development Bank, "Judicial Independence Overview and Country-level Summaries," (2003), p. 2, http://www.adb.org/Documents/Events/2003/RETA5987/Final_Overview_Report.pdf. (noting lack of a common or even consensus definition of judicial independence and that there is no single agreed model or set of institutional arrangements for judicial independence, and showing diversity of institutions within nine Asian countries).

there are some well-established general principles and numerous statements of international best practices.[6] These guidelines generally cover similar grounds – appointments and promotions, removals and transfers, compensation, jurisdiction of the courts, judicial administration, budget, states of emergency, and warnings against misuse of military courts to try civilians. For such an immensely complicated topic, the list is surprisingly short. The U.N. Basic Principles contain just twenty-two articles, the Beijing Principles have forty-four articles, the International Bar Association standards are set out in forty-six provisions, some of which address judicial accountability and ethics, whereas IFES sums it all up in eighteen judicial integrity principles.

Most provisions are abstract and hortatory. Others are tautological. Some are both. Consider Article 4 of the U.N. Basic Principles: "There shall not be any inappropriate or unwarranted interference with the judicial process, nor shall judicial decisions by the courts be subject to revision." Without a statement of what constitutes inappropriate or unwarranted interference, the first part simply restates the issue, whereas the second part, depending on how it is interpreted, is at odds with practices in many countries where legislatures may pass laws that overturn court decisions. Or take Article 3 of the Beijing Principles: "The judiciary has jurisdiction, directly or by way of review, over all issues of a justiciable nature." So far so good, but are decisions regarding states of emergency and declarations of war justiciable in nature? Are socioeconomic rights justiciable in nature? Such broad principles are consistent with a wide variety of institutions and practices.

Turning from broad standards to actual practice, the extent and nature of judicial independence and the institutional arrangements for realizing it vary widely from country to country, even among liberal democracies with well-functioning legal systems. In the United States, courts are an independent branch with broad powers to hear all types of cases and strike down congressional laws or executive branch regulations. In parliamentary supreme states such as England or Belgium, the courts answer to parliament and have limited powers to overturn laws or government regulations.[7] In common law systems, courts play an active role in policy making; in civil law countries courts have limited (albeit growing) powers to make or interpret law. The degree of separation between law and politics and the forms it takes vary

---

[6] See, e.g., the U.N. Basic Principles on the Independence of the Judiciary (1985); Universal Charter of the Judge (1998); Beijing Statement of Principles of the Independence of the Judiciary in the Law, Asia Region (1995); IBA Minimum Standard of Judicial Independence (1982); IFES/USAID, Guidance for Promoting Judicial Independence and Impartiality (2002); IFES, Regional Best Practices: A Model Framework for a State of the Judiciary Report for the Americas (2003).

[7] See Doris Marie Provine, "Courts, Justice, and Politics in France," in Herbert Jacob et al. eds., (*Courts, Law and Politics in Comparative Perspective*, New Haven: Yale University Press, 1996), p. 177: "In France, as in other countries that follow a civil law tradition, courts are not a coequal branch of government. . . . The courts were on the losing side of the French Revolution, and they suffered a tremendous loss of power and prestige in its aftermath. Two centuries later, the commitment to independence from the other branches is still in doubt. Courts in France are not known for standing up to government officials, and no one expects them to play an active role in government."

from place to place.[8] There is, for example, surprisingly wide variation with respect to the crucial issue of appointment of judges.[9] In some systems, judges are career civil servants who must pass an exam to enter the judiciary. In other countries, academics or political figures without any prior practice as a lawyer or judge may be appointed to the bench, with the executive, legislature, judiciary, and/or the ministry of justice responsible for appointments or involved in the appointment process. Alternatively, judges may be elected. Some countries allow judges to be members of political parties and even to hold simultaneous posts in the executive branch or the legislature. Although political affiliation is important in appointments and elections in some countries, other systems strive to depoliticize the selection process.[10] Liberal democracies endorse freedom of thought and speech, yet many require judges to take an oath promising to uphold the constitution and to commit to regime norms such as rule of law and the promotion of human rights; and although some systems allow judges to speak out on political issues, others impose a duty of reserve.

With respect to the personal independence of judges, the United States grants judges life tenure, most others only provide for a fixed term.[11] As for collective independence, some courts are funded locally while others are funded centrally. In some countries, the judiciary prepares the budget, in others the executive and/or the legislature is involved in preparing or approving the budget.[12] Moreover, while

---

[8] Martin Shapiro has made a career pointing out that judges are political actors, even if they differ in significant ways from other political actors. See, e.g., Martin Shapiro and Alec Stone Sweet, *On Law, Politics and Judicialization* (Oxford: Oxford University Press, 2002).

[9] See, generally, IFES/USAID, Promoting Judicial Independence, pp. 12–20. Article 2.14 of the Universal Declaration of the Independence of Justice acknowledges that: "There is no single proper method of judicial selection provided it safeguards against judicial appointments for improper motives."

[10] Between 1963 and 1992, 58 to 73 percent of federal appellate judges and 49 to 61 percent of federal district judges had a record of political activism before appointment. Moreover, the majority of state judges are elected in the United States. Herbert Jacob, "Courts and Politics in the United States," in Herbert Jacob et al. eds., (*Courts, Law and Politics in Comparative Perspective*, New Haven: Yale University Press, 1996), p. 19. Query whether the practice in the United States of presidents nominating Supreme Court justices based on political affiliation constitutes an improper motive. Compare then these practices to China, where the party approves or vetoes candidates, the vast majority of whom are party members, but where party membership is often ideologically insignificant, as discussed below.

[11] Christopher L. Eisgruber, "Constitutional Self-Government and Judicial Review: A Reply to Five Critics," *University of San Francisco Law Review*, vol. 37, p. 156 (2002) ("the United States is virtually unique in allowing its constitutional court judges to serve indefinitely"). Of twenty-seven European countries, only six provide for life tenure whereas twenty-one provide for fixed terms. Lee Epstein et al. "Comparing Judicial Selection Systems," *William & Mary Bill of Rights Law Journal*, vol. 10, p. 1 (2001).

[12] IFES/USAID, Promoting Judicial Independence: "There are two basic models defining the relationship of the judiciary to the rest of the government: (1) a judiciary dependent on an executive department for its administrative and budgetary functions; and (2) a judiciary that is a separate branch and manages its own administration and budget. Although there are clear examples of independent judiciaries under the first model, the trend is to give judiciaries more administrative control, to protect against executive branch domination." But see Asian Development Bank, "Judicial Independence," noting that in the end legislatures must approve the judiciary's budget and thus it matters little whether the budget is drawn up by the executive branch (Ministry of Justice) or the Supreme Court; moreover, in most developing countries, including in Asia, the judiciary is low on the list of funding priorities.

judges must enjoy a certain degree of independence, they must also be held accountable. Different systems employ various means to keep judges in line. Some rely on supervision by the legislature or the executive; some are self-regulating, with judges responsible for policing and disciplining themselves; others rely on media scrutiny and elections.

Legal systems also differ with respect to the degree of internal independence. Courts tend to be more hierarchical in civil law countries than in common law countries. Accordingly, the views of senior judges may carry more weight in practice if not according to law. Senior judges in civil systems may also exercise greater control over important administrative matters such as assignment of cases and personnel issues. Many countries have judicial councils; others do not. Of those that do, powers and functions vary widely.[13]

In light of such wide variation among liberal democracies considered exemplars of rule of law, significant divergence between countries with different conceptions of rule of law is to be expected. China explicitly endorses the principle of a socialist rule of law state, although there are competing conceptions within China.[14]

On the other hand, considerable convergence between countries with different conceptions of rule of law is to be expected. Notwithstanding significant variation with respect to judicial independence among similar and competing conceptions of rule of law, excessive dependence of the courts on political entities or interference by other actors in specific cases undermines the ability of the courts to impose meaningful restraints on political actors and runs afoul of both general rule of law principles such as the supremacy of the law and equality of all before the law and the need for impartial and fair outcomes based on law.

COLLECTIVE, PERSONAL, INTERNAL, AND DECISIONAL INDEPENDENCE IN CHINA

Collective Independence

The collective independence of the Chinese courts has been strengthened through increased budgets, more streamlined and efficient processes, and efforts to increase the authority of the courts.

The government has increased funding for the judiciary. However, costs have also risen. Many courts have relied on litigation fees to make up the difference. As a result, courts in developed areas such as Shanghai, Beijing, or Guangdong that handle a large number of cases have had many more resources at their disposal than courts in other areas. They have been able to invest in computers and other infrastructure and

---

[13] Violaine Autheman and Sandra Elena, "Global Best Practices: Judicial Councils – Lessons Learned from Europe and Latin America," *IFES Rule of Law White Paper Series*, 2004.

[14] See Peerenboom, *China's Long March toward Rule of Law* (Cambridge: Cambridge University Press, 2002).

to pay higher salaries, thus attracting and retaining highly qualified judges. Facing greater financial hardship, courts in remote areas have at times sought to increase litigation fees by stretching or ignoring jurisdictional rules, discouraging parties from withdrawing lawsuits, and preventing parties from joining in class action suits so as to charge each plaintiff a separate filing fee. In response, the government experimented with a system whereby all litigation fees are sent to the provincial and central level and then redistributed through the finance bureau and high level courts, and also increased central funding.[15] In December 2008, the State Council announced that funding of the courts would be centralized, although it remains to be seen whether funding will be adequate and reach lower level courts.

The spending increase has been matched by an attempt to reduce costs by increasing judicial efficiency. The total number of cases handled by the courts grew dramatically throughout the 1980s and much of the 1990s before leveling off at around 8 million cases a year. In response to heavier caseloads and increasing backlogs, the Supreme People's Court (SPC) has encouraged greater use of simplified and summary procedures in both civil and criminal trials. Almost 40 percent of criminal cases and 70 percent of civil cases are heard using these procedures.[16] There has also been a push to establish small-claims courts.[17]

Many other reforms have aimed at increasing judicial efficiency. In the past, the same judge frequently was in charge of accepting a case, carrying out pretrial investigations, and then trying it. To increase efficiency and curtail corruption, the functions of accepting, hearing, supervising, and enforcing cases have been separated. Some courts are now experimenting with pretrial judges who hold pretrial conferences, facilitate discovery and exchange of evidence, and carry out mediation. In any event, partiality in case assignment does not appear to be a significant problem.

The authority of courts has also increased over the last twenty-five years. This is evident in the high rate of administrative litigation cases where courts quash administrative agency decisions or a case is withdrawn after the agency changes its decision. Plaintiffs are much more successful in China than in the United States, France, and Taiwan.[18] The greater authority of the court is also evident in the low number of cases supervised by the procuracy or people's congress that result in a changed verdict – less than 0.3 percent.[19] The enhanced stature of the court is also evident in high acquittal rates for lawyers in cases where police and procuracy prosecute lawyers on

---

[15] China has experimented with different ways of funding the courts. See Zhu Jingwen ed., *Zhongguo falü fazhan baogao (1979–2004)* [China Legal Development Report (1979–2004)], (Beijing: People's University Press: 2007).

[16] Information Office of the State Council, China's Efforts and Achievements in Promoting Rule of Law, February 2008.

[17] The SPC's Second Five-Year Agenda (2004–2008), available at http://www.law-lib.com/law/law_view.asp?id=120832.

[18] See Chapter 6.

[19] Peerenboom, "Judicial Accountability and Judicial Independence: An Empirical Study of Individual Case Supervision in the People's Republic of China," *The China Journal*, vol. 55, p. 67, 2006.

trumped up charges of falsifying evidence.[20] Clearly the courts are increasingly able to stand up to the people's congress, procuracy, and police.

The growing independence and authority of the court is also evident in the public's increased reliance on the courts for dispute settlement. There has been a clear and marked trend toward greater reliance on courts with declining interest in mediation and arbitration.[21] In the past plaintiffs in labor suits often lost, with the court upholding the decision of the labor arbitration committee. Today, the majority wins in court – with plaintiffs enjoying a higher success rate in courts than in arbitration.[22] The enhanced authority and stature of the courts, which are responsible for enforcing judgments in China, is also evident in higher enforcement rates. Faced with a rise in parties refusing to comply with court judgments in the late 1990s, the courts acted aggressively, adopting a number of measures to increase their powers. The number of people detained in conjunction with compulsory enforcement actions rose to more than 50,000 in 1999, after which both the rate of noncompliance and the rate of people detained in enforcement cases dropped dramatically.[23] In keeping with general patterns of development, enforcement is much better in urban than in rural areas.[24]

At the same time, courts are exerting their authority and protecting their turf and reputation by resisting attempts to channel controversial socioeconomic disputes into the court.[25] These cases are difficult to resolve because they are fundamentally economic in nature and the state lacks the resources and institutions (such as a well-developed welfare system) to provide an effective remedy.

Personal Independence

The personal independence of judges has also increased. The Judges Law sought to strengthen the independence of the judiciary by providing that judges have the right to be free from external interference.[26] In fact, few judges are prosecuted or subject to administrative sanctions. According to the Supreme People's Court 2002 Work Report, 995 judges and judicial personnel violated laws and rules in 2001. It bears emphasizing that this number is only a tiny fraction of the total number of judicial personnel, includes both judges and all other court personnel, and includes major as well as minor infractions. Of the 995 cases, the infractions were sufficiently serious to result in criminal prosecutions in only 85 cases. In 2002, only forty-five judges

---

[20] Fu Hualing, "When Lawyers are Prosecuted: The Struggle of a Profession in Transition," 2006, http://ssrn.com/abstract=956500.

[21] Zhu, *China Legal Development*.

[22] See Ronald Brown, "China Labor Dispute Resolution," in *Dispute Resolution in China*.

[23] Zhu, *China Legal Development*, pp. 243–249.

[24] He Xin, "Enforcing Commercial Judgments in the Pearl River Delta of China," *Journal of Empirical Legal Studies* (forthcoming). On the general relationship between improvements in the legal system and development, see Zhu, *China Legal Development*.

[25] See Chapters 6 and 9 in this volume.

[26] PRC Judges Law, art. 8.

were subject to criminal sanctions. Moreover, according to the Supreme People's Court 2003 Work Report, the number of judges who violated the laws or rules decreased from an already low 0.067 percent in 1998 to an even lower 0.02 percent in 2002.

National regulations have also sought to strengthen the personal independence of judges by limiting the practice of penalizing judges for reversals on appeal. As in other countries, judges are sanctioned for intentional misbehavior or negligence in carrying out their duties. Some local courts have created an extensive incentive structure for judges. Although most requirements are uncontroversial, some are at odds with national norms established by the SPC and might impinge unduly on the autonomy of judges or create perverse incentives, depending on how the standards are interpreted and applied.[27] There does not appear to be any systematic evidence that the standards are leading to excessive sanctioning of judges for making honest mistakes in the handling of cases. In any event, judicial independence is not a goal in itself but rather a means to a just and efficient judiciary. Judges may be independent but incompetent, lazy, inefficient, or corrupt. Accordingly, even if an incentive system for judges impinged to some extent on judicial independence, the question would remain whether doing so was worth it in terms of fostering a more efficient, professional, honest, and just judiciary.

Appointments and promotions are now also more merit-based, with a greater role for higher level courts in the decision-making process. New graduates must start in lower courts and work their way up. Supreme and high court judges are now selected from lower level judges with at least five years experience and from academics and elite lawyers. In basic level courts, presidents who in the past were often appointed based on their political background rather than their legal skills are now supposed to meet the qualification requirements for judges and to be selected from the best judges on the court.

Nevertheless, as in many countries the criteria for becoming a judge and for being promoted are not publicly available, nor is the selection and promotion process transparent or subject to public monitoring.

Internal Independence

Internal independence refers to judges' ability to decide cases without regard to administrative hierarchies within the court and without interference from senior judges. A contentious issue has been the independence and authority of the judges hearing the case to issue a final decision without approval from the adjudicative committee or senior judges on the court. The advantages and disadvantages of the adjudicative committee review system have been debated for more than a decade.

---

[27] See generally Carl Minzner, "Judicial Disciplinary Systems for Incorrectly Decided Cases," in Mary Gallagher et al. eds., *Chinese Justice: Civil Dispute Resolution in Contemporary China* (Cambridge: Harvard University Press, forthcoming).

Supporters argue that review by more senior judges is necessary in light of the low level of competence of some judges. They also suggest that the system reduces corruption. Some claim that the system enhances the independence of the judiciary because the adjudicative committee, which includes the president and other high-ranking party members within the court, may be better able to resist outside influences than more junior judges.

On the other hand, critics complain that under the current system the judges who decide the case are not the ones who hear it. Accordingly, the judges who do hear the case feel they have little power. Further, critics claim judges hearing the cases become timid and are quick to hand over tough cases to the adjudicative committee rather than working through the issues themselves, even though doing so may result in delays.

One significant reform has been implementation of a system where presiding judges are selected based on merit through a competitive process and given more authority within the court. The second SPC agenda introduced further reforms. One change was to have the adjudicative committee hear directly major or difficult cases or those with general applicability. Another was to have the court president or head of the division join the collegial panel. Still another change was to create separate committees for civil and criminal cases to avoid the problem of criminal law judges hearing civil cases and vice versa.

Local courts have implemented additional reforms. For instance, Yuexiu court in Guangdong has recorded detailed rules for approval of cases to be heard by the adjudicative committee. The court also uses these cases as a pedagogical tool for lower courts by periodically publishing guiding opinions based on the results.[28]

EXTERNAL INDEPENDENCE IN CHINA

Discussions of judicial independence often begin and end with a litany of complaints about external interference, particularly by the party, or focus on isolated problematic cases that are politically sensitive or involve contentious social issues. As such, they fail to do justice to, if not completely ignore, significant improvements on other subcomponents of judicial impedence. Even in the area of external independence, however, there have been considerable improvements.

The Party's Influence on the Judiciary

The party's role in the legal system and its impact on judicial independence is generally overstated and assumed – without a close examination of the party's actual role and its consequences – to be pernicious. In a single-party, socialist state, the

---

[28] See Yueshou Court Adopts Several Measures to Actively Promote Reform of the Adjudicative Work, http://www.gzcourt.org.cn/court_info/court_info_detail.jsp?type=1&code=1625.

party will exercise some degree of influence over the courts. However, that does not mean that courts are simply party organs or that the party controls every action of the courts or determines the outcome of all or even most cases.

In practice, the party influences the courts in various ways and through various channels. The party exerts influence in ideology, policy, and personnel matters, although it sometimes is involved in deciding the outcome of particular cases.[29]

Examples of party-led or -inspired policies include the various strike hard campaigns to reduce crime, the SPC's "Opinions on Playing Fully the Role of Adjudication to Provide Judicial Protection and Legal Services for Economic Development," the Guidance Notice regarding Lawyers' Handling of Multi-party Cases, issued by the All China Lawyers Association, prohibitions on accepting Falun Gong cases, efforts to reduce judicial corruption and improve enforcement, and renewed emphasis on mediation.

Some of these policies enhance the independence and authority of the court vis-à-vis other actors. Some of them may impede judicial independence to achieve other important social goals. Generally, such policy statements do not ask lower courts to violate or set aside the law when deciding cases. Rather, lower courts are exhorted to ensure the cases are handled in accordance with law. To be sure, if party organs get carried away in their zeal to crack down on crime or root out corruption and pressure the courts to meet certain quotas, judges will feel they are being asked to deny the accused their rights or at least that their professional judgment is being sacrificed to satisfy political objectives.

Some of these policies aim to limit access to courts and steer disputes to other channels. In some cases, this is problematic and reflects the limited independence of the courts when it comes to politically sensitive cases, as in the rules prohibiting suits by Falun Gong disciples. But in other cases, limiting access to the courts may be justified and may actually enhance the authority of the judiciary. For instance, a number of measures have sought to steer socioeconomic disputes away from the courts toward other mechanisms such as administrative reconsideration, mediation, arbitration, public hearings, and the political process more generally, when it became apparent that the courts lacked the resources, competence, and stature to provide effective relief in such cases. Forcing the courts to handle such cases had undermined the authority of the judiciary and contributed to a sharp rise in petitions and mass protests.

When it comes to judicial appointments and promotions elsewhere, the general trend has been toward increased emphasis on professional skills and a greater role for judges in the same level and higher courts in decision-making. In any event, to conclude that the party's ability to vet judges determines the outcomes is much too simple. Because many party members joined the party for personal advancement rather than out of ideological commitment to socialism or the party, being a party

---

[29] For a more detailed discussion, see Peerenboom, *China's Long March*.

member tells us little about a judge's political or legal views; one could be a reformer or conservative. It is possible that party members are more likely to follow the party line more readily than nonparty members to avoid jeopardizing their career. But most cases turn on legal issues for which there is no party line or no clear party line. Of course, even in liberal democracies judges may be appointed and promoted based on their political views – the appointment of U.S. Supreme Court judges is one of many examples.

Most worrisome is direct interference by the party or political organs in the courts' handling of specific cases. Although party organs are not legally allowed to interfere in specific cases, in practice party organs or individual party members do on occasion become involved in pending cases. Usually, the party intervenes through the Political–legal Committee (PLC). However, party influence may also be brought to bear through the party committee, individual party members, the adjudicative committee, or the president of the court.

The PLC might become involved in politically sensitive cases or cases involving conflicts between the courts and the procuracy or government. Even when the PLC becomes involved, it does not necessarily dictate the outcome. Rather, it recommends action to the court. It also may express an opinion on certain aspects of the case, such as the guilt of the accused, but leave it to the court to determine punishment.

The extent of direct party intervention should not be overstated.[30] According to a survey of 280 judges published in 1993, party organs or individual party members were the source in only 8 percent of the cases. In contrast, government organs were the source of interference in 26 percent of the cases and social contacts in 29 percent. In a survey of administrative law judges in Jiangsu, only 14 percent cited interference from the party as a factor. Still another survey of eighty-nine arbitral award enforcement cases in China found that party interference was rare and usually only occurred when there was a personal connection between an individual party member and the respondent against which enforcement was sought. The nature of the interference and its impact on the final decision also matter: Were judges told to act in accordance with law, to bear in mind the impact on social stability or the consistency of the decision with economic policies, or to decide in favor of one party notwithstanding the law?

The party's main interest in the outcome of most cases, whether commercial, criminal, or administrative, is that the result be perceived as fair by the parties and the people. Accordingly, the CCP only rarely intervenes in the handling of specific cases. In any event, party involvement in specific cases does not necessarily mean that justice is sacrificed. Party intervention may ensure that the case is handled in accordance with law. In the aforementioned arbitration survey, most lawyers felt

---

[30] These surveys, discussed in Peerenboom, *China's Long March*, are from the 1990s and thus in need of updating in light of reforms during the last fifteen years.

that the CCP on balance played a positive role. The explanation why this is so is straightforward: the ruling regime has invested considerable resources in attracting foreign investment and does not want China's reputation sullied by negative publicity.

Of course, the CCP has a significant stake in cases that threaten sociopolitical stability and more specifically its right to rule. The courts' ability to decide such cases independently is severely restricted at best, as discussed in the next chapter.

People's Congresses and the Judiciary

As in other countries where the parliament is supreme, China rejects U.S. style separation of powers. In China, the National People's Congress (NPC) is the highest organ of state power. Thus, although the judiciary enjoys a functional independence, the NPC has the right to supervise the judiciary. The NPC influences the judiciary through its role in the appointment and approval process. It also exercises various forms of supervision. Every year, the SPC must submit a work report to the NPC for review.

People's congresses may also address inquiries to the courts regarding general issues, although they seldom do. Much more common and controversial has been their role in supervising individual cases – a practice which has now fallen into disfavor with the passage of the Supervision Law. Individual case supervision (ICS) inevitably diminishes the independence of the court to some extent. At minimum, the courts must devote resources to reviewing applications for responding to inquiries of the people's congress and retrying cases protested by the procuracy. The possibility of retrial also encourages outside parties to attempt to persuade the courts to readjudicate.

Although ICS inevitably diminishes the independence of the court, the extent will vary depending on how often cases are supervised and how supervision is conducted; ICS was always rare.[31] The method of ICS could also be more or less intrusive. People's congresses often responded to a petition by asking the court to handle the matter in accordance with law. They asked the court to report back or investigate on their own in only a small percentage of cases. In 2001, Gansu People's Congress Letters and Visits Office made 459 telephone calls and sent 306 letters to expedite cases, asking for a report in 102 cases. In the rare case where the people's congress conducted its own investigation and then issued a formal supervisory opinion, the nature of the opinion varied from general advice pointing out issues that require attention to specific advice on how the court should decide the case. In some cases, the committee investigating the case offered its own interpretation of the law, facts, or opinion on contested issues like the amount of damages or the proper sentence of criminals.

---

[31] For statistics, see Peerenboom, "Judicial Independence and Judicial Accountability."

Regardless of whether the supervision is by the procuracy or the people's congress, the court in theory has always retained the right to decide the case. Local regulations often stressed that people's congresses were not supposed to substitute their judgment for that of the courts, and people's congresses usually abided by this principle. However, in some cases there is sharp disagreement on specific legal or factual issues, and the people's congress or the procuracy might believe that the court is wrong or even suspect corruption. In such cases, the supervising entity may not be able to avoid addressing specific issues. Even if it did not reach a conclusion on a particular issue, its position may be apparent from the fact that it challenges the court, especially when there are only two possibilities.

Whether the people's congress should be able to set out in its opinion specific findings on legal or factual issues is debatable. However, it should not be able to compel the court to adopt its findings or continually challenge the court if the court upholds its original decision.[32] Ultimately, the people's congress and procuracy must defer to the SPC's judgment to avoid undermining the independence of the court.

In practice, the response of the courts to ICS by the people's congress varied widely. Some courts regularly ignored the people's congress's request for a report whereas others reported more often than not.[33] While in some cases judges appeared to cave in even when they did not agree with the advice of the people's congress, there were many more cases where judges resisted even specific advice from the people's congress. In fact, prosecutors and members of the people's congress regularly complained that courts did not take their advice seriously. As a result, some recommend greater powers for the procuracy and people's congress, including allowing the procuracy to attend adjudicative supervision committee deliberations.

In all legal systems, there is a tension between judicial independence and judicial accountability, and the two goals must be balanced. Given the current circumstances in China, particularly in some lower courts, the need for supervision is greater than in some other countries. However, advocates of greater judicial independence were able to argue successfully that there were other more suitable mechanisms for ensuring accountability than ICS by people's congresses.

Local Governments and the Judiciary

Local protectionism may take many forms, some more serious than others. Local government officials may pressure a court to decide a case in favor of the local party, deny an outsider's application for enforcement, or just drag out the enforcement

---

[32] SPC Notice on the Correct Application of the "Regulations on Issues Relating to People's Courts Remanding for Retrial and Ordering Retrial of Civil Cases," November 12, 2003.

[33] Cai Dingjian reports that rates vary from less than 10 percent to 75 percent. Cai Dingjian, "Renmin daibiao dahui gean jiandu de xianzhuang ji qi gaige" [The Current State of Individual Case Supervision by the National People's Congress and its Reform], in Cai Dingjian (ed.), *Jiandu yu sifa gongzheng*, [Judicial Fairness and Supervision] (Beijing: Falü Chubanshe, 2005).

process, usually by requesting additional documents or by leaving a case pending. Local protectionism is therefore a matter of degree: it may impede or be an absolute bar to recovery. To be sure, local governments are not free to engage in protectionism as they wish. Similarly, local courts cannot simply take their orders from the government, even if they are so inclined; they must also answer to higher courts, the media, and the court of public opinion. In fact, the SPC has adopted numerous measures to address local protectionism and interference by government officials.[34]

Although various factors contribute to local protectionism, the main causes are the way courts have been funded and judges appointed. It follows logically – and is widely accepted in practice – that local protectionism is a problem in basic level courts. The main proposals for dealing with local protectionism are to change the way courts are funded and judges are appointed, or to create federal or regional courts. The SPC Second Five-Year Agenda opted for both approaches, calling for changes in the way cases that cross jurisdictions are to be handled and recommending that the central and provincial level be responsible for funding the courts. As noted, the State Council centralized funding in 2008. As in other areas, there is a clear relationship between local protectionism and economic development, with protectionism more severe in poorer rural areas than in richer urban areas.[35]

The Procuracy, Public Security, and Police

Historically, public security was the strongest institution, especially during the Cultural Revolution when the procuracy was shut down and the judiciary weakened. Even now, the head of the PLC is often the chief of public security. Moreover, under China's constitution, the procuracy has the right to supervise the courts. On the other hand, reforms have given the courts an increasingly important role, particularly with respect to commercial matters. Judges tend to be better educated than procuratorates and police and enjoy a higher social status.[36] Moreover, procuratorates appear before the court as a party to a dispute, observe the rules of the court, and obey the court's orders.

As in other countries, there are also institution-based differences in the worldviews of judges, prosecutors, and police. The rank and file of the procuracy, public security, and police tend to be more sympathetic to the need for law and order than judges. Not surprisingly, the increase in the authority and importance of the courts during the last decade has led to tensions between the courts and the public security and police. The struggle for power has led to the judiciary and procuracy issuing

---

[34] Peerenboom, *China's Long March*; He, "Enforcing Commercial Judgments"; Zhu, *China's Legal Development*.

[35] Mei Ying Gechlik, "Judicial Reform in China: Lessons from Shanghai," *Columbia Journal of Asian Law*, vol. 19, p. 100 (2006); He, "Enforcing Commercial Judgments."

[36] Zhu, *China Legal Development*, p. 34.

inconsistent interpretations of key legislation and the procuracy objecting during the drafting of the Law on Legislation to the SPC's practice of interpreting laws. The police and prosecutors have also been accused of failing to cooperate with judges in trials by not appearing when they are supposed to or by not turning over evidence or documents as requested. There are also numerous reports of police harassing and physically abusing lawyers who try to meet with their clients, as well as reports of lawyers arrested on trumped up charges of harboring criminals or conspiring in crimes. As the prevailing dominant authority, the party is often forced to intervene in such disputes between the various institutions.

Procuracy supervision of individual cases remains controversial. There has been a change in the pattern of procuracy protests (kangsu) over the years. The number of criminal cases retried through adjudicative supervision has decreased, while the number of civil and economic cases has grown. Civil and economic cases now constitute more than 80 percent of all cases retried through adjudicative supervision, while criminal cases account for less than 10 percent, with administrative cases making up the remainder. In criminal cases, the procuracy often seeks heavier sentences. Regardless of the type of case, the procuracy loses the vast majority of the time, challenging the common if outdated and superficial view of the courts as subservient to the police and procuracy.

The Relation between Higher and Lower Level Courts

Normally one does not think of higher level courts as a threat to judicial independence. However, judicial independence may be undermined when higher courts exert undue influence on lower courts outside the normal channels of appeal.

In China, higher courts often engage in a longstanding practice of responding to inquiries from lower courts for advice regarding legal issues in particular cases currently before the lower court. Lower court judges may request advice formally in writing or less formally by phone. The lower courts are not bound by the higher court's answer, although in most cases the higher court's advice will be followed or at least given great weight. Scholars have criticized the practice for depriving the litigant the right to appeal because the higher court has already decided key issues, albeit in the absence of a complete record and without the parties having the opportunity to present their case. In practice, lower level courts reportedly seek instruction from higher courts less and less, with the frequency varying from court to court and judge to judge. In part, this reflects the increased confidence of judges but it is also in part the result of increased caseloads and stricter time limits for concluding cases so that busy judges simply do not have time to seek instructions from higher level courts.

The Second Five-Year Agenda recommended that lower courts submit cases involving generally applicable legal issues to the higher court directly for hearing rather than seeking advice. This would eliminate the problem of the higher court deciding issues in cases that it does not hear and would also preserve the integrity of the appeal process.

Social Pressures

Social pressure from relatives, friends, and acquaintances is a major source of outside interference. In a society that places a premium on guanxi (personal networks) and renqing (human feelings or empathy), judges often find themselves besieged by intermediaries seeking to intervene on behalf of a criminal suspect or one of the parties in a commercial dispute (see Chapter 11).

To be sure, personal connections come into play to some extent in every country, as do human feelings. Judges, however, must resist social pressures to render a fair verdict in accordance with law. Chinese citizens must appreciate, as have citizens in Taiwan, Hong Kong, and other Asian countries, that there are limits to empathy and personal connections.

Media coverage of legal cases has also been controversial, as it is elsewhere. IFES has noted: "Investigative journalism projects have not always been successful. Even when journalists are well-trained and media is independent from government control, the owners, with their own biases and connections, often control content."[37] In China, judges complain that the media, often paid off by one side to the dispute, presents a skewed picture of the facts and legal issues.[38]

Off-the-shelf guidelines for international best practices are so general as to be useless. Consider for example the IBA's advice: "It should be recognised that judicial independence does not render the judges free from public accountability, however, the press and other institutions should be aware of the potential conflict between judicial independence and excessive pressure on judges. The press should show restraint in publications on pending cases where such publication may influence the outcome of the case."[39]

An Asian Development Bank report provides a more useful rule of thumb: criticizing judges for unpopular decisions impedes judicial independence and is bad; exposing judicial corruption, judicial incompetence, or other judicial misbehavior is good, even if it also impedes judicial independence. Of course, in many cases it will not be clear at the time of reporting whether judges were in fact guilty of corruption

---

[37] IFES/USAID, Promoting Judicial Independence, p. 36.

[38] See Benjamin Liebman, "Watchdog or Demagogue? The Media in the Chinese Legal System," *Columbia Law Review*, vol. 105, p. 1 (2005); see also Liebman, "A Populist Threat to Chinese Courts," in *Chinese Justice*, suggesting that public opinion may affect court decisions in some cases, particularly high-profile criminal cases. However, the influence of the public is in most cases limited given the difficulty of mobilizing the public, differences of opinion among the public, and the fact that public opinion is frequently ill-informed about the legal issues. Controls on the press and civil society also limit public pressure. In addition, the government has attempted to relieve pressure on the courts by channeling controversial socioeconomic disputes away from the court.

[39] IBA Minimum Standards, arts. 33 and 34.

or misbehavior. Nor will it be clear in many legal cases whether a controversial and unpopular judicial decision was nonetheless correct as a matter of law. In any event, after reviewing several instances where the media exerted a negative influence on the judiciary, the report concludes on a more ambiguous note:[40]

> The country-level findings demonstrate that there is no single preferred model of the relationship between judicial independence and the media, organized interest groups, and civic organizations, or with other sources and mechanisms of external influence and control. Instead, they may present challenges and threats to, no less than support structures for, judicial independence.

SUMMARY CONCLUSIONS

Decisional independence – the ability of judges to decide cases independently in accordance with law and without (undue, inappropriate, or illegal) interference from other parties or entities – is in effect the sum of all other subcomponents. Notwithstanding problems in politically sensitive and socioeconomic cases or institutional weaknesses particularly in lower level courts, there has been a significant increase in decisional independence of the courts overall as measured by various indicators. It is incorrect to conclude (or to assume) that the Chinese judiciary is unable to decide any case independently, especially commercial cases and many other routine civil, administrative, or criminal cases.

As economic and legal reforms have progressed, the role of the courts has changed. Economic reforms have produced a more divided and pluralistic society, growing social cleavages, and a rapidly expanding middle class with significant economic interests to protect. As a consequence, citizens are increasingly looking to the courts to resolve disputes and to provide a neutral forum for reducing social tensions. The judiciary therefore is being asked to play a larger and more crucial role than in the past. Moreover, in today's modern market economy, companies can no longer tolerate long delays in concluding commercial cases or judges who lack the competence to decide complex legal issues. As Hu Jintao and the Politburo have forthrightly acknowledged, there is no choice but to continue with and deepen the process of reform.

Thus, although wary of the implications of deeper institutional reforms, the government has enacted a wide range of measures to create a more independent, competent, and authoritative judiciary. As we have seen, the last decade has witnessed a flurry of reforms, many of them initiated by those in the judiciary in response to the suggestions of judges working on the front lines as well as to the suggestions and criticisms of academics and citizens, but which could not have been carried out without the express or tacit consent of government leaders.

---

[40] Asian Development Bank, "Judicial Independence," p. 9.

As a result of these many incremental reforms, the judiciary has become more competent, authoritative, and independent. However, as with economic reforms, China has taken a pragmatic approach and avoided the temptation to accept the one-size-fits-all solutions that have produced such spectacular failures elsewhere.[41] Instead, it has tailored reforms to China's particular circumstances and adopted a number of more measured responses to increase judicial independence that addresses specific issues.

There are many reasons for such an approach. Like other developing countries, China lacks the institutional capacity and resources to implement one-size-fits-all solutions based on the institutions and practices in wealthy countries. Institutional conflicts between the procuracy, police, people's congress, and the courts, and between central and local governments, have also influenced the pace and direction of reform. More fundamentally, there is something of a chicken-and-egg aspect to judicial reforms: a competent and clean judiciary infused with a sense of professional pride requires a high degree of independence and authority; and yet an independent and authoritative judiciary assumes a competent and clean corps of judges. To be sure, there has been significant progress in raising the professional qualifications of judges. Would-be judges must now meet higher educational standards, pass a unified national exam, and undergo three months of training before they assume their post. In 2004, 97.7 percent of the 20,000 candidates who passed the unified judicial exam had a bachelor's degree or higher.[42] The improvements in judicial competence and accountability have allowed for increases in independence and authority.

We can expect further positive changes in the future, including deeper institutional changes that will inevitably alter the balance of power between the judiciary and the party as well as the legislature and executive branch, including local governments, the procuracy, public security, and the police.

China's experiences shed light on several more general law-and-development issues. First, disaggregating judicial independence provides a more accurate picture of the complex reality in China than simple generalizations about the lack of independent courts. However, many reforms undertaken to increase judicial competence, authority, and independence are highly technical. It is not likely most business people, foreign observers, or even many Chinese citizens will understand

---

[41] On the poor results, see Transparency International, *Global Corruption Report 2007: What can be done about corruption in the judicial sector?* http://www.eldis.org/go/what-s-new&id=33536&type=Document; Javier Couso, "Judicial Independence in Latin America: The Lessons of History in Search for an Always Elusive Ideal," in Tom Ginsburg and Robert Kagan eds., *Institutions and Public Law* (New York: Peter Lang, 2005); IFES/USAID, Promoting Judicial Independence; Carlos Santiso, "The Elusive Quest for the Rule of Law: Promoting Judicial Reform in Latin America," *Revista de Economia Politica/Brazilian Journal of Political Economy*, vol. 23, no. 3, pp. 112–134 (2003).

[42] 2004 nian sifa kaoshi canjia renshu ji tongguo lü [Number of Participants and Pass Rate in the 2004 Judicial Examination], http://education.163.com/edu2004/editor_2004/training/041223/041223_1709 87.html.

such reforms or even be aware of them.[43] Studies relying on subjective perceptions of judicial independence are likely to be biased therefore by the technical nature of reforms as well as media reports of nonrepresentative cases of judicial corruption or influence.[44]

Second, although there is no shortage of off-the-shelf guidelines for promoting judicial independence, there is a danger of description passing as prescription – that is, of taking institutions in the United States or Europe as necessary and sufficient for other countries. Conversely, any deviations from this standard model are condemned. Thus, China's regulatory innovations – including individual case supervision, adjudicative committees, an extensive incentive structure for judges, and, most of all, the role of party organs in the court system – have all been widely criticized. Yet the wide variation in legal systems calls into question what is needed, as do the poor results when developing countries try to mimic institutions and practices that have evolved over centuries in certain developed countries.

China's path toward greater judicial independence once again demonstrates that establishment of rule of law is a long-term process involving incremental reforms and considerable political struggle among competing interest groups. As such, it is largely a domestic process. Foreign actors lack the local knowledge and the influence to significantly shape the outcome.

Third, studies that use judicial independence as a dependent variable or as an independent variable to test the effect on economic growth or human rights necessarily assume there is a reasonably accurate way to measure judicial independence.[45] Yet the wide variation in legal systems and the many different aspects of judicial independence raise a number of thorny methodological issues for social scientists. What aspects are most important? How do you weigh the various factors and combine

---

43 IFES/USAID, Promoting Judicial Independence, p. 38, makes a similar point.

44 Selective use of data is common. For example, reports often provide absolute numbers of cases involving sanctions of judges but do not note that this is a small percentage overall given the size of China's judiciary, that it involves members of the judiciary who are not judges or who do not hear cases, and that the statistics include, and do not distinguish between, corruption and other misbehavior such as poor performance.

45 See, e.g., Rafael La Porta, "Judicial Checks and Balances," *Journal of Political Economy*, vol. 112, no. 2 (2004) (using tenure of high-court judges and the role of precedent to measure judicial independence). Compare Linda Camp Keith, "Judicial Independence and Human Rights Protection Around the World," *Judicature*, vol. 85, p. 195 (2002). Keith found that provisions for guaranteed terms for judges, separation of powers, bans on military courts and other exceptional courts, and fiscal autonomy were associated with better protection of civil rights, although a provision for exclusive authority of the courts to determine their own competence, a provision enabling courts to issue final decisions not subject to review other than by appeal in accordance with law, and a provision enumerating qualifications to be a judge were not significant. The various factors were coded on a scale of 0–2. However, many of the variables are vague or subject to wide variation in different systems. Consider the wide range of differences with respect to the key issue of separation of powers. Similarly, guaranteed terms of office encompass systems that provide life tenure and systems where judges are employed for a period of years, with the number of years varying from country to country. Nor is it clear how these various components are to be weighted and aggregated.

them into a single score? How do you design an index that will also capture significant differences in the types and level of courts, types of cases, and sources of interference? How do you move beyond formal measures of de jure independence to measures of de facto independence?

The limited attempts to do so thus far have produced surprising results: one study found that not a single country in the top ten of the de jure judicial independence index was in the top ten of the de facto judicial independence index; not one OECD country was in the top ten of the de jure index, whereas the United States was thirtieth; and Armenia, Kuwait, and Turkey were in the top ten of the de facto index. There was also a negative correlation between de jure judicial independence and a weak positive correlation between de facto judicial independence and other indexes that ostensibly measure similar things, such as rule of law, transparency, accountability of the legal system, and protection of civil and property rights. The authors concluded that the "irritatingly low correlations" suggest that the relationship between judicial independence and these other things may not be as straightforward as sometimes assumed.[46]

Fourth, measuring judicial independence, whether de facto or de jure, assumes there is substantive agreement on how independent the courts should be. There are, however, many controversial issues that undermine the assumption of an accepted normative standard of judicial independence and the assumption that the more independent the better.[47] What is the proper balance between judicial independence and accountability? How should that balance be obtained? Should courts be allowed to decide controversial social issues involving distribution of resources, or should such decisions be left to other political branches? Should the government be able to issue policy statements to guide judicial decision making? Given China's limited resources, how should the courts be funded? What would constitute an adequate budget?[48] How much of the budget should go for new buildings, computers, and

---

[46] They also note that they did not attempt to weight the various factors and point out various difficulties with trying to do so. See Lars Feld and Stefan Voigt. "Making Judges Independent – Some Proposals Regarding the Judiciary," in R. Congleton ed., *Democratic Constitutional Design and Public Policy: Analysis and Evidence* (Cambridge: MIT Press, 2006); Feld and Voigt, "Economic Growth and Judicial Independence: Cross Country Evidence Using a New Set of Indicators," *European Journal of Political Economy*, vol. 19, no. 3, 2003.

[47] IFES/USAID, Promoting Judicial Independence: "No judiciary is completely free to act according to its own lights; nor should it be. Ultimately, the judiciary, like any other institution of democratic governance, has to be accountable to the public for both its decisions and its operations."

[48] IFES/USAID, Promoting Judicial Independence, pp. 25–26: "Once again, there is no easy recipe for making this determination [as to what constitutes an adequate budget]. What is adequate varies from country to country and is based, among other things, on the resources available to the government, the stage of development of the legal system, the size of the population, the number of judges per capita and of organizational units included within the judiciary's budget (i.e., judges, judicial council, prosecutors, police, public defenders, military courts, labor courts, and electoral courts), and the extent to which courts are being used, or would likely be used if they were perceived to be fair and effective. Because of all these variables, comparisons among countries are virtually impossible.... If a judiciary's budget is inadequate to meet its needs, funds generated by the judiciary can provide an alternative

infrastructure and how much to higher salaries? Reasonable people in China and elsewhere can and do disagree about these fundamental issues.

Fifth, and related, judicial independence is a means to an end (or ends) rather than an end itself. The goal is not simply to maximize judicial independence. Some limits on judicial independence may be justified in terms of other social values or may not have an impact on the performance of the legal system. As an Asian Development Bank report has noted:[49]

> [There is a need to focus] attention on the actual performance of the judicial system, irrespective of whether the judiciary enjoys a high level of independence or not. This line of inquiry highlights the importance of understanding the specific ways in which judges are not independent and whether such specific constraints impede the system's ability to deliver justice. If the lack of independence does impede performance in specific ways, then it is necessary to ascertain how and to what extent it is impeded. Just as some are tempted wrongly to judge judicial systems as either "independent" or "not independent," so too many assume that any given structural constraint on independence will necessarily affect the performance of the judiciary across-the-board. This assumption is challenged [in the present study of legal systems in Asia].

Halliday et al. describe a threefold threat to judicial independence from the state, from markets (e.g., corruption), and from the public. In each case, too much independence is also a problem:[50]

> In relation to the executive arms of the state, too few benefits to state administration or reputation render them dispensable; too great an affinity with state politics renders them impotent. In relation to political parties, too distant a position from the policy ideals of parties renders courts irrelevant; too deep an immersion of judges in party politics converts courts into yet another arena of politics and subverts justice from within. In relation to the bar, too attenuated a relationship leaves courts vulnerable; too integral a relationship with lawyers diminishes courts' authority [and contributes to corruption]. In relation to the public [and media], too little public support denies judiciaries a primary source of legitimation; too much sensitivity to public opinion makes courts manipulable.

These issues demonstrate the need to think more deeply about the proper role of the courts in China at this stage of development. A closer examination of the specific role of party organs, which provide a pragmatic assessment of the advantages

---

to augment those resources. The United States provides an example of this practice. Trial courts in the United States were at one time insufficiently funded through state and local governments. Facing popular resistance to increasing direct support to the judiciary, the courts, with legislative approval, instead instituted user fees." Recognizing resource constraints in developing countries, the IBA does not attempt to specify a particular allocation of resources to the courts other than vaguely noting that the needs of the judiciary be given a "high priority." IBA Principles, art. 44.

49 Asian Development Bank, "Judicial Independence," p. 3.
50 Terrence Halliday et al., "Struggles for Political Liberalism: Reaching for a Theory of the Legal Complex and Political Mobilisation," in Halliday et al. eds., *Fighting for Political Freedom: Comparative Studies of the Legal Complex and Political Change* (Oxford: Hart Press, 2007).

and disadvantages of various forms of party involvement, is also needed. As Zhu Suli points out in his chapter, rejecting any role for party organs is neither feasible nor desirable. Efforts to promote judicial independence and rule of law have failed in many countries because of turf battles between the executive, legislative, and judicial branches.[51] In China, the CCP is the only entity with the authority to overcome such conflicts.

China's reforms have been successful due in large part to the government's pragmatic approach and willingness to resist, selectively adopt, and adapt as needed the ideologically driven prescriptions offered by Western states and international donor agencies. China has sought to develop its own variant of socialist rule of law compatible with the current form of government and contingent circumstances, including existing cultural norms and level of institutional development. Yet they have also realized that institutional reforms were needed, including a more authoritative and independent judiciary.

There are of course risks to this approach, including that political reforms will be too limited and too slow. For instance, although a high degree of judicial independence is possible within a single-party system, it requires a highly disciplined party to resist the temptation to interfere in cases that threaten its own survival. Until the handover to China in 1997, the Hong Kong legal system was widely considered to be an exemplar of rule of law, notwithstanding the lack of democracy and a restricted scope of individual rights under British rule. Even after the handover, the legal system continues to score high on the World Bank's Rule of Law Index, and the judiciary continues to enjoy a reputation for independence.

Much more likely is a high degree of judicial independence in some areas, combined with at times excessive restrictions in politically sensitive cases, as true for South Korea and Taiwan prior to democratization, and still true for Singapore. Singapore – a democracy, albeit dominated by the People's Action Party (PAP) – is generally ranked as one of the best legal systems in the world by investors, yet there are still highly problematic defamation suits against opposition figures and other limitations of civil and political rights.

Whatever the pace and limits of political reform under the current political system, democratization alone would clearly not ensure an independent and authoritative judiciary. In Indonesia, corporatist ties between judges and the political, military, and business elite have undermined the authority and independence of the judiciary.[52] In the Philippines, the courts continue to be so heavily influenced by the politics of populist, people-power movements that basic rule of law principles

---

[51] Daniels and Trebilcock argue that political-economy obstacles, including opposition by key interest groups, have been the biggest barriers in Latin America and Central and Eastern Europe. Ronald J. Daniels and Michael J. Trebilcock, "The Political Economy of Rule of Law Reform in Developing Countries," (2004), available at http://www.wdi.bus.umich.edu/global_conf/papers/revised/Trebilcock_Michael.pdf.

[52] Howard Dick, "Why Law Reforms Fail: Indonesia's Anti-corruption Reforms," in Tim Lindsey ed., *Law Reform in Developing and Transitional States* (London: Routledge, 2007).

are threatened.[53] Across Latin American democracies, efforts to increase judicial independence have fallen short time and again. In India and many other developing countries, judges are independent but corrupt and inefficient.

Nor is an independent court in a democratic state necessarily a force for political liberalism and protection of individual rights. In Japan, judges are independent but have played a minimal role in restraining political actors or protecting human rights. In Hong Kong, independent judges have often sided with the corporate sector and socially conservative forces. In the United States, courts have deferred to the executive branch in the war on terror, much to the dismay of civil libertarians. In Eastern Europe and Latin America, rising crime rates have led to a curtailment of protections afforded criminal defendants.

POLICY RECOMMENDATIONS

To challenge common assumptions and myths is not to deny the need for reforms to increase the independence and authority of the courts in China. Nor is it to deny that there are serious threats to judicial independence from various public and private sources or that judicial independence is severely constrained in some types of cases. But it does suggest the need for a more nuanced approach.

Efforts to increase judicial independence should be based on four general principles. First, reforms should be designed and proceed in light of a careful consideration of China's actual circumstances rather than ideology and the blind transplantation of universal best practices. Second, given the inherent tension between judicial corruption and judicial independence, both problems must be addressed simultaneously. Third, increased judicial independence and authority should be tied to levels of competence and integrity, beginning with judges in higher level courts in urban areas. Fourth, different types of cases produce different sources of interference, and therefore efforts to increase judicial independence require solutions targeted to the specific type of threat, as discussed in the next chapter.

Judicial corruption can be decreased by (i) ensuring that the recruitment and promotion of judges is based on merit and that judges are provided continuous on-the-job training; (ii) ensuring that the courts are adequately funded and that judges are paid a reasonable salary; (iii) reducing the discretion of judges and court staff by reducing barriers to the acceptance of cases, by adopting a case management system that assigns cases within a division randomly, and by reducing the complexity of pretrial and trial procedures; (iv) strengthening the mechanisms for accountability, including more prosecutions and heavier punishment of corrupt judges while at the same time ensuring that judges enjoy due process rights and will not be removed

---

53 Raul Pangalangan, "The Philippine 'People Power' Constitution, Rule of Law, and the Limits of Liberal Constitutionalism," in Randall Peerenboom ed., *Asian Discourses of Rule of Law* (London: Routledge, 2004).

from their jobs or denied promotion for whistle-blowing on other corrupt judges; (v) making full use of the rules for withdrawal in cases of real or perceived conflicts of interest; (vi) enhancing scrutiny of judges by civil society, including the establishment of consultative committees that include citizen representatives to investigate allegations of corruption and conflicts of interest while educating the media and the public about the value of judicial independence and the need to avoid trying cases in public; (vii) increasing transparency: publication of more judgments; wider and easier access to court documents by the public and media; more information about the process for nominating, appointing, and promoting judges, including selection criteria and reasons for appointing or rejecting candidates; and (viii) fully enforcing a requirement that judges report their and their immediate family members' income, with the information available to the public and media.

Judicial independence could be strengthened in various ways. Some of these overlap with recommendations for dealing with judicial corruption: (i) ensuring that the recruitment and promotion of judges is based on merit and that judges are provided continuous on-the-job training; (ii) allowing a greater role for higher level courts, the bar association, and other legal professionals in the nomination and appointment process; (iii) ensuring that the courts are adequately funded and that judges are paid an adequate salary; and (iv) publishing more judgments with reasoned opinions. Other ways include (v) changing the incentive structure for judges so that they are not penalized in terms of bonuses or promotions for reversals on appeal provided that their decisions were based on a plausible interpretation of law rather than due to ignorance of the law, negligence, or corruption; (vi) ensuring that judges are not fired or removed for deciding cases in ways that are politically controversial but in compliance with the law; (vii) eliminating the adjudicative committee in higher level courts and greatly restricting its role in lower courts; (viii) defining more specifically, and making more transparent, the role of party organs with respect to ideological guidance for the court, appointments, and involvement in particular cases, and ensuring that party policies are transformed into laws and regulations; (ix) eliminating or restricting supervision of the courts by the procuracy, again, beginning with higher level courts; and (x) increasing supervision by the media and civil society and restricting defamation cases against the media for criticism of government officials and judges while at the same time raising the professional standards of the media and eliminating the practice of reporters accepting fees from an interested party to a dispute; encouraging the emerging practice of having spokespeople from the courts hold press conferences to explain controversial cases to the media and the public; and more generally providing more information about the activities of the courts, including overall caseloads, the types of cases handled, and the results.

In addition, the SPC could further enhance the authority of the court by expanding the scope of judicial review to include abstract acts and by allowing the courts to annul lower level legislation inconsistent with superior legislation. As in other countries, efforts to increase the authority of the court at the expense of other institutions will be resisted. A newly empowered court could force a constitutional crisis if it were to challenge directly an NPC law (falü), State Council administrative regulation (xingzheng fagui), or even a ministry-level rule (guizhang). Thus one possibility would be to limit the ability of the courts to invalidate abstract acts to all normative documents (guifanxing wenjian).[54] Over time, as the courts gained in confidence and experience, their scope of review could be expanded, first to rules then to local people's congress regulations and State Council administrative regulations. Most of the problems are with regulations below the level of the State Council anyway. Moreover, the courts could expect support from the central authorities because conflicts between lower level regulations and laws or State Council administrative regulations do not benefit the nation.

Many of these recommendations are consistent with the general trend of judicial reforms over the last decade or are already being implemented. It is a matter of scaling up the reforms and carrying them out more thoroughly, a challenge made difficult by the size and diversity of China and the uneven development in rural and urban areas and between the eastern region and the rest of the country. Other recommendations are more contested, including increasing the amount spent on the judiciary, altering the balance of power between the courts and other state organs, decreasing the power of senior judges within courts, and defining the proper role of the party vis-à-vis the courts.

If all or most of the above changes were implemented or more fully implemented, judicial independence would increase over time. As in other East Asian states, judicial independence would deepen and the range of cases in which judges could decide cases independently would increase. Nevertheless, it is unlikely that the courts would gain the authority to handle politically sensitive cases independently. It is also unlikely that the courts would have the ability to provide an effective remedy in many socioeconomic cases. These cases are best handled in other ways, including through the establishment of an adequate social welfare system, by mediation, and through other political and administrative channels.

---

[54] This is essentially the approach taken in the PRC Administrative Reconsideration Law.

6

A New Analytic Framework for Understanding and Promoting Judicial Independence in China

Fu Yulin and Randall Peerenboom

This chapter develops a new analytical framework for understanding and promoting judicial independence in China. As noted in the previous chapter, general denunciations of the "lack" of (meaningful) independence in China do not capture the complexity of the situation. Attributing the lack of meaningful independence primarily if not exclusively to the nature of the political system also misstates and overstates the role of the party and ignores more common sources of pressure on the courts. The likely source of interference, the risk of interference, and the impact of interference all differ depending on the type of case.

Given the diverse nature of the problems, there is no single solution – no silver bullet – that will ensure meaningful judicial independence in China (whatever that means in light of the substantive disagreements about how independent courts should be at this stage of development). Reforms to facilitate judicial independence must be tailored to the particular circumstances and include a wide range of changes that affect not just the judiciary as an institution but substantive and procedural law, the balance of power among state organs, party–state relations, and social attitudes and practices. Judicial independence is, however, not an end itself, and the courts are not the sole, most effective, or most appropriate venue for resolving all disputes. Thus, we also provide policy recommendations for each type of case, including in some cases recommendations that emphasize nonjudicial mechanisms for resolving certain issues or that limit judicial independence in an effort to reduce corruption, promote sociopolitical stability, and enhance justice and judicial accountability.

Part I introduces the analytical framework and summarizes the results in table form. Part II discusses each type of case in more detail. Part III concludes.

THE ANALYTICAL FRAMEWORK

Types of Cases

The first distinction is between (pure) political cases and politically sensitive cases. The former are political in the straightforward sense of directly challenging the authority of the ruling regime. These include, for example, cases involving Falun Gong, attempts to establish an independent China Democracy Party, corruption among senior government officials, and national security cases involving terrorism, secession, endangering the state, and state secrets.

Politically sensitive cases affect sociopolitical stability, economic growth, China's position in the world and international reputation, or broad public interest. They are political but less directly political than the type of case that challenges the authority of the ruling regime.

These cases include socioeconomic cases such as land taking and compensation disputes, some entitlement claims (pension, unemployment, medical care, education), and some environmental and labor disputes. They also include class-action suits or cases involving a large number of plaintiffs, which often lead to protests, many of them increasingly violent, thus threatening social stability.[1] And they include some new economic cases or cases resulting from the transition to a market economy. Such economic cases present novel issues for the courts and have broad ramifications for economic growth and development, poverty reduction, China's efforts to create a "harmonious society," and China's relationship with other global economic actors. They include shareholder litigation suits and other types of securities litigation, bankruptcy claims (particularly involving large state-owned enterprises), and antidumping, price-setting, antimonopoly, and other types of competition law cases.

Political or politically sensitive cases may take the form of criminal, civil, or administrative cases. However, the Chinese courts handle more than 8 million first-instance cases a year, including more than 700,000 criminal cases, more than 4 million civil cases, and almost 100,000 administrative cases. Only a small fraction of them are political or politically sensitive. Moreover, not every political or politically sensitive case results in direct interference. On the other hand, routine cases are not necessarily free from interference. But the risk, nature, source, and impact of interference are different. Failing to draw these distinctions leads to misleading generalizations. Accordingly, we discuss separately routine criminal, civil, and administrative cases.

In addition, we discuss labor cases as a separate category. Although they are a type of socioeconomic dispute, and many are collective or mass-plaintiff cases,

---

[1] China allows for suits by multiple plaintiffs, although they differ in various respects from class actions in U.S. federal courts.

a significant number are routine in nature, involve only individuals, and present straightforward legal issues for which the courts can provide a remedy. Further, we treat them separately because of the unique nature of the labor dispute resolution process, which involves in most cases mandatory arbitration before parties can go to court.

Sources of Interference

In general, interference may come from:

(i) party organs: the party committee; political–legal committee; organizational department; and disciplinary committee;

(ii) the judiciary itself: the president of the court, head of division or other senior judges, the adjudicative committee, or higher level courts;

(iii) people's congresses and the procuracy;

(iv) (local) government and administrative entities;

(v) the media, public, and academics;

(vi) social acquaintances (relatives, friends, classmates, colleagues, members of community, golf club); and

(vii) parties, their lawyers, and hired consultants and experts with an interest in the case.

In every legal system, judicial independence must be balanced against the need for judicial accountability. Thus, every legal system has various review mechanisms. Sources of interference may be classified as systemic and nonsystemic depending on whether there is a legal basis for such intervention in particular cases.

As described in the previous chapter, the Chinese legal system authorizes certain forms of systemic intervention in specific cases by higher level courts, the adjudicative committee within courts, people's congresses, and the procuracy; there is a constitutional and statutory basis for such intervention, although there may be controversy about the wisdom and value of such intervention or particular aspects of it, and detailed rules regarding procedures or key issues may be lacking.

In contrast, the party's role is more controversial because there is no explicit constitutional or legal basis for the particular types of intervention in specific cases or in other ways. Nevertheless, various forms of party intervention are systemic and reasonably formalized, both through practice and party policies, directives, and guidelines. They are part of China's "living constitution."[2]

---

[2] The "living constitution" as used in American legal discourse usually refers to a method of statutory interpretation of the constitution that reads the broad purposes and principles of the constitution in light of contemporary circumstances and thus contrasts with the "original meaning" method that emphasizes the framers' intent. See Michael Dorf, "Who Killed the Living Constitution?" (March 10, 2008), http://writ.news.findlaw.com/dorf/20080310.html. In this context, "living constitution" refers to the existing constitutional order, including institutions, rules, and practices as they operate in practice.

Government officials and administrative entities have certain formal powers that affect the independence of the jury. For example, they can pass regulations, and under the current constitutional structure where the courts do not have the power to review abstract acts or strike down legislation for inconsistency with higher laws, they are often responsible for interpreting such statutes and maintaining consistency. Thus, in deciding cases, courts may have to refer certain issues to them and defer to their interpretations.[3] Until recently, courts were funded by the same level of government, although the government has recently announced that funding will be centralized. The ability to determine a court's budget clearly influences or affects the judiciary. Nevertheless, government entities and agencies have no formal or systemic powers to interfere with courts in handling specific cases.

Similarly, the media, academics, and citizens may comment on cases. Academics may take part in drafting laws or be asked to advise as experts on particular issues before the court. Lawyers obviously have a role in representing parties in particular cases. But the media, academics, social acquaintances, parties, and lawyers do not have formal or systemic powers to interfere in the way courts handle specific cases.

Not all systemic intervention is legitimate, and not all nonsystemic interference is illegitimate. In general, systemic interference (or, more neutrally and accurately, intervention) is legitimate when the intervention is on behalf of the entity rather than in the personal capacity of an individual member of the organization, when the nature or substance of the intervention is within the scope authorized by law, and when the manner of intervention is consistent with legal procedures (i.e., when the intervention is carried out in accordance with proper procedures). Conversely, intervention is illegitimate when an individual in one of the organs with power to intervene acts in his own capacity or for his own benefit, when the intervention exceeds the authorized scope, or when procedures are not followed.

Nonsystemic interference in specific cases is generally illegitimate, apart from public discussion of particular cases by the media, academics, citizens, or government officials. Nonsystemic intervention, particularly by parties, lawyers, and social acquaintances, is the most common source of corruption, although the various mechanisms of supervision also create opportunities for rent-seeking.[4] Illegitimate (nonsystemic) intervention by government officials in commercial cases, usually by local officials in lower level courts, is known as local protectionism.

---

[3] Courts rarely ask for interpretation of laws, and the National People's Congress Standing Committee has rarely issued interpretations. The SPC has been delegated the authority to issue interpretations of laws, and often does. The SPC files its interpretations with the NPC Standing Committee Legal Affairs Committee and generally obtains its consent on key issues. For a general discussion of mechanisms for ensuring consistency of administrative regulations and rules, see Randall Peerenboom, *China's Long March toward Rule of Law* (Cambridge: Cambridge University Press, 2002).

[4] The various supervision channels create opportunities for rent-seeking but are increasingly difficult to invoke and the likelihood of success is very low, making them worth pursuing only when the amount in controversy is large.

Impact of Interference

Just because intervention occurs does not mean it has an impact on the outcome of the case. When it does, the impact can range from ensuring judges decide cases according to law to minor changes in the outcome consistent with law to a decision that is at odds with law. Judges may also react to outside pressure by refusing to accept controversial cases[5] or by trying to steer parties to higher level courts, to courts in other jurisdictions, or to political, administrative, or civil channels for resolving the dispute. They may also try to mediate a settlement. Courts have responded to public pressure and criticism by increasing efforts to explain legal issues to the public. In some courts, for example, the president of the court or court spokesperson will hold press conferences or regular meetings open to the public. Courts have also published court judgments and opinions or articles written by academics and even judges discussing important cases or major issues on their Web sites.

Some Qualifications and Caveats

Several general caveats are in order. First, there is some overlap in the types of cases. For instance, many socioeconomic cases take the form of multiparty collective suits. In general, cases that fall into multiple categories are more likely candidates for intervention.

Second, these categorizations are ideal types. Although most people will agree how to categorize most cases, reasonable people can disagree how to categorize cases

---

5   See, e.g., Chapters 7 and 9 in this volume. A Supreme Court training manual suggests general guidelines for determining whether a case should be accepted: "The merits of the case by the Courts must be measured against two criteria: (1) legal criterion: whether it falls within the scope of laws and regulations . . . (2) political criterion: for questions that involve national defense, foreign relations, state interest, and other matters that go beyond the scope of the power of the judiciary and are not suitable to be adjudicated by the courts, cases should not be accepted. This is dictated by the place of the courts . . . in the political system." Huang Lirong, "Guan yu minshi libiaozhun de fali sikao" [Legal Theory Considerations on the Standards of Case Filing in Civil Litigation], Case-filing Office of the Supreme People's Court ed., *Guide on Case-Filing*, (Beijing: People's Court Publishing House, November 2004) (China Trial Guide series), pp. 89–91, cited in Human Rights Watch, "Walking on Thin Ice," fn. 50, p. 21, (http://www.hrw.org/reports/2008/china0408/5.htm). The Supreme Court has limited jurisdiction with respect to land-taking claims and securities litigation, as discussed below. One media report widely discussed on the Internet in China claims that Guangxi courts would not accept thirteen types of cases including securities litigation, land-taking claims, and compensation for resettlement, disputes arising out of illegal Ponzi schemes and other chain sale scams, cases involving laid-off workers and retraining as a result of economic transition or as a result of bankruptcy, large-scale government cancellation of rural responsibility system contracts, and remaining problems regarding how to divide collectively owned assets. These cases fall into the socioeconomic and transition to market economy categories discussed below. Many of them also involve large multiparty suits. In most if not all cases, the parties would have available a variety of political, administrative, and private channels to pursue their claims, each of which has advantages and disadvantages, none of which ensures success. See "Guangxi fayuan bu shouli 13 lei anjian; shenggaoyuan cheng you guoqing jueding" [Guangxi courts refuse to accept 13 types of cases; High Court claims decision in accordance with national conditions], *Zhongguo nianqing bao, Zhongqing zai xian*, Aug. 24, 2004.

closer to the margins – for example, whether a particular case is routine or raises issues that rise to the level of politically sensitive.

Third, nonsystemic interference may lead to systemic interference. The Chinese legal system allows various parties to seek supervision of individual cases by applying to the courts, the people's congress, or the procuracy.[6] Interested parties or citizens may also take advantage of an extensive petitioning system to raise complaints and in some cases, albeit few in practice, trigger the supervision mechanism.[7]

Fourth, reasonable people may at times also disagree about whether intervention is authorized or whether the particular intervention was within the authorized scope or in accordance with proper procedures. For example, there are no detailed national rules for intervention by people's congress, although some local congresses have passed implementing regulations. Many commentators take issue with some local provisions. In any event, the regulations are still vague on many key issues. Similarly, there is a great debate in China and many other countries regarding media coverage on pending cases and trials.

Fifth, legitimate intervention may be unwise or counterproductive; conversely, illegitimate intervention may be desirable or beneficial. Determining whether a particular form of intervention is harmful or beneficial requires assessing the costs and benefits of specific instances of such intervention and of the practice as a whole.

Summary of Results

In general, party and government influence determines, either directly or indirectly, results of political cases.

In politically sensitive cases, courts may be subject to intense pressure from various sources, including the media and public. The impact of various forms of influence on the outcome is difficult to predict, however, because the cases are complicated and there is often no adequate remedy available. As a result, courts often limit access to the courts in such cases, push the disputes toward other channels, or attempt to mediate a settlement.

Protectionism has decreased in economically advanced urban areas and is less of a factor in higher courts, but it remains a concern especially in lower courts in rural areas. Judges are generally able to resist other forms of nonsystemic intervention, particularly by parties, lawyers, and social acquaintances, but also increasingly from

---

[6] See Randall Peerenboom, "Judicial Accountability and Judicial Independence: An Empirical Study of Individual Case Supervision in the People's Republic of China," *The China Journal* vol. 55, p. 67 (2006).

[7] Carl Minzner, "Xinfang: An Alternative to the Formal Legal System" *Stanford Journal International Law* vol. 42, p. 103 (2006). A disgruntled party may complain about a court's handling of a case, including the refusal to hear the case, to many different entities, including higher level courts, the procuracy, government, and party entities. All of these noncourt entities may refer complaints to the court to trigger supervision.

senior judges within the court, as a result of improvements in education and professionalism, and an increase in their authority and stature. Judges are unlikely to decide a case in a way that is manifestly at odds with the law based on nonsystemic influence, although they may reach a different outcome that is consistent with law. Local protectionism and nonsystemic interference from the parties appear to be more severe in lower level courts and in poorer areas.

Although nonsystemic intervention generally does not have a significant impact on the outcome, it is the major source of corruption, and it erodes public confidence in the court. Although parties generally believe they prevail because they have the facts and law on their side – that is, they won on the merits – they frequently believe they lost because of bias and influence by the other party (see Chapter 11). Nonsystemic intervention also adds to the burden of judges, who in responding to and warding off intervention must spend time and energy attending to the social and professional relationships involved.

The table attached as Appendix A provides a summary of the results and a roadmap for the ensuing discussion.

DETAILED DISCUSSION OF EACH TYPE OF CASE

Pure Political Cases

Pure political cases threaten, or are perceived to threaten, the authority of the ruling regime. These include cases involving Falun Gong, attempts to establish an independent political party, high-level corruption, terrorism, secession, endangering the state, and other national security cases.[8] Many of these cases involve the exercise of civil and political rights. They often involve political dissidents, social activists, and their lawyers and representatives engaged in "political lawyering,"[9] including the more radical wing of weiquan lawyers.

Fu Hualing and Richard Cullen have provided a useful threefold classification scheme for lawyers in China who are part of the weiquan movement, a loose term that refers to activist lawyers engaged in efforts to protect citizens' rights and promote legal and political reforms. Activist lawyers can be moderate, critical, or

---

[8] For a brief discussion of several such cases, see Randall Peerenboom, *China Modernizes: Threat to the West or Model for the Rest?* (New York and London: Oxford University Press, 2007), pp. 100–118; Peerenboom, *China's Long March*, pp. 91–102.

[9] Political lawyering emphasizes first generation civil and political rights – the negative rights of freedom of speech, thought, religion, movement, and association – and the political institutions of (primarily economically advanced Western) liberal democracies that protect these rights. See Stuart Scheingold and Austin Sarat, "Something to Believe," in S. Scheingold and A. Sarat eds., *Politics Professionalism and Cause Lawyering* (Stanford: Stanford University Press, 2004); Terrence Halliday et al., "Struggles for Political Liberalism: Reaching for a Theory of the Legal Complex and Political Mobilisation," in T. Halliday et al. eds., *Fighting for Political Freedom: Comparative Studies of the Legal Complex and Political Change* (Oxford: Hart Press, 2007).

Type of case	Source of interference	Impact	Policy recommendation
Political	Party organs	Generally decisive; result usually restriction of rights, criminal punishment	(i) allow political organizations to resolve key issues (ii) clarify role of party (iii) clarify civil and political rights and limits (iv) if cases go to court, provide due process (v) better central control of local government
Politically sensitive	Party organs; government (ministry in charge; local government); higher level courts (limit access for certain claims but may also hear appeals). Adjudicative committees within court. Media and scholars.	Depends on particular circumstances, but party and government intervention often decisive with SPC following their lead; media and academics may have some impact. Results can range from plaintiffs obtaining no relief to a court judgment in their favor to a mediated result.	(i) prevention: more resources; strengthen welfare system (ii) strengthen nonjudicial mechanisms, including public hearings and mediation (iii) increase political participation and procedural fairness (iv) limit access to court: tight standing requirements; jurisdiction to IPC or HPC (v) strengthen court vis-à-vis executive agencies; power of review over abstract acts for higher courts (vi) more public education about issues and role and limits of courts
socioeconomic	Same; public security if social protests	Courts often respond to external pressure by limiting access and trying to mediate disputes; government sometimes intervenes to provide remedy/ resources	(i) same as above; (ii) specific actions for specific types of cases: e.g., land-taking – increase funding for local government, so they don't need to rely on land takings; require higher level of approvals with funds from sale paid to higher level; enforce auction requirements, etc.

Type of case	Source of interference	Impact	Policy recommendation
class action	Same; public security if social protests; MOJ to coordinate with lawyers and parties to ensure stability	Courts often try to break down into individual cases or cases with fewer plaintiffs; court leaders meet with media and parties to explain legal aspect of cases or elicit opinions from legal scholars; but parties more likely to be successful if number of plaintiffs large and media attention	(i) same as above (ii) clarify standing rules and rules regarding class actions
new economic cases	Same but with greater role for agencies dealing with economic issues, and more input from technocratic advisers, including academics, foreign business associations, international donor agencies on policy issues	Ministries often interfere; ostensibly to further public interest but often to protect own interests; courts must seek interpretations from agencies who pass rules; often conflicting views resulting in delays; cases often resolved through mediation	(i) same as above (except lack of resources is not the issue) (ii) clarify when parties have right to private action (iii) SPC in conjunction with other branches provide judicial interpretation of key issues (iv) SPC decide key cases to serve as models for lower level courts
Criminal: *politically sensitive* There are relatively few such cases. Such cases include citizens and lawyers charged in relation to socio-economic	Same as other politically sensitive; greater role for public security, procuracy, political-legal; Party discipline committee if case involves corruption; media and legal scholars	Party influence mainly through general policy guidance rather than intervention in particular case. Influence in particular case of Party or government depends on particular circumstances, rare but if occurs often decisive;	Not the same as other politically sensitive cases; most of reforms are just to deal with shortcomings in criminal justice system (see below)

(continued)

Type of case	Source of interference	Impact	Policy recommendation
disputes and class-action suits; cases involving corruption or govt malfeasance; major cases that capture the public's attention and have an impact on general policies or social issues such as capital punishment cases, the BMW case, Liu case		corruption cases involving Party members/government officials generally decided by Party discipline committee and then turned over to court for formal ratification; media and academics may have some impact; sometimes both point out problems but often media reflects popular desire for harsh punishments and scholars call for more respect for due process	
Criminal: routine	Limited or no systematic interference from Party organs; some systemic intervention from Procuracy through *kangsu* procedure; non-systemic interference from public security or procuracy; Interference from social acquaintances who know defendant	Limited impact on outcome; interference by parties or acquaintances may be corruption; if so, impact may on occasion result in wrong outcome (usually innocent) but more likely reduced (or more severe) punishment	(i) improve criminal procedure laws and criminal law, including rights of parties to access dossier and obligation of procuracy and police to provide exculpatory evidence; access to witness and power to compel testimony (ii) strengthen role of, and protections for defense counsel (iii) elevate the status of the courts relative to the public security; appoint member of judiciary as member of politburo; eliminate or limit right of procuracy to see review of court

Type of case	Source of interference	Impact	Policy recommendation
			decisions in both civil and criminal cases (iv) increase support from criminal law reforms by educating public about rising crime rates, rate of violent crime, likelihood of being subject to crime by strangers, etc. (v) limit media coverage of ongoing trials or ensure more balanced coverage by greater reliance on experts to cover stories or appear on tv and radio programs; in addition, to deal with non-systemic interference: see also general recommendations to combat corruption and increase judicial independence in Chapter 5
Civil: politically sensitive These include the socio-economic, mass plaintiff and new economic cases.	Same as politically sensitive cases above	Same as above	Same as above
Civil: routine	Limited or no systemic interference from Party organs. Sometimes non-systemic abuse of people's congress review or procuracy review particularly	Impact varies. (i) People's congress and procuracy review: judges increasingly independent; pressure rarely leads to reversal of original outcome; sometimes introduces corruption	*People's congress and procuracy review*: eliminate or reform; *local protectionism*: change way courts are funded and increase budgets (as is now happening); change way judges are appointed; long term, outgrow non-systematic interference/corruption same as above for routine criminal cases

(continued)

Type of case	Source of interference	Impact	Policy recommendation
	when amount at stake is large. Some local protectionism particularly in lower level courts in rural and economically less developed areas. Non-systemic interference from Party members or government officials with personal interest in case (may be their own business or business of relative or result of corruption). Nonsystemic interference from parties, lawyers, and social acquaintances who know parties.	(ii) local protectionism increasingly less of a problem (iii) parties, lawyers and acquaintances: not likely to result in manifestly wrong decision; can have impact when law unclear or judges have discretion; outright wrong decision more of a problem in lower courts, higher courts influence more subtle; may have no impact on outcome but still be corruption (decide case and then collect)	
Labor: politically sensitive	Same as other politically sensitive; greater role for Labor Bureau; Labor Arbitration Commission; ACLU (especially in mediation)	Courts often respond to external pressure by limiting access and trying to mediate disputes; govt sometimes intervenes to provide remedy/resources; enforcement often difficult	(i) prevention: more resources; strengthen welfare system; increase jobs, training for new jobs and services to find new jobs (ii) increase political participation and procedural fairness (iii) strengthen non-judicial mechanisms: mediation, arbitration, administrative review, labor associations (iv) allow workers to bring more cases directly to court – especially back pay and excessive mandatory overtime; dangerous

APPENDIX A *(continued)*

Type of case	Source of interference	Impact	Policy recommendation
			work conditions, sexual harassment, discrimination (v) strengthen collective labor disputes: strengthen unions, let collective suits start in IPC
Routine	Limited interference from parties, lawyers and acquaintances	Pressure by employers may occasionally lead to wrong decision or lower damages but nowadays plaintiffs/workers usually win	(i) allow parties to bring more cases directly (ii) increase enforcement powers; hold employers who withhold backpay criminally liable unless company is insolvent or in dire economic condition
Administrative: politically sensitive	Same as other politically sensitive	Same; court now allowed to mediate outcome	Same
Routine	May be interference from officials but decreasing; parties, lawyers and acquaintances may interfere but rare	Judges increasingly independent but officials may have some influence; parties unlikely to have much impact in most cases	Address *doctrinal limitations. Most problems are systemic.* Need to increase powers of court and other systemic reforms

radical depending on the type of the cases they handle, their objectives, and their approach.

Moderate lawyers are not overtly political. They select cases involving consumer protection, labor rights, or discrimination that are not terribly politically sensitive. They operate within the limits of law, rely on legal arguments, and seek to promote rule of law.

Critical lawyers are often more critical of the political system, but they are also pragmatic in their acceptance of the lack of viable alternatives. They want to ensure that the system lives up to expressed ideals, often pushing for systemic reforms. They are willing to take on more politically sensitive cases involving free speech, religious freedom, and freedom of association, but not politically prohibited cases such as Falun Gong or representing dissidents calling for the overthrow of the Chinese Communist Party (CCP). They rely on both legal and political methods, including greater mobilization of the media, support from foreign NGOs and organizations, and the use of mass protests and sit-ins, although they are divided about mass protests and sit-ins. They "prefer gradual institutional transformation, hoping to end the endemic abuses of the authoritarian state through reforming it from within, avoiding direct confrontation with the CCP/state."[10]

Radical lawyers take on highly sensitive political cases involving dissidents and Falun Gong. Their methods are more extreme, including organizing mass demonstrations and social movements, or even advocating violence. Their goals may include overthrowing the party-state. Radical lawyers "mobilize against the law and against the grain of mainstream politics."[11] As a result, they tend to alienate the general public and their fellow lawyers and provide a pretext for the government to delegitimize and suppress the weiquan movement, as many less radical lawyers have pointed out.[12]

Not every political case gives rise to direct interference, although some form of intervention is likely in most cases. These cases are generally decided through political channels or at least with heavy input from political entities. Party organs play a large and generally decisive role in determining the content of laws, in issuing policy statements, or in some cases intervening in specific cases. There is a trial, but the results are easily predicted in advance. In general, courts continue to impose severe limitations on civil and political freedoms when the exercise of such rights is deemed to threaten the regime and social stability. The lines of what is permissible and what is not are clear and fixed in some areas but vague and fluid in others. The time, place, and manner of expression are as important as the subject matter. What may be tolerated in some circumstances may be subject to greater restriction when there are certain aggravating factors present, such as attempts to organize across regions or to hook up with foreign organizations.

In addition, there are often serious due process violations both before and after the trial. Lawyers may be harassed and in some cases arrested on trumped up charges. Some lawyers have also been beaten by thugs, in some cases linked to the authorities, or by police, or members of the security bureau.[13]

Limitations on the independence of the courts in political cases reflect the nature of the regime, the current state of sociopolitical stability, the dominant conception of law/rule of law, China's model of development, and the political contract between central and local governments.

A single-party state is less likely than a democratic state to tolerate challenges to its authority, although the differences are easily overstated. Democratic states also

[10] Fu Hualing and Richard Cullen, "*Weiquan* (Rights Protection) Lawyering in an Authoritarian State: Toward Critical Lawyering," http://ssrn.com/abstract=1083925 (accessed March 15, 2008).

[11] Austin Sarat and Stuart A. Scheingold, "State Transformation, Globalization, and the Possibilities of Cause Lawyering: An Introduction," Sarat and Scheingold eds., *Cause Lawyering and the State in a Global Era* (Oxford: Oxford Socio-Legal Studies, 2001).

[12] Eva Pils, "Asking the Tiger for His Skin: Rights Activism in China," *Fordham International Law J.* vol. 30, p. 14 (2007).

[13] Fu Hualing, "When Lawyers Are Prosecuted: The Struggle of a Profession in Transition," (2006), http://ssrn.com/abstract=956500 (accessed March 15, 2008).

react to social instability and perceived threats to national security. A number of quantitative studies demonstrate that the third wave of democratization has not led to a decrease in political repression, with some studies showing that political terror and violations of personal integrity rights actually increased in the 1980s.[14] Other studies have found that there are nonlinear effects to democratization: transitional or illiberal democracies increase repressive action. Fein described this phenomenon as "more murder in the middle" – as political space opens, the ruling regime is subject to greater threats to its power and so resorts to violence.[15] More recent studies have also concluded that the level of democracy matters: below a certain level, democratic regimes oppress as much as nondemocratic regimes.[16] Moreover, the recent war on terror in the United States, England, and Europe demonstrates that even in consolidated democracies the legislative and executive branch, often supported by a compliant or intimidated judiciary, will not hesitate to restrict civil liberties when national security is perceived to be threatened.[17]

Ironically, the argument of many liberal critics that China is unstable tends to undercut their opposition to restrictions on civil and political rights. China clearly faces a number of threats to stability, including increasing rural poverty, rising urban employment, a weak social security system, and a rapidly aging population that has pushed the elderly into the streets to protest for retirement benefits. The number of mass protests has risen rapidly, from 58,000 in 2003 to more than 74,000 in 2004. Such protests, many of them violent, are a threat to social stability and thus to sustained economic growth. According to the state media, more than 1,800 police were injured and 23 killed during protests in just the first nine months of 2005. The desire for greater autonomy if not independence among many Tibetans and Xinjiang Muslims, the rise of Islamic fundamentalism in the region, and the difficulty of separating Buddhism and politics in Tibet also present risks that cannot be dismissed, even if they should not be exaggerated.

In addition, ideological differences, including the dominant conception of rule of law, also play a role. The stated goal is a socialist rule-of-law state, not a liberal

---

[14] James McCann and Mark Gibney, "An Overview of Political Terror in the Developing World, 1980–1991," in David Cingranelli ed., *Policy Studies and Developing Countries.* (Greenwich: Jai Press, 1996); David Reilly, "Diffusing Human Rights: The Nexus of Domestic and International Influences," paper presented at the annual meeting of the American Political Science Association (2003), http://www.allacademic.com/meta/p62741_index.html.

[15] Helen Fein, "More Murder in the Middle: Life-Integrity Violations and Democracy in the World," *Human Rights Quarterly* vol. 17, p. 170 (1987).

[16] Bruce Bueno de Mesquita et al., "Thinking inside the Box: a closer look at democracy and human rights," *International Studies Quarterly* vol. 49, p. 3 (2005); Christian Davenport and David Armstrong, "Democracy and the Violation of Human Rights: A Statistical Analysis of the Third Wave," (2002), http://apsaproceedings.cup.org/Site/abstracts/011/011002ArmstrongD.html; Linda C. Keith and Steven C. Poe, "Personal Integrity Abuse during Domestic Crises," (2002) http://apsaproceedings.cup.org/Site/papers/046/046004PoeSteveno.pdf.

[17] Nor is the post-9/11 war on terror exceptional. For other examples, see Peerenboom, *China Modernizes,* pp. 99–100.

democratic rule of law. One of the key differences between the two lies in the conception of rights, and in particular how to resolve the inevitable tension between the exercise of individual civil and political rights and the need for social stability.[18]

The tight restriction on civil and political rights also reflects the East Asian model of development. Chinese leaders no doubt are aware that sociopolitical instability has inhibited economic development and led to the downfall of many regimes (whether democratic or authoritarian) in Asia and elsewhere. Conversely, the successful Asian countries have followed a two-track system that combines rapid development in the commercial law area with tight restrictions on civil and political rights.[19]

These cases are also influenced by an implicit political contract between the central and local governments. The central government has created an incentive structure for local officials that emphasizes, among other things, economic growth, social stability, and the one-child policy. Yet it has failed to provide local governments the necessary funds to support the schools, hospitals, pension plans, and other institutions needed to ensure social stability or to build the roads, factories, and R&D centers needed to promote economic growth. As a result, local officials are given considerable leeway in how these goals are achieved. At times, they violate central laws or abuse their powers. The central government will prosecute local officials who cross the line – for example when police kill protesters or when local practices, such as use of child labor in factories or poor safety standards in mines leads to accidents, resulting in national scandals. But this only further encourages local officials to cover up the problems, often by harassing whistle-blowers or arresting or intimidating the leaders of mass protests. Thus, local government officials are directly or indirectly responsible for some of the worst abuses, including beatings and other serious due process violations.

Courts in all legal systems have various ways of avoiding conflict with other political organs. In the United States, for example, courts may rely on the political question doctrine to avoid hearing certain disputes. Even when they formally retain the right to hear cases and review executive or legislative decisions, courts may defer to the executive or legislative on issues, particularly in national security.[20]

In China, the party is responsible for major political decisions, including deciding the types of issues raised in these cases. The courts' role is to carry out the party's decisions. In most cases, the party line is clear and reflected in laws and regulations, so there is little need for party organs to intervene in specific cases. But in some cases the outcome may be less clear because the law or policy is unclear, the facts

---

[18] See Peerenboom, *China's Long March*, pp. 71–109.

[19] This is only one aspect of the East Asian Model. For a more in-depth discussion, see Peerenboom, *China Modernizes*.

[20] This is particularly true in Asia. See Peerenboom et al. eds., *Human Rights in Asia* (New York: Routledge, 2004). However, U.S. courts have not been aggressive in reviewing executive and legislative actions in the post-9/11 war on terror.

are uncertain, or the nexus between facts and the type of harms contemplated in the law and policies is uncertain. Accordingly, party organs may intervene.

To insist on judicial independence in these cases would be futile given the political system. Nor would it necessarily be wise, as many of these issues are essentially political and arguably best decided through political channels by political entities. Nevertheless, that does not mean that party organs may do whatever they want or that there is no role for the court. Although party organs may be responsible for deciding the general law and policies that determine the outcome in these cases, they could (and should) leave the application of the law and policies in the particular case to the courts. If cases raise new issues, then the courts could seek interpretation on the laws and policies from the entities that passed them, as is now contemplated. These political organs could consult party organs. Alternatively, the courts could seek clarification directly from party organs such as the political–legal committee on some issues, as now happens in practice. Either way, the respective roles of party organs and the courts should be further clarified and formalized in law.

A greater role for the courts in applying laws and regulations to the facts in these cases would also require that the limits of civil and political rights be clarified in laws and regulations. For instance, a judicial interpretation of subversion and related charges, and a narrower definition of state secrets, would go a long way toward clarifying the scope of impermissible activities and expanding the range of legitimate activities without detriment to state interests. Similarly, it made little sense for the authorities to set up protest zones for demonstrators during the Olympics and then refuse all or virtually all applications for demonstrations and arrest or harass some of those who applied.[21]

Even without further clarification of laws and regulations, the courts could play a greater role in reviewing the facts, establishing a nexus between the acts and the alleged danger, and ensuring that the procuracy has met its burden of proof. The danger of relying on broad allegations of subversion or endangering the state is readily apparent in this era of heightened sensitivity to terrorism. Yet in some cases courts have not closely examined statements offered by the procuracy as evidence of subversion. Similarly, in deciding whether time, place, and manner restrictions on freedom of assembly or speech are necessary in particular cases, the court could more closely scrutinize the likelihood that the anticipated harm will occur. Although acknowledging the possibility of instability, many court decisions fail to provide any discussion of how the particular acts in question will lead to instability or endanger the state or public order. A more considered analysis of the nexus between the acts and disruptions of the public order or harm to the state would expand the range of civil and political rights without harming national security or state interests.

[21] "China's Olympic pride and lessons learned," *South China Morning Post*, Aug. 25, 2008.

Moreover, whatever the outcomes on the substantive merits, the many due process violations even under China's own laws – including incidents of torture, the lack of transparency and a public trial, and excessively long periods of detention – violate both international and domestic laws. Nor should lawyers be harassed and prosecuted for trying to protect the legitimate rights of their clients, or environmental organizations and human rights groups unable to register or shut down simply for raising issues of genuine public concern. Courts could and should play a greater role in holding government actors accountable by enforcing procedural law and strictly applying evidentiary rules.

In addition, the existing political contract should be revisited. Government officials and police who rely on excessive force in dealing with demonstrators or who turn a blind eye to local thugs who beat and intimidate protesters should be held liable and given stiff punishments as a deterrent to others. These cases should be handled by higher level courts or courts in other jurisdictions to ensure impartiality.

Politically Sensitive Socioeconomic Cases

Socioeconomic cases include pension and other welfare claims, labor disputes, land takings, and environmental issues.[22] Like other politically sensitive cases, they attract the attention of party organs, government officials, administrative agencies, the media, public, and scholars. Because of their sensitive nature, the adjudicative committee is likely to be involved in the decision. Higher level courts are also likely to be involved, either on formal appeal or when lower level courts seek advice on new or controversial issues.

Dispute resolution of socioeconomic cases has been characterized by: (i) notably less effective resolution than the vast majority of commercial cases; (ii) a trend toward dejudicialization, in contrast to the judicialization of most commercial disputes as reflected in the rising rates of litigation and the expanded range of litigable commercial cases: that is, the government has steered socioeconomic disputes away from the courts toward other mechanisms, such as administrative reconsideration, mediation, arbitration, public hearings, and the political process more generally, when it became apparent that the courts lacked the resources, competence, and stature to provide effective relief in such cases; (iii) a sharp rise in mass-plaintiff suits; (iv) a dramatic rise in letters, petitions, and social protests in response to the inability of the courts and other mechanisms to address adequately citizen demands and

---

[22] For a discussion of pension and welfare claims, and land-taking and compensation disputes, see Randall Peerenboom and Xin He, "Dispute Resolution in China: Patterns, Causes and Prognosis," in R. Peerenboom ed., *Dispute Resolution in China* (Oxford: Foundation for Law, Justice and Society, 2008), http://www.fljs.org/section.aspx?id=1931. For an excellent study of various efforts to address environmental issues, ongoing problems, and policy recommendations, see Benjamin van Rooij, *Land and pollution regulation in China: law-making, compliance, enforcement; theory and cases* (Leiden: Leiden University Press, 2006).

expectations; and (v) a reallocation of resources toward the least well-off members of society as part of a government effort to contain social instability and create a harmonious society, combined with a simultaneous increase in targeted repression of potential sources of instability, including political dissidents, NGOs, and activist lawyers.

China is not alone in having difficulties resolving socioeconomic cases. These types of cases are difficult for low- and middle-income countries because expectations have risen, yet resources are scarce and institutions relatively weak. Citizen expectations have risen as a result of the human rights movement and in particular the greater (albeit still secondary) emphasis on socioeconomic rights in addition to civil and political rights. In the 1980s and '90s, the conception of development shifted from aggregate growth to sustainable, equitable, humane growth, growth that allows individuals, including socially vulnerable groups and individuals, to flourish and realize their capabilities. Amartya Sen's *Development as Freedom* championed this new, broader conception of development. The UNDP developed the Human Development Index, which measures health and longevity, education and literacy rates, and poverty. The World Bank and other international development agencies began to emphasize poverty reduction, legal empowerment, and access to justice.

The capabilities approach promises citizens more than even traditional socioeconomic rights, which have been and still are in most countries considered to be nonjusticiable. In ratifying the International Covenant on Economic, Social and Cultural Rights, for example, states agree only to realize socioeconomic rights to the maximum of their available resources with a view to progressive achievement. The capabilities approach pressures developing countries to deliver results immediately. Citizens have increasingly turned to the courts to pursue their individual socioeconomic rights and broader social justice goals. Most developing countries have struggled to make good on these commitments.[23]

In Indonesia, for example, reformers flush with optimism after the fall of Suharto wrote into the constitution some of the most forward-leaning ideas of the human rights movement. Accordingly, the constitution now provides that each person has the right to physical and spiritual welfare, a home, a good and healthy living environment, and the ability to obtain health services. Each person is entitled to assistance and special treatment to gain the same opportunities and benefits in the attainment of equality and justice. Unfortunately, the Megawati government in low-income Indonesia was not able to live up to such broad commitments or even to effectively deal with terrorism and rising crime rates. Her successor is not doing much better.

India offers another cautionary tale. The Bharatiya Janata Party (BJP) government was voted out of office despite overseeing a period of rapid economic growth. The

---

[23] Dam notes that the expansion of the 1988 Brazilian constitution to allow a wider range of plaintiffs to bring a wider range of constitutional rights claims, including social and economic guarantees, led to massive backlogs and calls for reforms to limit cases to those where the court could actually make a contribution. Kenneth Dam, *The Law-Growth Nexus* (Washington D.C., Brookings Institute, 2006), pp. 104–105.

vote reflected a deep dissatisfaction with growing income disparities and widespread poverty amid the growing wealth of some segments of society. The BJP's campaign slogan of "India Shining" only highlighted the discrepancies between the haves and the have-nots. By way of comparison, in wealthy South Korea, which has not made social rights justiciable, the government only made good on its promise to provide an equal education for all by providing nine years of compulsory education free of charge in 2003.

Citizen expectations have clearly risen in China. When the reform era began in 1978, people were equal – the Gini coefficient, a measure of income equality, was remarkably low. But they were equally poor. In introducing market reforms, the authorities announced that "to get rich was glorious" and cautioned that some would get rich first. Nevertheless, China remains, at least in name, a socialist state. The central authorities could not simply ignore poverty, rapidly increasing inequality, or the plight of state-owned enterprise employees and the socially vulnerable who have not benefited from globalization and the transition to a market economy. Accordingly, after years of focusing on aggregate growth, the government has now begun to emphasize social justice and sustainable growth as part of its commitment to create a harmonious society. The government has also long promised citizens the rule of law and sought to raise legal consciousness and public awareness of rights through numerous legal education campaigns. Yet China remains a lower middle-income country, with GDP per capita around $2,500. In keeping with the general correlation between wealth and institutional development, governance institutions remain relatively weak, at least in comparison to developed country standards. According to the World Bank's World Governance Indicators, China ranks in the forty-second percentile of all countries on rule of law, slightly outperforming the average lower middle-income country on most indicators, including rule of law.[24]

The long-term solution to socioeconomic cases is growth, although growth alone is not sufficient. As the government has realized, development raises many social justice issues, including how the wealth generated by development is to be distributed. Policy recommendations to mitigate some of the concerns must encompass at least seven major aspects.

First is prevention. Given the growing social tensions, the increasing pluralism of society, and the inadequacy of current mechanisms for dealing with such tensions, there is a need to prevent disputes from arising in the first place. This entails improving the welfare system and increasing resources to address some of the major social cleavages, including the rural–urban income gap, the regional income gap, and the intraurban gap between those who have benefited from economic reforms and those who have lost out.

---

[24] Kaufmann, Daniel et al., Governance Matters III: Governance Indicators for 1996–2007, http://www.govindicators.org.

Second, the increasing pluralism of society means that there will be a growing number of issues over which reasonable people may disagree. Procedural mechanisms must be developed and strengthened to handle the increasingly diverse views in society. In particular, there needs to be greater political participation in the decision-making processes, whether through public hearings, consultative committees, or participation in the nomination or election of officials. Empirical studies have found that procedural justice, including a sense of having a say in the outcome, is frequently more important to determining perceptions of legitimacy than the substantive outcome.[25] This is borne out by village elections in China, which have demonstrated that people generally are more willing to compromise or accept decisions that are not in their interest when they believe they had a fair opportunity to be heard and participate in the decision-making process. This approach is also consistent with the efforts to expand public participation as reflected in the Law on Legislation, the drafting of an Administrative Procedural Law, the experiment with access to information acts, and the increasing reliance on social consultative committees.

Third, given the courts' inability to provide an effective remedy in what at bottom are economic cases, access to the courts should be limited. The Supreme Court should clarify what cases the court will not accept or which cases it will accept only after administrative remedies have first been exhausted. Standing rules should be clarified and where necessary limited to minimize the social impact of particular cases. Given concerns about the impact of these cases on social stability or the national economy, jurisdictional rules should be changed so that the cases are heard by higher level courts, with initial jurisdiction in intermediate courts at minimum depending on the type of case and the amount in controversy.

Fourth, when higher courts are allowed to hear cases, they should be given the authority to reach an effective decision by striking down where necessary local legislation that is inconsistent with higher level laws. In particular, higher level courts should be given the right to strike down local legislation that fails to provide minimal standards of protection with respect to poverty, education, minimum wage, and safety standards and gross environmental violations. For instance, the central government has repeatedly prohibited schools from charging various fees, and yet the practice remains widespread. Many current laws and regulations set high standards – often as high as in the United States or other developed countries with per capita incomes ten to twenty times greater than in China – but then provide for local discretion in realizing these standards. For courts to play this role, there would have to be a clearer articulation of the bottom line – that is, minimum requirements in laws and regulations.[26]

[25] Tom Tyler, *Why People Obey the Law* (New Haven: Yale University Press, 1990).

[26] We are under no delusions that this will be an easy task or solve all of the problems. For instance, van Rooij has shown how the government first tried passing general but weak environmental laws and then more specific and stricter laws. Neither approach worked well. Not surprisingly, national-level laws often failed to adequately account for local circumstances, leading to low levels of compliance. A

Fifth, with access to the court and the courts' role restricted, nonjudicial mechanisms for addressing citizen concerns in these types of cases would have to be strengthened. In addition to increasing public hearing and public participation in the law- and rule-making processes, these alternative channels include administrative reconsideration, the letter and petition system, supervision by the administration, people's congress and party, mediation, and arbitration. In addition, new governance mechanisms that rely on public–private hybrids and self-regulation should be increased, as discussed below.

Sixth, greater attention must be paid to procedural justice in mechanisms for resolving disputes, whether through mediation, the letter and visits system, court cases, or other means. Participants must perceive the mechanisms to be fair, regardless of the outcome in the particular instance.

Seventh, greater efforts should be made to explain the proper role and limits of the legal system and rule of law. The legal system is not the proper forum for resolving all contentious issues. Moreover, the traditional emphasis on substantive justice – expressed through the heavy reliance on letters and visits – leads to unrealistic expectations from the legal system. The unrealistic expectations undermine trust in the judiciary when the legal system then fails to resolve each and every social problem, to ensure social justice, or to provide a substantively just outcome in the eyes of all parties to a conflict.

In addition to these general recommendations, specific types of cases give rise to specific issues and require specific policy responses and reforms.[27] For instance, reforms to address land taking and compensation disputes include increasing funding for local governments so that local governments do not need to rely on revenues from the sale of lands to operate; requiring higher level of approvals for land taking with all funds from the sale paid to the provincial or central level government and then redistributed; strictly enforcing and improving rules regarding public auctioning of law, and so on.

---

variety of other factors also undermined compliance: weak institutions, the lack of regulatory capacity, local power configurations, and the nature of the company involved, with small companies the most likely to violate environmental laws. However, the biggest factor was economic. Enforcement of national laws often meets fierce resistance by local government officials who are promoted based on their ability to achieve high levels of growth and by local residents dependent on the polluting industry for jobs.

[27] Van Rooij's policy recommendations for addressing environmental problems include more extensive empirical research prior to passing new laws; more participation from civil society in making law and monitoring compliance; introduction of an integrated permit system for pollution; adoption of a mixed system of enforcement that uses both a cooperative and deterrent approach; more tolerance of NGOs including allowing them to initiate public interest litigation; and adoption of a case-precedent system, which would allow courts to take into consideration local circumstances when applying national laws and thus allow for the emergence of bottom-up norms. Although most of these reforms are consistent with the general principles and recommendations we have proposed, we place relatively more emphasis on nonjudicial mechanisms.

Politically Sensitive Class-Action or Multiple-Plaintiff Suits

There were 538,941 multiparty suits in 2004, up 9.5 percent from 2003.[28] Many socioeconomic cases involve multiple plaintiffs. Land takings, labor disputes, and welfare claims are three major types of multiparty suits. In 2004 alone, Shanghai Intermediate Court No. 1 handled twenty-one multiplaintiff cases, of which seventeen involved land takings, relocations, and real estate disputes. In 2006, there were 14,000 collective labor disputes involving 350,000 workers, or more than half of the total number of workers involved in labor disputes.

Although the courts obviously hear many multiparty suits, they have developed a number of techniques to reduce public pressure, including breaking the plaintiffs up into smaller groups, emphasizing conciliation, and providing a spokesperson to meet with and explain the legal aspects of the case to the plaintiffs and the media in the hope of encouraging settlement or even withdrawal of the suit. Some courts also try to pacify the protesters by providing accelerated procedures to access government-sponsored funds. Basic level courts also often work closely with higher level courts and other government entities through the Social Stability Maintenance offices.

Worried about instability, the government will sometimes allocate more funds to a particular problem. However, this "oil the wheel that squeaks the loudest" approach creates the perverse incentive from the government's perspective of encouraging other disgruntled groups to engage in demonstrations and public protests. Accordingly, government officials have also sought to deter such efforts to organize and mobilize by detaining, intimidating, and harassing the ringleaders. They have also closed down or put pressure on some NGOs and law firms that have become too active in pressing for change.[29]

In a related move, in 2006 the All China Lawyers Association issued guidelines that seek to reach a balance between social order and the protection of citizens and their lawyers in exercising their rights.[30] The guidelines remind lawyers to act in accordance with their professional responsibilities. Lawyers should encourage parties and witnesses to tell the whole truth and not conceal or distort facts; they should avoid falsifying evidence; they should refuse manifestly unreasonable demands from parties; they should not encourage parties to interfere with the work of government organ agencies; they should accurately represent the facts in discussions with the media and refrain from paying journalists to cover their side of the story; they should report to and accept the supervision of the bar association. On the other hand, bar associations shall promptly report instances of interference with lawyers lawfully carrying out their duties to the authorities and press authorities to take appropriate

[28] Peerenboom and He, "Dispute Resolution in China."
[29] See Fu, "When Lawyers Are Prosecuted 2006."
[30] Guidance Notice of the All-China Lawyers Association regarding Lawyers' Handling of Multi-party Cases, March 20, 2006.

measures to uphold the rights of lawyers. Where necessary, local bar associations may enlist support from the national bar association.[31]

The policy recommendations for socioeconomic cases also apply to multiplaintiff cases because many multiplaintiff cases involve socioeconomic issues. To the extent that these cases raise freedom of assembly and speech issues, many recommendations for addressing pure political cases also apply. Additional policy recommendations include clarifying the rules regarding class actions and adjusting the reward structure for judges so that they no longer have an incentive to break up a large case into many smaller ones to meet year-end performance requirements based on the total number of cases resolved.

Politically Sensitive New Economic Cases

New economic cases result from the transition to a market economy and raise novel issues that have a significant impact on the national economy. As a result, they attract the attention of party organs, government officials, scholars, media, and the public. However, given their often technical nature, there is a greater role for administrative agencies responsible for economic matters and more input on policy issues from technocratic advisers, including international development agencies, and foreign and domestic academic experts, advisers, and business associations. Examples of such cases include securities litigation, bankruptcy, antidumping, antimonopoly, and other competition law cases.

For instance, shareholder rights were until recently mainly protected through criminal sanctions and fines.[32] The 1993 Company Law appeared to limit private shareholders to injunctive relief rather than damages. In 2001, the Supreme People's Court (SPC) issued an interpretation preventing shareholders from bringing suits and then four months later issued another interpretation allowing shareholders the narrow right to sue for misrepresentation where the China Securities Regulatory Commission had issued a report finding misrepresentation. The restrictions were justified on a variety of policy grounds, including that the judges lacked experience handling such cases, jurisdictional rules had yet to be worked out that would prevent different courts from issuing different awards for suits arising out of the same cause of action but brought by shareholder plaintiffs located in different areas, and large

---

[31] The passage of this notice produced a hailstorm of criticism from human rights organizations and liberal critics, who dramatically condemned China for the lack of rule of law. Yet the notice appears to have had little impact according to one of China's leading activist lawyers, Li Heping. "The river turns eastward to the sea: my views on the amended Lawyers Law," *Chinese by China Human Rights Lawyers Concern Group* (November 2007), http://www.chrlcg-hk.org/?p=214 (noting that the notice, denounced as destructive to rule of law and humanity, has not been implemented, much less undermined rule of law).

[32] Wang Jiangyu, "Rule of Law *and* Rule of Officials: Explaining the Different Roles Played by Law in Shareholders' Litigation and Anti-dumping Investigation in China," in Randall Peerenboom ed., *Dispute Resolution in China* (Oxford: Foundation for Law, Justice and Society, 2008).

damage awards against listed state-owned companies would result in significant loss of state assets.

In 2003, the SPC issued a third, much more detailed, interpretation. Although the interpretation did not expand the subject matter for litigation, it did clarify a number of procedural and evidentiary issues. After experience had been gained from further study of the issues and the handling of several cases, the Company Law was amended in 2005 to strengthen the rights of minority shareholders to bring suit, as discussed in detail in the next chapter.

Bankruptcy provides another example of the interplay between litigation and government policy.[33] The 1986 Enterprise Bankruptcy Law was limited to state-owned enterprises and was not very effective in practice. There were on average only 277 bankruptcies a year from 1989 to 1993. Banks objected to provisions that gave priority to workers; local government officials were worried about social unrest from laid-off employees; judges lacked independence and the specialized training in bankruptcy proceedings; and the support network of trained accountants, lawyers, and bankruptcy specialists was lacking.

Rather than relying on creditor-initiated bankruptcy proceedings to resolve the problem of insolvent state-owned enterprises (SOEs), the government opted for an administrative approach, with the State Council encouraging the merger of weaker SOEs with stronger ones and carefully allowing selected SOEs to go bankrupt based on a regional quota that allowed government officials to factor in the likelihood of social unrest in deciding which companies could enter bankruptcy proceedings. The government also reversed the preference for workers by reassigning the priority for the proceeds from the sale of secured land use rights to the secured parties, in most cases Chinese banks.

Over time, the vast majority of state-owned enterprises were sold off, with many of the remaining ones, having been exposed to increasing competition, less of a burden on the state. More generally, the private sector (including collective enterprises) played an increasingly dominant role in the economy. These changes were reflected in the 2006 Enterprise Bankruptcy Law (EBL), which applies to both state-owned and nonstate-owned companies, except for 2,116 SOEs that are either at particular financial risk or in a sensitive industry and small, unincorporated private businesses. The courts oversee bankruptcies, aided by the private professions of lawyers, accountants, and other bankruptcy specialists.

Although the government's role has been diminished, there are still various opportunities for the government to intervene to pursue noneconomic policy goals such as social stability. These include special approvals for certain SOEs and financial companies to commence bankruptcy proceedings, possible pressure on courts from

---

[33] Terrence Halliday, "The Making of China's Bankruptcy Law," in Randall Peerenboom ed., *Regulating Enterprise: The Regulatory Impact on Doing Business in China* (Oxford: Foundation for Law, Justice and Society, 2007), http://www.fljs.org/section.aspx?id=1880.

local governments to decide that companies are not technically insolvent or to simply refuse to accept the case, and government pressure on banks to issue policy loans to prop up ailing SOEs. Nevertheless, the 2006 EBL provides creditors the means to initiate bankruptcy proceedings, and, on the whole, represents a large step forward in clarifying and strengthening their rights.

Whereas the general trend in securities litigation and bankruptcy proceedings has been to provide a more rule-based system that strengthens the hand of private actors, antidumping remains an area that is much more politicized and dependent on administrative discretion.[34] China is one of the most frequent targets of antidumping claims and appears to pay a rising-power premium.[35] On the other hand, China has increasingly turned to antidumping actions against others doing business in China. The Ministry of Commerce (MOFCOM) is charged with both investigating the existence of dumping and recommending whether duties should be imposed. Antidumping proceedings remain shrouded in mystery. Parties are not allowed access to confidential information subject to protective order, to staff reports in particular cases, or even to MOFCOM's standards for calculating the dumping margin and industry damage. As in other countries, decisions appear to be driven by domestic political concerns to protect certain vulnerable industries rather than by principles of free trade or legal considerations.

The handling of new economic cases shows signs of two conflicting regulatory trends. On the one hand, there is a large role for administrative agencies, which is both a reflection of the historically powerful role of agencies in China's centrally planned economy and typical of East Asian development states.[36] At the same time, the role of agencies has clearly changed and become more limited as a result of the transition to a market economy, a more comprehensive and invasive international trade regime that has prohibited or restricted many of the tools used by East Asian developmental states in the past,[37] and a global trend toward new governance and a postregulatory state characterized by polycentric governance. Thus, there is a greater role in economic matters for commercial and administrative litigation as well as various forms of alternative dispute resolution (mediation, arbitration), public–private hybrids (corporatist and negotiated rule-making approaches that involve key stakeholders in the law-making and implementation processes), and a greater role

---

[34] Wang, "Rule of Law *and* Rule of Officials."

[35] Chad Bown and Rachel McCulloch, "U.S. Trade Policy Toward China: Discrimination and its Implications," (2005), http://ssrn.com/abstract=757124.

[36] See John Gillespie and Randall Peerenboom, "Pushing Back on Globalization: An Introduction to Regulation in Asia," in Gillespie and Peerenboom eds., *Regulation in Asia: Pushing Back on Globalization* (New York and London: Routledge, 2009).

[37] See generally, Ha-Joon Chang, *Bad Samaritans: The Guilty Secrets of Rich Nations & the Threat to Global Prosperity* (London: Random House, 2008). Chang discusses various ways rich nations have "kicked away the ladder" by prohibiting many of the policies and techniques used by rich nations to get rich.

for nonstate state actors, including business associations, standard setting agencies, consumer protection groups, and NGOs as part of the "contracting out of the state."

For the moment, the authorities continue to lean toward administrative agencies and decision making by technocratic elites, although there is also a tendency to provide private parties greater rights to litigate commercial suits and to diversify and open up the policy making and implementation processes. As in other politically sensitive cases, more must be done to clarify which institutions will be responsible for resolving which type of disputes. In many cases, different agencies compete with each, often passing conflicting regulations that promote their own institutional interests. Both the Securities Law and the Anti-Monopoly Law took more than a decade to pass in part because of turf struggles between agencies seeking to claim enforcement powers.

Similarly, rules regarding when parties have a private right of action must be clarified. The SPC, in conjunction with other branches, should (and no doubt will at some point) issue judicial interpretations on key issues raised by the Bankruptcy Law, the Anti-Monopoly Law, and other laws and regulations, as it has done for securities litigation. The SPC could also decide and publish key cases to serve as models for lower level courts.

Criminal Cases

As noted, some political and politically sensitive cases are prosecuted as criminal cases. Political criminal cases include, for example, cases involving parties that seek to overthrow the state or endanger the state and major corruption scandals involving high-level officials or a large number of people. Politically sensitive criminal cases include citizens and lawyers charged in relation to socioeconomic disputes and class-action suits; lesser corruption or government malfeasance; and high-profile cases that capture the public's attention and have an impact on general policies or social issues such as capital punishment cases; the BMW case where a woman from an allegedly influential family drove her car into a crowd, killing one and injuring twelve;[38] the Liu Yong case, where a former NPC delegate depicted as a mafia boss was sentenced to death subject to a two-year suspension, resulting in a public outcry demanding the death penalty;[39] and the tainted milk scandals that left several children dead

---

[38] The woman received a suspended sentence for negligence rather than a much harsher penalty, including perhaps the death penalty, for intentional murder. Many people believed she received the lighter sentence because of her family connections. Indicative of the special nature of the case, the government established a committee to review the decision. "'BMW Case' Reinvestigation Ends," *China Daily*, March 28, 2004, http://www.chinadaily.com.cn/english/doc/2004–03/28/content_318657.htm; see also Christopher Bodeen, "China's 'BMW Collision Affair' Draws Out Anger, Suspicions Against Newly Wealthy," *Associated Press*, April 6, 2004.

[39] In a highly unusual move, the SPC retried the case, found Liu guilty, and imposed the death penalty. See generally "Chinese Agency Gives Details of Alleged Crime Boss' Trial, Execution," *BBC* INT'L REP. (ASIA), Dec. 23, 2003, (discussing the unusual court procedure).

and thousands injured, resulting in several death sentences and the imprisonment for life of the head of one of the major milk companies implicated in the scandal. However, such cases account for only a tiny fraction of most criminal cases. For instance, endangering the state accounts for less than 0.5 percent of crimes.[40]

In general, whereas the same entities are involved in political and politically sensitive criminal cases as other political and politically sensitive cases, public security and the procuracy also play a significant role. Party influence in such cases is primarily through general policy guidance rather than intervention in particular cases. However, the political–legal committee may be involved in high-profile cases, particularly when they lead to an investigation, as in the BMW case. In addition, the party discipline committee will be involved in cases involving corruption by senior government officials. In fact, it will generally take the lead in the investigation, often relying on the legally dubious shuanggui (nonjudicial detention) procedure.[41] The case will be turned over to the courts only after the committee has collected ample evidence to determine that a crime has been committed.

The media, public, and legal scholars may also take an active interest in these cases, which are often widely discussed on the Internet. Public pressure is at times effective in politically sensitive cases, although it rarely seems to have much effect in political cases other than perhaps to secure a lighter sentence for the accused. In the Sun Zhigang case, for example, a college graduate died while detained pursuant to a form of administration detention known as custody and repatriation. The State Council eliminated this form of compulsory detention, retaining only the social service functions, in part in response to widespread public criticism and a petition signed by prominent legal scholars. Several officials were also arrested.

In contrast, Du Daobin was arrested for posting twenty-eight articles on the Internet, including some that opposed limitations on democracy and civil liberties in Hong Kong, and for receiving funding from foreign organizations.[42] His arrest also led to a petition, signed by more than one hundred writers, editors, lawyers, philosophers, liberal economists, and activists, calling for a judicial interpretation to clarify the crime of subversion. Nevertheless, Du was convicted of inciting subversion, although his three-year sentence was commuted to four years of probation.[43] The

---

[40] Robin Munro, "Judicial Psychiatry in China and Its Political Abuses," *Columbia Journal Asian Law* vol. 14, p. 67 (2000). Similarly, only a tiny percentage of administrative detention cases involve political or politically sensitive issues. Less than 1 percent of those subject to Education Through Labor (ETL) could be considered political prisoners, excluding Falun Gong disciples charged with violations under the generally applicable criminal laws. Including all Falun Gong cases, the percentage of political prisoners subject to ETL is around 2 percent. See Peerenboom, *China Modernizes*, pp. 98–99.

[41] Flora Sapio, "*Shuanggui*: Extra-legal detention by Commissions for Discipline Inspection." *China Information* vol. 22, p. 1 (2008).

[42] "Security Official Confirms Chinese Man Arrested for Internet Subversion," BBC MONITORING ASIA PAC., Feb. 17, 2004.

[43] "Internet Dissident Found Guilty of Subversion, but Given Probation," AGENCE FRANCE-PRESSE, June 11, 2004.

detention of Liu Di, a student at Beijing Normal University known by her Internet name Stainless Steel Rat, led to two online petitions signed by more than 3,000 people. Liu was detained for operating a popular Web site and posting satirical articles about the party. She was later released.[44]

Public opinion is a double-edged sword. Although public outcry over the Sun Zhigang case may have played a role in ending custody and repatriation, the public's demand to strike hard at crime simultaneously supports a harsh penal system and administrative detentions. More than 99 percent of Chinese favor the death penalty, with more than 20 percent thinking there should be more executions.[45] In the Sun Zhigang case, two officials were given the death penalty. There are many cases in addition to the Sun Zhigang and Liu Yong cases where courts have cited the anger of the public and the demand for vengeance to justify death sentences. Many judges have complained that public uproar over cases interferes with judicial independence and undermines rule of law, either directly by putting pressure on judges to decide a certain way or indirectly by inducing political actors to take up the issue and interfere with the court.

As in most countries, most criminal cases are routine. Whereas media coverage in China as elsewhere would suggest otherwise, most crimes are property crimes, with most murder, rape, and other violent crimes committed not by strangers but by persons known to the victim. China's crime rates are relatively low by world standards, even allowing that they have increased significantly during the last twenty years.[46] The percentage of defendants receiving heavy punishments of five years or more (including life sentences and death penalty) has also decreased from a high of 43 percent in 1996 to 19 percent in 2004.[47] Nevertheless, the public continues to list rising crime as one of the major issues confronting society and supports the government's relentless "strike hard" campaigns against crime.

There is limited systemic interference from party organs in routine criminal cases. The procuracy is given the right to supervise and challenge court decisions in both criminal and civil cases pursuant to a procedure known as kangsu. As noted in the previous chapter, the number of criminal cases retried through adjudicative supervision has decreased whereas the number of civil and economic cases has grown. Criminal cases account for less than 10 percent. In most criminal review cases, the procuracy seeks heavier sentences. However, the procuracy loses the vast

---

[44] Philip P. Pan, "China Releases 3 Internet Writers, but Convicts 1 Other," *Washington Post Foreign Service*, Dec. 1, 2003.

[45] Hu Yunteng, "Application of the Death Penalty in Chinese Judicial Practice," in Chen Jianfu et al. eds., *Implementation of Law in the People's Republic of China* (The Hauge: Kluwer Law International, 2002).

[46] Borge Bakken, "Comparative Perspectives on Crime in China," in Borge Bakken ed., *Crime, Punishment, and Policing in China* (Lantham: Rowman and Littlefield, 2005).

[47] Zhu Jingwen ed., *Zhongguo falü fazhan baogao (1979–2004)* [China Legal Development Report] (1979–2004) (Beijing: People's University Press, 2007).

majority of the time. Nevertheless, many commentators recommend eliminating the kangsu procedure or at least prohibiting the procuracy from challenging sentences imposed by the court that are within the range stipulated by law.

Nonsystemic interference in criminal cases is most likely to come from public security officials or prosecutors who informally contact judges to press their case and from relatives, friends, and legal representatives of the accused or relatives and friends of the victims. In general, such interference is unlikely to have a significant impact. However, it does open the door to corruption, which may result in some of the accused receiving a different sentence (usually lighter), the rare case of a wrong outcome (usually an innocent verdict), or favorable treatment while in prison.

Policy recommendations for dealing with politically sensitive criminal cases differ from those for other politically sensitive cases because of the limited involvement of party organs; the problems in criminal cases are not fundamentally due to scarce resources; such cases do not involve multiple parties that threaten social stability; and they clearly fall within the proper scope of the courts. Thus, the main policy recommendation is to improve the criminal justice system more broadly. As is well-known, the criminal justice system is beset by problems. A by-no-means-exhaustive list of reforms would include:

(i) improve laws and regulations, including the criminal law, criminal procedure law, and evidentiary rules; in particular, clarify the rights of the accused to access the dossier and the obligation of the procuracy and police to provide exculpatory evidence; improve the rights of the accused to access witnesses and strengthen the court's power to compel in-court testimony;

(ii) strengthen the role of, and protections for, defense counsel;[48]

(iii) elevate the status of the courts relative to public security; appoint a member of the judiciary, rather than the public security, as a member of politburo; eliminate or limit the right of the procuracy to challenge court decisions (kangsu) in both civil and criminal cases;

(iv) build support for criminal law reforms by educating the public about rising crime rates, the rate of violent crime, the likelihood of being subject to crime by strangers, and;

(v) limit media coverage of ongoing trials or ensure more balanced coverage by greater reliance on experts to cover stories or appear on TV and radio programs.

In addition, proposals to deal with nonsystemic interference from interested parties would include strictly enforcing ex parte rules, promoting judicial ethics, punishing judges found guilty of corruption, and changing social norms to discourage use of

---

[48] The recent amendments to the Lawyers Law do afford defense counsel greater protection against harassment and liability. However, additional steps are likely to be necessary.

social connections to influence judges. More generally, recommendations to combat corruption and increase judicial independence in the previous chapter should also be adopted.

Civil Cases

Politically sensitive civil cases include the socioeconomic, mass-plaintiff, and new economic cases discussed above. They, too, are but a small fraction of the more than 4 million civil cases handled by the courts every year. There is little systemic interference in the vast majority of civil cases. Party organs rarely take a formal interest in such cases. Supervision by the people's congress and procuracy is rare, with few cases resulting in overturning the original decision. Supervision by people's congress and procuracy may, however, in some cases lead to corruption or abuse, usually when the amount at stake is high and the parties involved are well-connected.

There is a much greater likelihood of nonsystemic interference in civil cases than systemic interference. Such interference may take various forms, including local protectionism, particularly in lower level courts in rural areas; illegitimate interference by individual party members or government officials who take a personal interest in the case because the case involves their own company or the company of a friend or relative, or because they have been bribed or influenced in other less direct ways; and attempts by parties, lawyers, friends, and acquaintances who seek to bribe or influence judges or simply seek to meet ex parte with judges to persuade them of the merits of their case without any quid pro quo (see Chapters 10 and 11).

Empirical studies demonstrate that local protectionism is not a significant factor in urban courts in economically advanced areas.[49] Similarly, enforcement has improved in urban areas.[50] Moreover, the main reason for nonenforcement is that defendants are judgment proof; they are insolvent or their assets are encumbered.[51] No legal system is able to enforce judgments in such circumstances.

---

[49] He Xin, "The Enforcement of Commercial Cases in the Pearl River Delta," *Journal of Justice* 72 (2007) (finding high rates of enforcement comparable if not superior to other countries, in urban courts in the Pearl Delta); Peerenboom, "Seek Truth from Facts: An Empirical Study of the Enforcement of Arbitral Awards in the People's Republic of China," *American Journal of Comparative Law* vol. 49, p. 249 (2001) (an empirical study of enforcement of arbitral awards found that local protectionism was not a statistically significant factor in the final outcome and that enforcement was more likely in economically wealthy urban areas); Mei Ying Gechlik, "Judicial Reform in China: Lessons from Shanghai," *Columbia Journal of Asian Law* vol. 19 p. 2006) (study of more than 20,000 cases in Shanghai found that less than 0.14 percent involved attempts to use outside connections to interfere with the court; interviews conducted by a foreign legal scholar corroborated the results of the study).

[50] Xin He, "Enforcing Commercial Judgments."

[51] Peerenboom, "Seek Truth from Facts."

Conversely, the main reasons for improving enforcement and the decrease in local protectionism are changes in the nature of the economy;[52] general judicial reforms aiming at institution building and increasing the professionalism of the judiciary; and specific measures to strengthen enforcement.[53] The economy in many urban areas is now more diversified, with the private sector playing a dominant role. The fate of a single company is less important to the local government, which has a broader interest in protecting its reputation as an attractive investment environment. As a result, the incentive for governments to engage in local protectionism has diminished.

The ability of particular individuals to influence the outcome depends on the individual, the parties involved, the nature of the case, the amount at stake, the level of the court, and the professionalism of the judges involved. One notable phenomenon has been several corruption cases involving the presidents of high courts. This may represent a rational strategy for those seeking to influence the outcome of the case. Most cases will be handled by three judges. If there is disagreement or the case is complicated, the adjudicative committee might become involved. To influence the outcome of the case, a party would have to influence at least two members of the panel and key members of the adjudicative committee. Parties may believe that they get the most "bang for the buck" by trying to influence the president of the court, particularly the higher level court that will hear the appeal or have the discretionary authority to supervise the final decision.[54] Of course, parties may be wrong about the president's influence. Recent changes have strengthened the autonomy of the panel of judges that hears cases, and adjudicative committees decide by majority vote, with the president only having one vote. Moreover, even where the president is able to exercise influence, there will always be other review mechanisms available to thwart efforts to influence the decision – as evidenced by the prosecution of several court presidents. In any event, Li Ling shows in her chapter that most court presidents have been convicted for behavior such as accepting kickbacks to build courthouses or bribes to support the promotion of judges rather than to influence the outcome of a particular case.

Attempts by parties, lawyers, and acquaintances to influence judges are not likely to result in a manifestly wrong decision given all of the possibilities for review. However, illegitimate influence may have an impact when the law is unclear or

---

[52] On the general relationship between improvements in the legal system and development, see Zhu, *China Legal Development*.

[53] For instance, the 2007 amendments to the Civil Procedure Law have strengthened enforcement by, among other things, increasing penalties for people who obstruct enforcement. The number of people detained during compulsory enforcement proceedings reached a high in 1999, the same year the number of people refusing to comply with court judgments peaked. Since then, both the number of cases in which parties refuse to voluntarily comply with the judgment and the number of people detained have decreased. Zhu, *China Legal Development*, pp. 248–249.

[54] They may also feel that the president is most susceptible. Others have noted that senior government officials who are close to retirement are most likely to accept bribes. Although there has been a trend to appoint younger people as president, particularly in lower level courts, the president of the court in higher level courts is likely to be somewhat older.

judges have discretion. In other cases, corrupt judges may first decide the case on the merits but then still seek benefits from the prevailing party.

A portrait of the legal system as so riddled by corruption and other problems that citizens have lost faith in the judicial system is however at odds with opinion surveys that show people generally trust the courts.[55] One large survey using GPS readings to generate a representative sample concluded: "Courts are generally perceived as effective and fair, despite the popular lore about corruption." In a survey of business people in Shanghai and Nanjing between 2002 and 2004, almost three of four gave the court system a very high to average rating, compared to 25 percent who rated the system low or very low. Still another survey found that Beijing respondents are more trusting of the courts than their Chicago counterparts and evaluate the performance of the courts more positively. Respondents in Beijing were twice as likely as Chicago residents to agree with the claim that courts are "doing a good job." Moreover, whereas more than 40 percent of Chicago residents disagreed or strongly disagreed that the courts generally guarantee everyone a fair trial, only 10 percent of Beijing residents and 28 percent of rural residents held similar negative views. And whereas 43 percent of Chicago residents disagreed or strongly disagreed with the statement that judges are basically honest, only 9 percent of Beijing residents and 29 percent of rural residents held similar views.

To put these numbers in a broader comparative context, barely half of Belgians believe court decisions are just, whereas 60 percent lack confidence in the judiciary. More than 40 percent of British citizens have little or no confidence in judges and the courts. In France, only 38 percent of the public trusts the judiciary, with only 21 percent believing judges are independent from economic circles and only 15 percent believing they are independent from political powers.

Moreover, if Chinese courts generally failed to provide an adequate forum, then there would not be more than 4 million civil cases a year, as there now are, given the availability of mediation, arbitration, and other mechanisms for resolving disputes.

Labor Cases

The transition to a market economy, the jarring process of SOE reform, and the pressures of economic globalization have resulted in a rapid rise in labor disputes. Labor disputes grew from fewer than 20,000 in 1994 to more than 300,000 in 1996.[56] Once again, there are significant regional variations. The more economically advanced areas such as Guangdong, Shanghai, Beijing, Jiangsu, Zhejiang, and Shandong have more disputes, as do the areas with significant heavy industry and a large number of SOEs, such as Liaoning, Hubei, Fujian, and Chongqing. The subject matter of labor disputes ranges, in descending order, from wages, to termination, insurance, and work injury.

---

[55] For this and the next paragraph, see Peerenboom and He, "Dispute Resolution in China."
[56] Ronald Brown, "China Labor Dispute Resolution," in *Dispute Resolution in China*.

The resolution of labor disputes involves voluntary mediation, mandatory labor arbitration, and litigation if the parties are unsatisfied with the results of arbitration. Although still common, mediation has declined in importance. Workers do not trust mediators, who are usually dominated by the union, which is closely allied with the employer.

Workers win the vast majority of arbitration cases; they prevail in nearly four cases for every one by the employer and partially win a majority of the other cases.[57] Nevertheless, employees are also the most likely to appeal, either because they were not satisfied with the arbitration result or the arbitration award was not enforceable.

Litigation of labor disputes plays a role somewhere between the role of litigation in commercial disputes and other socioeconomic disputes. On the one hand, litigation has become increasingly prevalent and effective, as in commercial law. Litigation cases increased to 122,405 in 2005. Whereas in the past, plaintiffs in labor suits often lost, with the court upholding the decision of the labor arbitration committee, today the majority wins in court – with plaintiffs enjoying a higher success rate in courts than in arbitration.[58]

On the other hand, the courts are often unable to provide effective relief for many of the same reasons that apply to other socioeconomic disputes. Cases involving back pay and pension claims are particularly difficult to enforce in large part because many companies are operating on thin margins or are even insolvent. Not surprisingly, many disputes are resolved through mediation at various stages of the process. In addition to the disputes resolved through enterprise mediation, about one-third of the disputes brought to arbitration are resolved through mediation, whereas about one-quarter of the cases resolved through litigation are mediated settlements. The courts will often work with government officials to resolve labor cases, particularly those that involve pension or unemployment benefits and affect many people, as demonstrated in the wake of the global economic crisis that led to widespread company closures, a sharp rise in unemployment, and many public demonstrations.

The inability of the courts to provide effective relief may also explain the reluctance to do away with the requirement that workers first go through arbitration before going to court. Although labor advocates have long called for the abolition of mandatory arbitration, a Supreme Court interpretation in 2006 provided only limited relief, allowing workers to go directly to court in wage arrears cases where they have written proof of unpaid wages from the employer and no other claims are raised.[59] In contrast, the 2007 Labor Dispute Mediation and Arbitration Law went the other way, providing for binding arbitration in certain cases including failure

---

[57] Brown, "China Labor Dispute Resolution."

[58] Ethan Michelson, "The Practice of Law as an Obstacle to Justice: Chinese Lawyers at Work, *Law & Society Review* vol. 40(1) p. 1 (2006).

[59] Several Issues Concerning the Applicable Law for the Trial of Labor Disputes Cases, August 14, 2006. Granted, one should not expect the SPC to forge new rights. Even the limited change in the SPC's interpretation would appear to be at odds with the Labor Law and thus technically invalid.

to pay wages or worker's compensation. Whether the law will provide relief for the courts remains to be seen. The law also emphasized mediation; the range of cases subject to final arbitration is limited; and, rather oddly, the law still allows workers and even employers to challenge in the courts the limited range of cases subject to final arbitration.

In general, influence is most likely in collective labor cases involving many parties and comes from the same sources as other socioeconomic cases, although the Labor Bureau, Labor Arbitration Commission, and All China Federation of Trade Unions may play more significant roles in policy setting and dispute resolution. Policy recommendations generally track those for other socioeconomic cases. Thus, disputes could be prevented by allocating more resources to address fundamental problems, including the need for a better welfare system (unemployment insurance, retraining expenses, medical care, and retirement benefits). Nonjudicial mechanisms for dealing with labor issues should also be further developed, including strengthening mediation arbitration and administrative supervision, as should postregulatory mechanisms including greater reliance on the private sector and self-regulation by businesses (including promoting corporate responsibility acts).

At the same time, and in contrast to other types of socioeconomic disputes, workers should be able to directly access the courts in an expanded range of cases, including for back pay, excessive mandatory overtime, dangerous work conditions, wrongful termination, worker's compensation, sexual harassment, and discrimination claims. Most of these claims involve individual employees or dangerous conditions that require immediate action.

In addition, workers' right to bring collective action suits should be further developed by strengthening unions and requiring collective labor contracts. Allowing parties to collect legal fees if successful would help in both individual and collective cases, as many workers cannot afford lawyers. Providing for initial jurisdiction in intermediate court for collective action cases would also help overcome pressure on judges from local government officials who want to maintain high growth rates and an investor-friendly business environment. Because local governments produce most of the regulations relating to workers, higher level courts should also be given the right to review normative acts for consistency with higher level legislation and to enforce minimal standards.

Administrative Cases

The number of annual administrative litigation cases has ranged from 80,000 to 100,000 over the last decade. Determining how often the plaintiff wins is difficult because about one-third of the cases are settled in other ways, such as rejecting the suit or mediation. However, even counting all such results, as well as all cases where the plaintiff withdrew the suit as a loss for the plaintiff, and setting aside all plaintiff victories on appeal or through retrial supervision, the plaintiff would have prevailed in 17 to 22 percent of cases between 2001 and 2004. These success rates stand in sharp contrast to success rates in the United States, Taiwan (both 12 percent), and Japan (between 4 and 8 percent).[60]

As in other areas, although there are politically sensitive administrative cases, the majority of them are now routine. Although routine cases are more likely than civil cases to give rise to interference from government officials whose decisions are being challenged, over time officials have become more comfortable and less threatened by judicial review of their actions. Again, the nature and severity of the problems differ by region, level of court, and type of case. It is more difficult to file cases and prevail in basic level courts, and then to enforce decisions against the government, in less developed areas where the local governments exercise more control over the courts.

Higher level courts are also less likely to be influenced by pressure from local governments. Not surprisingly, the number of administrative litigation cases appealed has risen steadily to almost 30,000 per year, or about 30 percent of all such cases.[61] Plaintiffs prevail, as measured by decisions quashed or cases remanded to the lower court, in approximately 17 percent of appellate cases.[62] Ever after appeal, parties may petition for retrial pursuant to a discretionary supervision procedure. Rates of success, measured by reversal of the appellate decision or remand for retrial, ranged from 27 to 36 percent between 2002 and 2004.[63]

All else being equal, cases that involve commercial issues such as the denial of a license or imposition of excessive fees are easier for the courts to handle than socioeconomic cases. Plaintiffs in the former type of case might still run into problems with local protectionism, government interference, or retaliation. Whereas such problems might also affect administrative litigation cases involving politically sensitive socioeconomic issues, plaintiffs are also likely to confront all additional obstacles that arise when courts handle socioeconomic cases, including conflicting policy goals, central–local tensions, an insufficiently developed regulatory framework, and most fundamentally lack of resources to provide an adequate remedy. Once accepted, judges are often pressured to resolve such cases through mediation. Mediation of administrative litigation cases has not been allowed under the Administrative Litigation Law (ALL) because of the fear that government officials would intimidate plaintiffs into settlement. However, in recent years, mediation of administrative litigation cases grew despite the prohibition, and an amendment of the ALL is being considered that would permit mediation.

Another response to problems in administrative litigation suits has been to emphasize administrative reconsideration and other political or administrative channels as

---

[60] Peerenboom, *China's Long March*, p. 400.

[61] Zhu, *China Legal Development*, p. 236.

[62] This number has declined over the last ten years, as has the success rate for appeals in criminal and civil cases, suggesting perhaps that judges in first instance cases are becoming more qualified.

[63] Zhu, *China Legal Development*, p. 242.

an alternative. Unlike in some countries, China allows parties to initiate an administrative litigation suit without first exhausting administrative remedies, except in a narrow range of circumstances. Regulations now require parties to first seek administrative reconsideration of the amount of compensation in land-taking cases before turning to the court. More generally, the government has sought to encourage administrative reconsideration by making it more appealing.

Despite the relatively high plaintiff success rates by world standards, there remain serious problems with administrative litigation. Some are due to doctrinal limitations. For instance, parties may only challenge specific acts that infringe their legitimate rights and interests, which has been interpreted to mean personal or property rights. Other important rights are thus excluded, most notably political rights such as the rights to march and to demonstrate, freedom of association and assembly, and rights of free speech and free publication. Moreover, the requirement that one's legitimate rights and interests be infringed has also been construed narrowly to prevent those with only indirect or tangential interests in an act from bringing suit. The narrow interpretation prevents interest groups or individuals from acting as "private attorneys general" to challenge the administration.

The main limitations, however, are systemic, and thus addressing them will require far-reaching changes that will alter the nature of Chinese society and the current balance of power between state and society, party and government, the central government and local governments, and among the three branches of government.

Market reforms have already shifted the balance of power away from the state toward society. The balance will continue to shift with the further separation of government and enterprises, the elimination or reduction of administrative monopolies, and the creation of a professional civil service in which government officials serve the public as regulators rather than extracting rents or competing with private companies in the marketplace. At present, most economic and social activities continue to be subject to licensing requirements, despite the passage of the Administrative Licensing Law and the streamlining of the approval process and registration requirements set out in the lists issued by various government entities to comply with the Licensing Law. However, the general trend is toward less regulation. Laws such as the Administrative Licensing Law are helping delineate the boundaries of individual autonomy and freedom. Holding government officials to clearly defined substantive and procedural standards allows citizens to take full advantage of whatever freedoms they are granted.

Administrative law reforms have empowered society to some extent by giving citizens the right to challenge state actors through administrative reconsideration, administrative litigation, and administrative supervision. The next step is to increase public participation in the rule-making and decision-making processes. The Law on Legislation opens the door slightly for greater public participation in the making of national laws. Local congresses now actively experiment with hearings. The

Administrative Procedure Law may go even further in providing the public access to administrative rule-making and decision making.

A more robust civil society, a freer media, and greater reliance on private actors would all benefit the cause of administrative law reform but would require a further shift in power toward society. A more robust civil society would provide the interest groups that play such a central role in bottom-up alternatives to command and control regulation. Along with a more independent media, interest groups could shoulder more of the responsibility for monitoring administrative behavior.

Administrative litigation could be strengthened in a variety of ways. In addition to allowing courts to review abstract acts and enhancing the independence of the courts, the scope of review could be expanded to include rights other than personal or property rights, such as political rights. Although China need not adopt a private attorney general theory of standing, a clearer and more liberal interpretation of standing would be useful. Enhancing the stature of the judiciary will help the courts overcome their reluctance to take full advantage of the Administrative Litigation Law's rather broad review standards. For example, they may take a broader view of what counts as inconsistent and use the abuse of power standard to examine purpose, relevance, reasonableness, proportionality, and so on. A more expansive interpretation and aggressive application of current standards would go a long way toward achieving a review of the appropriateness of agency decision making without substituting the judgment of the court for that of the agency. Although beyond the scope of this chapter, other mechanisms for controlling administrative behavior could also be strengthened in various ways, including legislative oversight, administrative supervision, and administrative reconsideration.

CONCLUSION

When commentators, particularly human rights organizations, claim that courts lack (meaningful) independence in China, they usually have in mind political cases, with the dominant role for party organs, the tight restraints on civil and political rights, and the limited power of the courts even to uphold procedural rules. A number of reforms have been suggested to improve handling of these cases. Yet the experiences of authoritarian regimes in East Asia and elsewhere suggest that the outcomes in these cases will continue to be determined by political organs, in this case, for better or worse, party organs.

Politically sensitive cases raise concerns about the proper role of courts in developing countries and whether the global trend toward judicialization of controversial economic and social policy issues is appropriate given the weak state of the courts and their limited ability to provide an effective remedy given scarce resources. As such, they shed light on the general relationship between law and development and are particularly important for international financial institutions and donor agencies in the development and rule of law promotion industries.

Whether courts are the proper forum for resolving certain disputes will depend on a number of factors, including the level of economic development, the status of the court, the relation of the judiciary to other political organs, and the competence and integrity of judges. In general, forcing the courts to hear socioeconomic cases for which they are unable to provide an effective remedy does not help the parties and undermines trust and confidence in the judiciary. Although the long-term solution is to outgrow such problems, in the meantime nonjudicial channels for addressing citizen needs must be strengthened. Nevertheless, the courts will still play a role, enforcing minimal standards and reviewing decisions by administrative or government agencies after parties have exhausted their judicial remedies or sought to resolve their disputes through mediation or other political and administrative channels. Over time, the role of the courts may be increased.

Most cases, however, are neither political nor politically sensitive. There is therefore still considerable room to improve the courts' handling of such cases, although the reforms required go far beyond prescriptions for increasing judicial independence.

7

Judicial Independence and the Company Law in the Shanghai Courts

Nicholas Calcina Howson

The essence of corporate and commercial laws is to protect business and commerce from the threat of political power.

– Zheng Guanying (1893)[1]

This chapter draws on a detailed study of corporate law adjudication in Shanghai from 1992 to 2008. The purpose of the study was to better understand the demonstrated technical competence, institutional autonomy, and political independence of one court system in the People's Republic of China ("PRC") in a sector outside of the criminal law. The study consisted of a detailed examination and comparison of full-length corporate law opinions for more than 200 reported cases, a 2003 Shanghai High Court opinion on the 1994 Company Law (describing a decade of corporate case outcomes),[2] a 2007 report on cases implementing the Company Law in 2006 (more than 760 cases),[3] and extensive interactions with Shanghai court officials handling such disputes[4] – all for a wide diversity of Shanghai

---

[1] Li Yu, *Wan qing gongsi zhidu jianshen yanjiu* [Development of the Corporation System in the Late Qing], (Beijing: The People's Press, 2002), p. 100.

[2] Reviewing cases from the previous decade (1993–2003), see Shanghai High Court ed., *Gongsifa yinan wenti jiexi (di san ban)* [*Company Law Issues: Problems and Analysis (3rd Edition)*], (Beijing: Law Press China, 2006), pp. 231–236 ("Shanghai Company Law Opinion").

[3] Shanghai High Court No. 2 Civil Division ed., "Shanghai fayuan xin 'gongsifa' shishi yi zhounian sifa diaocha" ["Judicial Investigation of Application of the New 'Company Law' in the Shanghai Courts After One Year"] in *Gongsi falu pinglun (2007 nianjuan)* [*Company Law Review (2007)*], pp. 38–51 ("Shanghai Company Law Report").

[4] Corporate law cases heard in the Shanghai courts vary. In 2006, Shanghai courts heard 768 corporate law-related cases. The three claims addressed most often and accounting for 76 percent of the total were: (i) shareholders rights (241 cases, or 31 percent of the total); (ii) share transfers (261 cases, or 34 percent of the total); and (iii) information rights (81 cases, or 11 percent of the total). Among the remaining 24 percent, the Shanghai courts heard suits involving: dividend distributions, distribution of residual assets on liquidation, shareholder qualification, share inheritance, and – in a direct response to changes in the 2006 Company Law – shareholder applications for corporate dissolution, invalidation of shareholders' resolutions, and challenges to "illegally" convened shareholders' general meetings.

jurisdictions[5] and procedural postures.[6] Due to space limitations, this chapter focuses on the demonstrated independence, and to a lesser extent autonomy, of the Shanghai courts when faced with a completely altered Company Law.

THE NEW JUSTICIABILITY OF THE COMPANY LAW

Corporate law theory holds that in jurisdictions like the PRC, where the judiciary is regarded as underdeveloped, buffeted by political and other external pressures, and deficient in handling complex cases, company law must be largely self-enforcing and may not be structured to "depend on fast and reliable judicial decisions."[7] China's first post-1949 company law, effective in 1994,[8] was a textbook expression of this

---

The High Court acknowledged that the Shanghai courts took relatively few cases involving corporate management rights and obligations – breach of corporate fiduciary duties – because of the relative complexity involved. The totality of the cases reviewed for the 1992–2008 period reveal much the same case composition (December 2008, Chief Judge of the Shanghai High Court No. 2 Civil Division; Shanghai Company Law Report, pp. 39–51; and Shanghai Company Law Opinion, pp. 231–236.)

[5] The courts include every district in Shanghai, from the expected Pudong New District (situs of the Shanghai Stock Exchange) to far off Baoshan, and even special courts like the Shanghai Rail Transport intermediate court. In many cases, the Shanghai courts are forced to deal with competing proceedings and/or prior rulings from other jurisdictions, especially courts in the Yangtze River Delta.

[6] The procedural postures are consistent. Most start at the district level, whence they are subject to appeal (to the intermediate level) at the litigants' initiative. Less frequently they begin in intermediate court, with appeal to the Shanghai High Court. In only one example in the sample does the case reach the Supreme People's Court. Many of the case opinions indicate seemingly endless rehearings, often by the same court level (but by different panels of judicial officers). For instance, one case shows a dispute heard twice by the district court, an appeal to the intermediate court, remand to the original district level, and then appeal again to the higher intermediate court. The Chinese courts do not hold to the fact-law distinction between trial and appellate courts known in the United States, England, and many non-Chinese jurisdictions. Accordingly, PRC appellate proceedings allow de novo pleadings of law and fact. Yet in the many cases reviewed for the study, very few show reversal at the second level of adjudication. Certainly higher level courts demonstrate how free they are to undertake factual investigations de novo and often apply different law and/or remedies, but the final judgments rarely change. That being said, the proportion of reversals or differentiated judgments seems higher in corporate and commercial cases when compared to criminal prosecutions or criminal appeals. For just 2006, the Shanghai High Court reported the following with respect to corporate law cases: among first hearing cases, 55 percent gave rise to judgment, 11 percent were concluded through mediation, and 33 percent were subject to some kind of order; for cases subject to rehearing and/or appeal, judgments were issued in 43 percent of the cases, only 1 percent were resolved through mediation, and a much larger proportion – 55 percent – subject to court order. In its report, the Shanghai High Court asserts that the higher percentage of cases concluded by court order on rehearing/appeal is a result of settlement reached between the parties or the litigants withdrawing the case. This is rather unsurprising, as many Chinese litigants would probably work to settlement once they have understood – via the results of the first proceeding – how their claims will fare on appeal. The phenomenon is also an indication of the relatively low success rate of appeals in overturning the initial court's decision. See Shanghai Company Law Report.

[7] Bernard Black and Reinier Kraakman, "A Self-Enforcing Model of Corporate Law," *Harvard Law Review*, vol. 109, p. 1914 (1996).

[8] Adopted December 29, 1993, and with minor amendments on December 25, 1999, and August 28, 2004.

self-enforcing model. There is little in the 1994 statute inviting judicial participation in corporate disputes, whether for external actors (e.g., veil-piercing) or internal participants (e.g., fiduciary duties). The 1994 law's self-enforcing character was deemed entirely appropriate given common perceptions of PRC judicial institutions and the resource constraints of its more competent but overworked securities regulator, the China Securities Regulatory Commission ("CSRC") or the public prosecutor, the People's Procurate.

Notwithstanding continued real and perceived shortcomings of the judiciary, on October 27, 2005, the PRC's national legislature passed a wholesale reworking of the 1994 Company Law, effective January 1, 2006 (the "2006 Company Law"). In a head-spinning departure from the self-enforcing model of corporate law and governance, the Company Law was suddenly replete with broad invitations for sophisticated judicial involvement, including derivative lawsuits, invalidation of corporate resolutions, ex post application of corporate fiduciary duties, information rights, appraisal rights, a right for shareholders of companies limited by shares to sue senior management for any breach of law, regulation, or the company articles of association, and corporate veil-piercing. Even mainstream PRC corporate law scholars saw in the 2006 Company Law a robust invitation to judicial involvement, divining for instance a private right of action to enforce corporate social responsibility standards or check the degree of Communist Party involvement in company management.[9]

CORPORATE LAW IN THE PEOPLE'S COURTS: AUTONOMY
AND INDEPENDENCE

Implications of the 2006 Company Law

Aside from the expanded technical mission foisted on the Chinese courts, the 2006 changes in the Company Law also signaled potentially significant impacts on the autonomy and independence of the judiciary. Specifically, the statute gave courts the bases and authority to act in corporate cases with a degree of expertise and autonomy far beyond the traditional role of China's Communist-era courts and in disputes with significant material interests at stake. The courts will now be asked to apply the newly justiciable corporate law in contests between independent commercial litigants and other more powerful political–economic actors. Consider, for example, a shareholder's lawsuit against a director representing the interests of a state agency-backed controlling shareholder – or the controlling shareholder itself – for breach of corporate fiduciary duties or minority shareholder oppression. Here the judiciary will be called upon to protect legal norms against the heretofore superior power of

---

[9] Luo Peixin, "Judicial Plights in the Context of the New Company Law of China," in Asian Law Institute ed., *The Development of Law in Asia: Convergence Versus Divergence* (Shanghai: Collected Papers from the 3rd Asian Law Institute Conference: May 25–26, 2006).

the government (or party controlling it) – which power comprises administrative and fiscal domination of the courts hearing the case. The question is whether PRC courts can take up, or be permitted to take up, this provocative challenge.

Competence, Autonomy, and Independence Differentiated

The proposed effects of the 2006 Company Law require definition of three distinct concepts invoked here: competence, autonomy, and independence. Competence is the easiest to describe and goes to the technical expertise of judicial institutions in evaluating factually and legally complex disputes.[10] More important in this volume are the seemingly synonymous concepts of judicial autonomy and independence. Autonomy is the ability of courts to act with their own institutional authority, even when on occasion they have no legal basis to act. An example is where Chinese courts accept, hear, and decide cases involving fiduciary duties, veil-piercing, petitions for dissolution, etc., without authority under statute or judicial regulations. Judicial independence is still another idea and goes to the ability of courts to act independently of, and against the interests of, political and military power. For example, a Chinese court might act autonomously to pierce the corporate veil and assess direct liability against the controlling shareholder of a debtor firm and yet prove

---

[10] The findings on competence are positive, as the Shanghai courts evidence increasing skill in adjudicating corporate matters (with the occasional blunder). Sometimes that skill is demonstrated by judges choosing not to apply the law for corporations to what are really closely held corporate partnerships (instead intelligently applying partnership law principles) or adeptly handling business forms "left over from history" and firms formed spontaneously by entrepreneurs with no basis in any law. The study shows there is no connection between the relative level of a given court and its demonstrated competence, as the most expert adjudication in corporate matters is often performed by district courts far from the more sophisticated action in downtown Shanghai or the exalted premises of the High Court. This indicates that the education, intellect, and personal qualities of judicial personnel are important variables in determining competence and that the court system's higher reaches may be staffed by bureaucratically adept administrative cadres rather than expert lawyers. The data also show that there are significant numbers of corporate law cases where the courts have no opportunity to demonstrate competence, or lack of it, because case complexity is so daunting. For instance, the Chief Judge of the No.2 Civil Division of the Shanghai High Court reported at the end of 2008 that the Shanghai courts have been cautious in accepting shareholder/creditor petitions for dissolution, even though the 2006 Company Law provides a clear legal basis for such suits, and the Second Supreme People's Court Regulations on the Company Law were issued specifically to provide the principles of application. The same official also expressed the need for a higher level of expertise in handling liquidation matters, especially where creditors are involved and firm principals have moved on, and the need to involve other departments such as the State Administration of Industry and Commerce (the registration authority), the State Taxation Administration, the banking regulator, etc. A related competence problem identified by the Chief Judge is the mandatory prior mediation requirement in dissolution actions. The Shanghai courts see this as something they are ill-qualified to undertake in a situation where they lack sufficient information, and a waste of judicial resources with movement to the inevitable lawsuit. The same phenomenon is reported with respect to the use of judicial resources in mandatory pretrial mediation in labor disputes. See "Zhongguo zui mang de fating" [China's busiest court], *Nanfang zhoumo*, Dec. 4, 2008 ("China's Busiest Court").

unable to act independently in enforcing that liability if the controlling shareholder is a powerful instrument of the state, party, or military.

Two other aspects of judicial practice in corporate cases provide a window into the degree of judicial independence manifested by Shanghai courts. First, there is a way courts act without independence when they implement state or party policy in contravention of what the law provides. In discussions of judicial independence in China, this failure is often exemplified by the application of criminal law in the service of social–political control and without regard to the rights of criminal defendants. Many would understand the 1983 Strike Hard campaign or the initial stages of the crackdown on Falun Gong as embodiments of this kind of failure.[11] Yet, as demonstrated below, even in the context of corporate law application, Chinese courts may be seen acting in the service of state or party policy and in contravention of the law. Second, and on the side of affirming judicial independence, court support for market and/or market–actor autonomy (including self-ordering) over the mandates of the state may express a kind of judicial independence. To the extent the judiciary has a role in applying such notions in modern China, it can be understood as a bulwark against an economic and financial system overwhelmingly dominated by the state and party as owner, manager, and regulator.

JUDICIAL INDEPENDENCE

Determining Political Background

As noted, my broader study focuses on the degree of competence and autonomy demonstrated in Shanghai corporate law adjudications. This focus is occasioned by the lack of transparency about the political power of litigants involved in the reported cases. The inability to obtain information about the political background of cases makes it exceedingly difficult to evaluate the demonstrated independence of judicial bodies in handling corporate law-related civil or criminal matters. The task is made doubly difficult because (i) many cases are simply not accepted due to public or internal bureaucratic direction or precisely because of the case's political coloration, or (ii) even if initially accepted, such cases are not subject to adjudication (or not reported as such) again for fear of bumping up against extralegal power.[12] Thus, it may be assumed that the most politically sensitive cases never make it into the body of data analyzed.

---

[11] As Peerenboom has shown, the campaign against Falun Gong was at least partially "legalized" subsequently. Randall Peerenboom, *China's Long March toward Rule of Law* (Cambridge: Cambridge University Press, 2002), pp. 91–102.

[12] The author, when a practicing lawyer, remembers representing a European bank in the mid-1990s against a large Shanghai financial institution where all levels of the Shanghai court system proved unable to act decisively or issue a final judgment for fear of ruling against the municipal government, which controlled the defendant.

There are two other reasons for the lack of identifiably political cases in the corporate sphere. First, many of the most politically powerful firms are still organized as state-owned enterprises ("SOEs"), or wholly state-owned company limited liability companies under the Company Law, and so they do not have shareholders or any separation of ownership and management. There are thus no shareholders to sue on governance concerns, or against corporate insiders, and most disputes are addressed between government departments in a wholly political forum. Second, only those SOEs that have been corporatized and then engaged in public capital-raising will conjure up a group of potential shareholder plaintiffs. Yet, as described more fully below, cases with respect to companies limited by shares with a public float are largely kept out of the courts by fiat or voluntary denial. As such, corporate lawsuits involving state- or party-backed firms, even corporatized, are almost nonexistent (although the picture is richer in securities law actions).

Intimations of Judicial Independence

Even with this limited ability to discern the political background of corporate cases, there is evidence of Shanghai courts ruling against political actors – cases where private litigants do battle against both government departments[13] and SOEs or apparently commercial actors/investors with substantial political backing. In fact, in all of the more than 200 full opinions reviewed, where there is a discernable political interest, the Shanghai courts supported the nonstate/party interest.

This conclusion is illustrated by two examples, which, perhaps not surprisingly, are contract cases implicating state investment vehicles. In 2003, a district-level court enforced the rights of an industrial site occupier against a condemning local government agency because the relocation contract at issue was validly formed under law, and the rights arising thereunder were "to receive the protection of the law" (i.e., against the government).[14] The defendant government agency's unsuccessful defense against payment of compensation under the contract went directly to state power: it asserted execution of the contract "on behalf of the district government" and that it had failed to perform pursuant to the "instructions of higher [administrative] levels." The court nonetheless ruled for the plaintiff against the government.

Similarly, a 2007 veil-piercing case went against the interests of a large central state entity, albeit in the more expected circumstance of a ruling against a non-Shanghai government power.[15] There, a Renminbi ("RMB") 32 million yuan creditor pierced

---

[13]   And distinct from administrative claims under the Administrative Litigation Law.

[14]   *Shanghai Kangpais Enterprise General Company v. Shanghai Municipal Administration of Industry and Commerce Huangpu District Branch, Shanghai Pushun Shunzhe Development Company and Shanghai Huangpu Market Development General Company* (Shanghai No. 2 Intermediate People's Court, 2001, upheld by the Shanghai High Court, 2003).

[15]   *Shanghai Huaxin Electric Wire and Cable Company v. China Tietong Group Company* (Shanghai No. 2 Intermediate People's Court (No. 4 Civil Division), 2007, upheld by the Shanghai High Court, 2007).

to the Beijing-based SOE parent of an undercapitalized Shanghai limited liability company debtor, with the Shanghai High Court specifically upholding the assertion of parent liability by litigation (i.e., by ex post application of standards by the judiciary) based upon "abuse of the corporate form" under Article 20 of the 2006 Company Law.

Shanghai courts have also proven able to grapple with the fraught circumstance resulting from SOEs existing alongside SOE-invested corporate vehicles and independently financed and nonstate corporations. Thus, the courts seem empowered to disregard formal corporate structures when they are offered as a defense against state or party cadre misfeasance. One 2007 case shows the trial-level court and the Shanghai High Court dismissing a first defense seeking to distinguish SOE-subsidiary enterprise department actions from the interests of the SOE itself, and then a second defense that seeks to protect a corrupt cadre from prosecution because he has diverted funds to a (commercial) limited liability company promoted and controlled by him.[16]

A similar case from 2007 dismissed the defendant's pleadings that admitted corporate misfeasance and breach of corporate law and regulation in respect of an SOE, but posited that such actions have nothing to do with the crime of "private misappropriation of public assets" because they occurred with respect to the internal affairs of a corporate entity (albeit a registered SOE).[17] The court would have none of this theory and sentenced the defendant to prison and disgorgement of diverted income.[18]

As noted previously, another indication of judicial independence in the corporate sphere is the ability of the courts to protect some area of semi-autonomous activity against direct state regulation. In the many opinions reviewed, there is abundant rhetoric upholding market actor autonomy against the state and frequent invocation of private ordering in opposition to mandatory business regulation. A statement to this effect appears in one intermediate court's 2007 commentary on a 2003 case,[19] where the court had to choose between protection of statutory rights of first refusal due existing shareholders and the rights of a good faith transferee under a fraudulently approved transfer agreement:

> First and foremost, the thing we must clarify is this: the jurisprudential logic underlying the giving of priority to the [right of first refusal] over the purchase rights of the transferee is absolutely not because the former right is in statute, and the

---

[16] *PRC v. Xue Henghe* (Shanghai Rail Transport Intermediate People's Court, upheld by Shanghai High Court, 2007).

[17] *PRC v. Wang Haiqing et al.* (Shanghai Hongkou District People's Court, 2007).

[18] This is consistent with the same sensitivity and approach taken in a 2001 criminal case, where the establishment of a new, private, enterprise (by an SOE manager) designed to skim transfer value from the SOE's sourcing transactions is a violation of the Criminal Law's prohibition against "illegally engaging in the same business" (as an SOE where the criminal defendant is posted), see *PRC v. Shen XY* (Shanghai High Court, 2001).

[19] *A. Investment Development Company v. Wang and Other Shareholders* (Shanghai No. 1 Intermediate People's Court, on appeal, 2003).

latter is merely a contract right. This is because statutory rights are not always supe-rior to contract rights – in fact, it is just the opposite. Approaching it systemically and adhering to the orientation which protects private ordering, regulation of the market requires that application of the law fully respect the freedom to contract to encourage successful transactions. . . . There is significant meaning in this.[20]

This is a remarkable rhetorical position in the context of recent Chinese history and a departure from common views of Chinese law even through the 1990s.[21] And the position is more than rhetoric, as seen in many Shanghai corporate cases. One 2005 opinion provides an excellent example where self-ordering memorialized in the articles of association completely swallows statutory norms like the fiduciary duty of loyalty.[22] A 2006 opinion shows the extraordinary weight placed on partnership agreement-like articles of association as an expression of private ordering, which triumph over larger default provisions or doctrines contained in the Company Law itself.[23] Even with identification of fiduciary duties breach and fraud by a control-ling shareholder, resolutions passed by a dissident shareholders' meeting are ruled invalid because the meeting was not called, and the voting was not effected, in technical conformity with the articles of association. The same heavy privileging of apparent self-ordering expressed in articles of association and entity regulations approved by the board is seen in another case that completely disenfranchised a shareholder [24] and a separate 2007–08 opinion where the intermediate court stated "the courts should not use the coercive power of the state to interfere with matters within the scope of a company's self-governance."[25] Although this weighting of pri-vate ordering over statutory mandates does not constitute the sharpest expression

---

[20] Shanghai High Court ed., 2005 *nian Shanghai fayuan anli jingxuan* [2005 Selection of Shanghai Court Cases], (Beijing: People's Court Publishing House, 2007), p. 111.

[21] Or nineteenth-century reform officials, see Wellington K.K. Chan, *Merchants, Mandarins, and Mod-ern Enterprise in Late Ch'ing China* (Cambridge: Harvard University Press, 1977), pp. 67–68 (two basic premises inherent in the views of officials and literati regarding commerce and industry were "that the state had the right to run, or at least intervene in, the affairs of any major business enterprise, and that the state had prior prerogatives over its profits . . . ").

[22] *Shanghai Yingdafang Service Company v. Shanghai Yingdafang Zhangjiang Service Company et al.* (Shanghai Pudong New District People's Court and Shanghai No. 1 Intermediate People's Court, 2005).

[23] *Yu Xiaoqi and 18 Shareholders v. Shanghai Changxin Accountancy Limited and Guo Hongtao* (Shang-hai Changning District People's Court and Shanghai No. 1 Intermediate People's Court, 2006).

[24] *Shanghai Shenmao Dianci Factory v. Wang Longbao, Shanghai Shengmao Xiancai Company, Shang-hai Guanlong Electrical Machinery Assembly Company and Taicang Municipal Guanlong Dianci Company* (Shanghai Nanhui District People's Court, 2004, upheld Shanghai No. 1 Intermediate People's Court (No. 3 Civil Division), 2004, overturned Shanghai No. 1 Intermediate People's Court (No. 3 Civil Division) 2006 on rehearing). In this case, the defendant actually pleads that assertion of law over the agreement memorialized in board regulations and the articles of association amounts to state interference.

[25] *Sun X. v. Li Y. and Shi Z.* (initial court hearing case and intermediate court hearing appeal not identified, but latter probably Shanghai No. 2 Intermediate People's Court (No. 3 Civil Division)), 2007 or 2008).

of political independence, in the context of China's historical political development and its reform-era legal construction program it shows a decidedly independent orientation at the courts.

In another demonstration of judicial independence, there are indications of the Shanghai courts acting as the guardians of a new corporate–commercial space. One April 2006 opinion considering the new Article 183 judicial dissolution mechanism refuses to grant relief to shareholder plaintiffs and yet directly scolds the directors of the subject firm for their failure to comprehend they are not political cadres operating a collective but rather shareholders with an economic interest – or corporate directors acting as fiduciaries of the owners – who have a radically different relationship to their coshareholders (the former worker–participants in the collective):

> But, the court has also noticed that the three defendants, as directors of the com-
> pany, have not really made the transition from their former role as leader-cadres
> of a collectively-owned enterprise to that of shareholders in a limited liability com-
> pany. For instance, in calling shareholders' meetings they have not conformed to
> their notification obligations, have failed in bringing about discussion of corporate
> operating policies, and ignored the other related rights of the seven plaintiffs. In
> addition, in managing corporate finances, there seems to be in evidence action
> which includes the transfer of corporate funds into personal accounts and the hold-
> ing out of corporate automotive vehicles as personal assets. And, the expenditures
> by the company have not been handled transparently, etc. The above-described
> actions by the defendants have certainly brought about the lack of trust by the
> plaintiffs, which has resulted in the disagreement [between shareholders].[26]

This opinion shows a PRC court striving to remind participants in an altered economic–corporate law system that the new order entails real separation of enterprise and administration, which the same judicial institutions seek to protect and enforce. Insofar as it works directly against the interests of preferred political actors, it is also an expression of judicial independence.

Failures to Demonstrate Judicial Independence

There are several ways in which the Shanghai courts evidence serious independence limitations in the sense proposed above, most notably (i) by acting as the handmaiden of policy implementation in contravention of what the Company Law allows or directs, and (ii) by blanket rejection of public company/large plaintiff cases.

First, the 1992–2008 survey shows a large number of cases – and in every instance of shareholder petition for judicial dissolution – where the courts actually work against the law in the service of state policy aims. A 2006 judicial dissolution case[27] is indicative of this value choice cum doctrinal approach. It is the same approach

---

[26] *Yang Lizhi et al. v. Cao Zhengjie et al.* (Xuhui District People's Court, 2006).
[27] *Tang Chunshao v. Zhou Huizhong* (Shanghai No. 1 Intermediate People's Court, 2006).

adopted two years later in the Second Supreme People's Court Regulations on the 2006 Company Law,[28] articulated directly by the Chief Judge of the Shanghai High Court No. 2 Civil Division in December 2008 when discussing the courts' hesitancy in accepting and allowing dissolution–liquidation pleadings,[29] and the policy direction signaled in a December 2008 ten-point notice distributed by one Shanghai intermediate court. The case involves Article 183 of the new Company Law, where the court rejects plaintiff's suit for judicial dissolution of a thoroughly deadlocked company. In the expanded reasoning behind the simple judgment, the court declares it is loath to order dissolution of a corporate legal person – even a dysfunctional one – because such action would "necessarily impact in different degrees on market order and stability."

Another 2006 case, where shareholders of a limited liability company (transformed from a collectively owned enterprise) also sought judicial dissolution, evidences much the same approach by the Xuhui District court.[30] There the application for dissolution is also refused because it is seen as a drastic and disruptive remedy, and – perhaps most importantly – it would alter arrangements whereby salary was being paid to laid-off workers. The Shanghai High Court in a commentary lauded the court's refusal to grant dissolution relief because of the negative impacts on market stability and the attendant social costs.

The consistent approach in these cases may be contrasted with an economic approach that encourages efficient redeployment of capital when shareholder relations become so difficult that they make firm operations impossible.[31] Instead, what these case opinions evidence is the courts acting as administrative units – often directly in conformity with bureaucratic instruction – prioritizing national social and economic policy over and above more specific mandates (and rights) set forth in the Company Law.

Far more illustrative of potential limitations on judicial independence is the pronounced absence in the sample of case opinions having anything to do with

---

[28] Article 5, which for petitions under Article 183 directs the courts to emphasize mediation and then strongly pushes the courts to support an agreed buyout among the shareholders, reduction of capital, and exit of one or more partners, or any method which is not in contravention of a mandatory article of law or administrative regulation, to serve the overriding priority of maintaining entity existence.

[29] "We strive to keep the company in existence; we have to think about creditors, the social responsibility of the corporate person, and the fate of the employees."

[30] *Yang Lizhi et al. v. Cao Zhengjie et al.* (Xuhui District People's Court, 2006).

[31] Compare *Shanghai Jingfa Enterprise Development Company v. Shanghai Haining Petroleum Products Company* (Shanghai No. 2 Intermediate People's Court, upheld on appeal at the Shanghai High Court, 2003) where the put of equity interests owned by complaining shareholders to the other (breaching) shareholders is ordered to allow the company to continue normal operations and maintain employment of the company's accumulated value but also implicitly to allow the complaining shareholders to redeploy their capital to continuing productive uses. In this case, the rhetoric about market stability and continued use of productive assets is similar, but the court feels emboldened to fashion its own, implicitly, economically far more efficient, remedy.

companies limited by shares (joint stock companies)[32] or such companies with listed capital, or their shareholders – less than 1 percent of the case opinions reviewed in detail between 1992 and 2008.[33] One result of this apparent rejection of public cases is that whole swaths of the Company Law are simply not used,[34] including numerous provisions supporting basic claims one expects to see in the application of a company statute in a country with two active stock exchanges.[35]

Does this mean that companies limited by shares and their shareholders and directors and officers (and controlling shareholders) are not getting into trouble or are being operated without discord and in perfect conformity with the highest standards of modern corporate governance? Absolutely not, as divined from the daily reports in China's muckraking financial press of corporate governance sins too manifold to mention.

When considering why so few such cases appear in the Shanghai courts – which is after all the situs of the Shanghai Stock Exchange – there are a number of reasons that have little to do with judicial independence concerns. One explanation – focusing on the plaintiff, not court bureaucracy, side – is a substitute enforcement structure

---

[32] It appears that Shanghai courts have had no particular problem dealing with the limited liability company form that actually predated China's entire corporate law system, the foreign-invested enterprise ("FIE") forms dominated by Chinese–foreign equity and cooperative joint ventures, each of which have their own specific statute and/or regulations governing certain aspects of their legal identity, operations, and shareholder relations. One of the reasons FIE-related cases are not seen in the Shanghai courts is that foreign investors and their PRC partners almost uniformly choose exclusive arbitration for dispute resolution.

[33] See *Zhang X. and Other Shareholders of Shanghai A Company Limited v. Shanghai A Company Limited* (first and rehearing courts not identified, 1995); *Lu Jianming v. Shanghai Light Industry Machinery Company, Limited* (Shanghai Jingan District People's Court, Shanghai No. 2 Intermediate People's Court, 2006); and *PRC v. Fang Kun, Ni Chunhua and Zhang Mingxia* (Shanghai Pudong New District Court, upheld by the Shanghai No. 1 Intermediate People's Court, 2007). In the 2003 Shanghai Company Law Opinion, reviewing more than a decade of corporate law cases in Shanghai, the only mention of public company cases is the allusion to "suits by public company shareholders to invalidate corporate resolutions" in a long list of "continuing difficulties," indicating that the courts receive such pleadings but perhaps do not accept them.

[34] For both companies limited by shares (listed or not) and limited liability companies (even the close corporation/corporate partnership form so prevalent in China's enterprise reality), the following are also absent: shareholders' civil suits against other shareholders for oppression; claims against control or actual control parties for harm to the company; specifically pleaded breaches of duty of care or duty of loyalty (including funds misappropriation, illegal lending or guarantees, self-dealing, corporate opportunity, corporate secrets); specifically pleaded claims against directors, officers, or supervisory board members for compensation; specifically pleaded derivative actions; adjudication of actual control person status; failure to make financial reports to shareholders; company dividend distributions; or breach of duties by court-confirmed liquidation group. Given the politicized capital structure of even nonpublic companies in the PRC, this paucity of claims may also be determined by political factors and thus have implications for the exercise of judicial independence.

[35] Equally glaring is the omission of any cases involving the new garb given SOEs, the wholly state-owned company subgenus of limited liability company. The absence of wholly state-owned limited liability companies conversely has everything to do with the reality of these firms as administrative units wholly controlled by state and party actors (even though reclad under the Company Law), with no shareholders' meeting.

for listed companies' cases via the public prosecutor[36] and the securities regulatory authority,[37] each prodded by the aggressive financial media in China. Another explanation, equally unrelated to judicial independence concerns, is what might be called the demand-side theory, where shareholders do not bring actions against the companies limited by shares they invest in either because of familiar collective-action problems or because they themselves do not understand that courts – as contrasted with the securities regulator – are the appropriate forum for hearing their claims.[38] The latter attitude is exemplified in the straight-faced pleadings reported in a 2008 private action against the CSRC.[39] There a defendant director, obviously negligent in fulfilling his corporate fiduciary duties, asserted he was not one of the named persons with a fiduciary duty under the PRC Securities Law – thereby completely ignoring the application of the Company Law to his role as a director of a public company limited by shares. Flawed in the legal sense, the defense highlights a common understanding in China of the separate worlds of limited liability companies on one side and companies limited by shares with listed stock on the other.

More likely explanations for the absence of public company cases are that the Shanghai courts (i) voluntarily avoid taking such cases, and (ii) are specifically directed not to take such cases. The distaste for public company cases, whether self-directed or ordered from the higher regions of the judiciary, was exemplified in the posture famously taken by the Pudong New District Court when it refused to accept the first public shareholders' suit against a capital markets issuer (and

---

[36] See, for example, the use of criminal law to punish breach of duty of loyalty in the prosecution of former New China Life chairman Guan Guoliang, "Yi shen Guan Guoliang" [First hearing for Guan Guoliang], *Caijing*, Dec. 8, 2008.

[37] Only one case sees a Shanghai court diminishing the power of the China Securities Regulatory Commission and taking a uniquely activist approach: *Lu Jianming v. Shanghai Light Industry Machinery Company, Limited* (Shanghai Jingan District People's Court, Shanghai No. 2 Intermediate People's Court, 2006).

[38] One Shanghai High Court judge told the author that the great proportion of closed company (limited liability company) cases and the absence of company limited by share/listed company cases are a result of "the relative completeness and clarity of the Company Law in addressing companies limited by shares" and because limited liability companies experience recurring problems of shareholder oppression and dual shareholder–employee status. This explanation seems dubious, especially as there is ample evidence of policy guidance constraining lower level courts from accepting such cases.

[39] Shenzhen Shenxin Taifeng Co., Ltd., where a fined director brought suit against the CSRC in a Beijing intermediate court pleading that he was "only a director appointed by a shareholder, and did not really participate in operation and management of the company" and so did not directly manage or operate the company, and thus is not one of "the only two kinds of people who can be fined under the PRC Securities Law." "Shang shi gongsi dongshi beifa zhuangao zhengjianhui" [Fined listed company director sues the CSRC], *Xinjing bao*, Dec. 7, 2008. See also the "flower vase director" case described at Nicholas C. Howson, "The Doctrine That Dared Not Speak Its Name: Anglo-American Fiduciary Duties in China's 2005 Company Law and Case Law Intimations of Prior Convergence" in Hideki Kanda, Kon-Sik Kim, and Curtis J. Milhaupt eds., *Transforming Corporate Governance in East Asia* (Oxford: Routledge, 2008), pp. 226–228.

its board, officers, and accountants) for false disclosure in 1999.[40] As the court wrote, "The plaintiff's case regarding behavior in violation of laws and regulations in the stock market should be handled by the CSRC. The plaintiff's suit regarding a securities dispute does not come within the jurisdiction of this court." More recently, evidence of self-restraint comes both from discussions with Supreme People's Court and Shanghai court officials between 2006 and 2008 and similar blanket refusals in respect of transferred nonperforming loan collection cases since 2005,[41] as well as thousands of cases by public stock purchasers seeking remedies for capital markets manipulation and fraud between 1999 and 2003.

There is both documentary and oral evidence suggesting that the Shanghai courts have been specifically directed not to accept public company cases. These instructions can come via openly issued regulations or local-level opinions, such as the December 12, 2002, ban on acceptance of securities actions, the January 9, 2003, Supreme People's Court regulations forbidding claims on manipulation and insider trading, and the June 2003 Shanghai Company Law Opinion command that Shanghai courts temporarily not accept shareholders' claims seeking invalidation of resolutions by companies with listed shares.[42] These instructions are also communicated internally, as noted in late 2008 by the president of one of Shanghai's most expert district-level courts when alluding to the existence of an internal instruction from the Supreme People's Court (not the CSRC) and apparently justified as part of the effort to discourage vexatious shareholder litigation nationally.[43]

Regardless of the mechanisms the Shanghai courts use to shunt aside public company cases, rationales supporting the rejectionist stance are fairly well understood and relevant to a consideration of judicial independence. One rationale dictates that courts be told to decline or voluntarily refuse listed company cases for fear of large plaintiff groups, and the attendant perceived threat of social instability or impact on the "super-value" in Chinese administrative–political culture: social harmony. This is seen in the Shanghai High Court's rejectionist response to group plaintiff actions (e.g., shareholders' suits) generally and to shareholders' suits to overturn resolutions, force dividend distributions, cause judicially mandated sale of equity, or spur dissolution, all at companies limited by shares or companies with publicly listed stock. The No. 2 Civil Division of the Shanghai High Court alludes to this

---

[40] The case against Hongguang Enterprise Co., Limited. See Xu Zhaoxiong and Zheng Hui eds., *Zhengjuan anli jingjie* [Selection and Explanation of Securities Law Cases], (Shanghai: Oriental Publishing Center, 2001), pp. 58–64.

[41] See "Buliang daikuan chuzhe xin guiding liang nan" [Two difficulties for new regulation of non-performing loan arrangements], *Caijing*, Nov. 24, 2008 ("NPL I") and "Buliang daikuan zhuan-rang susong 'jiedong'" ["The 'unfreezing' of litigation relating to the transfer of non-performing loans"], *Caijing*, Dec. 8, 2008, http://caijing.com.cn/2008–12–04/110034693.html (reviewed Dec. 2008) ("NPL II").

[42] This instruction was reversed upon adoption of the 2006 Company Law.

[43] Remarks of the Shanghai Changning District People's Court President, Dec. 5, 2008.

apparent redline in its grudging reversal of a pre-2006 policy barring lawsuits that seek to invalidate public company resolutions:

> In view of the fact that these kinds of cases may give rise to issues related to mass litigation and volatility in the securities markets, [the Shanghai courts] have taken an especially cautious attitude towards accepting these cases; in accepting these cases, we ask that the shareholders provide related evidence showing why the shareholders or board resolution is invalid or should be invalidated, and we will examine this evidence strictly so as to protect against vexatious shareholder litigation.[44]

A second rationale can also be perceived, albeit more subtly, in the Shanghai court system's consistent bias in favor of stability (including, as noted above, business entity preservation at all costs) over other values that might be held high in corporate law application, like transactional efficiency, redeployment of capital to most efficient uses, or fairness. Thus, even in the world of corporate law jurisprudence, where law, regulation, and fairness (often invoked by the Shanghai courts in corporate law cases) should be dispositive, there is a strong concern in the courts for political or social order, which either causes them to disregard the power they are clearly authorized to wield under the 2006 Company Law or causes their political and administrative masters to limit their jurisdiction in bald contradiction with the scope of their statutory power.

A third, largely unspoken rationale perhaps informing the rejectionist stance toward public company cases is twofold: (i) that such firms involve what were state-owned assets (albeit corporatized and repackaged as listed companies), and (ii) that the promoters, controlling shareholders, and directors, officers, and supervisory board members and other insiders are tied to superior political power, whether the state, the party, or the military. There is evidence that the courts will avoid cases concerning state-owned assets.[45] There is no document that describes the latter, sharper, political sensitivity, and no Shanghai court official approached in the course of the study alluded to it other than tangentially in connection with a discussion of the function of political–legal committees.[46] Yet it seems safe to speculate that

---

[44] Shanghai Company Law Report, p. 44.

[45] For instance, where a 2004 report by the head of the Hubei High Court warning of irregular activity and loss of state assets through transfers of nonperforming loans to asset management companies and then to third parties caused the courts to simply stop accepting or ruling on such cases in 2005. See NPL I and NPL II.

[46] According to officials at the Shanghai courts, most corporate and commercial case opinions are first drafted and then filed (beian) with the political–legal committee. Yet the same officials noted that if a specific case is particular (teshu) – potentially impacting on social stability (wending) or conflicting powers – the panel actually hearing the case and its court level administration will seek the opinion of the political–legal committee before accepting or deciding a case. These same officials declared that the notion of conflicting powers does not accommodate political conflict or political–economic privilege versus civil society, but instead conflicting jurisdictions (for instance, CSRC regulation against application of the corporate law by the courts).

the fear of involving far stronger political actors (and court paymasters if the defendants have organized the corporate entity in the same jurisdiction) or attempting to enforce against them animates the profound disinterest on the part of the court system toward application of the corporate law with respect to these firms.

The foregoing may explain the paucity of public company cases in the Shanghai courts, yet it does not excuse the same phenomenon. That lack of application constitutes a tragedy for China's corporate governance reform, precisely because it was the dire state of corporate governance at public companies that occasioned the 2006 Company Law amendments and the statute's new justiciability.[47] Indeed, one question for the future of the Chinese judiciary is the Chinese legal system's ability to sustain this defensive posture against mass-plaintiff cases.[48] Aside from the urgings of reformist intellectuals and lawyers, and despite older studies in 2001 and 2002 showing litigation adversity among China's urban and rural citizens,[49] individuals continue to push into the courts en masse. In late 2008, the Shanghai No. 1 Intermediate Court announced that it alone has seen skyrocketing numbers of group (qunti) lawsuits accepted in the past few years: from twenty-seven group cases suing on the same cause of action and 1,047 claimants in 2006 to fifty such cases (1,671 claimants) in 2007 and sixty-two such cases (1,449 claimants) by October 1, 2008.[50] Most of these cases pertain to labor disputes, residential housing management, administrative condemnation of land and buildings, and rural contracting. Other data demonstrate similar patterns nationally, with large numbers of group suits brought with respect to labor rights,[51] official misfeasance,[52] environmental torts, food contamination,[53] securities violations, etc. In response, one intermediate court in the Shanghai system

---

[47] Shanghai Stock Exchange ed., *Zhongguo gongsi zhili baogao (2003) nian* [China Corporate Governance Report 2003], (Shanghai: Fudan University Publishing House, 2003).

[48] See "Huajie minyuan: sifa ying ti zhengzhi huachu 'huanchongdai'" [Assuaging popular anger: the judiciary should be a 'conflict resolution area' substitute], *Nanfang zhoumo*, Nov. 13, 2008, and "Qunti peichang: quan yi yü yong an" [Mass compensation: rights and stability], *Caijing*, Oct. 13, 2008 (both doubting the long-term political sustainability of the current situation, even if justified at present by overburdened judicial resources).

[49] "Celiang shehui de hexie chengdu" [Measuring the degree of harmony in society], *Nanfang zhoumou*, Nov. 20, 2008.

[50] A doubling of cases in just twenty-four months, with no data on cases of the same type refused. "Shanghai shi di yi zhongyuan tansuo shenpan xin jucuo" [Shanghai Municipal No. 1 Intermediate People's Court explores new adjudication measures], *Xinmin wanbao*, Nov. 4, 2008 ("New Adjudication Measures").

[51] One report in late 2008 shows how overburdened a very local-level court in Guangdong Province is. To November 15, 2008, a basic level court serving a subdistrict of Dongguan with only thirteen judges had to process 7,540 cases (mostly labor contract cases and disputes regarding laid-off workers), against a national average of forty-two cases/judge. That case acceptance and adjudication rate was already a 100 percent increase over the count for the same district in all of 2007. See China's Busiest Court.

[52] "Parents of schoolchildren killed in China quake confirm lawsuit," *The New York Times*, Dec. 23, 2008.

[53] See "Milk scandal in China yields cash for parents," *The New York Times*, Jan. 17, 2009, and "Class action suit, rare in China, is filed over tainted milk," *The New York Times*, Jan. 21, 2009.

has now developed special procedures to handle such cases. The procedures are designed to provide an early warning system to the entire Shanghai court system of approaching group lawsuits.[54]

JUDICIAL AUTONOMY

This chapter cannot present in detail the study's findings on the demonstrated degree of institutional autonomy in Shanghai corporate law cases from 1992 to 2008. In summary, the Shanghai courts showed increasing autonomy after the promulgation of the 1994 Company Law and through the end of 2005. This is shown by the acceptance of cases in areas and the fashioning of remedies without authorization under statute or judicial regulations. Immediately after the 2006 Company Law took effect, there was a notably aggressive invocation of the new statute, even with respect to claims arising prior to January 1, 2006.[55] However, in the years following 2006, there has been an authorization-constraint dynamic at work where the Shanghai courts draw back from acceptance and adjudication of cases they are now explicitly authorized to hear and did hear when they were not authorized to.

Important in any institutional autonomy discussion are the bureaucratic instructions liberally issued in the PRC court system. First are judicial regulations issued by the Supreme People's Court – often incorrectly called judicial "explanations" – that provide a procedural and substantive basis for claims rooted in explicit statutory provisions.[56] Second are local-level opinions like the Shanghai High Court opinion on the handling of corporate law cases distributed internally in June 2003. Third are occasional notices and opinions issued by individual court systems, some publicly, others internally. For example, during the accelerating financial crisis in late 2008,

---

54 New Adjudication Measures.

55 In the Shanghai High Court study of 2006 corporate law adjudications, of the 318 cases producing a judgment after a first hearing, 164 (52 percent) used the new Company Law in the judgment; of those 164 cases, 102 cases (62 percent) issued a final judgment based on the 2006 statute, whereas 62 cases (38 percent) issued judgments using the preamendment 1994 version. This result is noteworthy because fully 88 percent of this litigation arose from circumstances prior to January 1, 2006. It indicates that the Shanghai courts felt free to implement the new 2006 Company Law on claims arising when the governing statute lacked affirmative legal bases for such claims. The Shanghai High Court is explicit about this when it coyly points to several cases where it applied expanded legal rights bestowed in the new Company Law, even though the case arose from a time when only the much narrower rights granted in the 1994 law were available. (See Shanghai Company Law Report.)

56 The Supreme People's Court issues three kinds of explanatory documents with something like the power of law or regulation: explanations (jieshi), regulations (guiding), and approving responses (pifu). Explanations by the court elaborate "law" (fa); regulations are issued to provide judicial institutions with direction on how to apply "law" to certain kinds of cases or common problems; and approving responses are Supreme People's Court responses to queries regarding correct application of "law" by Provincial High Courts and People's Liberation Army courts. To date, the Supreme People's Court has issued two regulations on the 2006 Company Law, the first on how courts should handle actions that straddle January 1, 2006, and the second on shareholder petitions for company dissolution. A third, on the derivative action mechanism, is expected in 2009.

when many of China's export-oriented producers in the Yangtze River Delta area experienced difficulties, the Shanghai High Court publicly issued an eleven-point document calling for heightened sensitivity to the impact of case decisions on distressed industries, reduction or elimination of litigation fees, deposit exemptions, and an emphasis on speedy adjudication of labor rights and compensation cases and enforcement. On December 2, 2008, one Shanghai intermediate court even issued its own ten-point document explaining how it would conform to the policy commands enunciated by the High Court, whose measures included unified and accelerated financial crisis-related case acceptance, hearing and enforcement, sensitivity to the capacity of firms to bear enforcement actions or asset attachment, and attention to the highest value of all noted above in the discussion of judicial independence: finding a way for distressed enterprises to keep operating even if technically insolvent or in default.[57]

Supreme People's Court regulations can impact the application of a "law" (fa) in three important ways: (i) providing specific authorization for claims already described in principle in statute;[58] (ii) forbidding the acceptance of certain claims;[59] and (iii) providing new legal bases for adjudication beyond what is set forth in statute. For instance, the May 2008 regulations on application of the 2006 Company Law forbid the acceptance of shareholder petitions for dissolution of companies based on factors not explicitly included in Article 183; yet the same regulations provide for expanded justiciability of claims beyond what is permitted in the statute.[60] Regulations can also prod courts to restart adjudication on cases they have voluntarily refused to accept.[61] Local-level instructions like the 2003 Shanghai opinion on corporate law cases show how local court bureaucracies may not wait for

---

[57] See "Jinrong weiji anjian youle kuaishen tongdao" [Financial crisis cases have an accelerated hearing channel], *Dongfang zaobao*, Dec. 3, 2008.

[58] As in the January 9, 2003, Supreme People's Court regulations allowing private lawsuits against false or misleading disclosure in the securities markets.

[59] As in the January 15, 2002, Supreme People's Court regulations mandating rejection of private shareholders' suits on securities law claims.

[60] Expanded justiciability with respect to creditors' lawsuits seeking confirmation of debts owed by the company subject to dissolution, and creditors' claims for joint and several liability for shareholders and controlling shareholders arising from their misfeasance or manipulation of residual assets in the dissolution and liquidation process. Another example is the 2003 draft regulation on Company Law adjudication issued before enactment of the 2006 Company Law, which regulation provided the basis for mechanisms absent from the 1994 Company Law, including: corporate veil piercing, derivative actions, shareholders' information rights, fiduciary duties, liquidation procedures, shareholders' lawsuits for invalidation of resolutions, etc. If the Company Law had not been amended in 2006 to include these items, and the draft had been actually issued as Supreme People's Court regulation, then the regulations would have provided the basis for a whole host of claims and procedures going far beyond the spare legal bases explicitly set forth in the 1994 law.

[61] A good current example of this kind of regulation is the continuing effort to issue a document instructing the courts to recommence handling creditors' collection actions on nonperforming loans sold by commercial banks to asset management companies and then to third-party buyers. See NPL I and NPL II.

central approval before adjudicating claims not explicitly justiciable and similarly will not wait for regulations even on newly justiciable items. For example, in the 2003 Shanghai Company Law Opinion, there are detailed provisions on judicial veil-piercing, disregard of the corporate form, and derivative actions – none of which had any legal basis under the 1994 Company Law, Supreme People's Court regulation, or in statute until the adoption of the 2006 Company Law. At the same time, the Shanghai Opinion also eliminated consideration of certain claims that courts were not authorized in statute to examine.[62] One Shanghai High Court official acknowledged to the author that the Shanghai court system indeed issues its own explanations – sometimes openly, usually internally. The official acknowledged that although such documents are normatively not as authoritative as Supreme People's Court regulations, in reality they can be more powerful in the handling of actual cases at the noncentral level.[63] The same judge also admitted that these local explanations are often issued before central bureaucracy instructions and thus gain authority by the mere fact of being in existence long before the national authorities get around to issuing a well-vetted regulation for the guidance of lower level courts.

There continues to be a fierce dispute in China on the real effect of judicial regulations. In the most common view emanating from the Chinese courts and academic circles, Supreme People's Court regulations are a condition precedent to application of certain provisions of law or doctrine by courts. For instance, many Chinese academics, lawyers, and judges hold that important provisions of the 2006 Company Law – such as corporate fiduciary duties, veil-piercing, or the derivative lawsuit mechanism – simply cannot be applied until regulations specifically addressing use of the provision have been issued. This broadly accepted notion is an important block in many other areas of Chinese law, for instance with regard to the use and application of the new PRC Bankruptcy Law,[64] with the Chinese courts openly refusing to accept bankruptcy cases without a judicial regulation. Yet even the shallowest inquiry, the many cases reviewed in the period 1992–2008 for Shanghai,[65] and the rich body of subnational level court opinions available demonstrate that this perception is not vindicated in the reality of lower-level adjudication and that the courts habitually accept and adjudicate cases relating to claims and mechanisms they have no authority to hear.

That being the case, it makes the negative authorization-constraint dynamic in the Shanghai courts after 2006 all the more striking. That dynamic is the situation where courts do not apply doctrines specifically authorized in the 2006 Company

---

[62] For instance, the Shanghai Company Law Opinion's temporary prohibition against accepting corporate resolution invalidation claims for public companies.

[63] Shanghai High Court judge, October 2008.

[64] See http://chinacourt.org/html/article/200707/11/256034.shtml (reviewed Dec. 2008).

[65] And see Howson, The Doctrine That Dared Not Speak Its Name (early adjudication of corporate fiduciary duties claims and allowance of derivative suits).

Law after January 1, 2006, even though they freely employed them before when there was no legal basis for them.[66]

Speculation on the reasons behind this counterintuitive reaction by the Shanghai courts is difficult. The purported civil law affiliation of the Chinese legal system is not helpful, precisely because Shanghai judges have demonstrated their autonomy in hearing claims without a formal statutory basis (or reference to academic or superior authorities) while even evidencing a common-law equity courts style of law application. Of course the courts may refuse to accept such cases or use such now-authorized doctrines because of some opaque political sensitivity – either by virtue of the parties involved or the ever-present risk of brushing up against state assets (as in the simple contract law nonperforming loan collection cases blocked since 2005). A more benign explanation may be the (temporary) reassertion of the Chinese court's basic bureaucratic identity. Before the 2006 authorization of key doctrines, courts may have felt relatively free to range about and implement common sense or justice- (fairness)-oriented solutions such as invocation of corporate fiduciary duties against obviously opportunistic or inattentive directors or ad hoc permission of a derivative suit even if not pleaded. With some of these doctrines now included in formal "law," even if in principle, the courts as embedded bureaucratic actors wait to see how the apex of their bureaucracy system (the Supreme People's Court) will instruct implementation of these newly declared instruments. This view is not wholly satisfactory, however, as some Shanghai courts continue to implement new corporate law doctrine and remedies without regulations or superior direction (for instance, in adjudicating fiduciary standards, permitting derivative lawsuits, and veil-piercing). This explanation goes some way to describing the basis for the pronounced reversal in one kind of autonomy after 2006 and also reminds us of the origins and context of party-directed, bureaucratically embedded actors lacking the fuller freedom of more autonomous judicial institutions.

CONCLUSION

In North-Weberian terms,[67] China is still far from the complete rule of law state with seamless protection of property rights and expectations. Yet the corporatization program – and the implementation of a justiciable corporate law calling for ex post

---

[66] Space limitations make it impossible to detail the cases, pre- and post-2006, that show this. Aside from the cases reviewed for this study and information related by Shanghai judicial officials, the dynamic is noted in the remarks of professor Zhu Ciyun, Tsinghua Law School, at the East China University of Politics and Law in November 2008 (citing an internal Supreme People's Court study showing that the courts have shied away from accepting veil-piercing and derivative lawsuits even after such mechanisms were formally established in the 2006 Company Law).

[67] See "Self-Government, Law and Capitalism" in Max Weber, *The Religion of China: Confucianism and Taoism* (1922), pp. 84–104 (Hans H. Gerth, trans., 1964); Douglass C. North, *Institutions, Institutional Change and Economic Performance* (1990); and Donald C. Clarke, "Economic Development and the Rights Hypothesis: The China Problem," *American Journal of Comparative Law*, vol. 58, p. 89 (2003).

application of law by a judiciary – has spurred the nation's formal legal institutions to develop real competence, substantial autonomy, and hints of political independence in application of one kind of law so important for growth. Those developments and the expectation of future progress in the same direction have clearly provided the initial assurances necessary for growth-enhancing investment and participation in China's capital markets. The critical question remains whether, in the technically complex world of corporate law adjudication, Chinese courts must achieve even greater judicial autonomy and independence to assure continued economic growth and hoped-for social stability, not to mention the equally important effect of enhanced institutional legitimacy for the judiciary itself.

8

Local Courts in Western China

The Quest for Independence and Dignity

Stéphanie Balme[1]

All justice emanates from the King. It is administered in his name by the justice whom he nominates, and whom he institutes.

– A constitutional adage in France until the 1830 Constitutional Charter

INTRODUCTION

In the north-central province of Shaanxi, as I was waiting to interview a judge, I noticed a small exercise book on his office desk. The same sort of notebook, brown and cheap, that Chinese children use for their homework. To start the conversation, I gently asked what he used the notebook for and was told that it was for his political homework assignments. The last page the judge had filled in was a handwritten copy of the Charter of the Chinese Communist Party (CCP).

As I decided to further explore the issue of grassroots judges' political culture in predominantly rural areas, I observed that although most of them share similar political and intellectual references, they do not have a strong common legal culture. For example, most of them believe that one-party rule is the key to stability, that party members are the elite of the country, that law's main goal is to be punitive, that the state constitution is purely ornamental, that judges are above all civil servants, and that the judiciary must be supervised by the people's congresses. Those recurrent political references reflect the judges' knowledge of the world. Put differently, their legal backgrounds appear highly politicized. Consequently, local level judges lack

[1] I wish to express my gratitude to court President Gu and Judges Chang, Pang, Hu, and Wang. Their constant support over the years speaks to their level of open-mindedness. I am also thankful to my institution, Sciences Po Paris, and to former director at CERI, Christophe Jaffrelot. Zhang Han from the Tsinghua University Law School deserves special thanks for her constant help, as do Alexandre Ziegler, Christine Cornet, and Jean-Luc Quinio. I gratefully acknowledge the fruitful discussions I had with Odile Pierquin on Chinese rural culture. Richard Balme, Edith Coron, and Peter Ford have provided useful comments on an earlier version of the chapter.

the professional skills and attitudes that would earn them the social status that one might expect a judge to enjoy.

After decades of neglect, the Chinese state is reforming its judicial system at the basic level. The uneven level of professionalism and the often corrupt attitudes of grassroots judges give rise to the question: How much independence should be given to the judiciary at the local level? Furthermore, are judges struggling for their professional dignity or is the CCP promoting it? Is the issue of ordinary courts' independence crucial? Why is it so difficult to address?

It is indeed crucial because it could motivate judicial activism and rights awareness among citizens and lead to a general political opening of the regime. Nonetheless, grassroots judicial independence would be tremendously difficult to implement even if the regime undertook a comprehensive doctrinal reform of its judicial system or a political democratization process. This would deeply affect the foundations of the judicial system whereas a lot of judges, at least at the local level, may not be professionally ready to act independently. In interviews, judges often express their wish to become more administratively independent but also their genuine fears about any new system that would require more professional transparency. As elsewhere in the world, the public in China is demanding more legal accountability from its judges. Although perfectly legitimate, the issue of transforming the status of judges within the state is not addressed as such by the media or by the political sphere.

Outline of the Chapter

Considering the relatively limited firsthand data available on people's tribunals, even in Chinese,[2] this chapter's main purpose is analytical and descriptive.

First, I argue that judges in China are not formally required to be independent if independence is understood as being guaranteed by the highest laws and entails that judges are individually free from the other branches of government as well as from political and social interests. Judicial independence is not officially prohibited or taboo, but the issue is so ambiguously tackled by political authorities that it is de facto unacceptable. Moreover, after the Sixteenth Party Congress in 2002 and under Hu Jintao's leadership, the judiciary as a whole, and more precisely courts of the "new socialist countryside" located in the Western, rural, or poor parts of the country have been assigned a new political role. They are now to contribute directly

[2] See, for example, Ding Wei, *Jiceng Sifa De Kunjing Jiqi Biange, Yi Qinzhen Renmin Fating De "Tebei Xietiaoyuan" Weili* [*Judicial Predicament and the Reform of Basic People's Courts: An Empirical Study on the Judicial Procedure*], vol. 2, (Beijing: China Legal Publishing House, 2007); Zhao Xiaoli, "Guanxi/Shijian, Xingdong Celue He Falu De Xushi" ["Relation/Event, Strategy of Action, and Narration of Law"], in *Xiangtu Shehui De Gongzheng, Zhixu Yu Quanwei* [*Justice, Order, and Authority of Rural Society*], (Beijing: China University of Political Science and Law Press, 1997); Wang Chenguang et al., *Nongcun Fazhi Xianzhuang, Laizi Qinghua Xuesheng De Shijiao* [*The Rule of Law in Rural Areas, In the Eyes of Tsinghua Students*], (Beijing: Social Sciences Academic Press China, 2006).

to social harmony and stability (hexie wending). Local justice is a key dimension of the authorities' objective to improve the quality of services in rural areas and to avoid open confrontation between citizens and the government.

Second, I show that, despite recent reforms, grassroots judges still work within the framework of the system of employment units typical of the collectivist and socialist legacy: the danwei. The court, as a work unit, is an institution that socially, politically, and culturally binds judges collectively to the CCP, the state, and the people. It provides them with a minimum "iron rice bowl" but is crucial to the implementation of government policy. In addition, the institution of the adjudicative committee (shenpan weiyuanhui) embeds judges more deeply in a collective system in which responsibility is shared and thus reduced.

Third, the extremely decentralized administration of the judiciary makes it harder for local judges to work independently. A significant number of ordinary courts are actually handicapped by the failure of local governments to provide adequate funding for the courts and judges with professional backgrounds. Also, the absence of vertical solidarities with upper level judges reinforces their dependence with local administrative systems. Strictly economic and social factors, such as a lack of prestige and decorum, tend to count for more than the political constraints of the one-party state. Nonetheless, the growing professionalization of the local judiciary and the policy of building new courts are contributing slowly to the affirmation of judges' dignity. A Goffmanian interpretive analysis of different aspects of the judges' interactions in their work places shows that new tribunals tend to produce new judicial rituals.[3] Accordingly, the way in which the judges in ordinary work situations present themselves and the ways in which they guide the impression they form of themselves will be analyzed.

Objective and knowledgeable judges in ordinary courts struggle to be more impartial notably by preferring alternative dispute resolution procedures such as judicial mediation or by emphasizing rational legal reasoning. This sort of mild activism on the part of judges is itself an outcome of their low financial status in contrast with their assigned political role.

Without causal factors external to the political system, the party's statist conception of the judiciary as an obedient agent of the administration is likely to remain unchanged. Nevertheless, the new national policy to recentralize local judicial funding paves the way for more financial independence at the microorganizational level.

The chapter concludes that in today's China, judicial independence cannot be an end in itself. Certain legal and ethical conditions must be realized so that judicial independence prohibits corruption rather than facilitating it. Moreover, the central state must be strong enough to guarantee a higher sense of dignity for grassroots judges.

---

[3] See Erving Goffman, *The Presentation of Self in Everyday Life* (New York: Doubleday, 1959).

Fieldwork and Methodology

Based on intensive fieldwork conducted mainly in Gansu and Shaanxi from mid-2005 to early 2009, this chapter focuses on the specific context of the governance of ordinary justice in China's basic people's courts (jiceng renmin fayuan) and basic people's tribunals (jiceng renmin fating). Despite recent growth, both provinces lag behind other parts of the country in terms of economic development. For 2007, Shaanxi's nominal GDP ranked twenty-second in China (equivalent to the Philippines) and twenty-sixth for Gansu (a level comparable with India).

People's tribunals are subdivisions of the county courts generally located in rural areas or semiurban districts. According to the Organic Law of Courts, this level represents the lowest of the four-tiered system of courts consisting of the national Supreme People's Court (SPC), provincial high courts, intermediate courts, and basic level courts. China counts approximately 3,130 basic people's courts and more than 12,000 basic people's tribunals. The latter have original jurisdiction over all civil, administrative, and criminal cases in a county except when the law provides otherwise.

In the course of China's legal metamorphosis since 1978, judicial reforms have mainly focused on national and provincial-level jurisdictions. Nevertheless, most litigation (almost 80 percent) occurs at the village and county levels, for the most part in the countryside where the fewest lawyers and professional judges are available.[4] Between 50 percent and 60 percent of the cases handled at this level involve divorce cases, domestic violence, traffic accidents, labor contract law issues, and criminal offences like murders, drug trade or trafficking, armed robbery; a further 25 percent to 30 percent involve land disputes. Within this, there are a growing number of cases dealing with defense of rights (weiquan).

Logically, a majority of Chinese judges are local judges from basic level courts. Most would describe themselves as a silent majority. In Shaanxi province, for example, in 2008 there were 11 intermediate courts, 109 basic courts and 394 basic tribunals. Of the 10,207 people working within the provincial judicial system, 5,913 were judges (almost 58 percent), 724 were "police law officers" (facha), and 2,222 were secretaries or clerks. More than 79 percent of the judges were local judges from intermediate courts and, mostly, basic courts.[5] In Gansu, similarly, 384 tribunals worked under the supervision of ninety-five basic courts and fifteen intermediate courts.

This chapter provides a portrait of more than ten basic people's tribunals located in China's colorful, culturally rich, if financially poor, and politically significant Western regions. As under Mao but for different reasons, Gansu, Shaanxi, and Sichuan provinces remain important experimental sites for the rural policy of the

---

[4] Zhu Jingwen ed., *Zhongguo Falü Fazhan Baogao (1979–2004)* [China Legal Development Report (1979–2004)], (Beijing: People's University Press: 2007), pp. 347–348.

[5] Situation of the whole provincial court system's personnel, inner Shaanxi courts' document, May 27, 2008. Documents not published.

current leadership called the "New Socialist Countryside Policy" (xin shehui zhuyi nongcun, hereafter NSCP). I witnessed numerous popular and judicial mediations as well as open trials in (mostly) civil, criminal, and administrative cases. As described elsewhere,[6] basic people's courts are staffed by thirty-five to sixty judges plus another 200–250 personnel. People's tribunals are run by one president, one vice president, one or two clerks or secretaries, as well as one or two additional judges. Based on the 2007 statistics, a people's tribunal in Shaanxi province, on average, is responsible for 78,000 inhabitants.[7]

During these years, I contacted hundreds of judges. Successive visits (including in other parts of China such as Beijing, Shanghai, Shenzhen, and Hebei province) were carried out for various purposes such as judges training programs, lectures in various local universities, research activities, and the task of "publicizing the law" (pufa).[8] The courts visited appeared to be quite typical of local courts in predominantly rural provinces such as Sichuan, Guizhou, Yunnan, Guangxi, or Anhui. This chapter does not purport to present results representative of all the 12,000 people's tribunals around the country.

The conditions and circumstances in which this research was made possible must be explained. First and foremost, the intellectual curiosity and support of certain grassroots judges themselves, including various court presidents and heads of political committees, have been decisive. The ethnographic methodology of this study required long and repeated stays. It allowed me to explain the academic purpose of the project, which was also supported by my status as a visiting professor at a prestigious law school in Beijing. I have always interacted with the judges in a way that they could themselves become active partners in this study. It required endless negotiations to make them accept that I needed to pay for my expenses or, conversely, that I would be honored to stay the night in the judges' dormitory. I did so several times, always accompanied by a female judge. Those "courageous acts" enabled me to gain the respect of the judges, who would then systematically mention to their colleagues how brave Western researchers are. Obviously, what was perceived as daring and brave was an invaluable opportunity to intimately experience the living conditions of grassroots judges. Respecting local customs of gift giving, I would take a lot of care choosing appropriate gifts for heads, deputy heads, clerks,

---

[6] Stéphanie Balme, "Ordinary Justice and Popular Constitutionalism in China," in Stéphanie Balme and Michael Dowdle eds., *Building Constitutionalism in China* (New York: Palgrave McMillan, 2009).

[7] Shaanxi Province High Court, "Statistics of the Shaanxi Basic People's Courts in 2006," (July 2007). The tribunal of Yin Town in the Changan District (Xian City) has a jurisdiction with the biggest population in the whole province, 909,500 inhabitants. The tribunal of Lianghe, in Shan county Ankang city has the smallest population with 38,000 inhabitants.

[8] See Stéphanie Balme and Wang Yaqin, *Ni Dui Falv Liaojie Duoshao* [*What do you know about Law and Justice?*], (Nanjing: Nanjing Normal University Press, 2009). Sponsored by CLD Beijing, this is a book to popularize legal knowledge and ideas of justice among Chinese children. Through drawings describing real-life scenarios, it explains in simple words judicial and legal procedures in China.

or other staff of the courts. Compared to the pressures and difficulties faced by the well-known filmmaker, Raymond Depardon, during his investigation of the ins and outs of the French judicial system,[9] I must acknowledge that I have generally been warmly welcomed and assisted in my research both in Shaanxi and in Gansu.[10]

I am aware, of course, that corrupt or unpleasant judges don't bother with academics. Some judges refused to allow me to attend court hearings despite their own superiors' endorsement. An interviewer remains dependent on the respondent's willingness to cooperate. An obvious limit is when one witnesses blatant corruption but is unable to further document it for lack of cooperation by the actors involved. Also, over time, few judges remained deeply interested in this research, leaving only a core group still willing to answer my awkward questions. Last but not least, this work has been facilitated because it focuses on distant areas where the usual sensitive questions raised by foreigners are not relevant. Locally, the potentially hot political issue of land expropriations challenges the local governments, not Beijing.

GRASSROOTS JUDGES BETWEEN SOCIALIST COLLECTIVISM AND LOCAL PROTECTIONISM

During a field trip in various Shaanxi courts in 2007, I organized a working visit for former Judge Garapon, general secretary of the Institut des Hautes Etudes sur la Justice (IHEJ) in Paris (see Chapter 3). Garapon delivered a speech to a large audience of mostly basic court judges. He decided to focus on the Outreau case, a devastating miscarriage of justice involving eighteen people accused of pedophilia, which occurred in France between 2000 and 2005 and ended with an extraordinary ad hoc parliamentary commission. What was intended as a public recognition of the victims' sufferings became a symbolic trial of the entire judicial system,[11] especially when Judge Burgaud refused to apologize, saying he was satisfied he had applied the letter of the law. Garapon characterized the appropriate relationship between judicial independence and accountability as "the stronger the former, the stronger should be the latter."

Following the lecture, a young judge stood up and wittily pointed out that if Chinese judges had to be accountable to a parliamentary commission each time

---

9 I have actually screened in Shaanxi some sequences of "Tenth District Court: Moments of Trials" to an audience of 300 judges and prosecutors in spring 2007. The commentaries that followed about the prestige of the Paris courtroom, the absence of policemen, the diversity of petty offenses, as well as the way the accused explain their side of the story or refuse to acknowledge their transgression to an experienced female judge, were very insightful.

10 Judges always insisted on welcoming me (using the official court automobile) upon my arrival at the airport or at the train station, for example.

11 The now famous Judge Burgaud had to swear in front of the Commission. His hearing was watched on TV by two-thirds of the adult population in France.

justice was denied, it would be impossible to manage and harmful to the political objective of social stability. On the contrary, he outlined that his profession in China was constitutionally under the scrutiny of local people's congresses (similar to a parliament). Substantially, his question was: Should the judiciary in China separate itself from such a strong link or does this supervision system (jiandu) ensure a judge's accountability? If so, is judicial accountability more important than judicial independence? During other meetings, notably with a local association of judges, the same hot issue of the relationship between independence and accountability was raised. Discussions showed that the issue of judicial independence was largely not viewed as a crucial step in the development of judicial professionalism. Also, it remained abstract and badly understood for a majority of judges and prosecutors both for reasons of legal culture and the nature of the political system.

"What Is Judicial Independence?" (Shenme shi sifa duli?)

Traditionally in Western civilization, the lady Justice is a goddess who holds three symbols: a sword depicting the court's coercive power, scales representing the weighing of competing claims, and a blindfold indicating impartiality. This last symbol is considered crucial. In China, the frightening animal of the cosmology who represents justice, xiezhi, expresses the value of impartiality in a rather different way. Xiezhi has a single horn and cleft-foot like a goat. The beast has the ability to discriminate between right and wrong, but it symbolizes a much more coercive approach to justice.[12] Under Qing rules of court, the robes worn by law superintendents and governmental censors were embroidered with the pattern of xiezhi as a badge of their duties. Today, xiezhi statues decorate the main hall of most of the newly built people's courts.

In socialist China, doctrinal foundations enshrined in superior laws do not provide a position of judicial independence to the judiciary. The Leninist conception of political institutions does not recognize the principle of separation of powers.[13] Contemporary ideology still does not meet the shared criteria of democratic rule of law states on the issue of judicial independence.[14] Relevant international conventions or treaties promulgated since 1945 all include the recognition of the independence

---

[12] Jonas Grimheden, *Themis v. Xiezhi: Assessing Judicial Independence in the People's Republic of China under International Human Rights Law* (Lund: Lund University, 2004).

[13] Xin Ren, Tradition of the Law and Law of the Tradition, Law, State, and Social Control in China (Santa Barbara: Greenwood Press, 1997), pp. 47–63; Margaret Y.K. Woo, "Adjudication Supervision and Judicial Independence in the P.R.C.," *The American Journal of Comparative Law*, vol. 39, p. 95 (1991); *Hikota* Koguchi, "Some Observations About 'Judicial Independence' in Post-Mao China," in R.H. Folsom and J.H. Minan eds., Law in the People's Republic of China (Boston: Brill, 1989), pp. 189–197.

[14] See Judicial Independence Minerva Research Group, "Documents under the auspices of governmental organizations," http://www.mpil.de/ww/en/pub/research/details/projects/minerva_jud_indep/intdocs.htm

of courts and of judges. The Universal Declaration of Human Rights (Art. 10), the International Covenant on Civil and Political Rights (Art. 14–1), the Universal Charter of the Judge, or the European Convention of Human Rights and Fundamental Freedoms (Art. 6), to name but a few, all recognize the absolute necessity to guarantee an independent and impartial trial to litigants through the independence of the courts (from the executive and the legislative power) and of judges (vis-à-vis internal hierarchies within the court system). In April 2003, the United Nations Commission on Human Rights brought "to the attention of Member States" the Bangalore principles of Judicial Conduct. In July 2006, the Economic and Social Council of the United Nations adopted a resolution in which it recognized the Bangalore Principles as complementary to, a further development of, the U.N. Basic Principles on the Independence of the Judiciary.[15]

Under the Chinese institutional framework, only the independence of courts and adjudicative committee are recognized. Yet both the independence of judges as a body and as individual judges is not clearly acknowledged in law. According to one commentator, "In the various versions of the People's Republic Constitutions, the judiciary has been a separate branch, but it is consistently treated as an ordinary state functionary fulfilling the role of 'proletarian dictatorship,' in parallel to the other functionaries that are primarily executive in nature, notably the public security [gongan] bureau and the procurator's [jiancha] office."[16]

The 1982 Constitution is essentially contradictory. On the one hand, it declares and ensures the supremacy of the ruling party. On the other hand, it proclaims that "judicial power should be exercised independently." Articles 126 and 128 are also confusing in nature. The first stipulates that "the people's courts (. . .) are not subject to interference by administrative organs, public organizations or individuals." Yet Article 128 stipulates that: "The Supreme People's Court is responsible to the National People's Congress and its standing committee. Local people's courts at different levels are responsible to the organs of state power which created them."[17] Moreover, the CCP is primarily responsible for initiating major political and legal reform activities. When they are party members, judges are subject to party discipline and the party secretary of the political and legal committee [zhengfa weiyuanhui], which supervises their judicial reward and punishment.

---

[15] Transparency International, Global Corruption Report 2007: Corruption in Judicial Systems (Cambridge: Cambridge University Press, 2007).

[16] Zhang Qianfan, Zhuanxingzhong De Renmin Fayuan: Zhongguo Sifa Gaige Zhanwang" ["The People's Court in Transition: The Prospects of the Chinese Judicial Reform"], *Journal of Contemporary China*, vol. 12, p. 69 (2003).

[17] Articles 131 and 133, which apply to Supreme People's Procuratorate (SPP), take the same approach. The SPP is responsible to the NPC and its Standing Committee. Local people's procuratorates at different levels are responsible to the organs of state power at the corresponding levels that created them and to the people's procuratorates at the higher level. Yet, "the people's procuratorates shall, in accordance with the law, exercise procuratorial power independently and are not subject to interference by administrative organs, public organizations or individuals."

Besides, the general provisions of the Judges' Law (2001) clearly asserts that people's courts should "independently exercise judicial authority according to law," which may be interpreted to mean that judicial power is restricted to judicial authority and also that courts rather than individual judges are deemed to be independent. The notion of judicial authority is related to the constitutional theory of most civil law countries, including socialist states. Their institutional framework is a mixed product of Locke and Montesquieu, Rousseau and Lenin's writings on the separation of powers. For Rousseau, citizens must be put under the charge of a general will, which is not reached through the separation of powers but through a sovereign legislative power. This implies a restrictive conception of the judiciary. Justice as a nonelected body is of a different nature than executive and legislative powers. Also, being the only power that can deprive people of their freedom, the judiciary cannot be assimilated to the others. In continental rule of law countries, there now prevails a flexible separation of powers where two constitutional powers (executive and legislative) cohabit with one constitutional authority (the judiciary). Whereas such a doctrine may guarantee the independence of the judiciary under a democratic rule, it might also create the conditions of its subordination because the judiciary cannot access the status of a third power but only of a public service.

"Court Is Just Like a Swill Barrel!" (Ganshui Tong)

Although not officially prohibited, judicial independence in China is de facto unacceptable. Notably, basic level judges address these issues more openly than the political sphere. The institutional channels for political interference are many. The method of nominating and appointing judges reflects their institutional dependence. Not only are local judges elected, appointed, and removed by local people's congresses, they are paid by local governments, and a large majority of them are members of the ruling party. Due to China's overall institutional design, the dependence of the Chinese judiciary on internal and external pressures at the local level is perceived as almost absolute by many of the actors themselves.

The phenomenon of local protectionism, where local court judges render judgments that favor local parties and interests, has been denounced by the judicial system itself. Over the years, the political–legal committee and the SPC have taken various measures to address this phenomenon. Nonetheless, as Chen Jianfu observes: "Local judicial protectionism is no more than an extension or a different form of interference by local administrative and party authorities."[18]

As expressed by a local judge on an Internet forum in 2007: "The court is just like a 'swill barrel' in which the conflicts of society, like garbage, are stuffed. It is the judge who is responsible for mixing them to balance law, society, and politics well."

---

[18] See Jianfu Chen et al. eds., *Implementation of Law in the People's Republic of China* (The Hague/Boston/London: Kluwer Law International, 2002), p. 100.

Petty ideological interferences with judicial work at various levels are a daily practice. Party and government officials who give doctrinal instructions are a reality. For
example, the slogan prior to the Olympics of the "three top priorities" (i.e., "giving
utmost priority to the party's work, the people's interests, the constitution, and the
law") was seriously studied within the local courts following a discourse by the head
of the central legal–political committee and politburo member Zhou Yongkang.

At the same time, judges' fidelity to the CCP should not be overstated or misun-
derstood. Membership in the CCP is not necessary to become a local judge or to
work as a civil servant. In addition, due to the high level of knowledge now required
to be a judge and/or a party member, one finds new judges and party members are
more educated and enlightened than court users including democratically elected
village leaders.

Considering their potential legitimacy, one would assume that village leaders'
level of rights consciousness would be high.[19] In practice, this is often not so. In
interviews, local judges have often expressed concern about the principle of village
self-government (cunmin zizhi) and its compatibility with local government power.
On one hand, courts must guarantee the constitutional principle of villagers' self-
government as well as their legitimate rights. At the same time, they shall protect
the rights of individuals when they are infringed upon by this principle. Judicial
mediations or trials of unfair land compensation cases are usually tense, particularly
when they involve collective actions. Villager committee members often refuse to
even participate or appear in court. Judges then criticize plaintiffs for having elected
committee members who are ignorant of law. The rudeness of village committee
members is illustrated by insults to the judges or pressures through the local government authorities to decide the ruling to their own advantage. As these cases
demonstrate, the juridification of cases involving fundamental rights at the local
level can give a much more activist shape to basic-level justice.

"Judges Are Those Who Eat at the People's Table!"

Besides political interventions, interference with judicial work by individuals who
have money and power is widespread at the local level. Local judges lack prestige and
social visibility. Therefore they are weak in standing up to such pressures. During
trials or even mediations, litigants can be openly aggressive, rude, or indifferent. It is
not rare to observe local folks sitting informally on the judge's bench, joking prior to
their arrival, or for judges to shout at parties, demanding to be shown more respect.
I have witnessed farmers offending judges by calling them "the poor guys who have
to eat at the table of ordinary people."

---

[19] Because the NPC passed the Organic Law of Villagers' Committees in 1986, local elections are
considered as a means to increase the accountability and legitimacy of local leaders as well as
implement "socialist democracy."

Once, the judges of a tribunal asked me to accompany them to visit a rich director of a private company who had been accused by his workers of pressuring them not to go to court even for civil disputes. The director imposed instead, in the pure Maoist tradition, a popular mediation system within the factory. The judges' mission was to convince the director to let the workers access formal judicial procedures. The man had cleverly arranged a lunch meeting. During an endless and sensational banquet, the company's boss insulted the poor condition of judges, encouraging them to seize the opportunity "to eat enough to be full." The long discussion in his office involved a series of sarcastic remarks about judges' poverty, incompetence, and corruption. Yet, if they would need any help, he would be delighted to use his connections if necessary. Back in the car, I hesitated to break the heavy atmosphere and asked the judges whether they felt their mission had been successful. One lady judge expressed her anger and frustration to see "local judges deprived of any basic face and honor."

Undoubtedly, local judges in China have a fragile status as they are intended to be the defenders of the people before the state as well as defenders of the state before the people. Their main weakness is to work within a system that combines an extremely decentralized administration in terms of daily management of the judiciary with a centralized legal system where national laws are abstract and local specificities given short shrift. As civil servants, they are supposed to work all their life in their danwei. Although judges are not often dismissed, they are often relocated from one court or tribunal to another depending on workloads and administrative needs. In addition, given the high number of clerks and secretaries within each province, the potential pool of staff is large enough not to be constrained by the decision to remove a judge from a given jurisdiction. In the courts visited, some judges had been removed from office for abuse of power, petty bribery, or both, whenever they lacked of solid networks to survive in the system.

A New Judiciary for the Sake of Social Harmony

As civil servants, Chinese judges, the vast majority of whom are party members, are accustomed and inclined to political mobilization as they have never been socialized to the figure of the neutral judge.[20] Basic people's courts and tribunals still fulfill various political and societal functions, such as publicizing party policies, assembling people to perform collective tasks, or teaching law. Based on a similar investigation in the 1990s, Zhao Xiaoli reached the conclusion that judges working at the people's tribunals displayed two faces: "On the one hand, they functioned as judges by settling various disputes and, on the other, they participated in law enforcement of local governments, such as directly taking part in the collection of bank loans,"[21] which may undermine judicial independence.

---

[20] Ren, *The Tradition of the Law and Law of the Tradition.*
[21] Wang et al., *Rule of Law.*

The political mobilization of judges might still occur today. Nonetheless, their official tasks are more legally oriented because access to justice at the local level became a priority of the state and the top leadership under Hu Jintao. Causes include rising social unrest due to injustices in the countryside and the high number of petitioners in Beijing. Since 2000, one of the main features of social unrest in rural areas has been people's anger at local governments.

In October 2005, the SPC enacted Second Five-year Reform Agenda of People's Courts (2004–2008), which listed more than fifty targets including administration and institutional reforms at the local level.[22] Then, in May 2006, a new decision was issued on Further Improving the Work of People's Courts and People's Procuratorates. As Xiao Yang, then president of the SPC, explained in 2006, "Judicial system reform is considered an important action for implementing the strategy of the rule of law, an important part of the political system reform, and an important aspect of improving the party's leadership competence . . . and developing socialist democratic politics." The document stipulates that "as part of the political reform, the reform of people's courts is, to a large extent, a political act." The report clearly states that: "The key tasks of the cause of socialism with Chinese characteristics in the first two decades of the 21st century are building a well-off society in an all-round way, developing the socialist market economy, socialist democracy and an advanced socialist culture, and constructing a socialist harmonious society." The report added: "The people's courts are an important part of the state apparatus and their primary task is to serve the overall objective of the country."[23]

In light of a growing number of disputes involving land expropriation, labor laws, or abuse of power, the central government has enacted ambitious policies regarding the countryside, as illustrated by the 2002 Rural Land Contracting Law, the Property Law, and the Collectively-Owned Construction Land Document, both issued in 2007. Usually, experts favor such laws because they aim to protect peasants from blunt violations by officials and strengthen their land tenure by prohibiting urban dwellers from purchasing so-called minor property right houses. Yet the laws and regulations are not always implemented, and court judgments are often not enforced.

To address issues of social stability and economic growth in rural areas, the top leadership has promoted the "New Socialist Countryside Policy (NSCP)." It is not totally a new concept as it combines long-term objectives such as the government's vision for the countryside in 2020 with a decisive immediate task: stability and prosperity. This "New Deal"-type policy has three main goals: increase rural incomes

---

[22] The first one was enacted in 1999 for the period of 1999–2003.

[23] Xiao Yang, "Shenru Xuexi Guanche Zhongyang Jueding, Jinyibu Jiaqiang Renmin Fayuan Gongzuo, Tuijin Renmin Fayuan Shiye Quanmian Fazhan" ["Studying and Implementing the Central Committee's Decision Intensively and Improving the Work of People's Courts for the All-round Development of the Cause of People's Courts"], People's Court, June 30, 2006.

(by investing in both agricultural and nonagricultural sectors), diminish farmers' financial burden, and establish a welfare system in the countryside. In sharp contrast with previous periods of the open-door era, the NSCP intends to be comprehensive and introduce a new way of considering rural issues.

In February 2006, the Opinions of the Central Committee of the CCP and the State Council on Promoting the Building of a New Socialist Countryside stated that the main goals were to promote a better balance between economic and social development and to narrow the economic gap between rural and urban areas. The opinions called for "a socialist society that is democratic and law-based." This program must be understood as the symbol of Hu Jintao's objective to build a harmonious society (hexie shehui) in the countryside. It calls for "building the countryside into areas characterized by well-off living standards, improving party development in a coordinated matter, promoting grassroots political democracy as enshrined in the constitution, promoting scientific planning, and providing social justice."[24]

Judges have been asked to contribute to this policy. The officials in charge of the judicial reforms stated that the court system should abide by the following core principles: upholding the CCP leadership and adhering to the people's congress system, which means that "the people's courts are accountable to and under the supervision of the National People's Congress" (NPC). Court reforms should be conducive "to improving and tightening the supervision of the NPC on the judicial organs . . . and advocating the unification of socialist legal system."[25]

Officials responsible for this policy insist that the reform should be carried out promptly and implemented from top to bottom: "The situation of 'each doing what he thinks is right' is not acceptable." Instead of a means of proletariat dictatorship as it used to be, judicial work has become "a basic means of punishing crimes, protecting citizens' rights and solving social conflicts."

Shaanxi and Gansu provinces are important sites for Hu Jintao's program. Under its auspices, the central government has already promoted the provision of more adequate and professional legal services in these rural areas. Between 2006 and 2009, the drastic reduction of litigation fees, the building of new courts, a growing acceptance of women farmers' discrimination cases, better training of local judges, and new slogans like "bringing judges closer to the citizens (faguan weimin)" and "justice for the people (sifa weimin)" have shown the key role judges play in the implementation of the NSCP.

[24] "Zhonggong Zhongyang Guowuyuan Guanyu Tuijin Shehuizhuyi Xinnongcun Jianshe De Ruogan Yijian" ["Opinions of the Central Committee of the CCP and the State Council on Promoting the Building of a New Socialist Countryside"], speech by Chen Xiwen, Deputy Director of the Office of Central Financial Work Leading Group, CCP Central Committee policy paper, N.1, 2006.

[25] Shen Deyong, Xinshiqi Zhongguo Sifa Gaige Jincheng ["On the Advance of China's Judicial Reform in the New Period"], *The People's Judicature*, vol. 6 (2004).

THE JUDGES' POLITICAL AND PROFESSIONAL CONDITION
AT THE GRASSROOTS LEVEL

The local judicial system was redesigned in the 1980s after the reforms of the 1940s "Ma Xiwu adjudication system," named after a CCP high cadre who invented a mode of dispatching itinerant tribunals to hear cases on the spot.

The People's Tribunal, an Institution that Binds Judges

According to Ma Xiwu, local judges were supposed to litigate anywhere, and especially outside of courtrooms. They would be average citizens, holding the same status and legal knowledge as court users. Unsurprisingly, it led to many instances of injustice, not to mention that during the repeated Maoist campaigns and until the beginning of the open-door policy, people's courts were designed as one of the most efficient repressive tools of the party–state's revolutionary policy. After the 1950s rightist rectification campaigns purged the judiciary of its best elements, courts were mainly run by military judges ignorant about law.

Since the 1950s and 1960s, the people's tribunals have been designed with one main room (the courtroom itself) and two or more small offices where local judges lived more or less permanently. Minimum facilities such as a bed, a water pot, a coal heater, food, legal books and some official newspapers, the CCP charter, and the state constitution, as well as more recently a secondhand computer, were usually provided. Because of local traditions that require guests be received in the main room of the house where relatives usually live, not to mention the need to reduce court administration fees, judicial mediations generally occurred in the judge's office (hence his/her bedroom). Official judgments and collective cases took place within the official courtroom. Such intimate conditions affected legal procedures and their contents.

Since 1978, the overall picture of the basic-level jurisdiction has changed dramatically enough that the Ma Xiwu system can be largely considered history. In 2002, a journalist from Shaanxi CCTV filmed a documentary about the life of a ruined and crippled farmer who decided to divorce his wife to give her and their daughter the opportunity to change their destiny and escape from a miserable life. The documentary shows a squadron of four local judges walking on the village's only red soil road carrying in a revolutionary style a desk and courts' official insignia along with the country's red flag. Another famous movie released in 2003 of a traveling law court in far-off Yunnan province, *Courthouse on Horseback*,[26] considered in Western countries one of the best movies on China's judicial system, is actually largely outdated. It shows the life of poor judges, virtuous cadres faithful to the CCP,

---

[26] Liu Jie, "Ma Bei Shang De Fa Ting," *Southern Weekly*, August 14, 2003.

who carry from villages to remote counties the court symbol on a tired horse to rule simple civil cases.

Those movies no longer represent the conditions of a growing majority of rural districts where an active policy of judicial modernization takes place. For instance, official reports state that "over 70% of courts across the country renovated or built office buildings, trial courtrooms and people's courtrooms since 2000. People's courts' conditions for trial and office work have greatly improved."[27] Most of the oldest local tribunals visited in Shaanxi and Eastern Gansu in 2005 and 2006 had been either destroyed and rebuilt by early 2009 or are in the process of being rebuilt.

Yet, in the fancy new courts and tribunals of China's countryside, one can still observe the remaining legacy of the Ma Xiwu style. For example, local residents – or village committee members – would insist on meeting the judges personally and, in some cases, offer gifts (such as cigarettes, expensive wines, banquets, and cash) and pay tribute to ensure their cases won't be ignored. Dormitories are still provided so judges can live at the court like in a danwei. Also they may offer better living conditions than judges' own private housing. In addition, there are no fixed working hours, which would imply a strict separation between private and public life. The contemporary use of the word adjudicator (shenpanyuan) instead of judge (faguan) is also a legacy from this period. Although the Judges' Law has made the use of the term judge official,[28] local citizens continue to call them adjudicators simply because it is what appears on the court desk. The word judge is also not mentioned in court judgments. During mediations, ordinary citizens use other terms to designate the judge responsible for their cases: lüshi (literally "master of law," the word for lawyer), ganbu (cadre), tongzhi (comrade), or kinship terms such as uncle, elder brother, aunt or elder sister, reflecting Chinese tradition. Lastly, local judges are still called to join the so-called popularization of law activities (pufa huodong). This is similar to Ma Xiwu's campaign to "send law to the countryside" (songfa xiaxiang). However, whereas judges locally still use the politically meaningful term of yundong (campaign or movement), popular under Mao, they are asked today to use the word huodong (activity) instead. Nowadays a relaxed atmosphere prevails (to a certain extent it might turn out to be a leisurely break for judges). However, to an external observer, the general philosophy largely remains the same. The doctrine is still to train the masses how to obey the law and fulfill their duties. Extremely formal legal speeches are delivered to huge audiences without giving the opportunity of a dialogue and asserting the idea that law is also a set of rights.

[27] Xiao Yang, "Renmin Fayuan Shiye Zai Buduan Fazhan Jinbu" ["Progress of the Cause of People's Courts"], *The People's Courts*, Jan. 6, 2006, p. 2.
[28] Article 2 defines judges (faguan) as "judicial personnel who exercise the judicial authority of the state according to law, including presidents, vice presidents, members of judicial committees, chief judges and associate chief judges of divisions, judges and assistant judges of the Supreme People's Court, local people's courts at various levels and special people's courts such as military courts."

A local judge still has a broader definition than in the contemporary Western conception. It designates someone who decides cases but also someone who manages internal court affairs. According to the law, the duty of judging is to take part in a trial within a collegial panel (heyi ting) or in certain circumstances to try a case alone (duren shenpan). Therefore, similar to the former planned socialist economic system, at the local level judges are both dependent on their danwei (the court) and protected by it. The inner court system based on the principle of the separation between the trial and the final decision (shenpan fenli) institutionalizes the fact that adjudicators seldom are in a situation to be individually accountable. The trial function is exercised by the shenpan zhang or trial head and one (or two) trial members (shenpan yuan) under the guidance of the presidents of the tribunal or the court and the chief of a particular division when there is one. In practice, the head of the court is too busy to try cases, whereas trials are part of the daily life of a head of tribunal.

Judges ultimately may not decide their cases and, conversely, those who finally decide their case may not have tried it. The system of adjudicative committees (shenpan weiyuanhui), generally used only for sensitive, significant, or difficult cases at the local level, is well described by Zhang Qianhan: "The hearing judges would report the facts of the case and their tentative decision to this committee to get its approval. The decision of the committee must also be approved by the head of the division and then the president of the court. For important or sensitive cases, a common decision would be discussed by people at many different levels: a panel of judges who actually tried the case, the trial committee (which usually did not try the case), the committee of the division to which the case belonged, and the administrative heads of the court."[29] As a consequence, Zhang notes, a judge is obliged "by his self interest to obey ranks and status rather than the voice of reason and law" and "become[s] little more than a bureaucratic clerk." According to court rules, court presidents have one vote like the other members. Yet, as the head of the court sits automatically on adjudicative committee, to the regular judges, he or she holds power of decision on literally every case. "This automatically alters our feeling of being independent," argued a judge during an interview. Judgments are never pronounced publicly, affecting their genuine independence. Litigants receive the ruling a couple of weeks after the trial or the mediation once it has been decided by the adjudicative committee.

In the new courts visited in Gansu or Shaanxi, an electronic surveillance system has been set up. Court presidents are proud to show their sophisticated "American-style video system." As one judge proudly declared, "I can check instantly different trials at the same time and from my desk. I can intercept on the spot potential wrong-doings in court." In response to my remark that such modern equipment could also alter judges' autonomy, he explained that its main purpose was "to better

---

[29] Zhang, "The People's Court in Transition."

train the judges, like coaches do with sportsmen... Important cases were decided by the adjudicative committee anyway... Modern technology was simply a way to save time and guarantee more transparency."

Whereas the SPC's first five-year reform agenda in 1999 sought to enhance personal independence of the judges, the adjudicative committee system was preserved. Its role was intended to be limited to "studying the problems with fundamental and systematic impact in the trial work and only provide authoritative guidance." In reality, at the local level, the system keeps young and professional judges in a situation of childish servitude.

As explained in an important article by Li Yuwen, Article 13 of the Judges' Code of Conduct[30] requires that "a judge may not comment on cases being handled by other judges and may not give suggestions or opinions on cases in which his interests are involved; he may not ask about or interfere in cases that are being handled by lower courts; and he may not offer personal opinions to the higher court for cases at second instance."[31] Article 14 requires that a judge, except in exercising his adjudication or management duty, may not ask for information about cases handled by other judges.

How Can Ordinary Judges Establish a Profession?

One of the most difficult issues for Chinese judges is to differentiate their areas of competence from those of other legal and administrative actors and therefore their own identity. Not only are judges called adjudicators, they are also simply referred to as "staff members of the courts" (fayuan gongzuo renyuan) or "courts cadres and police personnel of courts" (fayuan gancha). Since the 1950s and until the adoption of the judges' robe, an adjudicator looked just like a police or a military officer. Official court automobiles are still symbolically similar to public security ones. They are of the same shape and color with the only difference being the mention of the word court (fayuan) on one side. Local judges admitted that they had never considered that it might be confusing for citizens. Most even thought the confusion might help them in imposing respect for the law.

Today, at the local level in Gansu and Shaanxi, only during important trials do judges wear a robe, which they share with others. Their daily outfit is a dark blue or black Western suit (including for women) during the autumn and winter seasons and a dark grey Mao style suit during summer and spring. In the courtroom, if judges do not wear their professional robe but the dark suit outfit, it is impossible for litigants to distinguish them from the prosecutor. The new official red and gold insignia of

---

[30] Issued by the SPC in October 2001, the code contains fifty articles, divided under the headings of six basic principles: judicial impartiality, judicial efficiency, integrity of judges, judicial decorum, the self-improvement of judges, and the restriction of extrajudicial activities.

[31] Li Yuwen, *Professional Ethics of Chinese Judges* (Hong Kong: French Centre for Research on Contemporary China, 2006).

the Chinese judiciary is their only distinguishable symbol from other civil servants, although it still looks like the symbol of the NPC.

The administrative decentralization of the judicial system is designed in such a way that local judges cannot build vertical solidarities with upper level judges. In the absence of professional cooperation or professional consciousness, dependence on local authorities also prevents them from building institutionalized horizontal solidarities. Collective mobilization of the judges to defend their status or working conditions is almost impossible. Associations of judges at the national level (such as the Women Judges Association) hold neither legitimacy nor power. Each intermediate court is supposed to have a judges association. Yet, deprived of an independent budget, they barely manage to organize more than one or two conferences a year for their colleagues. Not surprisingly given these conditions, willingness for judicial reforms is witnessed through individual efforts and commitments more than judges' collective enterprises. Also, networking and mobilizing through the Internet appears much more powerful than any existing association of judges.

I have argued elsewhere that to compensate for shortcomings in the system, competent and committed judges may favor alternative dispute resolution procedures like judicial mediation.[32] Mediations allow judges to solve a case without external interferences. Mediations are much less bureaucratic and scripted. Judges and parties frequently engage in spontaneous, vigorous, and dramatic debates. One-third of the mediation process is often devoted to exploring orally the personal backgrounds and experiences of people involved. Whereas tribunal judges still ask particularly fragile plaintiffs to control their emotion, tears, expressions of anger, and other kinds of emotive appeals are generally acceptable during mediations. When judges empathize with certain litigants, tribunal-based mediation can be a popular form of adjudication among grassroots judges. They can personalize their decisions and promote their professionalized independence in a way they cannot during trials, and indeed it is often unclear whether these judges are using individual virtue or moral standards (daode) as a substitute for law. Mediated settlements may also be easier to enforce than court judgments. On the other hand, mediation can also open the door to coercion and corruption.

QUALIFICATIONS AND PRESTIGE

Often accused of protectionism, ignorance, and corruption by the general public, grassroots judges often feel slighted by colleagues in higher level courts. Nevertheless, it is not true anymore that almost anyone can become a judge. Judicial performance and judicial independence are interdependent phenomena. The professionalization of the judiciary contributes to its growing independence toward local powers, albeit only to a certain extent.

[32] Balme, "Ordinary Justice."

The quality of the large local judiciary is not as low as it used to be, although it remains uneven. The Judges Law amended in 2001 raised the qualifications bar for all judges by requiring them to have a college degree and pass a national examination. In October 2007, a notice was issued to all local courts forcing everyone working in the courts that had not passed the entrance examination for government employees or party and political institutions (dangzheng jiguan) (which have little to do with judicial work) to take the exam promptly. The grade of the government employee and the result of the exam affect a judge's salary. Those who failed would only be given one more chance to pass. Court presidents fully endorsed this professionalization policy.

However, they were also aware of the extreme difficulty of retaining young and well-trained judges in the countryside or in district areas where the work is both demanding and poorly compensated. Turnover remains high in part because judges are often sent for training to places where they do not want to be. Qualified judges who stay tend to be either passive or highly committed, or in some cases judges are being punished by court leadership. In 2008, the judiciary hoped to take advantage of the global economic crisis to attract young law graduates who failed to find jobs in the private sector.

The number of university graduates is steadily increasing, yet the percentage holding law degrees is still less than 50 percent. Data collected from the last available yearbook of Shaanxi Judgments (published in 1997) already show an evolution toward professionalization:[33] in 1990, only 29.4 percent of the 7,909 Shaanxi court staff, working in 118 courts and 648 tribunals, were junior college graduates; in 1996, 85 percent were. Between 1991 and 1996, 25 percent of the already appointed provincial judicial staff had received intensive undergraduate law training at local university law schools (mainly Northwestern University of Political Science and Law[34]) or within the courts.

Interestingly, in the courts visited a large proportion of presidents, because of their age, were former soldiers trained within the court in the 1990s. They are expected to retire around the year 2015. Their reputation is usually low among younger and better-trained judges. The following comment on one judge's forum in May 2007 is insightful: "Our new court president used to work in the Public Security Bureau. Faithful to this working style, he promised to the high court that we will enforce 100 percent of the judgments and close 100 percent of all cases this year otherwise the head of the enforcement division will be removed from office. This announcement has panicked all of us. The other reason is that we need more training about the new laws and regulations that have been promulgated recently."

---

[33] Yearbook of Judgment of Shaanxi Province: Judges' educational level, Shaanxi Shenpan Nianjian Zhengli: Faguan Wenhua Suzhi.

[34] The president is an open-minded scholar whose classmates at the beginning of the open-door policy were law students. They are now courts presidents and prosecutors spread over the whole province.

As in many civil law countries, Chinese courts do not possess the power to interpret laws or administrative regulations. The former rests with the NPC and the latter with the issuing agency. Article 64 of the Legislation Law (lifafa), promulgated in 2000, specifies that local rules and regulations conflicting with national law are invalid. However, the law does not provide an effective enforcement mechanism. Instead, the law rather weakly suggests that local legislatures and agencies should abolish any offending rules. This particularly affects the delivery of justice at the grassroots level.[35] In 2003 there was the famous case of the young female judge, Li Huijuan, from the Luoyang Municipal Intermediate People's Court in Henan. She nearly lost her job for declaring in a civil case that provisions of certain local regulations were invalid due to their conflict with national law.

Local rural judges are often called "basket judges" (lanzi faguan) or "generalist judges" (zonghexing faguan) as they have to preside over a full spectrum of legal issues rather than being able to specialize in particular kinds of cases as common in more urban courts. They also interact with grassroots lawyers who are not properly trained legal professionals.

In addition, the quasijury system involving one citizen assessor on the collegial panel and two judges remains in its infancy. Together with some local judges, we designed a questionnaire in 2007 for people's juries. Although the official reports stipulate that more than 270,000 citizen assessors participated in local tribunals in China in 2005,[36] our goal was to know what exactly their roles were within local judiciary. Our results show that with the exception of one case in three years, their role has been purely symbolic.

Professionalism and transparency are both an objective and a precondition for the independence of the judiciary. Therefore, lack of professionalism and the absence of independence are in a systemic relation. Corruption and lack of professionalism are the main impediments to effective reform, whereas the lack of independence is a main obstacle to the eradication of corruption and professional mediocrity.

REFORMING THE GOVERNANCE OF THE JUDICIARY

In terms of constraints and independence, contemporary grassroots justice in China shares common features with France's Ancien Régime. Meanwhile, in part for historical reasons described in relation to Ma Xiwu's system, there is no such thing as a local elite of legal professionals, and hence no social reproduction of a group like the "nobility of the gown" (noblesse de robe) prior to 1789. Most grassroots judges currently have neither the social resources nor the economic capital or long-established professional background to act fully independently.

---

[35] Balme, "Ordinary Justice."
[36] Renmin Wang, April 30, 2005.

The Iron Rice Bowl

Judges are paid as other civil servants according to a strictly hierarchical scale. The basic salaries of judges of the same rank are supposedly the same throughout China, although the reality is very different. Differences in remuneration lie in additional benefits, the amounts of which vary but are directly proportional to the standard of living of the locality in which the court is situated. For example, certain local governments guarantee their judges a free housing package whereas others do not or simply cannot. Yet, whatever compensation is provided, a judge's financial dependence on local government is still absolute as the purpose of the new policy to decentralize courts' funding is only to compensate courts for the loss of revenue to the reduction in litigation fees. Whether the funds will be adequate to pay directly their salaries to judges to ensure their economic independence remains to be seen.

Faithful to Ma Xiwu's principles, grassroots judges come from the grassroots. The social proximity between judges and litigants is particularly striking in court. Neither the judges' salaries nor their living conditions differentiate them from average citizens in the countryside. In Shaanxi and Gansu in late 2008, basic judges' salaries ranged from RMB 900 to 1,500 monthly without including housing compensation and a subsidy for children, which average RMB 90 per month but can be as high as RMB 150 per month. According to Shaanxi province's employment bureau, in 2005 the average monthly salary of a state-owned enterprise's worker was RMB 1,268. Yet in both provinces, a few tribunals could not even provide full salaries to judges for several months. Judges regularly complain about their low wages on BBS forums.[37]

Social proximity between judges and citizens can lead to unexpected results such as certain empathy toward weak parties and a growing recognition of victims' rights.[38] On the other hand, it can contribute to corruption.

Interestingly, when grassroots judges are not paid, the courts have few means to address the problem. Judges associations are powerless. The party committee may refuse to become involved, claiming separation between party and government. Nor can the local people's congress exert pressure on the local government. Simply put, the problems are most likely to be addressed when the court president has good relations with the local government.

The economic analysis of corruption stresses that people tend to respond to incentives. Low compensation and weak monitoring systems are traditionally considered the main causes of corruption. Conversely, organizational changes and salary increases tend to lead to more and better enforcement of anticorruption rules.[39] The anthropologist Marcel Henaff shows how money is a means to gain social recognition

---

[37] See, for instance, BBS of Fazhi Luntan, http://bbs.chinacourt.org.
[38] Balme, "Ordinary Justice."
[39] Edgardo Buscaglia "Corruption and Judicial Reform in Latin America," *Policy Studies Journal*, vol. 17.4, p. 273 (1997).

and authority. Contrary to the idea that money corrupts, Henaff demonstrates that the lack of money corrupts even more.[40]

In the case of Chinese local tribunals, inadequate salaries and the lack of transparency in the management of funds have led to institutionalized corruption. A significant number of local judges are also kept busy with extrajudicial activities because they are directly or indirectly involved in small businesses (usually together with relatives) such as restaurants or shops. In light of the low salaries of judges, such behavior is only punished when carried to an extreme. Interestingly, the Judges' Code of Conduct does not provide an exhaustive list of extrajudicial activities. Although judges are requested to report their property, this system is poorly implemented at the local level. In the tribunals visited, none of the judges had ever officially declared assets. Most acknowledged that petty financial judicial bribery is common, although they pointed out that basic level courts mainly handle small-scale cases generating small amounts of money. From their perspective, the higher in the hierarchy, the more corrupt the system can be. As Keith Henderson has pointed out, judges' disclosure of assets and incomes alone, "without public access or oversight or fair and effective enforcement, will likely have limited impact."[41]

Following is an excerpt from the diary of a female judge, vice president of the civil division of a court in Shaanxi. Although from a simple family background, she holds a university degree. What follows sheds light on ordinary life in people's tribunals:

> Although I am not a permanent working staff of this tribunal, I found its aging president somewhat dependent on me. He would ask for advice when he encounters difficulties during work or doesn't know how to solve a case. It was really a hard time for him when the litigation fees were reduced after the April 1, 2007 regulation. The tribunal's income decreased in such a way that our monthly allowance of RMB 400 was cancelled. People felt bad in their lives especially because simultaneously they had much more work to do. . . . Three staff members will be leaving soon. X refused to work on the new cases assigned by our chief because he needs time to prepare for the national judicial examination. Y is in a very bad physical condition. As for me, I have finished my internship in a basic jurisdiction and do not wish to stay. Only two permanent staff members will remain including the current vice-president. Though responsible and hard-working, she is more suitable for an urban life. Her low salary as a basic court's judge can not satisfy her life style. Therefore she is now running a teahouse with a friend. As she has put all her savings into this business, she has to put her energy into it as well. Because of this well-known situation, she will not be promoted to a higher level but, at least, the court provides her with an iron rice bowl. Anyway, she had told the chief she did not want to be promoted and was not expecting anything from her job at the tribunal. She will complete her cases on time. But she said, "I want to live a decent life, which is far away from

[40] Henaff Marcel, *Le Prix de la Vérité: Le Don, l'Argent, la Philosophie* (Paris: Seuil, 2002).
[41] "Asset and Income Disclosure for Judges: An Overview of the Issues with a Checklist," http://siteresources.worldbank.org/INTLAWJUSTINST/Resources/IncomeAssetDisclosure.pdf.

being a local judge. So please don't expect much from me. I will only work three days a week. That is all I can contribute." Both the chief and I felt very sorry about her attitude.[42]

Both in Gansu and Shaanxi, the court officials responsible for the disciplinary work did not consider their work that of an ethics committee. Judges' work evaluations seldom involve an ethical evaluation. Nonetheless, in 2007 and 2008 internal court examinations to recruit new judges focused on respect of judicial etiquette because they have observed that a lack of judicial rituals and traditions in court procedure contributes to their lack of credibility. According to the Code of Conduct, judges should not smoke, drink, or use their mobile phone in court. They shall use civilized language and comply with standards in their actions. Actually, in almost all people's tribunals the air is suffocating from heavy smoking, and mobile phones ring during trials simply because judges share the same lifestyle as the litigants. As such, they are closer to the Yamen offices in the Qing dynasty but without the formal decorum.[43]

Erving Goffman explains that "when an individual plays a part he implicitly requests his observers to take seriously the impression that is fostered before them. They are asked to believe that the character they see actually possesses the attributes he appears to possess, that the task he performs will have the consequences that are implicitly claimed for it." His observation is useful in understanding local level judges' nascent professional culture in China. The former Ma Xiwu style of people's tribunals nurtured professional disengagement. New courts may create the conditions for what Goffman identifies as "things that are make-believe." The hope is that legal rituals and a new judicial etiquette will follow in the newly built courts.

Slogans on wall posters clearly prohibit judges from meeting privately with litigants, accepting gifts, or attending banquets. The essence of the Judges' Law and the Code of Conduct for Judges is adapted to local dialects in colorful wall posters forbidding corruption. Judges should neither directly nor indirectly use their position to obtain improper benefits for themselves, their relatives, or others; judges should not accept entertainment, goods, and the like offered by parties to a case, their representatives, and defenders; judges should not become involved in commercial activities or other economic activities that may cause the public to doubt the integrity of judges; judges should make appropriate arrangements for their personal affairs and should not deliberately disclose their position as judge to obtain special attention and should not use the reputation and influence associated with the position for private interests either for themselves, their relatives, or others; and judges should not be part-time lawyers, legal advisers for companies, governmental institutions, or individuals, and should not provide legal advice or legal opinions on a pending case to parties.

---

[42] Stephanie Balme, *A Countryside Judge in China*, manuscript to be published in French (our translation), 2010.

[43] See "Faguan xingwei bu guifan" ["Judges actions are not standardized"], *The People's Daily*, October 31, 2006.

Rural Justice as a Common Good?

Whenever and wherever, judicial systems are costly. Yet the most direct threat to judicial independence has been the decentralized system of distributing judicial funds. As one judge explained:

> In recent years, queries by the mass media and the people about the court's high litigation fees contributed to our bad reputation . . . Yet, the public only pays attention to how much the court charges the litigants. One does not see that a large amount of these fees, charged in the name of the court, actually indirectly goes to the local government.

In some circumstances a judge may be asked to undertake an independent investigation if available evidence is insufficient to reach a decision. The cost of such investigative trips (banan fei) can be high in remote areas. The same Gansu judge added:

> In the past, litigants themselves paid for the judges' personal expenses through the litigation fees. Nowadays we are forbidden to do so. Yet, it may cost between RMB 300 and 1,000 to complete a case. Due to the 2007 decision on reducing the litigation fees, we simply cannot afford to do our job except if the litigant himself comes to us. This means practically that only people who can afford it have their cases solved, and also that we have no financial resources to ensure that judgments are enforced.

Limits of judicial funds make it difficult for courts to enforce judgments, as is well known by litigants who do not fear losing in court. One case in Gansu involved a young man who had fled with his young child. After a divorce ruling, the tribunal could not afford to pay for a trip to the man's village, given that the RMB 1,500 cost of the trip far exceeded the RMB 80 in litigation fees paid by the mother as the plaintiff.

Presidents of tribunals in Shaanxi and Gansu often need to subrent part of their building to small businesses (like haircut or mobile phone shops) to cover expenses such as electricity, staff lunches, and transport fees. Many court presidents struggle to find the supplementary funds needed to build their new tribunals ordered by SPC's directive, as they are allocated only part of the cost. I met several of them whose daily work was to raise funds, find a piece of land, design a budget, and bargain with the construction companies.

Between late 2006 and spring 2007, the litigation fees' management system was reformed, along with the idea of separating the collection of litigation fees from court's expenditures. In April 2007, a State Council decision promoted unified charging standards as well as (supposedly) unified bank accounts and litigation fees management system for all courts: a labor dispute now cost RMB 10, whereas fees for divorce, land, or road accident cases are RMB 50 maximum. Litigation fees are no longer paid directly to courts but to designated bank accounts.

The central government's decision to drastically reduce litigation fees "to diminish ordinary people's burden and facilitate access to justice" had a direct and immediate impact on local courts' sources of incomes. For courts whose economic situation was already fragile, their working budget severely decreased. By June 2007, a large number of intermediate court presidents in Shaanxi and Gansu had reported their dire financial situation to their superiors, noting complaints from basic level courts of losses ranging from 40 percent to 75 percent of their budget. At that time, in some areas judges' salaries were also delayed due to the local government's financial difficulties. The financial situation of most courts was serious due to the resulting increase in the number of cases and thus in courts' daily expenses (such as materials and maintenance). Outlays had almost doubled, whereas basic tribunal's incomes had steadily decreased.

The NPC Report on the Implementation of the Central and Local Budgets for 2006 and on the Draft Central and Local Budgets for 2007 states that "in 2006, the central authorities supported the strengthening of government authority at the county and township levels. Funds totaling RMB 5.93 billion were set aside in the central budget in 2006 to help lower-level procuratorial, judicial, and public security departments improve conditions for processing cases."[44] It also states that transfer payments to improve local governments' ability to provide basic public services will be increased. A total of RMB 6.49 billion (an increase of RMB 560 million above the amount of 2006) has been allocated in the central budget in assistance for public security, procaturatorial organs, and people's courts in financially strapped areas. In September 2007, an article in the Legal Daily explained that courts had lost an average of 54 percent of their revenues. Consequently, RMB 2.4 billion would be allocated to compensate local tribunals.[45]

Fieldwork in 2007 revealed a more differentiated picture. In some areas, the compensation policy had not yet been implemented. Courts still had to charge informal and arbitrary fees (luanfei) to meet basic expenses. Elsewhere, the provincial government provided some basic courts (those with better connections?) enough resources to fill their income gap.

In 2008, the situation drastically improved. Most respondents reported they had received partial or total compensation for lost revenues while claiming to have scrupulously implemented the regulation forbidding arbitrary fees. In November 2008, the Politburo issued an opinion on how to deepen the reform of the judiciary and its working system.[46] During that important meeting, Politburo members apparently agreed on the necessity to guarantee the new system. The Ministry of

---

44 Ministry of Finance, www.chinaview.cn, March 18, 2007, p. 9.
45 "Susongfei Xin Banfa Shishi" ["Experiencing the New Procedure of Litigation Fees"], September 22, 2007.
46 "Zhongyang Zhengfa Weiyuanhui Guanyu Shenhua Sifa Jizhi He Gongzuo Jizhi Gaige Ruogan Wenti De Yijian," [Various Opinions of the Central Politics and Law Committee Concerning Deepening the Reform of the Judicial System and Its Workings] Xinjing Bao, Nov. 29, 2008.

Finance, the SPC, and other state departments started centralizing funding for the courts from 2009.

CONCLUSION

"Being independent is easy. We are protected by a status. We are 'untouchables.' Who would ever dare to intervene in a judge's work (except the media)?"[47] Those words written by the prominent French judge Eva Joly show how the judiciary has slowly managed to become a counterweight power in today's France. This independence is now naively viewed as irreversible despite the fact that the 1958 constitution only ensures judicial authority (title VIII) and not judicial power. But perhaps more importantly, the concept of an independent judiciary is now understood as a fundamental right of both citizens and judges. This certainly departs from the traditions of the Ancien Régime, both popular and constitutional, which stipulated until 1830 that "all justice emanates from the king. It is administered in his name by the judges, whom he nominates, and whom he institutes."

In China today, although most local judges consider the general evolution of the judicial system to be positive, judicial reforms are usually more piecemeal than systemic and often slower than some would wish. It is also more oriented toward access to justice for citizens than toward improving judges' working conditions and bolstering the status and dignity of local level judges.

Nonetheless, the increasingly wide range of legal disputes brought to court and the nascent legal culture among judges frustrated about their profession are influencing the judicial agenda. Given the political context, reform of the governance of the judiciary could bring key reforms to judges' independence. Judicial independence cannot be an end in itself. Changing the courts' governance by centralizing the administration of judges is an important task that could have a great impact on the courts. Political changes are obviously vital to solve the issue of judicial dependence. But, more than new ideological slogans, it is the reform of the ordinary judiciary that is likely to affect the scope of its political independence.

Reforms should involve a conceptual change of judicial services as a public service and a common good. Almost (financial) cost-free access to justice, the transformation of courts from danwei to a distinct legal institution, as well as increased professionalism are key steps in a long-term evolution. Rose-Ackerman has stated that "corruption is a symptom that the state is functioning poorly."[48] In China, the central state must be strong to guarantee a higher dignity to grassroots judges. Undoubtedly, China will not become a state ruled by law without establishing the rule of law in the countryside.

---

[47] Eva Joly, *Notre Affaire à Tous* (Paris: Gallimard, 2002).
[48] Susan Rose-Ackerman, "Corruption and Development," *Journal of International Peacekeeping, Special issue on corruption and post-conflict peace building* (2008).

9

The Judiciary Pushes Back

Law, Power, and Politics in Chinese Courts

Xin He*

Despite the passage of hundreds of laws and the expansion of the judiciary since the late 1970s, a dominant theme in the literature is that Chinese courts have enjoyed little judicial independence.[1] The courts are often portrayed as little more than a loyal subordinate of the party–state that carefully carries out assigned tasks; they have virtually no will or capacity to resist the party–state's interference.[2]

However, recent developments have raised questions about how far, and under what conditions, the conventional wisdom that Chinese courts are incapable of resisting political pressure from superior powers holds up. The courts have refused to accept jurisdiction over some types of disputes that have arisen in China's unprecedented social transformation.[3] This strategic retraction rather than expansion of judicial power is surprising in light of the global trend toward judicialization and the trend in China to extend the government's policy of "governance in accordance with law" to a widening range of economic and social activities.

For some of these disputes, the courts' refusal to exercise jurisdiction may be explained by the inferior position of the courts: when superior political powers such as the party or the government do not want the courts to be involved in the dispute resolution process for political reasons, the courts have little room to disobey. This

* The author acknowledges the support provided by a research grant from City University of Hong Kong.

1 Xin He, "Ideology or Reality? Limited Judicial Independence in Contemporary China," *Australian Journal of Asian Law*, no. 6, p. 213 (2004); Kevin J. O'Brien & Lianjiang Li, "Suing the Local State: Administrative Litigation in Rural China," in N. Diamant et al. eds., *Engaging the Law in China: State, Society and Possibilities for Justice* (Stanford: Stanford University Press, 2005); Stanley B. Lubman, *Bird in a Cage* (Stanford: Stanford University Press, 1999).

2 Weifang He, "Zhongguo sifa zhidu de liangge wenti [Two Problems of Chinese Judicial System]," *Zhongguo shehui kexue* [Social Science in China] (1997).

3 See Chapter 6 in this volume.

has been well illustrated in the handling of urban housing demolition disputes. But for many other disputes, the courts' refusal to extend its reach cannot be adequately explained by the inferior position of the courts or the interference of the local governments or party committees. These disputes are not purely political cases that challenge the power of the Chinese Communist Party (CCP). They are usually civil in nature and involve infringement of rights and interests of a large number of socially unimportant people. These issues become legally or politically important only when these people effectively organize public demonstrations to protest their plight.

Moreover, in contrast to the cases where political powers limit the jurisdiction of the court, in these cases local party committees and governments, to relieve their own pressure and to maintain social stability, have repeatedly urged the courts to solve these major and complex disputes. Yet the courts have resisted the political pressure and refused to hear the disputes.

This development raises a number of questions: What is it about these cases that makes the courts so reluctant to accept them? How do the courts resist pressure from the party, government, and society to hear these cases? What light does this new development shed on the decision-making process of the courts and their evolving status in the Chinese polity?

This chapter explores these questions by examining in detail how courts in Guangdong province have handled disputes involving "Married Out Women" (waijianü, hereafter MOW). It shows that if the courts were to take these disputes, they would be forced to apply vague and inconsistent laws and regulations and would be incapable of enforcing many judgments in favor of MOW, leading to diminished legitimacy and public trust in the judiciary. Citing inadequate resources and procedural and substantive legal barriers to hearing such suits, courts have steered MOW disputes into political and administrative channels for preliminary settlement. At the same time, the courts have expanded their authority by insisting on the right to review government decisions in administrative litigation. By so doing, they not only reduce their workload and the administrative burden of hearing the disputes and enforcing the decisions, they also successfully reduce the number of complaints likely to result from their decisions and perhaps stir popular discontent against the townships, a result acceptable to the superior political powers. The judiciary's strategic maneuver to limit its own jurisdiction has allowed the courts to mitigate damage to their image while strengthening the judiciary's position in the power relationship between the courts and local governments and party organizations.

Part I introduces MOW disputes, which occur across the country but have been particularly prevalent in Guangdong province. Part II describes how the basic level or lower courts in Guangdong have resisted pressure from local party committees and governments. Part III assesses the effectiveness of the courts' resistance by tracing subsequent legal developments and how ultimately the courts have come to handle MOW disputes.[4] Part IV analyzes the results. Part V concludes with some implications for the relationship between the courts and the governments and for judicial independence and the prospect of the human rights movement in China.

MOW DISPUTES

"MOW" refers to peasant women who are married outside their home villages. MOW disputes must be understood against the backdrop of the urbanization process of rural China, where rural lands have been transformed into urban lands by state requisition. Prior to state requisition, rural land was collectively owned, although the land-use rights might have been allocated to individual households under the land-reform scheme implemented in the early 1980s. Consequently, when rural lands are requisitioned, the state acquiring the land usually compensates the village collective. The village collective is supposed to then compensate the individual members of the collective. However, how to divide the proceeds from the land sale, or the dividends or benefits derived from the use of the proceeds, has become an extremely controversial issue. The issue is whether MOW are eligible to a share of compensation, dividends, and other benefits of their home or destination villages.

One standard is household registration (hukou).[5] But the complexities of the evolving hukou policies and practices have rendered this seemingly simple test unworkable. In actual practice, there are many different types of MOW as a result of the hukou policy, and using hukou as the sole criterion could lead to numerous unfair consequences.

The term MOW broadly covers: (i) women who do not or cannot transfer their hukou after being married to men from other villages, urban areas, or

---

[4] The analyses and data are based on court judgments (including all the administrative judgments of the MOW disputes in a basic level court of Guangzhou in 2005), relevant administrative decisions, government documents and directives, news reports on the disputes, and in-depth interviews with seven judges who handled the disputes (five in a basic level court and two judges of the administrative chamber at an intermediate court), three township level officials, twelve MOW, five human rights activists who have unsuccessfully assisted the MOW to obtain justice, and four cadres of a village in the outskirts of Guangzhou during the years 2003–2006.

[5] People are officially provided either an urban or rural hukou based on where they were born. People with a rural hukou are usually permanently tied to the village they were born in, and they are entitled to have a portion of the land in their village but not entitled to welfare outside their village. One of the major functions of the hukou system is to restrict people in the rural areas from migrating into urban areas. People may change their hukou status or move their hukou to another place only through limited channels like marriage, work, and higher education, although the system has become much looser as a result of economic reforms. For a detailed description of the origin and development of this extremely complicated system, see generally, Kam Wing Chan, *Cities with Invisible Walls* (Hong Kong: Oxford University Press, 1994); Cheng Tiejun, & Mark Selden "The Origins and Social Consequences of China's Hukou System," *The China Quarterly*, no. 139, p. 664 (1994); Dorothy J. Solinger, *Contesting Citizenship in Urban China: Peasant Migrants, the State, and the Logic of the Market* (Berkeley: University of California Press, 1999); Fei-Ling Wang, *Organizing through Division and Exclusion: China's Hukou System* (Stanford: Stanford University Press, 2005).

overseas;[6] (ii) women who move their hukou to the destination village from their home village – in this sense, MOW also covers "Married In Women"; (iii) women who have married outside their home village and moved their hukou to their destination village but have now moved their hukou to their home village because they are divorced or widowed; (iv) women who are allowed to move their hukou to the destination village under the condition that they agree not to enjoy any benefits of that village; (v) children of these women, including those from previous marriages, illegitimate children, or children born outside the One Child Policy, and; (vi) men married into their wives' households; in this sense, MOW also includes "Married Out Men."[7]

According to the Organic Law of Villagers' Committees, it is the village members' meeting that shall, based on majority vote, make final decisions on such important issues, although the law also states that the decisions shall not contradict the constitution and other laws. In practice, the village meeting decisions usually exclude MOW from any benefits.

Most villagers do not regard MOW as their fellow villagers. Rather, they view MOW as "water splashed out from their parents' family," an idea deeply engrained in Chinese history and culture. According to the villagers, after getting married the women become members of their husbands' households, and thereafter they have no substantive relationship with their parents' households. As a result, even if many MOW still have their hukou registered at the home village, they are not regarded as village members by their fellow villagers.

However, a more direct reason for the villagers' view is that including MOW as part of the village will inevitably reduce each villager's share. Moreover, MOW are easily outvoted by the majority. Even in Guangdong province where the urbanization process is well under way, MOW only amount to a little more than 1 percent of the total population.[8]

For the same reason, the destination villages of many MOW also refuse to offer them benefits. As a result, some MOW and their children cannot get benefits from either their home or destination villages, leading to an extremely grave situation.

For two reasons, most MOW believe they deserve equal treatment for benefits and compensation at their home or destination villages. First, several important national laws, including the constitution and the Women's Rights Protection Law, clearly

[6] To restrict people from moving into the cities, the current hukou policy usually does not allow MOW to move their rural hukou to their husbands' households in the city, although moving an urban hukou back to rural areas is much easier.

[7] Sun Hailong et al., "Chengshi hua beijing xia nongchun waijianu quanyi jiufeng jiqi jiejue jizhi de sikao [A Meditation on Rural "MOW" Disputes and Their Resolution Mechanism in the Background of Urbanization]," *Falu shiyong* [Legal Application], no. 3, p. 26 (2004).

[8] The report in *Nanfang Agricultural News* states that there are 100,000 MOW in Guangdong province. See e.g., Nanfang Agricultural News, 5 December 2005, http://www.nanfangdaily.com. cn/southnews/dd/nc/sntt/200512050702.asp, last visited on 22 August 2006. This number apparently does not include MIW, MOM, and their children.

stipulate that female villagers shall enjoy the same rights as male villagers, according to the principle of gender equality. The MOW raise a very simple question: Why can men enjoy the benefits regardless of their actual residence whereas women cannot?

Second, according to General Principles of Civil Law, the country's basic general law governing civil law relationships, benefits, and obligations should correspond to each other. MOW have worked the land and contributed to the village collective, so when the compensation from the sale of collective land is distributed, they should also be entitled to a share. Adding insult to injury, MOW are required by their destination village to fulfill obligations as a village member, such as irrigation maintenance duty, simply because their households are located in the village; but when the members' meeting of the destination village distributes benefits, the MOW are excluded.

Indignant over village collectives' decisions that either denied or reduced their compensation and benefits, many MOW have sought help from any authority that might offer a remedy. They have gone to the township and district governments, where they were generally told the government could not interfere with the internal business of the village, and that the MOW should take the disputes to court. They have made their case to local women's rights protection committees. Although the committees have been sympathetic, they lack the authority to resolve the disputes. The committees could only urge local party committees, people's congresses, local courts, and some upper-level women's rights protection organizations to address the issue. Local people's congresses have also been ineffective in responding to the needs of MOW, although in some cases they have initiated an individual case supervision (gean jiandu) process and demanded a reply from the courts.[9] All these authorities have urged the courts to solve the disputes.[10]

Since the late 1990s, MOW have tried to file lawsuits. Their main cause of action was a civil one: the decisions of the village members' meeting violated the principle of gender equality and infringed their property rights. The courts, however, generally refused to accept the disputes, for reasons discussed in detail below.

Having failed to obtain redress through these various channels, many MOW fired the last missile in their arsenal. Assisted by human rights activists, they organized collectively and protested the decisions of their village collective through public demonstrations and sit-ins.[11] In the process of having their grievance heard, the

---

[9] For a general discussion of individual case supervision, see Randall Peerenboom, "Judicial Independence and Judicial Accountability: An Empirical Study of Individual Case Supervision," *The China Journal*, p. 67 (2006).

[10] Interview with a vice president of a basic level court on August 19, 2004. The request usually takes place in PLC meetings where the directors of various relevant institutions explain their difficulties.

[11] There have been occasional news reports of such protests, although MOW that I interviewed noted that this kind of protest occurs often. As MOW are obviously a very weak social group and their complaints have merit, the protesters usually are treated well when they meet with higher level officials, with the authorities often sending them home in official vehicles.

protesting MOW often break down into tears, lose control, and demand solutions from the highest authority in local affairs – the party committees. Luckily for MOW in Guangdong province, the rapid process of urbanization has generated a large number of such MOW, and their grievance is so obvious that their situation has generated wide attention and sympathy.[12] As a result, what began as the relatively minor disputes of a group of socially vulnerable women became transformed into a major and complicated issue in the eyes of the local party committees and government officials, which once again urged the courts to solve the disputes.

THE COURTS' RESISTANCE

Local party committees and governments can influence courts through the Political–Legal Committees (PLC) at corresponding levels. The committees are composed of senior officials from the local party committee, relevant government branches, procuracy, and people's congress. They are usually headed and convened by a senior party member who often serves in the government, such as the head of the police. The president of the courts, however, usually is only an ordinary member of the committees. PLCs usually become involved in significant and complicated cases.

As social stability has become an increasingly pressing issue in China, PLCs have required the courts, along with other government branches, to comply with a "social security and comprehensive governance responsibility" system (shehui zhian zonghe zhili). The goal is to hold them responsible for serious incidents in their jurisdiction. The PLCs periodically check and assess the situation, and reward and punish relevant officials accordingly. Officials in charge may be reprimanded if there are serious incidents that threaten social stability and their political career may be adversely affected. Although social security and comprehensive governance is not clearly defined, public demonstrations and massive petitions are generally causes for concern. When the MOW disputes have been discussed at the PLC meetings, the heads of the courts have often been grilled for not solving the disputes.

In the face of such political pressure, courts often try to find a compromise acceptable to all relevant parties in the dispute by balancing modern legal skills, traditional custom, and local knowledge.[13] But this does not mean that the courts will accept everything dumped on them. As a member of the PLC, the president of the court can always argue that although dispute resolution generally falls within the courts' scope of duty, the courts lack jurisdiction over, and the capacity to solve, MOW disputes. If other political actors want the courts to solve these disputes, they should first address the jurisdictional and capacity issues.

---

[12] There are numerous news reports on MOW, including in major official news outlets like *Guangzhou Daily* and *Yangchen Evening News* (December 28, 2005; November 24, 2006). A search of "waijialu" in search engines like Google or Baidu results in more than 500 links.

[13] Suli, *Songfa xia xiang* [Bring the Law to the Countryside], (Beijing: China's University of Political Science and Law Press, 2000), pp. 130–133.

More specifically, the courts have argued that there are legal barriers preventing them from hearing MOW disputes.[14] MOW disputes are neither civil nor administrative disputes, and thus there is no legal basis to accept them. Under the framework of China's procedural laws, there are three major types of litigation: civil, administrative, and criminal. Civil litigation involves disputes between parties with equal legal status; administrative litigation involves judicial review of specific or concrete administrative decisions and acts (as opposed to review of generally applicable administrative rules or regulations). MOW disputes are between the village collective and individual village members, but these two are not equal in legal status, and thus they are not civil disputes. The village collective is not a regular civil party because it also serves the administrative functions of managing community affairs and maintaining village order. On the other hand, the township government is the lowest level of government; accordingly, the village collective is not regarded as an administrative institution or agent. It is therefore impossible for the courts to review a decision of nonadministrative institutions through administrative litigation.

The courts have also argued that they do not have the authority to review the decisions of the village members' meeting. Although the village collectives are not allowed to make decisions contrary to the fundamental policies and constitutional principles of the nation, there are no laws explicitly authorizing the courts to review village collective's decisions. And they cannot do so simply because the decisions have violated some general and vague legal principles. If the courts accept such disputes and decide in favor of MOW, they may be usurping the autonomous decision-making power of the village collectives.

In addition, the courts argued that there are no clear regulations regarding MOW, and that existing regulations are contradictory. Although this argument seems odd in a common law jurisdiction, it makes sense in a legal system such as China's where the courts do not have legislative power and are charged with faithfully applying laws and regulations rather than creating law. With respect to MOW, a fundamental conflict exists between the laws protecting women's interests and the democratic decisions of village collectives. On the one hand, the principle of gender equality implies that women's property deserves the same protection as that of men. Article 30 of the Women's Rights Protection Law stipulates that "women and men in rural areas enjoy equal rights in agricultural lands and homestead lands allocation" and that "women's agricultural lands and homestead lands should still be protected after marriage or divorce." On the other hand, the Villagers' Organic Law also specifies that it is up to the village to make decisions on its internal affairs and the township governments shall not interfere. Although the law mentions that the decision made by the village collective shall not violate other laws, the law does not mention how to redress the situation when such violations do occur.

---

[14] Interviews with judges at one basic level court and an intermediate court of Guangdong province in the years 2004 and 2005.

Local regulations are also inconsistent. For example, Article 12 of The Guangdong Implementing Measures of Women's Rights Protection Law, issued by the Standing Committee of Guangdong People's Congress (Guangdong Measures), explicitly requires both household registration (hukou) and actual residence to enjoy dividends and other benefits. Most importantly, it also mentions that it is the township government's responsibility to address any problems. On the other hand, Article 8 of Several Stipulations of Women's Rights Protection of Guangzhou Municipality (Guangzhou Stipulations), issued by the Standing Committee of Guangzhou Municipality People's Congress and approved by the Standing Committee of the Guangdong People's Congress, simply refers to hukou plus places of living and working, without specifically requiring actual residence. Nor does the article mention which authority shall be responsible for addressing MOW problems, although it does state that MOW can take their disputes to the government or to the court.

There are also inconsistencies between upper-level laws and lower-level legal regulations. For instance, when the Women's Rights Protection Law specifies the principle of gender equality in protecting women's rights, it does not set out any preconditions or qualifications. But when the principle has been restated in the local regulations intended to implement the Women's Rights Protection Law, various preconditions and qualifications have been added with little justification. Tying benefits to both the place of actual residence and household registration, for example, significantly impairs the rights of MOW.

The second major argument raised by the courts is that they lack the capacity and resources to provide an effective remedy. A single district of Guangzhou has more than 8,000 MOW, and the number would be as high as 19,000 if their children are included.[15] If the courts opened the door to MOW, they would be overwhelmed.

Furthermore, because the disputes of MOW arise from various causes and the decisions of village collectives vary on criteria for benefits – the timing of moving in or out, the marital situation, and the legal status of the children – the cases are factually complicated. The courts do not have enough personnel and resources to examine all relevant evidence and go through an extremely complicated hearing process for so many disputes. Moreover, most village assets have already been distributed, and it is very difficult, if not impossible, to retrieve them from individual villagers scattered around rural areas. With a limited number of court sheriffs, who are supposed to deal with criminal suspects and enforce economic judgments, the courts lack the capacity to collect the minor amounts of money from individual villagers. The courts also lack the capacity to monitor the village members' meeting each time benefits are distributed.[16]

The third, and perhaps the most important, argument is that the courts are unable to provide an equitable and enforceable judgment to the MOW. If the courts hold the

---

[15] Sun et al., "Nongchun waijianu quanyi jiufeng [Rural 'MOW' Disputes]."
[16] Interview with a judge of the research department of a basic court in Guangdong, August 15, 2004.

decisions of the village collectives unlawful and subsequently offer specific remedies to the MOW, the village collective would likely resist and refuse to implement such a judgment. Village heads have little incentive to follow the instructions of the courts; they are elected by village members and have no direct relationship with the judicial system. But these village heads have every reason to act on behalf of the majority of their fellow villagers; without the support of the majority of villagers, the village heads may not be able to keep their positions. As far as this kind of dispute is concerned, most villagers believe that the division of benefits is an internal affair with which outsiders like the courts have no right to interfere. In my fieldwork interviews, many villagers have openly stated that they would not support a village head who agrees to share the benefits with MOW.[17] Under such circumstances, it is not likely that village heads would implement judgments favorable to MOW. Without a grassroots network, the judiciary may not even be able to locate the whereabouts of relevant villagers let alone convince them to implement the court judgments.[18]

With an unenforceable court judgment in hand, MOW are all the more likely to appeal to higher authorities. The courts, having already expanded considerable energy and resources on the case, will once again be blamed by these authorities for not really solving the disputes.

On the other hand, if the courts hold against the MOW, the MOW are likely to appeal to higher courts. Alternatively, they may turn to the petitioning system and claim that the courts have misapplied the laws. Either way, higher-level authorities may criticize the courts for mishandling the disputes.

In demonstrating to the local party committees and government officials practical and legal difficulties that arise in handling MOW cases, the courts are negotiating a solution. They are claiming that they will not be able to carry out their task unless steps are taken by other actors to address their concerns. Even if the court's resource constraints are addressed, the legislative inconsistencies would have to be addressed. In so doing, the judiciary is exploiting conflicts among the PLCs, higher level courts, and different levels of government. It is also taking advantage of the political space created for the courts by the commitment to rule of law.

SUBSEQUENT DEVELOPMENTS: ASSESSING COURT RESISTANCE

Although the courts initially rejected MOW disputes, this did not end MOW protests or the pressure to hear such cases. Partly due to pressure from MOW as well as from local authorities, lower courts sought internal instruction from higher courts to clarify various legal issues. In response to an inquiry raised by the Guangdong High Court, the Research Department of the Supreme People's Court issued a reply on

---

[17] Interview with villager cadres of a town in the outskirts of Guangzhou in June 2004.
[18] Jiang Shigong, "Falu bu ru zi di de minshi tiaojie [Civil Mediation in a Lawless World]," in S. Jiang, *Fazhi yu zhili* [Legal System and Governance], (Beijing: China's University of Political Science and Law Press: 2003); Suli, *Songfa xia xiang*.

July 9, 2001, stating that individual MOW and the village collectives have equal legal status. Consequently, the courts could hear MOW disputes as civil cases.

In less than one year, however, the Case Filing Department of the SPC issued another reply in response to a similar inquiry from the Zhejiang High Court, providing that disputes over land compensation between the collective and its members are not civil disputes, and the courts shall not accept them as civil cases. Although neither reply has the effect of law because they were not issued by the adjudication committee of the SPC, as required by the Legislative Law, in practice such replies would normally be followed by lower level courts.

In light of conflicting opinions from the SPC and, more importantly, to temporarily diffuse mounting pressure from MOW and PLCs, basic courts in Guangdong accepted a series of MOW cases. In 2002, a district court in Zhuhai awarded judgments in favor of more than fifty MOW.[19] Regarded as the first instance in which MOW won through civil litigation, the decision drew national attention. Inspired by this court decision, many MOW urged other courts in Guangdong to accept their disputes as civil cases. Nonetheless, after several months most basic courts dismissed these cases, citing the reasons discussed above.[20]

In 2004, the Guangdong High Court, after long debates inside and outside the judiciary, suggested a tentative solution.[21] MOW shall first request the township government address their complaints, and the township government shall make an administrative decision on the issue.[22] If the MOW believe the decision made by the township government is unfair, they may seek administrative reconsideration from the district government, the next higher level government. If the MOW are not satisfied with the results of administrative reconsideration, they may challenge the administrative decision in court through administrative litigation.

The solution thus includes three steps: a preliminary attempt to resolve the dispute by the township government, administrative reconsideration, and administrative litigation.[23] This three-step solution was indirectly upheld by a formal opinion issued

---

[19] "Collective Dividends Remained after Being Married," *Southern Metropolitan Daily*, August 29, 2002, Section A19; see also, http://www.cctv.com/program/lawtoday/20030826/100522.shtml (visited March 26, 2006).

[20] Panyu District Court in Guangzhou alone dismissed 213 such cases in 2003.

[21] "Guangdong High Court: 'MOW' Have New Way of Protecting Rights," *Guangzhou Daily*, April 5, 2004, Economic News Section.

[22] If the township government refuses to make a decision, MOW can file an administrative litigation suit based on the government's failure to act.

[23] The second step arguably does not have a sound legal basis because, according to the Administrative Litigation Law, the plaintiff can directly file a lawsuit unless required by a law or administrative regulation to first seek administrative reconsideration. However, in this case, suggesting the plaintiff go through administrative reconsideration prior to filing a lawsuit serves the interests of both the courts and the government. For the courts, administrative reconsideration can filter out additional cases. For the governments, this is one more chance to review the decision internally and thus perhaps avoid judicial scrutiny. In practice, not all MOW followed this instruction; some of them filed administrative litigation immediately after the township government had made a decision.

by the SPC in 2005, which confirmed the reply of the Case Filing Department in 2002 and nullified the 2001 reply of the Research Department of the SPC.[24]

The courts have therefore provided only limited access for MOW. Even so, the courts have heard a number of MOW cases. For instance, the Panyu district court in Guangzhou received eighty-eight applications for MOW administrative litigation suits in 2005. An examination of these judgments reveals several salient features.

First, courts have held that it was the responsibility of the township government to step in and redress the issue. In cases where the township government failed to make a decision after being requested by the MOW or village collective, courts have consistently held that this constituted administrative inaction, an improper administrative behavior in administrative law, and thus the government had to make a decision. The courts obviously wanted the government to also bear some responsibility for resolving these socially complicated disputes. This approach also solved the problem of the court directly reviewing a village collective decision, as the court now reviews the decision of the township government, which indisputably is an administrative entity over which the court has jurisdiction.[25]

Second, with regard to the substantive law on the issue, courts have consistently applied the so-called two-places principle – the places of hukou and actual residence as the precondition for benefits. That is, they simply applied the Article in the Guangdong Measures without giving an explanation why the more lenient standards under the Guangzhou Stipulations were not applicable. Nor have courts addressed other inconsistencies that might provide more benefits to MOW.

Rigid application of the two-places principle has inevitably led to many unfair consequences. Only those MOW and their children whose hukou and actual residence remained unchanged received benefits. If MOW move to another town for whatever reason, they lose their benefits, even though their hukou remains registered at the village. Similarly, a divorced woman would not receive benefits if her original house had been demolished by government and she physically had no place to stay in the village. A child of an MOW would not enjoy benefits simply because he went to school in another town and did not live inside the village.[26]

The court's reluctance to address legal inconsistencies and their application of the Guangdong Measures rather than other higher level laws or regulations that adopt a standard more favorable to MOW suggests that the courts reached an agreement with the government as part of a broader political compromise whereby MOW would receive some benefits but not as much as they demanded.[27]

---

[24] The Opinion of the SPC on Adjudicating Rural Contracted Land Disputes, July 29, 2005. Although the opinion does not explicitly address how to solve the disputes, it does state that they cannot be treated as civil disputes. It thus confirms the opinion of the Case Filing Department and nullifies the opinion of the Research Department of the SPC.

[25] Whether the township has the right to review village collective decisions, or whether such review constitutes undue interference with village autonomy, remains an issue.

[26] Interview with MOW on August 20, 2005.

[27] Many judges and officials that I interviewed admitted this, although the decisions apparently were made independently by court, party, and government officials in different local areas.

Third, despite the alleged inferior political position of the judiciary, the court frequently overturned government decisions. Among the eighty-one MOW cases completed in 2005, the courts upheld the government decision in only seventeen cases, or 21 percent. The plaintiffs prevailed in forty-three cases, the overwhelming majority, with eight cases dismissed and thirteen cases withdrawn. This result once again shows that the courts are not a rubber stamp or reluctant to challenge local government decisions.[28] With regard to the detailed issues in administrative litigation, the courts seem to have reversed their underdog role by asserting a supervisory position toward the governments.

Fourth, enforcement of these administrative judgments has not turned out to be a major problem. The townships and district governments have cooperated in implementing the judgments, even when the governments' decisions were revoked and when the court judgments were favorable to the MOW. When some judgments were resisted by the village collective, the governments sent special delegates to the village and persuaded and cajoled the villagers to accept and implement the judgments.[29]

Fifth, the courts' decision to provide relief to MOW was not the end of the story. The two-places principle left many MOW without relief. Accordingly, together with other social groups such as the China Confederation of Women, MOW lobbied successfully for the revision of the Women's Rights Protection Law. The revised 2005 law stipulates that women shall be treated equally in the division of benefits in rural village collectives.

Nevertheless, the courts' handling of MOW disputes has so far not been affected by the revised law, either procedurally or substantively.[30] Although the revised law arguably invalidates the two-places principle, Guangdong courts continue to argue that the Guangdong Measures have not been abolished and that the detailed regulations trump general stipulations in higher level laws.

Similarly, although the revised law explicitly stipulates that if such disputes are brought to the courts, the courts shall hear them, Guangdong courts contend that the revised law does not specify whether the disputes must be heard as civil lawsuits or administrative suits, and if administrative suits, whether MOW must first challenge government decisions through administrative reconsideration.

ANALYSIS

In applying the two-places principle, the courts established a clear standard to deter potential MOW disputants. The two-places principle limits the number of MOW able to bring suit, thus decreasing the courts' workload. Moreover, because

---

[28] Randall Peerenboom, *China's Long March toward Rule of Law* (Cambridge: Cambridge University Press, 2002), p. 400.

[29] Zhang Yongbo, "Nongchun 'waijianu' wengti de sifa yanjiu [Judicial Research on Rural 'MOW']," Panyu District Court ed., *Yushan Law Forum* [Yushan fatan], no. 2 (2006).

[30] *Nanfang Agricultural News*, December 5, 2005.

this filtering procedure is complicated, expensive, lengthy, and fragmented, and also because some MOW may believe (incorrectly as it turns out) that suing the government is likely to be futile, many MOW may settle their disputes or give up before the cases reach the courts. Early results seem to confirm this strategy. In 2005, Panyu court received only eighty-eight administrative cases. In contrast, during the three months of the year 2003 when the court agreed to hear the disputes as civil suits, it received 213 cases.[31]

Even for those cases that eventually reach the courts, the most onerous and laborious part of the case, including evidence gathering and particularly interviews with villagers, now becomes the responsibility of the governments. The courts only need to review the paperwork prepared by the governments and the plaintiff MOW. If the evidence and facts are clear, the courts make a judgment. Otherwise they simply remand the cases back to the governments. Thus, the courts have offloaded the most troublesome and thorny part of the disputes but have taken the easiest part.

The current practice also helps the courts avoid the difficulty of implementing judgments. Even if the disputes reach the courts and the courts decide in favor of the MOW, it is still the responsibility of the governments to implement the decisions. From the perspective of the courts, the governments are much better situated to enforce the decisions. Although village heads have every reason not to follow the orders of the courts, they will likely bow to pressure from the township government because they receive financial and other support from the township government.

Moreover, judgments based on the two-places principle are most likely to be accepted by the majority of villagers, thus decreasing the need for enforcement and minimizing damage to the court's reputation and public trust in the judiciary.

In adopting the two-places principle, the courts negotiated a compromise with local governments. Although the courts preferred to shift responsibility for MOW disputes to political and administrative channels, local governments wanted the courts to handle these socially contentious issues. It also seems unlikely that such a compromise could have been reached without provisional support from central authorities.

Although the compromise may have been acceptable to both local courts and political authorities, not everyone was satisfied. For example, disgruntled MOW may continue to threaten social stability by repeated mass protests and petitioning of central authorities. The mass media may continue to highlight their plight. Although local governments have treated MOW with care so far, they may react more harshly to repeated protests. MOW may also be able to continue to enlist the support of women's rights groups and human rights activists in pressing for further legislative reforms. Indeed, having been left out of the negotiation process, MOW allied with human rights activists and women's rights groups to push for revision of national

---

[31] Zhang, "Nongchun 'waijianu'[Rural 'MOW']."

laws to better protect their rights, invoking international human rights law in the process.[32] But the reality is that MOW remain a weak group whose interests are at odds with the interests of a majority of villagers. In short, the current compromise provides some protection for MOW and yet serves the interests of most villagers, the courts, and local party and government officials.

CONCLUSION: IMPLICATIONS FOR JUDICIAL INDEPENDENCE AND HUMAN RIGHTS PROTECTION

This study illustrates the complexity of the judicial decision-making process in contemporary China where elements of law, power, and politics all come into play. Judicial decisions, including whether to expand jurisdiction, cannot be adequately explained or assessed in the absence of thick descriptions of the sociopolitical context, and a detailed understanding of the legal arguments, resource constraints, and strategic interpretations are open to the courts within that context.

The examination of MOW cases demonstrates that although local party committees and governments exert considerable control over the courts' personnel and budget, the courts do not always follow their instructions. Local party committees and governments strongly and repeatedly request the courts to hear MOW disputes, but the courts effectively resist their pressure.

Moreover, whereas PLCs may provide a venue for nonjudicial political actors to exert influence on the courts, PLCs have also become an arena for the judiciary to resist such pressure and to advance its own institutional interests. In this interaction, legal doctrines and even the detailed wording of the specific laws and regulations become powerful weapons for the courts. By creatively and strategically interpreting the law, the courts can advance their own institutional interests and compete in the struggle for power and legitimacy with other political actors.

This study paints a more complicated and nuanced picture of the relationship between the judiciary and other powers in China than conventionally recognized. The courts are not simply a passive instrument of the governments and the party, yielding to various external forces that have been imposed on them. Under the seemingly peaceful surface of iron control exists dynamic turbulences of conflict, repression, resistance, competition, compromise, and cooperation in which law, power, and politics interact. There is room for the courts to maneuver in the current political structure.[33] Although the particular context differs, Chinese courts are

---

[32] See a report of an interview with Lu Ying, an expert in providing legal aid to the MOW, in http://www.ccrs.org.cn/article_view.asp?ID=1779 (Last visited March 27, 2006).

[33] This kind of resistance is by no means unique to MOW disputes. In addressing the difficulty of judgment enforcement, for example, the courts regularly complain that other powers are not coop- erative and the courts do not have enough resources. The strategy is twofold: to deflect blame and responsibility for ongoing problems and to obtain more resources.

similar in this respect to their counterparts in developing democracies and even to some extent to courts in Euro-America.[34]

This study also reinforces the findings of other studies that have emphasized the need to disaggregate the "party–state."[35] On this view, state power, including the role of the judiciary, is best understood by examining interactions between various authorities at multiple levels and how they interact with assorted social groups.

The judiciary as an institution and courts in particular cases are subject to pressure from various external sources. To reduce and resist the pressure, the courts have to rely on, and take advantage of, administrative power. By citing technical legal barriers and resource constraints, the courts are able to resist pressure from other actors and develop a significant form of judicial independence, even though they are still embedded in a complex political power structure. Their political embeddedness and resource constraints determine that they cannot pursue an aggressive power maximization strategy. But they nonetheless can fashion some degree of judicial autonomy.

Although the courts were reluctant to expand their jurisdiction in MOW cases, they enhanced their authority by claiming the right to review administrative decisions. Thus, in giving up some territory, they have regulated, disciplined, and rationalized a wider scope of social activities. This strategy is similar to that employed by many courts when they side with the legislator or the executive in the particular case on the substantive issues but expand their authority by claiming the right to review their decisions.

Perhaps unlike the situation in some other transitional countries, the MOW cases constitute a judicialization of administrative power and not a direct judicialization of politics.[36] This is perhaps a better path for legal development in a country in which administrative power is dominant but the state nonetheless needs to use the courts to handle more disputes. Were the courts to directly grab power in judicializing politics and confronting superior powers, they would encounter tremendous resistance that may even threaten their existence.[37] The relatively weak judiciary therefore must first rely on and cooperate with administrative power in fulfilling the social control function required by the state. It must be acutely aware of the circumstances where it executes its power.

---

[34] Rogers M. Smith, "If Politics Matters: Implications for a 'New Institutionalism,'" *Studies in American Political Development*, no. 6, p. 1 (1992).

[35] Neil Diamant, Kevin O'Brien, and Stanley Lubman, "Law and Society in the People's Republic of China," in *Engaging the Law in China*, p. 3. See also, Fu and Peerenboom in this volume.

[36] Tamir Moustafa, "Law versus the State: The Judicialization of Politics in Egypt," *Law and Social Inquiry*, no. 28, p. 883 (2003); Gretchen Helmke, *Courts under Constraints: Judges, Generals, and Presidents in Argentina* (Cambridge: Cambridge University Press, 2005).

[37] For example, when Li Huijuan, a midlevel judge of Luoyang, Henan province announced that a local regulation was void, she herself was almost removed from the position. "A Judge Tests China's Courts, Making History," *New York Times*, November 28, 2005.

More fundamentally, this line of cases demonstrates that before asking whether the courts are independent in adjudicating disputes, we need to ask whether the courts are capable of independently resolving the disputes. At least with respect to MOW disputes, but arguably also with respect to many other socioeconomic disputes, judicial independence is not a preferred option even for the courts themselves.

Finally, the story of MOW offers an opportunity to reflect on the limitation of the human rights movement in quasiauthoritarian states like China. Compared to the original situation in which no judicial remedy existed, MOW achieved some progress. The three-step process provides MOW a political channel, an administrative channel, and a judicial channel to bring their claims and have their voices heard. The efforts to mobilize and organize also resulted in useful links to human rights organizations and women's rights groups, leading to revisions in national laws. Accordingly, the case of MOW demonstrates that even under a rather conservative political system, average people may be able to obtain justice, if not in the courts than through other political, legislative, and administrative channels.

On the other hand, MOW, women's rights groups, and human rights activists did not obtain all they wanted. The progress for many MOW may be largely symbolic given the limited access to the courts and the constraints of the two-places principle. Human rights activism offers the courts an opportunity, or a push, to subtly adjust their power position in the political context. But when international human rights law is translated into local practice, the meaning of the law itself may be twisted and deformed.[38] The decision-making process of these courts suggests that although China is moving toward more protection of women's rights, the progress is likely to be incremental, and the road to justice long and bumpy, much as it has been elsewhere. Human rights groups may have to pay more attention to the dynamic of local politics to better understand their own role and potential in the complicated interplay of power, law, and politics.

[38] Sally Merry, *Human Rights & Gender Violence: Translating International Law into Local Justice,* (Chicago and London: University of Chicago Press, 2006).

10

Corruption in China's Courts

Ling Li[1]

INTRODUCTION

Corruption in China's courts is a neglected field of study in both Chinese and English language academic circles. Although scholars and commentators have pointed out various deficiencies in the operation of courts, their relation to corruption has never been closely examined, let alone systematically investigated.[2] Policymakers as well as scholars seem rather more ready to attribute judicial problems to external factors, such as undue interference from the Chinese Communist Party (CCP), lack of resources, and local protectionism. Even when scholars pay attention, they do so most often only in passing.[3] This casual treatment of corruption in the courts has resulted in the marginalization of the problem in academic discourse. As a result, corruption in the courts appears omnipresent yet untraceable and elusive.

[1] I owe thanks to Laurel Mittenthal, Jan Michiel Otto, Randy Peerenboom, Ran Jingfu, Benjamin van Rooij, and Friedl Weiss, who read earlier versions of the manuscript and offered me valuable feedback. I am also grateful to the generosity of the Leiden University Fund, which helped finance my fieldwork. Needless to say, errors and mistakes remain entirely my own.
[2] Edited volumes on this topic include Yaxin Wang et al., "Falü chengxu yunzuo de shizheng fenxi [A Positive Analysis to Practice of Legal Procedures]," (Beijing: Law Press China, 2005). Suli Zhu ed., Falü he shehui kexue [Law and Social Science] (Beijing: Law Press, 2006). Yefu Zheng et al., ed., Beida qinghua renda shehuixue shuoshi lunwen xuanbian [Selected Theses for Master-Degree in Sociology from Peking University, Qsinghua University and Renmin University] (Jinan: Shandong People's Publishing House, 2006).
[3] Yuwen Li, "Court Reform in China: Problems, Progress & Prospects," in Implementation of Law in the People's Republic of China ed., Chen Jianfu et al. (The Netherlands: Kluwer Law International, 2002). pp. 57–58; Dingjian Cai, "Development of the Chinese Legal System since 1979 and Its Current Crisis and Transformation," Cultural Dynamics 11, no. 2 (1999). pp. 152–154; Keyuan Zou, "Judicial Reform Versus Judicial Corruption: Recent Developments in China," Criminal Law Forum 11 (2000) pp. 328–329; Keith Henderson, "The Rule of Law and Judicial Corruption in China: Half-Way over the Great Wall," in Global Corruption Report 2007: Corruption in Judicial Systems ed., Transparency International (Cambridge: Cambridge University Press, 2007); Benjamin L. Liebman, "China's Courts: Restricted Reform," The China Quarterly 191 (2007), p. 627.

The relative scarcity of studies on this topic is perhaps attributed to the sensitive nature of the topic, which makes empirical research difficult. The fact that corruption is openly denounced and severely punished in China makes interviews with judges or other court officials difficult.[4] Even for punished and closed corruption cases against court officials, access to case files is highly restricted. For researchers, attending court trials sometimes may yield interesting findings.[5] However, what is seen in courtrooms provides little information on what happened behind the scenes. This lack of data makes any systematic analysis of corruption in the courts immensely challenging.

This chapter is the result of a comprehensive study of about 350 court corruption cases, spanning the years 1991 to 2008. These are supplemented by numerous media reports, diaries, and essays written by court users about their court experience during the same period of time. Unlike the policy- or solution-oriented approaches adopted in most current studies,[6] I attempt in this chapter to investigate, describe, and analyze the factual features of corruption in China's courts with a view to demonstrating corruption's varied and multifaceted nature to gain and foster a better understanding of the problems associated with corrupt practices. Such an investigation is a necessary precondition before normative or remedial solutions can be prescribed with sufficient accuracy. The investigation seeks to answer three main questions: What types of corrupt behavior exist in China's courts? Do the different types of corruption occur with equal salience in different court divisions, different types of cases, courts at different levels, and for different groups of judges? How can the findings be interpreted and explained? In answering these questions, I adopt an inductive analytical framework developed from studying relevant cases.

Analytical Framework

Corruption in this chapter is broadly defined as the abuse of public power for private gain, a definition used by many corruption-monitoring organizations, such as the World Bank and Transparency International.[7] I divide this understanding of

---

4 During my fieldwork I made several attempts to interview judges and other court officials. Some declined the request. Some agreed to be interviewed but were clearly reluctant to discuss corruption in the courts.

5 Liang's recent work provides a valuable "thick-description" of the operation of the courts by attending open court-hearings, shedding light on various discriminative and unfair court practices. Bin Liang, *The Changing Chinese Legal System, 1978-Present: Centralization of Power and Rationalization of the Legal System* (New York, London: Routledge, 2008).

6 Ting Gong, "Dependent Judiciary and Unaccountable Judges: Judicial Corruption in Contemporary China," *China Review* 4, no. 2 (2004). Xin He, "*Zhongguo fayuan de caizheng buzu yu sifa fubai* [Lack of Financial Funding and Judicial Corruption in China's Courts]," *Ershiyi shiji (21 Century Bimonthly)*, no. 2 (2008). Henderson, "The Rule of Law and Judicial Corruption in China: Half-Way over the Great Wall."

7 See Vito Tanzi, "Corruption around the World: Causes, Consequences, Scope, and Cures," *IMF Staff Papers* 45, no. 4 (1998). For Transparency International, see http://www.transparency.org/about_us.

corruption into three subcategories: Type A involves cases where corrupt judges have physically abused litigants, illegally seizing and detaining them by force. Type B represents corrupt conduct without exchange between the judge and litigants, such as embezzlement, misappropriation of assets, swindling litigants, and serious negligence. Type C represents mainly bribery and favoritism.[8] The cases investigated in this research include both those punishable and punished in accordance with Chinese Criminal Law and those that do not meet the minimum legal requirement for criminal indictment but involve violations of ethical, professional, or party disciplinary rules.

Data Sources

The data include 350 cases corresponding to 341 individual judges and 9 nonjudge court officials, including 4 court clerks, 4 court accountants, and 1 court bailiff.[9] In each of these cases, a judge or court official was punished for one or in some cases several corrupt acts according to the CCP anticorruption disciplinary regulations or the Chinese Criminal Law. Information concerning these 350 cases comes from media reports of court trials or press releases from courts or related investigated bodies, principally the procuratorates or the disciplinary inspection committees of the local CCP. Twenty-one of these cases are supported by court files, such as court judgments and statements by prosecutors or defendants. The cases were collected between 2005 and 2008 by regularly screening the legal sections of major Internet news outlets and newspapers or magazines focusing on legal affairs and corruption issues.[10] A supplementary number of cases have been located by using the popular Chinese domestic search engines Baidu and Google.[11]

Data Configuration

The data are summarized by when the corrupt act was detected rather than by the time the corrupt act was committed because many cases involve multiple corrupt acts, extending over several years. Among the 350 judges, 12 were accused of corruption in the period 1991–1999, 183 from 2000 to 2004, and the remaining 155 in the period 2005–2008. It is difficult to ascertain the cause of this imbalance. It could be that reports of recent cases are more visible and accessible online than reports

---

[8] These cases are often referred to as jinqian'an, renqing'an, guanxi' an (literally translated as money case, personal-feeling case, and connection case).

[9] Because the number of nonjudge subjects in the database is limited, for ease of reference this group is also referred to as judges.

[10] These sources include the legal sections of www.sina.com and www.xinhuanet.com, Fazhi Ribao (Legal Daily), Jiancha Ribao (Procuracy Daily), Jiancha Fengyun (Procuracy Affairs), Nanfang Zhoumo (Southern Weekly), Caijing Magazine, and Minzhu yu Fazhi (Democracy and Rule by Law) and Anti-corruption Weekly published on Zhengyi Wang, an Internet-based magazine run by the Supreme Procuratorate.

[11] A considerable proportion of the cases was initially posted at "tanguan dangánguan," a blog hosted by Zhang Hongjian, a procuratorator in Heilongjiang Province, whom I owe thanks to.

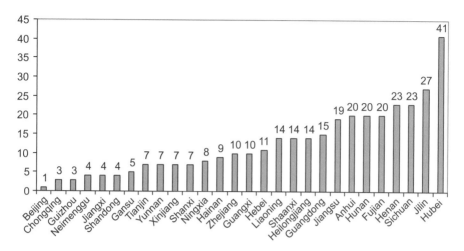

FIGURE 10.1. Regional Representation in the Database.

of earlier cases. It could also be the result of increasing incidences of violations, increased efforts against corruption, or both.

Concerning court levels, 55 of the 350 judges served in high courts (gaoji renmin fayuan) at the time of detection and 151 in intermediate courts (zhongji renmin fayuan). The remaining 144 judges served in basic level courts (jiceng fayuan), of which 63 were in urban districts and 81 in counties. The Supreme People's Court (SPC) is not represented in this database, although the openly reported ongoing investigation against SPC vice president Huang Songyou suggests it is highly likely that a corruption prosecution will be pursued.[12]

At the regional level, the data cover all provincial level administrative regions except Shanghai City, Qinghai Autonomous Region, and Tibetan Autonomous Region. Different regions have different rates of representation in the database. However, the regional representation in the database should not be mistaken with that of the actual occurrence of corruption.[13] Rather, it is more an indication of the visibility of corruption in public media, which is a mixed result of many factors that are beyond the scope of discussion here.

[12] Because the public media are under strict control by the central government, preprosecution media reports of corruption cases, especially those concerning high-profile officials, often serve as a means for the political leadership to prepare the public, providing guidance about how the case should be perceived. Among the cases studied, a prosecution is most likely to take place, followed by a conviction, when the media reports start to demonize the suspect already in the investigation period, which is exactly what is happening with the case of Huang Songyou.

[13] For example, Shanghai had reportedly investigated and punished eight court officials in 2006 and fourteen in 2005. See "Shanghai Court Officials Sign Anti-corruption Pledge First Working Day after Spring Festival (2007)," news.qq.com/a/20070226/000696.htm and "Shanghai Court Officials Sign Anti-corruption Pledge First Working Day after Spring Festival (2006)," http://news.eastday.com/eastday/node37/node189/node4644/userobject1ai163508.html. However, no publicly reported corruption cases were found during the research period concerning corruption in the Shanghai courts.

So-called political corruption,[14] or cases where judges render partial decisions in response to political pressure, is not represented in the database and hence not discussed in this chapter. What Wang describes as judicial corruption in a special environment,[15] that is, institutional corrupt practices carried out semiofficially by courts, such as illegal overcharging of litigation fees, is also not represented in the database. Crimes committed by court personnel but unrelated to the exercise of a court's function are also excluded.

Lastly, the database includes only cases for which official investigations had been completed and which were reported by official sources with specific allegations. Among the 350 judges, only 2 were acquitted on the grounds of lack of evidence.[16] Compliance with criminal procedure in the process of investigation has been considered in data selection. This resulted in the elimination of two cases; in one the evidence was unreliable due to having allegedly been procured by forcible means; in the other, there was competing evidence that the prosecution had acted out of revenge against the defendants, even though the prosecuted corrupt acts of the defendants may also have occurred.[17] For the remainder of the cases, compliance with criminal procedure requirements can only be generally assumed to have been observed in the absence of any observable indication to the contrary.

Limitations

Because most of the data was obtained from the media, the configuration of the cases is as much an indication of the slant of media coverage and different propaganda policies of different regions as of the frequency of actual instances of corruption. Due to the lack of up-to-date studies and, more important, due to the scarcity of data, this chapter must, inevitably, remain methodologically exploratory as well as tentative in its findings and conclusions. The lack of scientific sampling of the data means the result may be skewed by media bias and my selective and hence possibly imbalanced exposure to media coverage.

---

[14] Gong, "Dependent Judiciary and Unaccountable Judges: Judicial Corruption in Contemporary China."

[15] Yaxin Wang, "Sifafubai' xianxiang de yizhong jiedu [An Interpretation of 'Judicial Corruption']," Sixiang zhanxian 31, no. 4 (2005). p. 50. fn. 2.

[16] In this case, two judges from Gansu High Court were prosecuted for bribe-taking because their family members had purchased apartments from a litigant's company at a below-market-value price while the litigant's case was pending in their court. One judge was also given a mobile phone by the same litigant. In their defense, one judge argued that he had no knowledge of the purchase whereas the other argued that the price–benefit was not illicit because the judge's father-in-law was an employee of the litigant's company. The court acquitted the judges on the ground of "unclear facts" and "insufficient evidence." For details, see "Two Gansu High Court Judges Became Suspects of Bribery in Their Adjudication of A Civil Case." http://news.tom.com/1002/20040703-1058395.html.

[17] I would like to thank Christiane Wendehorst, who raised the issue at the Second Annual Conference of European China Law Association in Turin, Italy, in 2008, where an earlier version of this chapter was presented.

TABLE 10.1. *The SPC national figures for court personnel investigated for corruption*[*][†]

Year	1993	1994	1995	1996	1997	1998	1999	2000
No. of cases investigated	850	1094	962	1051	NA	2512	1450	1292
Year	2001	2002	2003	2004	2005	2006	2007	
No. of cases investigated	995	NA	794	461	378	292	218	

[*] *Note:* "Punished" refers to both criminal punishments and administrative sanctions. All numbers refer to court personnel only (so do not include corrupt prosecutors or police). The national figures for 2007 and a few local figures refer to judges only. The figure of investigated and punished judges in 2003 released in the SPC Report (2004) is 794 but 468 in the SPC Report (2008).

[†] *Source:* The SPC Annual Reports.

It has proved difficult to generate a sizable database from official press releases, the main source of information currently available for this kind of research.[18] However, representativeness of the database could be much improved if other reliable means of data collection could be accessed and used to expand the case coverage.

CORRUPTION IN CHINA'S COURTS: SCOPE AND PREVALENCE

How serious is corruption in China's courts? This has been the most frequently asked question during my research. Scale of corruption in the courts can be gauged by reviewing published data released by official sources. However, it is impossible to measure the actual scale with accurate quantitative data because many corrupt acts remain undetected. Because statistics concerning court affairs are officially considered confidential (jimi) or even absolute confidential (juemi) state secrets,[19] access to original court data of any kind is extremely difficult to obtain, let alone data concerning court corruption. The most visible index is the total number of court personnel investigated and punished for misusing or abusing adjudicative or court enforcement power for private benefit, as presented in SPC working reports each spring.

According to SPC reports, the number has continuously declined since 1998. Compared to the total of more than 190,000[20] judges in the country as a whole, the figure of 218 corruption incidents for 2007 appears moderate. However, as shown in Table 10.2, some of the data released by local courts through the local media cast doubt on the accuracy of the SPC figures in Table 10.1. For example, the number

---

[18] Media case reports have been used as the major source of data for statistic analysis in the following research studies on corruption: Yong Guo, "Corruption in Transitional China: An Empirical Analysis," *The China Quarterly* 194, June (2008). Alan P. L. Liu, "The Politics of Corruption in the People's Republic of China," *American Political Science Review* 77 (1983). Wenhao Cheng, "An Empirical Study of Corruption within China's State-Owned Enterprises," *The China Review* 4, no. 2 (2004).

[19] "[Regulation on Strengthening Judicial Statistics of People's Courts]," ed., The Supreme People's Court (1985). Part IX. Art. 29.

[20] Jingwen Zhu ed., *Zhongguo Falü Fazhan Baogao (1979–2004)* [*China Legal Development Report (1979–2004)*] (Beijing: People's University, 2007) p. 19.

TABLE 10.2. *Annual figures for court personnel investigated and punished (chachude) for corruption**

Year	Local figures released by local courts	National figures released by the SPC
2007	**252**	218
	4 provincial regions: Shaanxi, Hebei, Jiangxi, Hubei; 3 cities: Nanjing (Jiangsu), Linfen (Shanxi), Shizuishan (Ningxia) 1 basic court: Beilin District of Suihua city (Jilin)	
2006	**697**	292
	8 provincial regions: Shanxi, Henan, Ningxia, Hunan, Liaoning, Hubei, Hainan, Shanghai 2 cities: Ha'erbin (Heilongjiang), Xuzhou (Shandong)	
2005	**597 + 80**[†]	378
	8 provincial regions: Liaoning, Hainan, Zhejiang, Shanxi, Henan, Guangdong, Jilin, Shanghai	
2004	**298 + 31**[‡]	461
	5 provincial regions: Hunan, Hainan, Fujian, Jilin, Liaoning 1 city: Guilin (Guangxi)	
2003	**884**	794
	9 provinces: Shanxi, Liaoning, Shaanxi, Henan, Anhui, Hainan, Jiangsu, Hubei, Xinjiang 1 city: Cangzhou (Hebei)	
2002	**386**	NA[§]
	4 provincial regions: Hubei, Hunan, Liaoning, Neimenggu	

* *Note:* Some of the statistics from local courts only roughly correspond to the full calendar year as listed in the left column. For example, some figures only represent the results of an anticorruption campaign in a particular month. Some figures start and end in the middle of the calendar year. In two cases, the figures also cover the first half of the next calendar year; this is indicated where applicable.

[†] The figure for Guangdong Province covers 2005 and the first half of 2006.

[‡] The figure for Liaoning Province covers 2004 and the first half of 2005.

[§] *Source:* The SPC Annual Reports and local media reports on file with the author.

of court personnel investigated in 2006 for corruption in just five provinces (out of 32 provincial level administrative regions) is 585, or more than twice the SPC's total nationwide figure.

The origins of this discrepancy are difficult to explain. There is relatively little incentive for the local courts to inflate the number. Do the local courts perhaps shrink the numbers before they are submitted to the SPC, or does the SPC manipulate the data after collecting it from the local courts? Irrespective of the correct explanation for the discrepancy, it appears that the actual level of corruption in courts is more serious than SPC reports suggest.

Furthermore, when looking at these numbers, it should be borne in mind that the detection of corruption in the courts is usually, if not always, tied to a particular case.

When a judge is caught for corruption in one case, previous cases tried by the same judge will not normally be examined. It is only when a suspect confesses to other as-yet-undetected corrupt acts in exchange for lenient punishment that this case-by-case approach is modified to some limited extent. However, the total number of unlawful and unethical acts in a corrupt judge's career can never be accurately ascertained.

TYPE A: EXTREME CASES INVOLVING PHYSICAL VIOLENCE

Corrupt conduct involving physical abuse of the victim mainly refers to those acts that deprive the victim of her/his physical liberty, such as the illegal seizure and detention of litigants. There were 6 such cases among the total of 350. In a notorious case in Jiangxian County, Shanxi Province, the former vice president of the county court Yao Xiaohong instructed his subordinates to beat a litigant to death just because the litigant attempted to challenge Yao's arbitrary decision.[21] In another case in Rongcheng County, Hebei Province, Yin Hexin, then chief of the economic division of the county court, was "hired" by two plaintiffs to "enforce" payment of debt from their disputant, who resided in another province. Having accepted a RMB10,000 "litigation fee" Yin and his colleagues kidnapped the defendant from his home. Struggling and shouting for help, the disputant was handcuffed from behind and covered with the judges' clothes over his head. Hours later, the disputant was found suffocated to death.[22] In at least four cases, the judges committed violent corrupt conduct at the request of friends or relatives. At the moment of detection, all six judges served in basic level courts, five at the county level.

There are too few cases in this category to conduct a more segmented analysis. In reality there are most certainly more cases of this type, although not necessarily all with fatal consequences. Nonetheless, the comparatively low representation of this type of corruption in this database may suggest that the use of physical violence is not typical for corruption in China's courts. The explanation for the violence in these cases, both in terms of its existence and its low representation in the database, may well be that the courts enjoy only limited policing power via the judicial police (sifa jingcha),[23] whose formal purpose is to uphold court orders and assist in enforcing asset-related judgments. This feature of the distribution of power also separates corruption in courts from that in other law enforcement institutions, such as the procuratorates and the police, which enjoy a wider range of policing powers involving restricting an individual's physical freedom, and in which the deprivation of a victim's liberty is a more salient form of corrupt conduct.

---

[21] "How Can a Court Become the 'Palace of Hell'? (1999)," http://www.cyol.net/cyd/zqb/19990715/GB/9560°Q515.htm.

[22] "To Make Money Court Issues Quota to Judges, To Collect Debt Judges Killed Human Life (1998)," http://www.gmw.cn/01shsb/1998–07/27/GB/688^SH14–215.htm.

[23] Regulation of Judicial Police in People's Courts, The Supreme People's Court (1997).

TYPE B: CORRUPTION WITHOUT EXCHANGE (NONBRIBERY)

Corruption in this and the next category does not involve violence. However, the absence of physical force does not necessarily imply an absence of any kind of force, coercion, or threat. Instead, some acts in this category involve the use of symbolic power, which extracts deference through the presence of symbols of court power, such as a court document or a court official riding in a court vehicle. It is this kind of power, imbued with the threat of coercion, that enables some judges to compel voluntary submission or cooperation from their subjects to obtain their corrupt gain without needing to resort to physical violence or intimidation. Judges from basic courts continue to dominate in the category of Type B (forty-seven of the total of seventy-nine judges). Six judges were from high courts and twenty-six from intermediate courts.

The main form of corrupt conduct in Type B is theft. Sixty-nine judges were punished for embezzlement and/or misappropriation of court funds or seized assets. Nine judges were found guilty of fraud (four of them also conducted embezzlement and/or misappropriation). Six judges, including one who also conducted embezzlement, were involved in serious incompetence and negligence at work, such as losing case files and failing to hold an open trial for nineteen years.[24] Because there is no clear indication in the available materials that the judges had received external incentives to be deliberately negligent (although this is generally more likely), "effort-saving" is assumed to be the private benefit in these five cases.

Among the sixty-nine embezzlement and misappropriation cases, it is not surprising to find that more than one-third took place in enforcement divisions, where large volumes of seized assets are administered. In these cases, courts largely failed in discharging their mandated role as guardian of the seized assets for litigants. Instead, easy opportunities for embezzlement and misappropriation were nurtured by the lack of monitoring, especially monitoring by the litigants to whom the assets belong. Tan Yongxing, an enforcement judge in Longgang District (Basic) Court, Shenzhen City, misappropriated RMB 13 million for gambling in a year and had gambled away nearly half of it when he was caught.[25] Li Zhengda, an enforcement judge in Jilin High Court, embezzled RMB 40 million over eight years. Despite complaints from litigants, the investigation only started after he had retired from his job and was about to leave the country.[26]

Other than the enforcement judges, four court accountants and twenty court presidents or vice presidents were also apprehended for embezzlement or

---

[24] "Hainan Lingao Court Failed to Hold Open Trials for a Small Case for 19 Years (2006)," http://news.sina.com.cn/s/2006–07–29/09219601648s.shtml.

[25] "Thrown Millions in Gambling Judge Became Prisoner (2000)," http://gzdaily.dayoo.com/gb/content/2000–12/07/content_42133.htm.

[26] "Exploiting Loopholes, Jilin High Court Li Zhengda Embezzled Millions (2006)," http://news.qq.com/a/20060216/000869_1.htm.

misappropriation. Both accountants and court administrative leaders have easy access to the public coffers. Cheng Wei, an accountant in Tianjin Maritime Court, had successfully embezzled RMB 1.69 million and misappropriated RMB 140 million, mostly from court accounts of seized assets. Cheng ultimately left an RMB 100 million "black hole" at Tianjin Maritime Court.[27] There is no information about how the loss in these cases was settled with the litigants to whom these assets actually belong. It is surprising, though, that within Type B only one judge came from the case registration division, which is responsible for collecting litigation fees, the principal source of court income.

Apart from theft, seven judges were accused of usurpation of assets through deception and/or illegal seizure. One judge from Heishan County Court in Liaoning Province swindled RMB 990,000 from a gullible buyer who believed the judge's story of a fake court auction.[28] In Hunan Province two judges loaned money to a construction subcontractor commissioned by a corporate developer. Knowing that the developer had deep pockets, the judges raised the interest rate of the loan to twenty times above the market rate, which the subcontractor obviously would not be able to pay. The judges then brought a lawsuit against the subcontractor in their own court in the name of an acquaintance, rendered a court decision in their favor, and enforced the judgment by freezing the account of the corporate developer.[29]

In two cases, judges seized assets from nonlitigants just by dressing up in court uniforms and showing fake court documents. Li Shengyin, a county court judge from Hebei Province, used a forged court order to appropriate assets worth RMB 7 million from a bankrupt state-owned enterprise under the eyes of the factory guards. They invented a contractual dispute case against the enterprise after the usurpation, using remote relatives as plaintiffs and forging evidence.[30]

TYPE C: CORRUPTION THROUGH EXCHANGE

In this subcategory, corruption occurs in the form of an exchange. In this chapter, exchange is not limited only to monetary transactions, or jinqian case (cases influenced by monetary bribes), as in the SPC classification. It also includes exchanges performed in the form of a favor under the principle of reciprocity. Often such

---

[27] "No. 1 Biggest Judicial Corruption Case in Tianjin Involving More Than RMB 100Million (2006)," http://news.163.com/06/0418/14/2F0ES2P30001124J_3.html.

[28] "Liaoning Heishan County: Judge Chewed Receipt, Court Denied Responsibility (2004)," http://house.people.com.cn/xinwen/article_04_10_12_2340.html.

[29] See case digest in Shigui Tan, *Zhongguo sifa gaige yanjiu* [A Study on Judicial Reform of China] (Beijing: Law Press China, 2000) p. 123.

[30] The case drew media attention only when the employees of the state-owned company held a public protest and physical conflict ensued with the local police. An investigation by the local procuratorate followed. Xinhuanews Net, Fazhi News, December 12, 2003, available at http://news.xinhuanet.com/legal/2003–12/12/content_1228524.htm.

favors are not immediately or directly associated with a monetary value or payback. Nonetheless, these favors necessarily have great value for the recipients.

For example, Su Jiafu, the former chief of the criminal division of Gutian County Court, Fujian Province, confessed that he acquitted three defendants on a rape charge not just because he was offered the RMB 6,000. Rather, it was also because one of the defendants turned out to be the son of the director of the local police bureau, who had done a favor to Su before in a battery case involving Su's brother. Su considered that it was time for him to return the favor.[31] Su acquitted the defendants by recognizing the victim's cries as a form of sexual consent (out of pleasure) against all other contesting evidence. This is a typical example of what the SPC terms a "renqing case," a case influenced by an exchange of favors. Sometimes, the litigant does not yet have an established reciprocal relationship with the judge when the litigation is brought to court. In such circumstances, a favor exchange is often conducted through an intermediary, the so-called guanxi, a person who is familiar with both parties and guarantees that the favor is properly registered and returned. Jinqian, renqing, and guanxi cases are all denounced by the SPC and all three fall into the category of corruption through exchange in this chapter.

This section is arranged along the three phases of litigation, which also correspond to the three major functional court divisions: case registration (li'an), adjudication (shenpan), and enforcement (zhixing). A summary of litigation procedure in China's courts provides the context for this discussion.

Brief Introduction to Litigation Procedure in China's Courts

In the 1990s, the SPC launched an institutional reform, dividing courts into several divisions according to the chronological order of the litigating process. Before this reform, courts were only divided according to the nature of the case[32] and each court division was mandated to complete the entire process from case registration, court hearing, panel adjudication, and issuance of verdict to enforcement of the judgment. Under the previous system, the judge who registered a case might well be the same judge who heard and decided the case and who enforced the judgment. This concentration of power is believed to have increased opportunities for corruption in courts.[33]

Under the reform, a division of power was carried out resulting in three separate court divisions: case admission/registration, case adjudication, and judgment enforcement. Each performs different functional judicial power.[34] At the same time,

---

[31] Tan, *Zhongguo sifa gaige yanjiu [A Study on Judicial Reform of China]* p. 123.

[32] Namely, whether the case is civil, criminal, or commercial. The Organizational Law of People's Courts (1979), Ch. 2.

[33] Shouguang People's Court (Shandong Province), "'*Dali'an jizhi de yunxing moshi yu chengxiao* [The Operational Model and Effect of the 'Grand Case-Registering' Mechanism]," *Sifa shenpan dongtai yu yanjiu [Research on Judicial Development]* 1, no. 1 (2001), pp. 95–97.

[34] Jianxin Ren, "Annual Report of the Supreme People's Court," (1998).

a separate adjudicative supervisory division (shenpan jiandu ting) was also established, charged with correcting glaring mistakes and injustices in closed cases using a special procedure.[35]

The normal sequence of the litigation procedure is as follows. The plaintiff brings his statement of action to the case registration division (li'anting), where the case will be examined and archived and the litigation fee will be decided. Once the litigation fee is received, the case will then be assigned to the responsible adjudication division (shenpanting). The adjudication division will hold court hearings and issue the judgment after deliberating in a panel – either a small collegial panel set up within the court division (heyiting) or a grand collegial panel (shenpanweiyuanhui) set up at the court level – depending on the nature of the case. A few cases can be handled according to a simplified procedure and are subject to the decision of a single judge instead of a panel.[36]

A victorious plaintiff can go to the enforcement division of the first instance court to apply for enforcement if the defendant fails to perform his obligation voluntarily.[37] The enforcement division will examine the application and decide whether the enforcement will be carried out. Within two years after the court judgment has taken effect, if evidence of serious injustice can be provided, litigants are entitled to apply for zaishen, a reexamination, and retrial of a closed case at the adjudicative–supervisory division. The procedure can also be initiated by the court that had rendered the judgment, its superior court, or the procuratorate.[38]

Among the 350 judges included in the database, 304 were involved in corruption through exchange in the form of either specific monetary payment or unspecific reciprocity. One hundred seventy-nine judges were bribed for their favorable decisions in the adjudicative procedure; ninety-one were bribed for the same in the enforcement procedure, and seven in the case registration procedure.[39]

Adjudication Phase

One hundred seventy-nine judges rendered perceptibly favorable court decisions to favor-seeking parties in exchange for monetary bribes or other forms of favors. Usually, judges would render perceptibly favorable decisions to the party from whom they had taken or expected to take bribes, against the interest of the other party. However, a few especially greedy and manipulative judges[40] managed to take bribes

---

35 Zhu ed., *Zhongguo Falü Fazhan Baogao (1979–2004) [China Legal Development Report (1979–2004)]* p. 189.

36 Civil Procedural Law (1991). Ch. 12–13.

37 Civil Procedural Law (1991). Art. 207.

38 Civil Procedural Law (1991). Art. 177, 185.

39 The remaining twenty-seven judges conducted corrupt exchange in court administrative affairs, for example, taking bribes from subordinates in exchange for promotion or taking bribes from bidders in exchange for court procurement contracts.

40 For example, see http://news.sina.com.cn/c/2003–01–20/180136143s.shtml and http://news.tom.com/Archive/1002/2003/7/17–35160.html.

from both parties and yet made both believe that they had been treated favorably. The most infamous example is Meng Laigui, the then Chief of the Adjudicative–Supervisory Division of Shanxi High Court. Meng had conducted the "eating from the defendant after having eaten from the plaintiff (chile yuangao chi beigao)" in ten out of twenty-one cases, in which Meng had taken bribes.[41] Most of these cases underwent lengthy mediations presided over by Meng, who took advantage of asymmetric information of the litigants to play off the two sides and manipulate their expectations.[42]

Among the 179 judges bribed in the adjudication phase, at least 57 took bribes in criminal cases, and 111 in civil cases.[43] Among the 111 civil cases, 95 were about contractual disputes and tort. Court insolvency cases, in particular, always seem to attract a high volume of bribes. Having just passed the Bankruptcy Law and obviously lacking experience of such cases, the SPC established a pilot program in the Shenzhen Intermediate Court and Tianjin High Court. Both courts wound up with high-profile corruption scandals. Some lawyers revealed that in these cases the court insolvency proceedings are opaque, which makes it difficult for creditors to supervise and allows great discretion to the court in choosing the members of the insolvency committee.[44] In these scandals, where high volumes of assets are at stake, corrupt exchanges develop not only between judges and the creditors/debtors in exchange for a manipulated price of the auctioned items, but also between judges and professional service providers, such as auctioneers, asset-assessors, and lawyers, in exchange for court commissions. The SPC was alerted by similar practices detected in many other courts.[45]

No case reviewed in this research concerns administrative litigation. However, one case involving corruption in an administrative review procedure may be worth mentioning. Lou Xiaoping, who served as deputy director of the Justice Bureau of Hainan Province, was prosecuted for taking RMB 400,000 from a farm manager who had applied for an administrative review of a decision made by Sanya City concerning the confiscation of his land. Consequently, Lou rendered a decision in

---

[41] "Corrupt Judge Meng Laigui 'Eating from Defendant After Having Eaten from Plaintiff' (2007)," http://news.163.com/07/0703/03/3IEPKLR200011229.html.

[42] For similar practice, see the case of Cheng Kunbo, the former court president of Huanggang Intermediate Court. "Faguan de fubai tongmeng [Corrupt Coalition of Judges]," *zhongguo xinwen zhoukan* [*China Newsweek*], April 19, 2004.

[43] In some cases, there was no information concerning the type of case in which bribery took place. In other cases, judges took bribes in multiple cases, civil and criminal, and hence are counted twice.

[44] "Five Former-judges from Shenzhen Intermediate Court Suspected of Corruption, Three Sentenced (2007)," http://news.sina.com.cn/c/l/2007–03–24/093512601837.shtml and "Several Judges from Tianjin Courts Fall Due to Corruption (2008)," http://news.xinhuanet.com/local/2008–07/29/content_8834976.htm.

[45] The SPC referred to the practices as the "blowing wind of insolvency cases (guaqile pochanfeng)." See "Several Opinions of the Supreme People's Court on Strengthening the Adjudicative Ability and Raising the Standard of Adjudication (2005)," Note 13.

the farm manager's favor. When the bribery was detected six years later, Lou had already been appointed the vice president of Hainan High Court. Lou was sentenced to a term of imprisonment of 11 years for bribe-taking and for illicit enrichment, namely having a significant increase of his assets that he cannot reasonably explain in relation to his lawful income.

The low volume of administrative actions in China's courts in general[46] might be the direct explanation for the low incidence of corruption in administrative cases in the database. Nonetheless, Lou's case is special because we would normally assume that biased decisions in administrative disputes would be rendered only in favor of governmental institutions. However, as Fu has shown, the reason that there seems to be less corruption between plaintiffs and courts in administrative cases is more likely to be that most of the plaintiffs have no money or status.[47] If the plaintiff has substantial resources, as the farm manager in Lou's case, the decision may also be tilted in the plaintiff's favor.

Enforcement Phase

It is conspicuous that seventy-nine judges had conducted corrupt exchange in the enforcement phase. A law graduate, after having worked as an intern in a local law firm for a year, said in an interview, "I thought the operation of the adjudication procedure was dark. But now I realize that the darkness only begins when it comes to judgment enforcement."[48]

In practice, both plaintiffs and defendants can bribe the enforcement personnel to either expedite or delay the procedure, depending on which party is making the request. To help the plaintiffs, exceptional measures can be employed to facilitate the enforcement, including advanced enforcement (xianyu zhixing),[49] seizing assets located outside of one's jurisdiction (yidi zhixing),[50] designating a specific court to

---

[46] Detailed statistics can be found in Zhu ed., *Zhongguo Falü Fazhan Baogao (1979–2004)* [*China Legal Development Report (1979–2004)*]. Ch. 4.

[47] Hualing Fu, "Putting China's Judiciary into Perspective: Is It Independent, Competent, and Fair?" in *Beyond Common Knowledge: Empirical Approaches to the Rule of Law* ed., Erik G. Jense, Thomas C. Heller (2003), p. 212.

[48] Interview L013.1. More complaints and remarks from lawyers about court malpractice in the enforcement procedure can be found at "Truth of *zhixingnan*" http://12203.1cnlaw.com/Essay_Topic.htm?fn=20080927091446; "Judges, why don't you enforce the judgment when the defendant is solvent"; http://club.pchome.net/topic_1_15_1814718__.html; "Lawyer out of solutions," http://www.acla.org.cn/forum/printthread.php?Board=fzsp&main=702008&type=post.

[49] In one case, a well-connected plaintiff had her claimed assets seized and delivered even before the trial started through the xianyu zhixing (advanced enforcement) procedure. Court Judgment (2006) [Huaihua Intermediate Court No. 52], Ruanling People's Procuratorate v. Tang Jikai.

[50] In the so-called "*Changhang* incident" in Hubei province, several judges from Shiyan Intermediate Court once seized assets worth of millions from someone over whom the court had no jurisdiction and who had never been informed about, let alone heard, in the framed litigation. It was later found out that the judges had shares in the plaintiff's pledging business. "A Fraud Case Led to Discovery

enforce a particular case not necessarily within the court's jurisdiction (zhiding zhixing), and requesting that a case be transferred from lower courts to a superior court for the purpose of enforcement (tiji zhixing).[51] Some enforcement personnel, after taking bribes from the plaintiff, were also caught seizing assets from third parties unrelated to the litigation.[52]

Other than accelerating the procedure, plaintiffs also bribe enforcement judges to prioritize their court award in litigation involving multiple creditors. For example, after taking RMB 100,000 a former judge from Hunan High Court satisfied a creditor's court award by appropriating the amount from the defendant's account that had been frozen in another pending case for the benefit of a different plaintiff.[53] A lawyer expressed his concern in an interview that a court award was unlikely to be realized automatically if the plaintiff does not provide a monetary incentive to the enforcement judges, especially when there are many creditors and much is at stake.[54]

In some cases judges also accede to requests from losing defendants to stall the enforcement, temporarily or indefinitely. As a matter of common sense, requests from defendants for inaction or delayed action are much easier to satisfy than requests from plaintiffs for proactive enforcement, because the latter would naturally require more effort and resources. Another approach to the stalling of enforcement is to start a zaishen case, the exceptional retrial procedure mentioned in the introduction of the litigating process. Under the Civil Procedure Law, once a zaishen application is granted, enforcement proceedings are suspended.[55] A judge in Sichuan High Court was once paid RMB 160,000 by a defendant for this service.[56]

The enforcement procedure is likely to become precarious when both the plaintiff and defendant seek to influence the judge. In a contractual dispute between two real estate developers in the capital city of Guangxi Province, the disputed apartment building was seized and reseized several times, leaving the primary victims, the real estate buyers, totally unprotected.[57]

---

of Greedy Judges," *Worker's Daily Tianxun Online*, Nov. 29, 2003. More such examples include Li Zhengda, former judge from Jilin High Court; Wu Chunfa, former judge from Guiyang Intermediate Court; and the group corruption case of judges from Wuhan intermediate court, including former deputy court president Ke Changxin.

51 A more detailed local study about yidizhixing and tijizhixing written by a judge from Chongqing High Court is on file with the author.

52 See the report "Anci District Court of Langfang City Illegal Enforcing Non-Litigant's Property," *Legal Daily*, Jan. 11, 2002; "Enforcement Staff Ignore Defendant's Property for Months but Freeze Property of Owners Not Related to the Litigation," *Guangming Daily*, Nov. 25, 2005.

53 Court Judgment (2005) [Hunan High Court final No.129] Loudi People's Procuratorate v. Wang Kuang.

54 Interview L014.1.

55 "Opinions on the Application of the Civil Procedure Law (1991)," The Supreme People's Court. Art. 206.

56 "Two Judges From Sichuan High Court and Chengdu Intermediate Court Were Sentenced for Bribe-taking (2005)," http://www.justice.gov.cn/epublish/gb/paper147/5/class014700001/hwz672714.htm.

57 "A Guangxi Court Released Seized Assets, Plaintiff Got Nothing in Eight Years after Winning the Litigation (2006)," http://news.sohu.com/20060802/n244576787.shtml.

That enforcement procedures are particularly fertile ground for corruption stems in part from litigants' increasing willingness to pay as the fulfilment of their objectives draws closer. In addition, excuses for judges' corrupt conduct are easy to find. For example, when stalling the enforcement procedure after bribes have been taken from defendants, judges can justify their inaction by resorting to subterfuges such as local protectionism, the lack of vehicles and human resources, the lack of cooperation from the defendants, and the lack of authority.[58] On the other hand, if tough enforcement is meted out, the conduct can be described as a demonstration of the court's endeavors to realize litigants' rights and enhance its authority.[59]

Court auction procedures administered by enforcement divisions are also prone to corruption. In three cases involving three judges who had taken twenty-two bribes during enforcement procedures, eleven bribes were from plaintiffs, four from defendants, and seven from auctioneers. In the database as a whole, fourteen judges were punished for taking bribes either from auctioneers in exchange for the court commission or from buyers in exchange for a manipulated lower-than-market price of the auctioned item.

Case Registration Phase

This research uncovered only seven judges from case registration divisions (li'anting) who had engaged in corrupt exchange. Two were from intermediate courts and five from high courts. The seemingly low corruption rate in this court division, especially in the lower courts, is not surprising. With litigation fees constituting a major portion of the income for many lower level courts, charging litigants an additional "entry fee" on top of the litigation fee would risk deterring litigants from going to court all together, resulting in a loss of litigation fees for the court and consequently corruption opportunities for judges in other court divisions. To ensure that courts are the ultimate dispute-resolution institution, the Civil Procedure Law also clearly provides that "a court must accept a case if the plaintiff has indicated a specific defendant, the dispute and his claims"[60] and appeal is provided as a right

---

[58] After taking money from a defendant, Ke Changxin, the former vice president of Wuhan Intermediate Court, instructed to stall the enforcement of the defendant's case. The plaintiff resorted to the court president, who then pressed the vice president to proceed with the enforcement procedure. In order not to offend the court president but, at the same time, keep his promise to the defendant, Ke had a plan and instructed both the defendant and the enforcement personnel. On the day of enforcement when the court personnel arrived at the defendant's residence, the defendant resisted the court order and threatened the enforcement personnel by slaughtering a live rooster in front of them and told the enforcement personnel that whoever took his assets would be killed like the rooster. The enforcement personnel withdrew from the scene immediately. See "*Jiekai wuhan zhongyuan de heixiazi* [Uncover the 'Black Box' of Wuhan Intermediate Court]," *Minzhu yu fazhi [Democracy and Rule by Law]*, vol. 6, Issue 1, 2004.

[59] The aforementioned former enforcement judge Li Zhenda from Jilin High Court was even awarded a medal for his contribution to the court. These reasons were also mentioned in an interview with a judge and two other interviews with lawyers.

[60] Civil Procedure Law (1991) Art. 108.

of litigants.[61] Both leave comparatively little discretion to judges for manipulation, especially in the case of an application to appeal.

No litigant in the investigated cases was found paying monetary bribes to judges to obtain an appeal. In contrast, acceptance into the zaishen procedure is notoriously troublesome and is more likely to involve monetary bribes.[62] Because zaishen is an exceptional procedure, its acceptance is strictly controlled to ensure the authority, effectiveness, and predictability of court judgments. This creates a large gap between the demand for zaishen from litigants and the supply of this procedure by the courts. At the same time, the screening criteria for acceptance are vague and leave substantial room for manipulation.[63] Within the data sample, five judges responsible for reviewing zaishen cases were found to have taken bribes. Two of them reportedly boasted in identical terms to the bribing litigants, saying "Your case had reached its last stop here in my division."[64]

It should be noted that first instance case registration is not trouble-free for litigants and lawyers. Although it is not a procedural phase characterized by serious bribery, complaints abound as to the phenomena of "difficult [surly] court personnel; difficult to obtain entry into the court system; and difficult to get things done in the courts" (liannankan, mennanjin, shinanban),[65] which have been repeatedly denounced by the SPC.[66] Typical behaviors include the arbitrary rejection to file an action. A young lawyer once had the registration of an action rejected because, according to the chief of the registration division, "the length of the contract was too short."[67]

---

[61] Civil Procedure Law (1991) Art. 147.

[62] Discussions on this topic can be found in lawyers' online discussion groups; for an example, see http://www.fl365.com/gb/nhlaw/bbs/topicnew.asp?TOPIC_ID=98458&FORUM_ID=58&CAT_ID=&Topic_Title=%C1%A2%B0%B8%C4%D1.

[63] Because of the abundant judicial problems emerged in the procedure, the Civil Procedure Law was amended in 2008, aiming to improve the transparency and efficiency of the examining procedure over zaishen application. See "New Civil Procedure Law: Examination of Zaishen Application Better Regulated, More Transparent and More Efficient," People's Courts Daily, April 12, 2008. For further study on the zaishen procedure, see Yulin Fu, "Minshi shenpan jiandu zhidu de shizhengxing fenxi [An Empirical Analysis of the Supervisory System of the Adjudicative Process in Civil Litigations]," in Falü Chengxu Yunzuo De Shizheng Fenxi [A Positive Analysis to Practice of Legal Procedures] (Beijing: Law Press China, 2005).

[64] See supra note 41 on the case of Meng Laigui. See also http://www.chinavalue.net/Media/Article.aspx?ArticleId=9149&PageId=1.

[65] A couple of examples can be found at http://www.xici.net/b641398/d39976989.htm and chinahunyin.com/list.asp?unid=482.

[66] For details, see reports on the SPC's Guifan sifa xingwei zhuanxiang zhenggai huodong [special rectification campaign on regulating judicial behaviors].

[67] Interview L013.1. Similar complaints from lawyers can be found at "Descriptions and explanations of li'an nan, http://www.9ask.cn/blog/user/fyhaolvshi/archives/2008/41476.html and "Lazy Beijing judges," http://www.acla.org.cn/forum/printthread.php?Board=44&main=682368&type=post. For a summary of the problem of li'annan, see the interview with Professor Xu Xin in China Adjudication Magazine: "Jiejue "liánnan" yao lizu zhongguo guoqing [To Resolve the Problem of Difficulty in Case-Registration One Needs to Consider the Current Situation of the Country]," zhongguo shenpan [China Adjudication] 2007. An electronic copy can be found in the interviewee's blog: http://www.fatianxia.com/blog_list.asp?id=8057.

Several complaints of this kind were posted online against the Chaoyang District Court of Beijing. On one occasion, as revealed by lawyer Liu Xiaoyuan in his blog, the court rejected a medical negligence case because the lawyer did not provide proof of cremation of the deceased in addition to the death certificate. In another case involving a contractual dispute, lawyer Liu, after having provided the detailed postal address of the defendant, was told that the case could not be registered if he could not provide a special geographic code for that address, which is only commonly known to the police.[68] In an extreme case, a lawyer was even assaulted by a judge in Tianjin Nankai District Court when the lawyer tried to challenge an unjustified rejection.[69]

It is noteworthy, however, that rejections are hardly ever made in written form,[70] making it difficult for litigants or lawyers successfully to challenge such rejections. According to a report in the *Legal Daily*, one lawyer was left with no option but to appear in court accompanied by a notary officer to witness the rejection to secure evidence, an innovative and desperate measure.[71]

On the other hand, some court users report that if the litigant or lawyer has the right connections or guanxi in courts, the registration procedure can be surprisingly smooth and efficient. A lawyer proudly revealed in his blog that with the help of his "judge mates" (faguan xiongdi) he had once completed all court procedures and had a defendant's bank account frozen in less than two hours from the moment he began to draft the plaintiff's statement of case.[72] In another instance, Zhan Xiaoyong, the son of a former court president of the Hunan High Court, once successfully completed the notoriously difficult zaishen acceptance procedure on the same day, just a few hours after the announcement of the verdict of the appeal.[73]

---

[68] See the blog of Liu Xiaoyuan lawyer: http://blog.sina.com.cn/s/blog_49dafoea010005iw.html. Similar complaints about mishandling of case registration applications by the same court can be found in "Resolving the impasse of li'annan," http://club.news.sohu.com/r-fazhi-78818-0-0-10.html.

[69] The report on this incident stated that when the administrative court division of Tianjin Nankai Court rejected a class-action lawsuit, the lawyer representing the plaintiffs attempted to challenge the court's rejection by asking for an explanation and refused to leave the court. During the argument, the then chief of the administrative court division came to the scene and tried to strangle the lawyer with his hands. This notorious incident was widely disseminated because the judge shouted at the lawyer and litigants that "*wo jiushi fayuan; fayuan jiushi wo* [I am the court and the court is me]." For details, see "Tianjin Judge Assaulted Lawyer: Investigation Team Suggested Removing the Judge from Court Leadership (2006)," *Huaxia Shibao [Huaxia Times]*.

[70] There are also many complaints from lawyers and litigants that court clerks took evidence from them without issuing any acknowledgment about whether, when, and what has been submitted by litigants or their representatives and received by courts. This practice makes it difficult to hold courts responsible when files are found to be missing. For details, search "*fayuan bu gei shouju* (no acknowledgment of receipt of evidence by courts)" at http://www.baidu.com.

[71] "First Public Notary Case of Securing Evidence for the Act of Registering a Case in Court (2007)," http://www.legaldaily.com.cn/0705/2007–08/12/content_678775.htm.

[72] The Web page of this story has been removed from the Web site but is on file with the author.

[73] The information was disclosed as a piece of "side information" in the defendant's statement of Ao Wanquan, a former judge and deputy chief of the economic-case court division in Hunan High Court, who was later prosecuted for bribe-taking.

GENERAL FINDINGS AND INTERPRETATION

The first general finding of this chapter is the striking dominance of Type C corrupt conduct, corruption through exchange without any direct physical impact on the victim. Among the total of 389 corrupt acts (some judges were detected and punished, for example, for both embezzlement and bribe-taking) committed by the 350 judges, 303 acts, 78 percent of all, belong to Type C, corrupt exchange. This result is to be expected because Types A and B normally leave traces of evidence of corruption, such as missing assets or a direct victim, which makes the conduct riskier and its practitioner more vulnerable to exposure. Bribery and favoritism are instead based on a voluntary agreement between the exchange parties either in terms of a monetary transaction or an unspecified reciprocation, from which both parties benefit. This creates a sense of equilibrium, which sustains secrecy and makes the corrupt conduct more difficult to detect. Indeed, this form of corruption is widespread not just in the courts but in Chinese public institutions in general, as illustrated in Guo's recent work.[74]

This dataset also suggests that judges from intermediate and high courts appear to be more likely to engage in Type C corruption than in Types A and B. In fact, no judge serving in high courts or above in this database was involved in corruption described in Type A. Physical violence is rare and found mainly in basic courts, suggesting that upper court judges have a higher sense of professionalism and self-identity that inhibits such behavior. Higher court judges also appear to be less likely than lower court judges to engage in theft or misappropriation of funds. Judges from higher courts represent 8 percent of such Type B cases in the dataset, whereas intermediate court judges account for 33 percent.

In contrast, for Type C, exchange-based corruption, high court and intermediate court judges accounted for 17 percent and 47 percent, respectively. However, this finding does not necessarily suggest that fewer cases of corrupt exchange occur in lower courts than in higher courts. It is more likely that punishable corrupt-exchange activities in higher level courts are more visible than those committed by judges in lower courts. Greater sums or promises of reciprocal favors are likely to be required to influence judges in higher courts (overseeing higher-stakes cases). This attracts more attention from the media and the relevant judicial disciplinary committee that are generally more likely to focus on cases in which judges accept large bribes from litigants or their lawyers in major cities, rather than on cases where litigants try to influence judges in remote countryside courts by delivering to them, for instance, 5 liters of cooking oil.

The second and related finding is that few high court judges in the cases digested in this research committed the crime of rendering a court decision in violation of the prescription of law (wangfacaipanzui). In other words, few high court judges

---

[74] Guo, "Corruption in Transitional China: An Empirical Analysis."

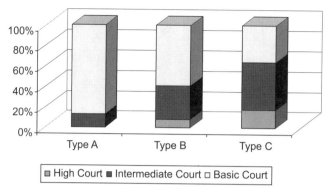

FIGURE 10.2. Representation of Courts at Different Levels in Types A, B, and C.

were engaged in corrupt activities that resulted in overt miscarriages of law, such as rendering favorable decisions for litigants by forging court documents or instructing litigants to forge evidence or commit perjury. Among the seventy-nine corrupt exchanges committed by basic court judges, the ratio between corrupt exchange resulting and not resulting in overt miscarriage of law is 1:1.5. In contrast, the ratio drops to 1:11 and 1:48 in intermediate courts and high courts respectively. One possible explanation for this could be that the complexity of cases presented in higher courts leaves more room for manipulation of discretion. Another possible explanation is that higher court judges are generally better educated and experienced in interpreting the law and hence more capable of exploiting the law for corrupt purposes.

On the other hand, "collective corruption" cases (chuan'an yao'an) are more often found in higher courts, such as the corruption scandals in the provincial high courts of Jilin, Hunan, Liaoning, Tianjin, and intermediate courts of major cities, including Changsha, Wuhan, Shenyang, and Shenzhen. These scandals are characterized by collusive and sometimes organized corrupt conduct of judges from different court divisions and from courts at different levels who shared clients and the resulting corrupt benefits.[75] In some of these courts, corruption was so deep-rooted that corruption scandals continued to resurface even after the courts had gone through anticorruption purges and the corrupt judges had allegedly been removed and replaced.[76]

The third general finding is that the occurrence of bribery relating to court-management affairs is closely correlated to the position of the offender. Fifteen

[75] For example, in the Changsha scandal, corrupt cooperation was found among judges from Hunan High Court and Changsha Intermediate Court. In the Wuhan scandal, cooperation existed among judges between Wuhan Intermediate Court and Shiyan Intermediate Court. The recent investigation against Huang Songyou, the former vice president of the SPC, also indicates that there was cooperation between the SPC and the Guangdong High Court.

[76] Such incidences have been found in the following courts: Fuyang Intermediate Court, Wuhan Intermediate Court, Shenzhen Intermediate Court, and Jilin High Court.

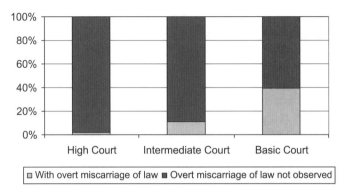

FIGURE 10.3. Numbers of Corruption Cases with Different Features in Courts at Different Levels.

judges took kickbacks from contractors in court construction projects; of these, thirteen were court presidents at different levels. Twelve judges, all of whom were court presidents, including four from high courts, took bribes from their subordinates for court appointment and promotion.[77] This finding is not surprising given that the decision-making power over court finances and personnel management is concentrated exclusively in the hands of top court leaders. This finding reinforces the conclusion of Ren and Du's work, namely that "first-in-command" officials in public institutions are highly susceptible to corruption as a result of the concentration of power.[78] Meanwhile, as the data discussed in this chapter show, the distribution of corruption in litigation-related affairs, although still dominated by court leaders (161 out of 273 are judges above the rank of deputy division chief), is more dispersed among all judges.

The fourth general finding is that, at least on the basis of the datasets reviewed for this chapter, the number of detected cases of corruption committed in the litigation process, including the adjudication and enforcement phases, has increased steadily in recent years compared to cases of corruption conducted in other court management-related areas. Notably, since 2005 the number of corruption cases detected in the enforcement divisions has equaled that found in the adjudicative divisions. It suggests that corruption in the litigation process, especially in the enforcement phase, is becoming more visible in media reports. Data collection methods will need to be improved to determine whether this also indicates an increase of the actual occurrence of corruption incidents in these procedural phases and court divisions.

---

[77] The four courts are Liaoning, Hunan, Heilongjiang, and Guangdong High Courts.
[78] Jianming Ren, Zhizhou Du, "Institutionalized Corruption: Power Overconcentration of the First-in-Command in China," *Criminal Law and Social Change* 49 (2008).

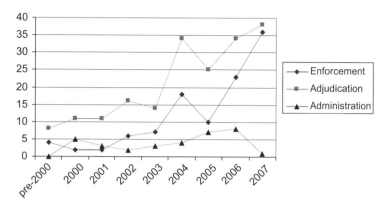

FIGURE 10.4. Numbers of Corruption Cases in Relation to Different Functional Powers.

Nonetheless, this trend would seem to coincide with the implementation of a series of SPC instructions aiming at strengthening the capacity of the enforcement divisions in higher courts.[79] The most important of these instructions was the decision taken in 2000 to establish enforcement bureaus.[80] This decision raised the administrative rank of the enforcement divisions and of their top administrative leaders, thereby turning the enforcement divisions into the most powerful divisions in the courts.[81] In contrast, the less powerful case registration divisions attract only petty forms of corrupt exchange, which is mainly achieved through "work-to-rule" practices, discharging the minimum amount of work possible and following the rules to the letter to impede progress rather than achieving the aim of the rules. The only exception to this pattern is the zaishen procedure, in which the acceptance of a case has an immediate benefit and value to applicants and hence is able to attract and justify the more serious bribes.

The last general finding is that although corrupt exchange can occur in either civil or criminal litigation, civil and particularly commercial litigation dominates. Among the cases studied, the number of corrupt-exchange activities detected in the adjudicative phase in civil litigation doubles that found in criminal litigation. However, taking account that the average first instance case-intake ratio between civil and criminal litigations in China is about 7.5:1,[82] the amount of corrupt activities taking place in criminal litigations, as suggested in this dataset, is much higher than

---

[79] "Announcement of the Supreme People's Court Concerning Issues Related to the Reform of Enforcement Divisions of People's Courts (2000)," SPC.

[80] Since the reform, the administrative rank of the chief of the enforcement court division has been a half-rank higher than those of other court divisions. "Announcement of the Supreme People's Court Concerning Issues Related to the Reform of Enforcement Divisions of People's Courts," (2000).

[81] Interview Z019.

[82] Zhu ed., Zhongguo Falü Fazhan Baogao (1979–2004) [China Legal Development Report (1979–2004)] p. 207.

what would be expected. Because the method for data collection in this research is not ideal, here one can only speculate the causes to this result. A possible explanation is that in criminal cases the defendants are more willing to bribe because of the high stakes involved. It could also be explained as that requests from bribers in criminal cases are easier to be granted because the resistance from antagonists in criminal cases is weaker than in civil cases. After all, in civil cases what is requested by one party has to come from the other party; however, in criminal cases if a judge grants a bribing defendant a shorter term of imprisonment, protests would be much weaker either from the victims[83] or the public prosecutors.[84] The data also show that more corruption was detected in commercial litigation (ninety-five cases) than in noncommercial civil cases most probably because commercial litigation involves much greater material interests, which more readily justify and better accommodate the costs of more expensive bribes as well as the higher transactional costs associated with illegal transactions.

As demonstrated above, corruption by definition shadows power. This is also demonstrated by the absence of corruption cases in courts involving the enforcement of judgments in criminal cases, over which courts do not enjoy full competence. In such cases, for example, in which a person is jailed and for how long may be tainted by corrupt decision making by individuals from other law enforcement institutions rather than the courts. In fact, as emerged in some of the investigated cases, resourceful convicts and their families may seek out opportunities for favored treatment through bribing prison administrators, which is akin to litigants in civil and commercial litigation bribing judges in courts. Such practices range from obtaining practical privileges in prison[85] to more substantive preferential treatment, such as grant of parole, bail on medical leave, and providing supportive evidence for sentence reduction.[86] In some prisons, the cost of a bribe is correlated to the amount

---

[83] According to Huang's conversation with a basic-court judge, what crime victims care most about is the civil compensation. Criminal punishment is and should not be their [the victims'] concern, said the judge. Jialiang Huang, "Falü zai jiceng gayuan zhong de shijian luoji [Logic of Law in Operation in Lower Courts in China]," in Beida Qinghua Renda Shehuixue Shuoshi Lunwen Xuanbian [Selected Theses for Master-Degree in Sociology from Peking University, Qsinghua University and Renmin University] ed. Yefu Zheng et al. (Jinan: Shandong Renmin, 2006) pp. 28–29.

[84] To judge from the annual working reports of the Supreme Procuratorate, the performance of public prosecutors is evaluated mainly by the number of prosecutions and convictions.

[85] See the report on Ma Jianguo, the convicted former governor of Jinniu District, Chengdu City. While serving his sentence in a local prison, he kept several prison administrators on his payroll. In return, Ma enjoyed the freedom of wearing his own clothes, having meals brought in, using his mobile phones to run his company businesses, and even attending banquets held for him in the city. See http://news.sina.com.cn/c/l/2006–09–08/072010953673.shtml. Another example concerns the convicted local gang leader Liu Wenyi, who was granted a reduction of sentence and released on the ground of "significant technology contribution" to the prison. It was later found that the so-called contribution was his purchase of a heating boiler for the prison. In addition to the boiler, Liu also contributed money to the deputy director of the prison and other prison administrators. See http://www.china.com.cn/law/txt/2007–11/08/content_9196874.htm.

[86] The shrewd businessman Zhou Zhengyi, who was directly linked to the fallen Shanghai Mayor Cheng Liangyu, bribed four prison administrators to obtain a sentence reduction. The effort only

of the reduction of sentence.[87] This change of habitat of corruption is because the enforcement of criminal judgments involving the punishment of imprisonment is administered by the Ministry of Justice and its branches rather than courts.[88] Courts, however, retain the discretion to grant probation, enforcement without imprisonment, and pecuniary penalties,[89] a field that in practice is far from corruption-free.[90] Customary practices had been found in some courts where a fixed-amount observation fee for probation (huanxingkaochafei) is collected semiofficially from criminal defendants and the profits are later allocated proportionally among all court personnel involved.[91]

CONCLUSION

The data analyzed in this research indicate that corruption exists in all main court divisions where key functional judicial power is exercised. The data also show that corruption occurs at almost all levels of the judicial system, involving all types of judges, regardless of their rank, level of education, and income, whereas differences lie in the type, manner, and frequency of corrupt activities. By classifying corruption in China's courts into three types, this chapter demonstrates that each type exhibits different features depending on their particular context in courts at different levels and in different court divisions. On the basis of the data collected, extreme cases involving physical coercion and overt miscarriage of law appear mostly in a highly visible manner in courts at the lowest level. More subtle forms of corruption seem more conspicuous in higher courts. Among court divisions, corruption is distributed unequally as well. According to the cases studied, corrupt-exchange activities are mostly concentrated in the adjudicative divisions of the courts. However, corruption

---

failed because of the high-profile nature and political sensitivity of his case in relation to the former mayor. See http://www.why.com.cn/epublish/node4/node12488/node12489/userobject7ai99708.html. For a review of these and similar malpractices, see Shixing Jiang, "*Jianyu ganjing zhiwu fanzui yufang duice* [Prevention and Counter-Measures against Professional Crimes Committed by Prison Cadre-Officers]," in *Zhongguo Zhiwu Fanzui Yufang Diaocha Baogao [Investigative Report on Professional Crimes and Its Prevention of China]* ed., Criminology Research Society of China (2004), pp. 381–382.

[87] A report revealed that the price of a one-year sentence reduction in the Dalian prisons was known to be RMB 12,000. Jiaxun Lü, Hu Qishu, "*Dui Liaoning Dalianshi sifa jiguan gongzuo renyuan zhiwu fanzui qingkuang diaocha ji yufang* [Investigation and Prevention of Professional Crimes Committed by Personnel in the Justice System in Dalian City, Liaoning Province]," in *Zhongguo zhiwu fanzui yufang diaocha baogao [Investigative Report on Professional Crimes and Its Prevention of China]* ed., Criminology Research Society of China (2004), p. 353.

[88] Law of Prisons of the People's Republic of China (1994). Art. 10.

[89] Criminal Law (1997) Ch. 3 and Ch. 4.

[90] Liu Yaming, "*Zhiwu fanzui anjian shiyong huanxing qingkuang diaocha fenxi* [An Investigation and Analysis of the Use of Suspended Sentence in White-Collar Crimes]," *Network of prevention of white-collar crime* (2004). See http://www.yfw.com.cn/shownews.asp?id=36265.

[91] "Rendering suspended sentences after taking money from defendants is illicit adjudication (2007)." See http://news.sina.com.cn/c/pl/2007–03–26/154612617436.shtml. See also Yaxin Wang, "'Sifafubai' xianxiang ce yizhong jiedu [An Interpretation of 'Judicial Corruption']," *Sixiang zhanxian* 31, no. 4 (2005) p. 50. fn.2.

has also grown rapidly in the enforcement divisions, making the enforcement and adjudicative divisions almost indistinguishable in terms of the salience of corruption. By contrast, due to their structural constraints, case registration divisions appear to be less prone to corrupt practices.

This research also shows that judges in executive positions constitute a major group of corruption offenders in the dataset. Possessing multiple functional powers, judges in this group conduct corruption through exchange in various types of court affairs, ranging from the rendering of biased decisions in litigation, the granting of court commissions, the assignment of court procurement contracts, to the appointment and promotion of judges. That bribery has played a role in the appointment and promotion of judges, especially in four high courts, is a concern. It is not difficult to imagine the effect on litigation in these courts under a leadership inclined to retain judicial posts for sale. This phenomenon suggests that at least in some courts corruption is not an isolated event but may become part of an organizational culture. This is further confirmed by outbreaks of corruption recurring in certain courts that had ostensibly already been purged of corrupt judges.

It is often claimed that the root of various judicial problems is the judiciary's lack of independence and authority. However, contrary to such claims, the judicial problems illustrated in this chapter are the result of the abuse and misuse of judicial authority and power. This chapter argues that the question of how to encourage and improve judicial integrity should be assigned a higher, or at least equal, priority as that concerning judicial independence. Otherwise we risk equipping the already corrupt or potentially corruptible with more power, leading to even more corruption. This chapter provides a modest initial contribution to the study of corruption in China's courts. Further systematic and sustained studies of corrupt behavior in the special legal/political setting of the courts are called for, especially of corrupt exchange, the most vigorous and resilient type of all.

11

A Survey of Commercial Litigation in Shanghai Courts

Minxin Pei, Zhang Guoyan, Pei Fei, and Chen Lixin[1]

The capacity of a legal system to protect property rights is generally considered one of the most important factors in economic development because commercial transactions will become unduly costly and risky in an environment in which contracts cannot be enforced by the state. An independent judiciary, in turn, is generally considered an essential element of an effective legal system and thus necessary for sustained economic growth. Chinese leaders have clearly recognized the critical importance of building a legal infrastructure that will facilitate commercial transactions in an increasingly market-oriented economy; they have also acknowledged the need to enhance the competence, authority, and independence of the judiciary. Yet scholars remain divided on the role of the legal system in development and how well it protects property rights.[2]

How well then is China implementing the declared policy of "ruling the country according to the law"? How are Chinese citizens and corporations responding to the new legal environment? What strategies do they use to win favorable outcomes in court? How independent are the courts in handling commercial cases? What are the sources and impact of outside influence in such cases? How do the parties assess the legal system and their experience in court? This chapter sheds light on these important issues by measuring various aspects of the civil proceedings in basic level and intermediate courts in one of China's leading urban commercial centers.[3]

[1] We wish to acknowledge the generous support from the Henry Luce Foundation that funded this project. We are grateful to the valuable editorial assistance from Kevin Slaten, a Junior Fellow at the Carnegie Endowment for International Peace in 2008–2009.

[2] See Donald Clarke, "Economic Development and The Rights Hypothesis: The China Problem," *American Journal of Comparative Law*, 51: 89 (2003); Donald Clarke, Peter Murrell, and Susan Whiting, "The Role of Law in China's Economic Development," (2006), http://ssrn.com/abstract=878672; Kenneth Dam, *The Law-Growth Nexus* (Washington D.C.: Brookings Institute, 2006); Randall Peerenboom, *China's Long March toward Rule of Law* (Cambridge: Cambridge University Press, 2002).

[3] We initially collected 574 judgments from basic level courts and 308 judgments from intermediate courts. We then sent questionnaires to the "natural person" litigants. Because of the litigants'

Numerous studies demonstrate that there are significant differences between urban and rural courts in the nature of disputes, level of competence of judges, local protectionism, and ultimately the willingness of parties to litigate and their satisfaction with their experience when they do litigate.[4] Similarly, empirical studies call attention to the need to distinguish between types of cases and levels of court in assessing the performance of the legal system.[5] This chapter draws on an empirical study of 190 corporate litigants and 214 individual litigants involved in civil proceedings (exclusively property or commercial disputes) adjudicated in Shanghai's courts from 1999 to 2003.[6] The types of property disputes included in these court cases range from typical contract disputes to debt collections. The stakes varied considerably. Of the larger pool of court cases from which these two samples were chosen, we found that of the cases tried in the courts of first instance, 11 percent involved monetary claims of under RMB 10,000; 32 percent involved claims of between RMB 10,000 and 100,000; 22 percent involved claims of between RMB 100,000 and 500,000; and 35 percent involved claims in excess of RMB 500,000. Of the appellate court judgments we collected, 15 percent involved claims of less than RMB 10,000; 38 percent involved claims of between RMB 10,000 and 100,000; 24 percent involved claims of between RMB 100,000 and 500,000; and 23 percent involved claims of more than RMB 500,000.

Part I presents the results for the corporate litigants and Part II the results for the individual litigants. Part III concludes.

---

understandable concerns regarding anonymity, we were unable to match the questionnaires completed by the "natural person" litigants with their original judgments. However, because the judgments reached at the basic level courts from the original pool were roughly double those reached at the intermediate courts, we are confident that at least two-thirds of the questionnaires returned were from those who litigated in basic level courts. In addition, the percentage of judgments reached in the basic level courts is likely much higher because natural person litigants tend to have smaller claims. On the other hand, legal person litigants, who typically have bigger claims, tend to litigate in intermediate courts. In soliciting response from them, we used identifying numbers to match their response to the court judgments we have collected. In our sample of corporate or legal person litigants, 77 percent of the judgments were reached at intermediate courts.

4 See, e.g., Ethan Michelson, "Dispute Processing in Urban and Rural China: Findings from Two Surveys," in R. Peerenboom ed., *Dispute Resolution in China* (Oxford: Foundation for Law, Justice and Society, 2008); He Xin, "Enforcing Commercial Judgments in the Pearl River Delta of China," *Journal of Empirical Legal Studies* (forthcoming); Mary Gallagher, "Mobilizing the Law in China: 'Informed Disenchantment' and the Development of Legal Consciousness." 40 *Law and Society Review* 783–816 (2006).

5 See, e.g., Fu and Peerenboom's chapter in this volume.

6 We mailed 882 questionnaires to the natural person and legal person litigants and received 214 completed questionnaires from natural person litigants and 190 completed questionnaires from legal person litigants, some of whom were interviewed. The combined response rate is roughly 45 percent. Detailed questionnaire and responses from the surveyed individuals and corporations are available online at http://carnegieendowment.org/publications/index.cfm?fa=view&id=22696&prog=zch.

CORPORATE LITIGANTS

Of the 190 firms surveyed in this study, 75 (or 40 percent) were state-owned; 6 (3 percent) were state-controlled (most probably through ownership of a majority of the shares). Roughly a third (64 firms) were private and about 10 percent (twenty-two firms) were collectively owned. This appears to be a fairly representative profile for firm ownership in Shanghai, where the state has a much greater presence in the economy than many other provinces in China.

In terms of the size of the firms based on revenue, the survey collected much less information because 43 percent of the respondents provided no answer to this question. To the extent that private or collectively owned firms tend to be small and their managers tend to know more about their companies' financial results than their counterparts in state-owned firms (which also tend to be very large), it appears that the 25 percent of the firms in the sample, most likely private or collectively owned, generate annual sales of RMB 1–5 million. Another 8 percent of the firms, also likely private or collectively owned, generate annual sales of RMB 5–10 million. In other words, about one-third of the sample consists of small firms. Medium-sized firms, defined here as those generating annual sales of RMB 10–50 million, represent about a quarter of the sample. Forty-two percent have fewer than 100 employees and 25 percent have between 101 and 200 employees. Seventeen percent have between 201–500 employees. Again, small- and medium-sized firms represent more than two-thirds of the sample.

The Decision to Litigate

We attempted to find out why firms decided to litigate. Unfortunately, the response rate was only 58 percent, calling into question the reliability of the results. Nevertheless, it appears that at least a quarter of the firms had tried other dispute resolution methods before deciding to sue. In slightly more than half of the cases (54 percent), the general managers or presidents of the firms made the decision to file a lawsuit. In 18 percent of the cases, the boards of directors made the decision. Legal advisers made the final decision in only 14 percent of the cases.

What is most interesting was the negligible role played by the Communist Party in the decision-making process. There are at least two possible explanations. First, roughly a third of the firms are private. Private companies typically do not have a Communist Party committee despite the party's efforts to recruit private entrepreneurs and set up party organizations in private firms.[7] Thus, the party's role

---

7 Although the party has stepped up its efforts to recruit private entrepreneurs, it has limited success in setting up organizational cells in private firms. See Bruce Dickson, *Wealth into Power: The Communist Party's Embrace of China's Private Sector* (New York: Cambridge University Press, 2008).

simply is nonexistent in these cases. Second, in many state-owned firms, the general manager or president also assumes the position of the party secretary and represents the interests of the party. As a result, the party committee's role is marginalized.

The surveyed firms reported obtaining information about the litigation process through a variety of channels. In roughly a third of the cases, the company's legal advisers were the source of such information. However, because many companies, especially private ones, cannot afford to hire in-house legal advisers, they retain outside counsel. Thus, lawyers provided such information in a quarter of the cases. Although some companies obtained information by checking out the experiences of a peer firm, by and large professional legal advice is the main source of information for decision makers in understanding the litigation process.

The way firms obtain their lawyers largely mirrors how they learn about the litigation process. Roughly a third of the firms use their in-house lawyers to represent them in court, whereas a quarter go directly to law firms to retain their legal counsel. Apparently, only a small number of companies (6 percent) would hire outside counsel on the recommendation of their in-house lawyers.

Administrative intervention by supervising government bodies appears to be rare. Only 2 percent of the firms report that their lawyers were directly appointed by their supervising agencies.

Only about 20 percent of firms believe they can competently represent themselves in court. The most important reason for corporate litigants not to hire lawyers for their legal proceedings is the cost. Almost 70 percent of the respondents cite excessively high fees demanded by lawyers as the main obstacle.

The majority of litigants gave relatively high marks to their lawyers. Sixty-two percent believed that their lawyers were professional and had a positive impact on the trial. A sizable minority (14 percent) thought their lawyers were highly qualified but had no substantial impact on the trial. Only a tiny minority (6 percent) of the litigants rated their lawyers as professionally unqualified.

Pretrial Maneuvering: Party Influence of Judges

Given the relative immaturity of the legal system in China, it is rational for litigants to try to gain an advantage over their adversaries even through questionable means. We tried to coax the respondents into disclosing some of the methods they used in influencing the outcome of the trial. Obviously, the sensitivity of the question inevitably deters many respondents from answering. As a result, the nonresponse rate, at 57 percent, is perhaps too high for the results to be reliable. Nevertheless, corporate litigants appear to take their cases seriously. In 25 percent of firms, top managers made frequent inquiries about the case whereas 8 percent set up a special task force to handle the lawsuits.

Only a small number of corporate litigants (seventeen altogether) admit that they initiated or attempted to initiate various apparently inappropriate contacts with the court outside the courtroom before the opening of the trial. Based on reports in the Chinese media, such inappropriate contacts with the presiding judges could include inviting the judges to banquets, calling the judges in their homes, and sending emissaries to meet with the judges. However, somewhat surprisingly, and inconsistently, 75 percent of respondents admit to attempting to influence judges before the trial. The most prevalent method used, according to 53 percent of the respondents, was to give gifts to, or hold banquets for, judges. Thirty-two percent of the respondents used unidentified methods to try to influence the judges. Only 5 percent asked someone from their head office to intervene on their behalf – this may suggest that Shanghai courts may have become more independent of state-owned enterprises and that local protectionism has decreased.

The large percentage of cases in which parties attempt to influence judges raises troubling questions about the integrity of judges and the effectiveness of regulations against accepting gifts or meals from litigants.[8] Even in Shanghai, often considered one of the least corrupt jurisdictions in China, such questionable practices appear to be widespread.

What impact did such activities have on the outcome of the case? Of the seventy-one litigants who responded, 60 percent believed their efforts "had an actual effect," whereas 35 percent believed that it had no effect, with only a few respondents reporting that the court rejected their overtures. Nevertheless, as discussed below, more than 95 percent of victorious respondents claimed that they won based on the evidence and legal merits. Conversely, 26 percent of losing respondents claimed they lost because of the other party's influence, although a surprisingly high 68 percent accepted that they lost because of lack of evidence or legal merit. This suggests that even in the case where parties thought such influence had an effect, the effect was not determinative of the substantive outcome of the case. Other possible effects include, for example, a more prompt resolution of the case, assistance in obtaining evidence or preserving assets, or a favorable decision on procedural issues within the judge's discretion. Finally, we cannot rule out that the litigants' influence on the judge was far more effective than they were willing to admit in a written questionnaire.

The Trial Process

Few studies have examined whether Chinese courts adjudicate cases according to established legal procedures or sought to assess the procedural fairness of the trial

---

[8] On paper, China has various regulations and laws that attempt to insulate judges from inappropriate contact with the litigants and their lawyers. Lawyers are explicitly forbidden, by the PRC Lawyers Law, which was passed in 1996 and amended in 2001, to "give gifts, banquets, or bribes to judges, prosecutors, arbitrators or other related government officials, or ask or encourage their clients to engage in bribery." In January 2009, the People's Supreme Court also issued a set of regulations that forbid court personnel from accepting banquets and gifts from litigants and from "inappropriate contact" with their lawyers. However, based on Chinese press reports, these regulations and laws may not be effectively enforced.

and impartiality of judges. Accordingly, we sought to ascertain whether Chinese courts follow established trial procedures and how judges are perceived by litigants.

Litigants learn the procedures of the trial from a variety of sources. Judges play as important a role as the litigants' lawyers in informing parties of the trial procedures. Nowadays many courts, including Shanghai courts, have posted materials on their Web sites outlining the litigation process, listing fee schedules and court dates, and tracking the enforcement process. Companies' in-house counsel is listed as the third most important source of such information. In any event, by the end of the trial process practically all litigants are familiar with the procedures.

Nearly all respondents (91 percent) report the timely opening of their trial. On the whole, the overwhelming majority (83 percent) of litigants report that the courts complied with the legal procedures throughout the trial proceedings. Procedural violations are reported by only a small minority. Seven litigants blamed their judges for failing to observe the procedures. Four suspected that their opponents influenced the judges.

Another encouraging finding from this survey is that a large majority of corporate litigants (63 percent) gave the presiding judges high ratings ("dignified conduct and high professional quality"). A sizable minority (17 percent) rate their judges as having performed with "acceptable conduct but low professional quality." Only a small percentage of judges (3 percent) were deemed as having both "poor conduct" and "low professional quality."

Outcomes and Enforcement

In explaining the main factors responsible for their court victories, roughly half of the winning respondents cited clear and abundant evidence, whereas 47 percent singled out the legal merits of their cases.

When asked to explain the reasons of their loss, respondents gave more varied – and interesting – explanations. The most important cause of defeat, identified by 47 percent of the respondents, was lack of evidence, whereas 21 percent blamed the lack of legal merit. However, 26 percent of the respondents attributed their loss to "preferential treatment" of the other party by the judge. Only a small number attributed their defeat to bad lawyers.

The response to this question suggests that evidence plays the most important role in Chinese civil proceedings. But it also reveals a disturbing aspect of the Chinese legal system – a significant minority of litigants believe that the judicial process is corrupt. Such a perception comes as no surprise given that roughly half of the respondents who participated in this survey report that they had dined with or given gifts to judges.

The perception of injustice or unfair treatment may be the cause of the high rate of appeal by litigants who fare poorly in the courts of first instance. In our sample, a majority of the losing litigants (57 percent) decided to appeal. Twenty-seven percent chose not to appeal because of concerns about costs in legal fees and time. Only a minority (16 percent) of the respondents acknowledged the lack of merit of a possible appeal and conceded defeat.

A large majority (76 percent) of the respondents who appealed their judgments hired or planned to hire lawyers because they believed lawyers would strengthen their cases. Notably, two respondents who did not retain lawyers during first instance proceedings decided to hire lawyers for their appeals. Only 24 percent of the respondents did not hire or plan to hire lawyers for their appeals because they felt that lawyers made little difference during the first instance proceedings or they were dissatisfied with the lawyers they had contacted.

After the conclusion of the first instance proceedings, only a third of winning plaintiffs report the execution of the judgments by the losing party in fifteen days. An overwhelming majority (77 percent) claim that it took the losing party more than fifteen days to execute the court's ruling. In fact, an overwhelming majority of the winning plaintiffs (77 percent) requested compulsory enforcement of judgments by the courts because the losing parties failed to carry out the court's judgment voluntarily.

Despite the often discussed difficulties of enforcing judgments in China, Shanghai courts appear to enforce court judgments in a timely manner.[9] About 80 percent of the winning plaintiffs that requested court enforcement report that their judgments were enforced within one year. Among this group, 26 percent report enforcement within 3 months and 35 percent report enforcement within 3 to 6 months. Only 21 percent claim that it took more than a year for their judgments to be enforced.

However, the actual results of enforcement are more mixed. Only 21 percent of the respondents seeking compulsory enforcement report that the court was able to collect fully. Thirteen percent report that the court collected two-thirds or more of their judgments. Nineteen percent report receiving between one-third and two-thirds of the judgment. Twenty-eight percent received less than one-third of the judgment. Nineteen percent report receiving nothing. Based on this finding, it appears that nearly half of the court judgments in Shanghai may be characterized as unsuccessfully enforced. Unfortunately, our respondents did not provide any details on why their judgments were not successfully enforced.

Finally, it appears that the majority of the corporate litigants have realistic expectations about the trial. Roughly two-thirds report that the court's ruling was what they expected. Only a minority (22 percent) report that the outcome of the trial was completely different from their expectations.

In sum, notwithstanding the well-publicized difficulties and problems besetting the Chinese legal system, Shanghai courts appear to be performing relatively well in

---

[9] Xin He also finds significant improvement in enforcement in economically developed urban areas. Xin He, "Enforcing Commercial Judgments." See also Mei Ying Gechlik, "Judicial Reform in China: Lessons from Shanghai," *Columbia Journal of Asian Law*, vol. 19, p. 100 (2006).

that the final outcome matches most corporate litigants' expectations of a subjectively fair and positive outcome.[10]

PRIVATE PARTY LITIGANTS

In this section, we report the findings from data gathered from the questionnaires completed by 214 natural person or individual litigants in civil proceedings in primarily basic level Shanghai courts. In terms of the socioeconomic background of the litigants, they are diverse, with the largest number being workers (35 percent). The second largest group was businessmen (20 percent), and only 6 percent were peasants.

In terms of income, most of the litigants (two-thirds) are lower middle class, with a family income of less than RMB 2,500 per month. A quarter have middle-class income (between RMB 2,500 and 4,000 a month); only 5 percent should be considered really well-to-do, with a family monthly income of more than RMB 7,000.

The education background of the litigants mirrors that of Shanghai residents more generally, with nearly 40 percent of litigants completing middle school and 20 percent graduating from high school or technical college. It is notable that 30 percent of the litigants have received three to four years of college education (in China, the corresponding figure is 5 percent).

In terms of political affiliation, the portion of Communist Party members is large (21 percent), three times the national average in urban areas (around 6–7 percent).[11] Given the concentration of managerial and administrative personnel in Shanghai, it is to be expected that the share of CCP members in the city's population may be higher than the national average. Nevertheless, the apparent overrepresentation of CCP members among the litigants may suggest that, to the extent that litigating in an emerging legal system requires political sophistication, courage, and resources, a CCP member may be in a much better position than an average citizen. Other studies, however, find that cadres, party members, and other political elites are less likely to have disputes in the first place, more likely to turn to the courts if they have disputes, but no more likely to be satisfied with the courts than other parties.[12]

The Decision to Litigate

Given the high costs of litigation (in terms of time, financial expenditures, and energy), litigation is usually not the first option for settling disputes. Roughly

---

[10] We reach this conclusion because roughly two-thirds of the plaintiffs win complete or partial victories. We suspect that two-thirds of the respondents who report that the trial outcomes match their expectations may be, for the most part, winning plaintiffs.

[11] This estimate is based on the following calculation. Half of the members of the CCP (with a total membership of 70 million) reside in urban areas. Chinese urban population accounts for 42–45 percent of the total population, so CCP members should account for 6–7 percent of the urban population.

[12] See Michelson, "Dispute Processing in Urban and Rural China."

one-third of survey respondents said they decided to sue after they had tried but failed to resolve their disputes through other means. Somewhat surprisingly, about 60 percent did not attempt other means of dispute resolution because they believed litigation was either the most authoritative or most effective means of resolving their disputes.

Because commercial litigation is a relatively new phenomenon in China, even in a cosmopolitan city such as Shanghai, it is expected that first-time individual litigants lack information about the process of litigation. In obtaining information on how to file a lawsuit, a slight majority of the respondents listed mass media, family, friends, and colleagues as their main sources. Due to the relatively large percentage of respondents who failed to answer this question (36 percent), it is conceivable that litigants may have also sought other channels of information.

We posed a series of questions to find out how lawyers are retained and how much value they create for their clients. Again, we see evidence of the importance of social networks. In obtaining the services of professional lawyers, social networks such as family, friends, and colleagues constitute the most important source of recommendations (41 percent of the litigants reported that their lawyers were recommended by members of these networks), and 24 percent of litigants contacted a law firm directly.

In deciding whether to hire a lawyer, the most important factor appears to be cost. Of the reasons cited by the sixty-three respondents who apparently did not hire a lawyer, almost half cited high fees as the reason. Nevertheless, a sizable minority, 36 percent, believed that lawyers would play a negligible role during litigation and that it would not be worth the money to retain their services. Unfavorable first impressions played a minor role in the decision-making process.

Although most private parties did not hire lawyers, those who did had largely positive opinions of their lawyers. In terms of professional qualifications, the overwhelming majority of the respondents (77 percent) ranked their lawyers as having "high professional quality." Roughly half of the respondents (45 percent) thought positively of their lawyers' professional quality and believed they made a positive contribution. About a fourth of the respondents believed their lawyers were unqualified and did not help their cases substantially. About one in five thought that even though their lawyers were highly qualified, they had no substantial impact on their cases. Intriguingly, 13 percent suspected that their lawyers probably had hurt their cases even though they were professionally qualified.

Party Influence of Judges

The responses to our questions whether the parties attempted to influence the judges before the trial are notable for two reasons. First, although only 5 percent of the parties admitted to actually influencing the judge prior to trial, a sizable minority – 28 percent – admitted that they thought about doing so but gave up on the idea because they "could not find the right way" to influence the judges. This most likely reflects in part the low level of legal representation in that lawyers, as repeat players, tend to have the connections and understand ways to influence judges. Indeed, it is common for judges to blame lawyers for seeking inappropriate access, whereas lawyers claim to be responding to direct or indirect hints from judges. Second, of the 129 respondents who answered the question whether they believe influencing judges would produce real results, a quarter firmly believed it would, whereas another quarter thought it would not. Half believed that whether one can obtain the desired results depends on the appropriateness of the methods used in influencing the judges.

Unfortunately, only twenty-four respondents (out of seventy-one who said they thought of influencing judges or actually did so) replied to the question regarding the ways of influencing judges. Based on the limited information provided, it seems that the most prevalent practice is to ask "influential people to intervene." Interestingly, no respondent admitted giving gifts or holding banquets, the preferred methods for corporate litigants.

In any event, the effectiveness of private litigants' efforts to influence judges appears limited. Of the twenty-eight litigants who answered the question whether any of the methods of influencing the judge worked, eleven thought their methods produced real results, whereas ten believed their methods had no effect. Seven were not sure.

The Trial Process

In terms of procedural fairness, about a quarter of litigants did not know anything about trial procedures, whereas a small minority learned about the procedures on their own. The courts were the main source of information for half of the litigants.

Again, as in the case of corporate litigants, 90 percent of the trials took place on time. The overall assessment of the trial procedures by the respondents suggests that legal reform in China's wealthiest city has made solid progress. Nearly three-quarters of the respondents said that the trial procedures formally complied with those stipulated by law. Only a small minority (7 percent) blamed judges for taking short cuts in trial procedures. And 8 percent cried foul because they suspected that the other party had influenced the judge, who in turn violated the legal procedures.

More generally, private litigants gave a relatively high favorable rating to Shanghai judges. Forty-one percent showed "dignified conduct and high professional quality." Twenty-two percent were thought to have "acceptable conduct but low professional quality," and 10 percent were rated as having "poor conduct and low professional quality." Thus, even in one of China's most developed cities, about a third of basic level court judges were perceived to have low professional quality. The most likely cause of the discrepancy in how private litigants and corporate litigants view their lawyers is the different courts in which their cases are heard. A majority of the case for private litigants is heard in basic level courts, which have less senior or well-trained judges than intermediate courts, where a majority of the corporate cases in this sample were tried.

Outcomes and Enforcement

Asked to explain what might be the reasons for their court victories, more than half (53 percent) cited abundant evidence and 42 percent believed their cases had legal merit. Surprisingly three respondents conceded that the judges gave them favorable treatment.

In comparison to corporate litigants, a much smaller percentage of losing respondents believed the reason they lost was lack of evidence (26 percent) or lack of legal merit (4 percent), whereas a much higher percentage (56 percent) believed they lost because of the other party's influence. Thus, most private party losers perceive the judicial process as corrupt and flawed, although party influence appears to be less frequent and the impact less significant than in cases involving corporate litigants. Notwithstanding greater and more significant influence, corporate litigant losers perceive the process as fairer and less flawed. This suggests corporate litigants have a more sophisticated understanding of the legal issues and the merits of their case, which may be the result of a greater use of more qualified lawyers.

The perception of unfairness was one of the main reasons for appeal. Twenty-four percent of the cases were appealed, roughly similar to the overall rate of about 20 percent for civil litigation in China. If we eliminate or exclude the litigants who were awarded satisfactory judgments, almost 40 percent of the litigants who were unhappy with their results or lost their case appealed. Their stated reason was to "get a fairer result." Of those who did not appeal, 31 percent (half in the adjusted sample) cited their concern with the costs (both in time and money) as the chief reason for not appealing. A small minority (7 percent) confessed that they did not appeal because they knew their cases were weak.

In terms of enforcement, after adjusting for the fact that only the respondents who won complete or partial victories would answer this question, 70 percent of the winning plaintiffs had to ask the court to enforce the judgment because the losing defendants failed to carry out the court's ruling. Only 24 percent of the losing parties voluntarily executed the court's judgments.

Again, Shanghai courts were relatively fast in enforcing judgments. Roughly 70 percent of the judgments were enforced within six months, and only 16 percent were enforced after one year. But the courts were less effective in terms of the amount of judgment collected. The courts collected "about two-thirds or more" of the judgment in roughly half of the cases and "between one-third and two-thirds" in about 20 percent of the cases. Notably, the courts failed to collect anything in 23 percent of the cases. Regrettably, our respondents did not provide specific information regarding the causes of noncollection of court awards.

Finally, we asked the participants in our survey whether the results of their litigation met their expectations. The results indicate that a large majority – two-thirds – thought that the results were "completely or basically" in line with their expectation. Thirteen percent reported that although the judgment was expected, the execution of the judgment was not expected (indicating perhaps a degree of disappointment at the incompleteness of the enforcement). A quarter of the litigants were clearly surprised by the judgments. Only a small minority, 12 percent, concluded that the whole effort was not worth it.

CONCLUSION

Given the nature and limitations of the data, we are unable to answer many important questions regarding the effectiveness of the legal system as a whole, or even about commercial litigation in Shanghai courts. Nevertheless, the studies do shed light on judicial independence in commercial suits in one of the most developed urban commercial areas in China. One would expect these cases, particularly those involving private parties, to be the least controversial and subject to the least outside interference. One would also expect judges in these courts to be among the most competent and professional.

In general, the results support these hypotheses. Most corporate litigants found judges competent and professional, about 80 percent believed that judges followed procedures and complied with law, and two-thirds felt that the outcome matched expectations. Similarly, two-thirds of private litigants also believed that the outcome met their expectations, whereas three-quarters believed that judges followed procedures and complied with law. Although a somewhat higher percentage of private litigants, about one-third, felt that the judges lacked competence, few believed it was a mistake to litigate. The higher level of dissatisfaction with the quality of judges could be due to a larger number of private cases starting in basic level courts. As generally true everywhere, higher level courts tend to have more qualified judges and adjudicate cases of greater commercial stakes. Alternatively, private parties may have a less sophisticated understanding of the legal issues – especially because a much higher percentage do not retain legal counsel – and thus may be unduly critical of judges who decide against them.

Nevertheless, enforcement and judicial independence, in particular influence from the parties, remain areas of concern. A high percentage of cases – upward of 70 percent – required compulsory enforcement.[13] Moreover, although Shanghai courts are reasonably fast and efficient in enforcing awards, parties often are able to collect only a portion of the judgment. Unfortunately, we were unable to ascertain whether this is because the losing parties are insolvent or for other reasons. Obviously, if the

---

[13] Recent regulatory and institutional changes have strengthened enforcement, including amendments to the Civil Procedure Law. The new measures include increased penalties for people who obstruct enforcement. The number of people detained during compulsory enforcement proceedings reached a high in 1999, the same year the number of people refusing to comply with court judgments peaked. Since then, both the number of cases in which parties refuse to voluntarily comply with the judgment and the number of people detained have decreased. Zhu Jingwen ed., *Zhongguo falü fazhan baogao (1979–2004)* [China Legal Development Report (1979–2004)], (Beijing: Renmin University Press, 2007), pp. 248–249.

parties are insolvent or their assets encumbered, there is nothing any legal system can do.

The influence of the parties on the courts is difficult to measure because parties generally will not admit to attempting to influence judges or discuss the details of any such attempts. Moreover, assessing the impact of influence is difficult. Nevertheless, this study revealed that a significant number of corporate litigants contacted or sought to influence judges, usually by giving gifts or holding banquets. In contrast, private litigants were less likely to influence judges – but not necessarily because they did not want to – most simply did not know how to do so effectively. Influence from party organs or government officials does not appear to have been a significant factor. In these relatively run of the mill commercial cases, most of the attempted influence comes from the parties, either directly or indirectly through their lawyers and other social acquaintances of the judges.

Significantly, almost all winning parties attributed victory to having the law and facts on their side, whereas losing parties, particularly private parties, believed they lost because of the other side's influence. Whether or not such attempts to influence the court actually affect the outcome, they clearly undermine public trust in the fairness of the judiciary. Although there are rules against gift giving or dining with judges, they are hard to police given the cultural context where gift giving and dining out are common practices, and parties can seek friends and social acquaintances to meet with judges or their relatives. Asset disclosure rules and other transparency measures may have some impact on curtailing such inappropriate behavior. However, in the end, rule of law requires the internalization of professional ethical norms on the part of judges and lawyers and respect for such norms on the part of parties and the general public.

The findings suggest that although still a work in progress, China's legal system provides some protection of property rights, and that both corporate and private litigants take their legal recourse very seriously. However, further reforms are required to address real and perceived corruption and party influence to avoid undermining public trust in the courts and the government's efforts to sustain economic growth by providing a just and efficient forum for resolving commercial disputes.

12

Judicial Independence in Authoritarian Regimes

Lessons from Continental Europe

Carlo Guarnieri

Judicial independence is often considered the simple by-product of a set of legal provisions aimed at wholly insulating the judge not only from state influence – usually the executive – but from the external environment: the more insulated the judge, the more independent she is deemed to be. A good example of this attitude can be found in one of the 1985 United Nations Principles of Judicial Independence:

> The judiciary shall decide matters before them impartially, on the basis of facts and in accordance with the law, without *any* restrictions, improper influences, inducements, pressures, threats or interferences, direct or indirect, from *any* quarter or for *any* reason. (Emphasis added.)

There is often little critical reflection about the extent to which this ideal can be realized in practice and its consequences for the administration of justice. Conversely, judges working in political systems where such guarantees are not present in full are thought to lack independence, often without any further investigation.[1]

To clarify the issue, a distinction should be introduced between institutional independence – that is, institutional guarantees of independence like the well-known during good behavior clause against arbitrary dismissal – and independence on the bench, that is, impartial behavior on the part of the judge.[2] Some degree of institutional independence is a necessary but not sufficient condition of judicial impartiality. Institutional independence is only one of several determinants of judicial behavior. This is one reason why it is not always easy to single out the "right" degree of (institutional) judicial independence. In fact, even in nondemocratic

---

[1] Tamir Moustafa, *The Struggle for Constitutional Power: Law, Politics and Economic Development in Egypt* (Cambridge: Cambridge University Press, 2007).

[2] Peter Russell, "Toward a General Theory of Judicial Independence," in Peter Russell and David O'Brien eds., *Judicial Independence in the Age of Democracy* (Charlottesville: University Press of Virginia, 2001), pp. 6–9.

countries, where institutional independence is often limited, judges can exhibit a variable degree of impartiality in deciding specific cases. Of particular importance is the reference group of judges, which varies depending on the nature of the political regime (democratic, authoritarian, or totalitarian) and the nature of the legal system (common or civil law).

Part I discusses the evolution of judicial independence in Western Europe, emphasizing the importance of reference groups within these different political and legal systems. Part II then applies the experiences of Western Europe to China.

JUDICIAL INDEPENDENCE IN DEMOCRATIC REGIMES

Judicial independence from political power is an essential trait of democratic constitutional regimes. Because one of the main objectives of constitutionalism is to limit the exercise of power and make it legally accountable, submitting the performance of public functions to the scrutiny of legal rules administered by an independent body can ensure the supremacy of the law and become an effective check on the exercise of political power.

The fact that judicial independence is mainly aimed at sustaining judicial impartiality in dispute resolution implies that it must be related to that end and cannot be understood in absolute terms.[3] Obviously, absolute independence – that is complete insulation from outside influences – is impossible to achieve; judges are social animals and not slot machines.[4] Also pursuing absolute institutional independence – an extremely difficult goal to achieve because institutional channels of influence are many and difficult to control – is in tension with the need to ensure judicial impartiality if it means allowing the judge to escape any form of check or responsibility for the way she discharges her institutional function, the administration of justice. Complete institutional insulation would mean that only informal – and often nontransparent – influence will matter.[5] In fact, in all democratic regimes judges are considered dependent on the law or, in any case, on the recognized norms of the political system. Thus, although it is not always easy to ascertain if a judge has really followed the law – because any legal text must be interpreted and interpretation is a complex activity – all democratic regimes exhibit some checks on judicial misbehavior or at least on serious breaches of shared norms.[6]

---

[3]   Russell, "Toward a General Theory," p. 3.

[4]   Jerome Frank, *Courts on Trial* (Princeton: Princeton University Press, 1949), p. 147.

[5]   This statement is supported, for example, by the results of studies in Latin America by Julio Rios-Figueroa, *Judicial Independence: Definition, Measurement and Its Effects on Corruption* (Ph.D. dissertation, New York University, 2006), and in a larger set of countries by Stefan Voigt, "The Economic Effects of Judicial Accountability: Cross-country Evidence," *European Journal of Law and Economics*, vol. 25, p. 95 (2008).

[6]   Different forms of judicial responsibility – and the way they can be compatible with a democratic arrangement – are carefully analyzed by Mauro Cappelletti, *The Judicial Process in Comparative Perspective* (Oxford: Clarendon Press, 1989).

Thus, some level of institutional independence should be considered a necessary but not sufficient condition for independence on the bench. Judicial behavior depends also on other elements, particularly the prevailing conception of judicial role – the way judges think they should behave – which in turn is influenced by legal education and, above all, by the reference group judges tend to adopt.[7] The reference group is composed of the "relevant others"[8] – in this case people whose opinion judges tend to take into account in their behavior – and its composition depends to a large extent on the general structural traits of the judiciary. More precisely, judge's impartial behavior seems to be related to her loyalty to the judicial organization, which is strongly influenced by her professional qualifications. As learning and experience increase a judge's competence to perform a specific role, they increase the process of internalizing the requirements of that role. People are more likely to internalize roles and rules that they fulfill effectively than those they do not.[9] Therefore, professionally qualified judges tend to identify more with their institutional role and to follow accepted rules of behavior. Moreover, well-qualified judges are likely to adopt their fellow judges and the legal profession in general as a reference group. An indirect check on judicial misbehavior is activated by the professional environment because judges tend to act according to the values and standards of the whole legal profession. In addition, a qualified judiciary, enjoying more prestige in society, tends to attract better candidates, generating a virtuous circle.

Two Legal Traditions in a Process of Change

The Western legal tradition shares common principles on the subject of judicial independence, such as appointment, at least in part, on merit, good working conditions, safeguards against disciplinary sanctions and removal.[10] Nevertheless some significant differences exist between the two main Western legal traditions: civil and common law. For example, because European continental judges are recruited without significant professional experience just after university studies, young judges are placed at the bottom of the judicial pyramid, and their organizational socialization is monitored through a career system; in other words, a pyramid of rank exists, and only judges who show they have internalized the requirements of the judicial organization, as defined by the senior judiciary, are promoted. This organizational setting affects the reference group of judges, which lies mainly inside the judiciary where judges tend to be professionally socialized. The hierarchical structure enables

---

[7] See, above all, Lawrence Baum, *Judges and Their Audiences: A Perspective on Judicial Behavior* (Princeton: Princeton University Press, 2006).

[8] Robert K. Merton, *Social Theory and Social Structure* (New York: The Free Press, 1968).

[9] James March, *A Primer on Decision Making* (New York: The Free Press, 1994) esp. pp. 65–68.

[10] See, for example, the Recommendation n. 12 (1994), adopted by the Committee of Ministers of the Council of Europe on "Independence, efficiency and role of judges."

high-ranking judges to influence the behavior of lower-ranking judges, because the higher ranks control promotions, transfers, and discipline. The influence of politics – usually the government, represented by the Ministry of Justice – tends to be restricted to the appointment of top judicial positions, whose occupants must be chosen among the senior judiciary. This institutional setting tends to promote a sort of executory definition of the judicial role: judges should be the mouth of the law and passively apply it as produced by the legislature. In practical terms, this conception supports a relatively passive stance of the judiciary vis-à-vis the political branches; creative judicial decisions are allowed only the extent to which they do not trigger negative reactions.[11]

In recent decades this picture has been altered. Judicial review of legislation has been introduced in many civil law countries. Although the final say is always entrusted to a special constitutional court staffed with prestigious lawyers, the change influences the way the judicial function is performed, increasing the creative role of judges and generally reducing the influence of the traditional senior judiciary.

In several countries, the role of higher judges has been influenced also by another significant institutional change: the creation of Judicial Councils, composed at least in part by judges elected by their colleagues, having wide competence on decisions affecting the status of judges. This institutional innovation has been motivated by the aim of strengthening judicial independence, because the traditional powers of the senior judiciary – and in some cases of the executive – have been correspondingly reduced. The innovation has brought about a significant strengthening of the institutional independence of the judiciary and, with the support of the Council of Europe and of the European Union, is presently adopted by an increasing number of European countries.[12]

On the other hand, in common law countries, because the practice is to appoint to the bench only professionally experienced lawyers, there is less emphasis on internal controls. Therefore, a civil law internal hierarchy does not exist, and the reference group tends to lie in large part outside the judiciary. However, there is a difference between the English judiciary, which tends to have a small professional reference group (traditionally, the Bar), and the American judiciary, which has a much more diverse composition and a recruitment process that incorporates different types of professional and political influences.[13]

---

[11] In other words, judges tend to act as simple executors of the legislature or as their explicit or implicit delegates. See Carlo Guarnieri and Patrizia Pederzoli, *The Power of Judges. A Comparative Study of Courts and Democracy* (Oxford: Oxford University Press, 2002), esp. pp. 68–71.

[12] See Carlo Guarnieri, "Autonomy and responsibility of the Council: should it be accountable for its actions?" (2007), http://www.coe.int/t/dg1/legalcooperation/judicialprofessions/ccje/meetings/Conferences/Conseils/Discours_en.asp.

[13] Recently England has radically reformed its system of judicial appointments. See John Bell, *Judiciaries within Europe* (Cambridge: Cambridge University Press, 2006), pp. 310–311.

Judicial Independence in Totalitarian and Authoritarian Regimes

The situation in nondemocratic regimes is different. Totalitarian regimes – characterized by a high degree of concentration of political power – try to enlist the judiciary in their attempts to exert control over society and implement deep social and political changes: courts tend to be simple tools of the regime. Judicial independence is extremely low, if not nonexistent, with judges appointed and dismissed at the pleasure of the regime. Judges are considered only an internal articulation of the whole state apparatus, and the judiciary is made up of members of the totalitarian party. Judicial elections, when present, only ratify the choice of the political leadership.[14] Hence, the values of judges necessarily mirror those of the regime, and their behavior is influenced accordingly, although there can be tension between central and local politicians. The administration of justice is therefore characterized by high politicization of judges, inadequacy of their professional qualifications, general public distrust of judicial institutions, and destruction of standards of impartiality in legal decision making. However, this situation also entails costs for the rulers of these regimes in that the legitimating function of the administration of justice is seriously impaired.[15] Moreover, the politicization of judges means that they are often elected at the local level and controlled by local political bosses. Therefore, to regain control of local courts, the center fosters a process of bureaucratization with a corresponding increase of hierarchical control but also of professionalism. However, more professional judges tend to have more consideration for the requirement of the judicial role and therefore, at least to some extent, for judicial impartiality, reducing somewhat the regime's room to maneuver. The result is often a continuous oscillation between politicization and bureaucratization.[16]

The picture of authoritarian countries is more complex. In comparison with totalitarian regimes, authoritarian regimes are characterized by limited pluralism and a lower degree of concentration of political power.[17] Concrete situations vary but, as a rule, the judiciary plays a minor role in the political system. The ordinary judiciary is only marginally involved in the policies of the regime and usually retains a modest degree of independence, as in Franco's Spain, Salazar's Portugal, and to some extent

---

[14] See, for example, the analysis of East Germany carried out by Otto Kirchheimer, *Political Justice* (Princeton: Princeton University Press, 1961) and of the USSR, by Peter Solomon, "Judicial Power in Authoritarian States: The Russian Experience," in Tom Ginsburg and Tamir Moustafa eds., *Rule by Law: The Politics of Courts in Authoritarian Regimes* (Cambridge: Cambridge University Press, 2008), pp. 261, 267.

[15] Peter Solomon, "Courts and Judges in Authoritarian Regimes," *World Politics*, vol. 60, p. 122 (2007).

[16] See the changing strategies pursued by the Soviet leadership described by Solomon, "Courts and Judges" and "Judicial Power."

[17] Juan Linz, "An Authoritarian Regime: The Case of Spain," in Erik Allardt and Yejo Littunen eds., *Cleavages, Ideologies and Party Systems* (Helsinki: Westermarck Society, 1964).

Mussolini's Italy.[18] The most interesting trait of these regimes is that the judicial system tends to show a bifurcated structure.[19] Politically significant cases are entrusted to regime-controlled courts or dealt with directly by the police or other security forces. In other cases – for example, those involving private parties or considered not to be of political significance – courts enjoy some measure of independence; in this way the regime can legitimize itself, at least to some extent. The bifurcated jurisdiction plays an important role: it assures the regime that politically significant cases will be dealt with by trusted courts and that its interests will not be threatened, with the consequence that a relative freedom can be allowed to ordinary judges in other cases. Thus, once a democratic transition begins, the ordinary courts are positioned to play a greater role in a broader range of cases. But even in the authoritarian phase, the scope of ordinary jurisdiction varies according to different factors, including the internal dynamics of the regime – with groups attempting to shield state organizations from political party influence – or the will of the regime in attracting foreign investments.[20] In any case, relatively independent courts play a positive but limited role in protecting citizens' rights and can be used by opposition groups as a forum for their grievances, because by going to court they can get significant visibility if not a favorable result.

Because judges are protected from blatant executive interference, they can develop a more professional outlook, with some emphasis on judicial independence and impartiality. This development is exemplified by the evolution of Franco's dictatorship in Spain. After the end of World War II, the regime – internationally isolated after the defeat of Nazism and Fascism – tried to legitimize itself by introducing a sort of "authoritarian rule of law."[21] In the intention of the regime, these changes were considered cosmetic. In fact, the ordinary judiciary began to enjoy a growing degree of autonomy: as a result, at the end of the 1960s democratic attitudes inside the judiciary were rising.[22] Thus, although the majority of Spanish judges were politically conservative or moderate, they welcomed the democratic transition.

Fascist Italy also demonstrates the complex role of the judiciary in authoritarian regimes. The Italian case is arguably more significant because the period between

---

[18] See Pedro Magalhaes, Carlo Guarnieri, and Yannis Kaminis, "Democratic Consolidation, Judicial Reform, and the Judicialization of Politics in Southern Europe," in Richard Gunther, Nikiforos Diamandouros, and Dimitri Sotiropoulos eds., *Democracy and the State in the New Southern Europe* (Oxford: Oxford University Press, 2006).

[19] This arrangement seems popular among authoritarian regimes. In fact, it has been adopted also in other cases, e.g., Egypt. See Moustafa, *The Struggle*.

[20] Moustafa, *The Struggle*; and G. Silverstein, "Globalization and the Rule of Law: 'A Machine That Runs of Itself,'" *International Journal of Constitutional Law*, vol. 1, n. 3, p. 427 (2003).

[21] Lisa Hilbink, "Politicising Law to Liberalize Politics: Anti-Francoist Judges and Prosecutors in Spain's Democratic Transition," in Terence Halliday, Lucien Karpik, and Malcolm Feeley eds., *Fighting for Political Freedom. Comparative Studies of the Legal Complex and Political Liberalism* (Oxford: Hart, 2007), pp. 418–423.

[22] José Juan Toharia "Judicial Independence in an Authoritarian Regime: The Case of Contemporary Spain," *Law & Society Review*, vol. 9, p. 475 (1975).

the two world wars was by no means favorable to democracy. However, ordinary judges continued to enjoy some degree of independence, even though the regime was becoming more totalitarian, especially after 1938. Most of all, there was no political penetration of the judicial corps. The traditional bureaucratic nature of the judiciary – with its emphasis on legal competence – was not altered and most judges remained faithful to the traditional stereotype of the judge as a nonpolitical professional whose task was to apply the law in a neutral way.[23]

In fact, the relative degree of independence enjoyed by the judiciary in author-itarian regimes allows the development of some form of professionalism. Much obviously depends on the organizational structure and on the fact that recruitment be based on merit with promotions based at least in part on professional evaluations carried out by judicial peers. The way professional socialization is organized and organizational rewards distributed is critical for the composition of the reference group of judges. For example, a system of promotions controlled by the senior judi-ciary – located at the center – is a way to check local influence. This is often the case, because national rulers are willing to employ courts as a check on local political bosses; the central government will try to establish some channels of influence with lower court judges, but it will allow some degree of independence of courts from local politics.[24] A hierarchical structure allows the regime to limit its influence to the top of the judicial hierarchy, entrusting senior judges with the task of day-to-day policing of the corps. In this situation, much depends on whether the judicial leadership consists of career judges or if external, more political appointments are allowed. Obviously, if only internal promotions are made, ambitious career judges will take into account the wishes of the political leadership, but they are unlikely to dismiss their rela-tionships with the judicial corps; they are likely to act as mediators – or buffers – between the regime and the judiciary.

The relative insulation of the ordinary judiciary from regime influence can have other significant consequences. First, the increasing professionalism of the corps – with judges spending most of their professional life inside the judiciary – is likely to support the development of a stronger corporate identity. Most of all, profession-alism means that the reference group of judges will be composed mostly of other lawyers, especially fellow judges and academics, with the consequence that it will be difficult for the regime to control the cultural orientation of judges. The influence

---

[23] This is true not only of the ordinary judiciary, dealing with ordinary civil and criminal cases, but also to a large extent of the top administrative court, the Council of State. See Guido Melis, "Il Consiglio di Stato," in Luciano Violante ed., *Storia d'Italia. Annali 14. Legge Diritto Giustizia* (Torino: Einaudi, 1998).

[24] An interesting example of this attitude is provided by Italy. When in the late 1930s the Fascist regime decided to "fascistize" the judiciary, the regime put pressure on judges to join the Fascist party. However, to avoid local party influence and to safeguard judicial impartiality, Fascist Justice Minister Grandi decided that all judges should have been affiliated with a special party unit located at the Ministry of Justice in Rome.

of the academy is particularly significant here, because – being more permeable to democratic influences – it can support a corresponding evolution in the judicial culture.[25]

The traditional nonpolitical definition of the judicial role may also have complex consequences. On the one hand, it limits the extent to which judges can defend citizens' rights, because they claim to be bound to the law, in this case a nonliberal authoritarian law.[26] On the other, it can shield the judiciary from political pressure and, with the return of democracy or liberalization of the regime, allows for a more liberal evolution of judicial decisions.

Another important element to take into account is the relationship between judges and prosecutors. In some civil law countries, judges and prosecutors belong to the same organization and tend to switch their roles often.[27] In any case, they tend to share the same institutional culture and are a significant part of each reference group. The consequences of this sort of setting are ambiguous. In the case of southern European authoritarianism, it has often fostered among ordinary prosecutors a "judicial" attitude, which is a relatively impartial posture toward the accused and, above all, a certain detachment from the police. On the other hand, the proximity between prosecution and adjudication can impinge on the appearance – and sometimes on the reality – of judicial impartiality. In this situation, much depends on the relative prestige of the two roles, which in turn is related to their respective professional requirements and the organizational rewards. More prestigious judges can become role models also for prosecutors, supporting their judicialization.

Summary

Judicial impartiality plays a role in assuring effective conflict resolution on the part of the judge. Institutional independence is, without a doubt, an important element in supporting judicial impartiality, but it is by no means decisive. The professional qualifications of the judge, her identification with the requirements of the judicial role – especially the impartial adjudication of disputes – and with the larger legal profession are even more significant.

Therefore, the composition of the reference group matters. In consolidated democracies, a distinction should be made between common law judiciaries where the reference group is composed mainly of legal professionals, in large part external to the judicial organization, and civil law systems where judges look mainly to their

---

[25] This has been, at least to some extent, the case of Spain and also Italy.

[26] See Lisa Hilbink, *Judges Beyond Politics in Democracy and Dictatorship* (Cambridge: Cambridge University Press, 2007), analyzing the failure of the Chilean judiciary to protect citizens' rights during the Pinochet dictatorship. Building on the Spanish and Italian case, she argues that only with the development of a sort of political mobilization inside the judiciary, which emerged later in the democratic context, could the judiciary overcome the limits of traditional legal positivism.

[27] Mirjan Damaska, *The Faces of Justice and State Authority* (New Haven: Yale University Press, 1986).

colleagues, especially senior higher-ranking judges. In the common law system, the stronger relationship with other legal professions will make the judge more responsive to the needs of the social environment. In the civil law system, "corporatism" – that is, the tendency to consider mainly the internal point of view – is more likely to prevail.

In both civil and common law democratic systems, politicians play a role, although in a way much less intrusive than in nondemocracies. Traditionally, in common law countries, political influence is channeled through the recruitment process. In the United States, for example, at the federal level the president and the Senate play a decisive role in judicial appointments, whereas at the state level judges are often directly elected. In civil law, political influence has traditionally been channeled through powers enjoyed by the Ministry of Justice in the appointment of the senior judiciary. However, top executives of the ministry, typically judges temporarily attached to the administration, often play a significant role in the process. In this way they act as influential mediators between politics and justice. As we have seen, in some civil law countries this role is today performed by Judicial Councils, composed of lay members – as a rule, appointed by the political branches – and judges elected by other judges. This development has increased the independence of the judiciary – especially internally, because the influence of the senior judiciary has been strongly circumscribed. It has also fostered political mobilization of the judicial corps, as in the growing role of unions and professional associations and the development of more activist conceptions of the judicial role.[28]

APPLICATION TO CHINA

What lessons can be learned from applying the preceding analysis of the transformation of European authoritarian regimes to China? The two situations are obviously very different. Chinese authoritarianism today is the result of the evolution of a totalitarian regime, in which the political penetration of courts was deep and judicial independence as well as judicial professionalism were all but nonexistent. Historically, China does not seem to have enjoyed a tradition of judicial independence and rule of law, even in the limited version of the civil law countries of continental Europe. Therefore, the point of departure is definitely less promising for rule of law and judicial independence than for Italy or Spain (or even, in some ways, for Germany[29]).

---

[28] Carlo Guarnieri, "Courts and Marginalized Groups: Perspectives from Continental Europe," *International Journal of Constitutional Law*, vol. 5, n. 2, p. 187 (2007).

[29] Although the Nazi regime was characterized by extensive and serious violations of the rule of law and courts were subject to all sorts of political interference, Germany still had a cultural tradition of government through law (Rechsstaat), which could – and has been – employed in the new democratic regime after the Second World War. See Guarnieri and Pederzoli, *The Power of Judges*.

On the other hand, many general institutional features of the Chinese judiciary are today similar to those of the civil law tradition: Chinese judges are above all civil servants. The judiciary is characterized by a general hierarchical bent, although the large size of the judiciary is an obstacle to strong central control. Moreover, the role of Chinese judges seems to be defined in relatively narrow terms: judicial review of legislation and administrative acts is limited and subject to significant restrictions.[30] All these traits point toward a relatively limited role of courts in Chinese politics.

Nevertheless, the limited political role of the courts should not be considered negative. In an authoritarian context, judicial review of legislation risks damage to the legitimacy of the courts. Courts are often posed a difficult dilemma: if they vigorously exercise judicial review, they collide with the regime and risk a dramatic reversal; if they do not, their prestige and legitimacy suffers, because they are seen as weak and supportive of the regime's policies. However, Chinese courts can play a positive role in supporting the development of a "thin" version of the rule of law. That is, courts may uphold the principle of legality; political power must follow general rules and, although it can alter those rules, it can do so only following previously enacted procedures (in Chinese, yifa zhiguo – government in accordance with law). Arbitrary deviations in specific cases are not allowed, and courts may quash government actions that lack a legal basis.[31]

As we have pointed out, the extent to which courts actually play an impartial role in a political system – for example, by faithfully applying a body of general rules – depends in a large part on the general organization of the judiciary and, more precisely, on the composition of the reference group of the judiciary. Recent reforms have strengthened the role of merit in recruitment and promotions, although the role of party organs remains significant, particularly in the appointment of the president of the courts and the promotion of the most senior members of the judiciary. The crucial point here is the way merit is defined and assessed: whether the most significant part in the process is played by higher-ranking judges or party officials, and in this last case the respective role of central versus local party branches. As for now, the judicial body seems to be split between higher-ranking judges, more professionally minded and whose points of reference seem to be other colleagues and the higher ranks of the party, and lower court judges, who take into account mainly the viewpoint of the local society and therefore of local party officials. The latter observation, however, is subject to two caveats. First, younger, more recently recruited judges in local courts tend to be better trained in law than older judges,

[30] My analysis of the Chinese case is based on Randall Peerenboom, "China's Judicial and Administrative Law Reforms in Comparative Context: Rising Expectations, Diminishing Returns and the Need for Deeper Reforms," the chapters in this volume, and the discussions at the December 2007 conference on judicial independence in China organized by the Oxford Foundation for Law, Justice and Society, Sciences Po, and the Institut des Hautes Etudes sur la Justice.

[31] See Martin Shapiro, "Courts in Authoritarian Regimes," in Ginsburg and Moustafa, *Rule by Law*, p. 329.

who are more receptive to local influence. Second, the professional qualification of judges in major urban areas even in lower courts may be quite high, particular in the civil division that handles commercial cases. Nevertheless, to strengthen the impartiality of courts, especially vis-à-vis local disputes, a greater role for the central judiciary seems crucial.

Less significant seems to be the role of the legal complex.[32] From this point of view China seems to exhibit to a large extent the state of "Balkanization" typical of the civil law tradition.[33] Lawyers, judges, and prosecutors pursue separate career paths and do not seem to engage in forms of coordinated activity. On the contrary, judges tend to distrust lawyers (and vice versa), sometimes with negative consequences for criminal defense lawyers or for those fighting for human rights.[34] There are also tensions in the relationship between public prosecutors and judges; judges are on the whole better educated and resent the extensive powers of the procuracy, especially the right of the procuracy to review final judicial decisions through the kangsu or protest procedure. In this case, however, the relative tension between these two actors can play a positive role in supporting a more detached stance of the judge toward prosecution and, possibly, more impartial decisions.

Unlike in other civil law systems, the role of legal academia also appears to be more limited. Although not without influence, especially on technical matters, academics are not unified in their political views or their stance toward legal reforms.[35] Some support the development of democracy and constitutionalism in China. Others are critical of democracy – at least in the Western meaning of the word – with some influenced by socialist and/or Marxist thinking. Others think that before introducing democracy China needs to strengthen the rule of law.

Generally speaking, in China national political leaders are interested in developing some sort of rule of law, therefore strengthening judicial independence. There are obvious economic reasons behind these attitudes because the certainty of the law is positively related to economic growth. Also, political considerations can play a role because courts independent from local bosses can act as a check on their power and, if organized in a way to be responsive to central interests, help the center control the periphery. In this endeavor, much depends on the process of professionalization and the way it will be organized, that is the degree of influence of the center – high court judges and central party officials – versus the local political systems. If successful,

---

[32] See Halliday, Karpik, and Feeley, *Fighting for Political Freedom.*

[33] See John Merryman, *The Civil Law Tradition* (Palo Alto, CA: Stanford University Press, 1985), p. 102.

[34] See Terence Halliday and Sida Liu, "Birth of a Liberal Moment? Looking Through a One-Way Mirror at Lawyers' Defence of Criminal Defendants in China," in Halliday, Karpik, and Feeley, *Fighting for Political Freedom*; and Chapter 6 in this volume.

[35] For the different positions inside academia see Randall Peerenboom, "Searching for Political Liberalism in All Wrong Places: the Legal Profession in China as the Leading Edge of Political Reform?" in Bryant Garth and Yves Dezalay eds., *Lawyers and the Construction of Rule of Law: National and Transnational Processes* (forthcoming).

the likely result will be a sort of "thin" version of the rule of law: a situation not far away from that prevailing in most continental European states before the middle of the twentieth century. Longer term, the system need not necessarily evolve into a stronger form of rule of law, at least not while the party remains in control of the legislative and constituent powers.[36] However, a judicial system assuring the certainty of the law – even though conceived as the product of positive legislation – is in any case an important achievement and, possibly, a step toward further developments.

POLICY RECOMMENDATIONS

Given the experiences of southern European authoritarian regimes, the following policies seem most likely to support the development of judicial impartiality in the context of an evolving or liberalizing authoritarian regime in China:

(i) an effort should be made to increase the guarantees of independence and, above all, the status of the judges, not so much by increasing institutional insulation but rather by introducing professional criteria in the recruitment process and by generally improving working conditions. This will have the additional positive consequence that bright and motivated candidates will want to become judges. This process is already under way but should be deepened and accelerated to instill professional values deeply into the judicial corps;

(ii) the general level of professionalization of judges should be strengthened not only in the recruitment phase but through a judge's career. This requires permanent training and a prominent role for professional evaluations in the promotion process. There has been progress on this front, although the complex structure of the Chinese judicial system makes ongoing training difficult. More could be done, however, to ensure that merit is the main, although not the exclusive, basis for promotion;

(iii) the fragmented nature of the Chinese legal complex tends to reduce the potential influence of lawyers and academics on the judiciary. Although their influence is likely to increase in the long run, it is also likely that judicial appointments and promotions will be subject to political considerations. However, the political appointment of top judges, if based primarily on merit, can have positive consequences. For example, an appointee with political capital may use that capital to defend judicial independence in individual cases or particular areas of law, to push for institutional changes that strengthen the judiciary vis-á-vis other organs of state power, and to provide effective leadership to the judicial corps;[37]

---

[36] The example of Singapore seems, from this point of view, particularly telling. See Gordon Silverstein, "Singapore: The Exception That Proves Rules Matter," in Ginsburg and Moustafa, *Rule by Law*.

[37] Shapiro, "Courts in Authoritarian Regimes," p. 332.

(iv) finally, as pointed out above, the reference group of judges is strongly influenced by the judicial organization. For instance, a centralized judiciary – in which senior judges at the center control promotions and the allocation of benefits – will be more responsive to the needs of national politicians and will likely ensure a higher degree of impartiality, at least in most cases. However, general working conditions must also be taken into account. If crucial resources – like judicial buildings, administrative staff, and so on – depend on the local government, local points of view will inevitably influence the behavior of local judges.

13

Judicial Independence in East Asia

Lessons for China

Tom Ginsburg*

Like many countries around the world, China is increasingly interested in promoting the rule of law and judicial independence. A competent and professional judiciary is a central component of the "socialist rule of law," and China has made significant investments in institutional quality. Scholars disagree, however, about the efficacy of these reforms to date.[1] Just as we have few appropriate points of comparison for assessing China, China has few points of reference for designing reforms.

This chapter explores the experience of China's East Asian neighbors with regard to judicial independence, with an eye toward drawing lessons for China's own reforms. Japan, South Korea, and Taiwan collectively provide a useful vantage point to examine developments in China because their rapid growth from the 1950s through the 1990s represents the greatest sustained example of rapid growth in world history. The only comparable period of growth is that of contemporary China, now nearing the end of its third decade. The East Asian cases are also relevant to China because the countries in the region share certain cultural traditions, and because many of them developed their judicial systems during periods of authoritarian governance. Finally, the East Asian cases, like contemporary China, seem to challenge the conventional wisdom that a powerful legal system is necessary for sustained economic development.[2] My argument is that these cases provide nuanced lessons for the Chinese case about the definition of and conditions for judicial independence.

---

* Thanks to Jianlin Chen for research assistance.

1 Compare Stanley Lubman, "Looking for Law in China," *Columbia Journal of Asian Law*, Vol. 20, no. 1, pp. 1–92 (2006) with Randall Peerenboom, *China's Long March Toward Rule of Law* (New York: Cambridge University Press, 2002).

2 John Ohnesorge, "Developing Development Theory: Law and Development Orthodoxies and the Northeast Asian Experience," University of Wisconsin Working Paper No. 1024 (2007), available at http://papers.ssrn.com/sol3/papers.cfm?abstract_id=916781; Randall Peerenboom, *China Modernizes: Threat to the West or Model for the Rest* (New York: Oxford University Press, 2007).

The chapter begins by considering the problem of judicial independence in general, focusing on authoritarian settings. It tries to unpack the notion of independence. It then describes the experiences of Japan, Korea, and Taiwan in some depth and concludes with thoughts on implications for the Chinese case. It argues that a realistic and achievable level of judicial independence can be realized should China structure its judiciary roughly along Japanese lines, as has already been done in Korea and Taiwan.

THE CONCEPT OF INDEPENDENCE

Judicial independence has become like freedom: everyone wants it but no one knows quite what it looks like, and it is easiest to observe in its absence. We know when judges are dependent on politicians or outside pressures, but we have more difficulty saying definitively when judges are independent. Still, the normative consensus suggests that there is something important about the concept.

And the normative consensus is clear. Virtually every developing country has some program of legal reform focused on the judiciary, and billions of dollars have been spent promoting independence. The General Assembly of the United Nations supports it, as do governments both democratic and authoritarian. All this suggests that there is a consensus that judicial independence is important, but also that the concept risks being diluted so thin as to be meaningless.

More rigorous definition is in order.[3] Nuno Garoupa and I have laid out a model in which a judiciary can shift along two dimensions: independence versus accountability and strength versus weakness.[4] A weak and politically dependent judiciary might, through careful decision making and institutional reforms, be able to build up a space for autonomy over time. As the courts become independent, however, they may expand their reach and intervene into matters of public policy. In some circumstances this can provoke reforms to enhance accountability of the judiciary, such as improved transparency and external involvement in the governance of the courts. This heightened access for outsiders, in turn, might reduce independence and strength of the courts.

The concept of independence can also vary across areas of the law, types of cases, and courts within a single jurisdiction. Judiciaries differ in their levels of independence and also the scope of activity over which they are independent. Independence is thus a two-dimensional problem: one can imagine an independent judiciary with a narrow scope of activity or a judiciary that is highly responsive to manipulation that governs a wide range of activity, as well as the inverse configurations.

---

[3] Stephen B. Burbank and Barry Friedman eds., *Judicial Independence at the Crossroads: An Interdisciplinary Approach* (Thousand Oaks: Sage Publications, 2002).

[4] See Nuno Garoupa and Tom Ginsburg, "Guarding the Guardians: Judicial Councils and Judicial Independence" *American Journal of Comparative Law* vol. 57, no. 1 (2009), pp. 201–232.

Notwithstanding all these nuances, at its core, judicial independence involves the ability and willingness of courts to decide cases in light of the law without undue regard to the views of other government actors. Given all the other values we might want out of a judiciary, such as consistency, accuracy, predictability, and speedy decision making, it is not clear that independence is the supreme quality we want to maximize. But it is, nevertheless, an important one in many definitions of judicial quality, and a judiciary that repeatedly decides cases in legally implausible ways under the influence of government actors is likely to suffer a decline in its reputation for independence and quality.[5] Furthermore, independence can enhance the overall reputation of the regime. This explains why a wide variety of regimes are willing to cede some autonomy to court systems.

JUDICIAL INDEPENDENCE IN AUTHORITARIAN STATES

It is becoming increasingly clear that democracy is not a prerequisite for judicial independence. Many general theories of judicial independence focus on the link with political competition, and it is probably true that judges as a general matter have greater levels of independence in democracies than in dictatorships. However, it would be an overstatement to say that democracy is required for any judicial independence at all. Courts in authoritarian Korea and Taiwan as well as Meiji Japan, for example, showed a willingness to rule against the government on occasion. The distinction between democracy and dictatorship has to do with the scope of judicial independence and the range of transactions over which independence is exercised.

There are several reasons an authoritarian government may want to empower the judiciary in certain areas and grant it genuine autonomy. For many years, scholars have believed that an independent judiciary is useful for economic predictability. Entrepreneurs who know that they can go to independent courts are able to transact with a wider number of market players and be less fearful of government arbitrariness. These things tend to encourage growth. A regime that wants to make a credible commitment to the market may set up courts with the power to rule against the regime in economic cases.

Another reason to empower courts is to provide a mechanism for monitoring the performance of lower level bureaucrats. All governments face the problem of monitoring their own employees, who may abuse their office. If enough lower level bureaucrats abuse citizens, the regime as a whole will lose legitimacy. But it is difficult for politicians at the center to monitor all their employees. A limited regime of administrative complaints by the public can shine the light on bureaucratic malfeasance, informing the regime center and improving the quality of government.

---

[5] Nuno Garoupa and Tom Ginsburg, *Reputation and the Industrial Organization of the Judiciary*, Manuscript.

A third reason regimes may want to empower courts is for legitimacy. Legitimacy comes in many forms, but having a court bless regime policies can help convince citizens that those policies are just. Courts can also legitimate the regime in the eyes of foreigners, be they donors or other powers with whom the regime must interact. Furthermore, high-quality justice can be provided to citizens and help legitimate the regime.

We see several examples of nondemocracies that demonstrate judicial independence over some scope of transactions. Singapore, for example, has a high-quality judiciary: indeed, by some survey measures it is the best judiciary in the world. Singapore's chief justice is perhaps the highest paid such official in the world, making more than U.S. $1 million per year in total compensation.[6] The courts regularly rule against the government in routine matters, and the government always obeys. Sometimes, obedience is purely formal. In one prominent case, the courts found that the government had failed to follow rules for an arrest under the Internal Security Act. The government released the prisoner in question – but immediately rearrested the prisoner following proper procedures.[7] The ruling was only possible because of a certain degree of judicial independence.

Notwithstanding this rosy picture, Singapore's courts avoid ruling against the governing party and indeed have been used to silence the opposition through libel actions. One can characterize the judiciary as having a good deal of independence over economic and administrative matters, but little in the realm of politics. This example highlights that the scope of independence matters as much as its level.

The Singapore model may or may not be transferable to China. There are obviously vast differences in terms of scale and manageability. Furthermore, Singapore's judiciary has the advantage of having come from the common law tradition, in which independence is a more longstanding ideological and institutional goal. Nevertheless, the case is important to consider because it provides a plausible model of a high-quality judiciary that nevertheless has avoided "judicializing" politics. Independence can be maintained for the vast majority of cases without directly threatening core regime goals.

One also sees relevant experience in the northeast Asian cases. Most accounts of rapid growth in the region do not emphasize the role of law or the judiciary. Instead, analysts focus on wise bureaucrats, political stability, trade policy, and the American security umbrella as the keys to rapid growth. But the northeast Asian countries also featured a particular form of legal system that, by conventional measures, was fairly independent. There may therefore be lessons for China in understanding the East Asian cases.

---

[6] Gordon Silverstein, "Singapore: The Exception that Proves Rules Matter," *in* Tom Ginsburg and Tamir Moustafa eds., *Rule by Law: The Politics of Courts in Authoritarian Regimes* (New York: Cambridge University Press, 2008).

[7] Silverstein, "Singapore."

NORTHEAST ASIAN EXPERIENCE

Japan

To understand the northeast Asian pattern, we must start in the nineteenth century when Japan undertook its decision to modernize after two centuries of isolation. Pressured from abroad and confronted by unequal treaties that immunized foreigners from Japan's "barbaric" courts, Japanese leaders in the Meiji period realized that national independence required a set of strong institutions. They built a strong bureaucracy, an industrial base, and a legal system along Western lines.

A leading legal history of the Meiji period divides legal reform into three phases.[8] The first phase was from the Restoration in 1868 to the promulgation of the Imperial Edict of 1881, which announced the formation of a national Diet and drafting of a constitution; the second phase was from 1881 through 1898, during which time the constitution and great codes were promulgated; and the third phase lasted from 1898 through the death of the Meiji emperor in 1912, a period of implementation and consolidation rather than dramatic legislative change.

It should be emphasized that the legal system was not demanded from within but rather was adopted as a response to the unequal treaties. Only when the Western powers viewed Japan as having a "civilized" legal system would the treaties be revised. The early Meiji reformers thus placed great emphasis on the adoption of substantive law and, crucially, the creation of a high-quality judiciary.

The appointment of Shinpei Eto as Minister of Justice in June 1872 led to a series of radical institutional changes. Eto, leader of the militant faction in the government that sought to mimic Western imperialism with an invasion of Korea (and later leader of a revolt against the new government), clearly saw formal legalism as crucial to maintaining national strength.[9] Eto was also a centralizer, trying to take away jurisdiction from the local governments and centralize it in the Ministry of Justice responsible for the courts.[10] In keeping with the notion of legal institutions as embodying "universally recognized principles," the judiciary was established as a separate branch of government under the supervision of the Ministry of Justice.[11] Professionals in the ministry would issue advice to judges of the courts when faced with questions of interpretation or application of law. The Minister of Justice was the presiding judge of the highest court, so separation of powers was incomplete in this early phase. Only in 1875 was the Great Court of Judicature established as the

---

[8] Ryosuke Ishii ed., *Japanese Legislation in the Meiji Era* 13 (tr. William Chambliss, Tokyo: Pan-Pacific Press, 1958).

[9] Hiyoshi Sonoda, *Eto Shimpei Den* (Tokyo: Taikōdō, 1968).

[10] Even this formal shift did not change the fact that actual establishment of prefectural courts under national administration was slow, leaving the prefectural authorities in control even after the abolishment of the *han*.

[11] The Shiho Shokumu Teisei (Justice Staff Regulations) issued in September 1872.

highest judicial authority.[12] In 1877, qualifications for judges and prosecutors were issued and executive officials barred from serving concurrently as judges.[13] Thus we see in this early period the first steps, if still tentative, toward establishment of autonomous legal institutions.

In 1881, the emperor issued a rescript calling for the creation of a national assembly and the drafting of a constitution.[14] This occurred in reaction to growing calls for more rapid reform and in the wake of internal challenges to central authority including the Satsuma rebellion of 1877. From then on, legal reforms become more coherent, less piecemeal, and centered around the nascent institutions that had emerged in the early Meiji years. The 1884 rules on appointment of judges and the 1886 Court Organization Act established an examination requirement for judges and prosecutors. Reappointment of existing judges and prosecutors was not required, so the movement toward a professional judiciary was not fully articulated, but by the mid-1880s the direction seemed clear. The judicial system was reformed by organic law in 1890 just after the adoption of the Meiji Constitution.

By the 1890s, the judiciary in Japan had emerged as a discrete branch of government, with a strong reputation for consistency and an insistence on resisting overt political pressure. An important test of the new reforms came in a famous incident in 1891 when a policeman attempted to kill the Russian crown prince at Otsu. Ordinarily, attempted murder was punishable only by life in prison, but the government sought the death penalty by analogy to offenses against the Japanese imperial household. Resisting this pressure, the courts declined to issue a death sentence, establishing the principle of judicial independence in the Japanese context. This ruling became a wellspring for the traditions of institutional autonomy and freedom from pressures that remain the hallmark of the Japanese judiciary.

The story of the development of judicial autonomy in Japan is a remarkable one in comparative terms. Before Eto's reforms of 1872, the notion of a distinct branch of government for judicial affairs seemed, to use the most appropriate term, foreign. Within two and a half decades, a profession had been created and judges had developed enough sense of professional autonomy to resist executive pressure from an authoritarian government. Although the initial motivation for creating a judiciary may have largely been symbolic, designed to satisfy foreigners that Japanese justice was not barbaric, it led to genuine institutional autonomy rather quickly. It is instructive that judicial independence was maintained to a greater extent in wartime Japan than in Nazi Germany.

---

[12] Much of the modern judicial structure can be traced back to the Choshu leader Kido Takayoshi, who secured the establishment of a supreme court at the same time the Genro-in was established in 1875. An initial proposal that the Genro have formal power to review legislation was rejected at Kido's insistence.

[13] Takkaki Hattori, "The Legal Profession in Japan: Its Historical Development and Present State," in *Law in Japan: The Legal Order in a Changing Society* ed., Arthur T. von Mehren (Cambridge: Harvard University Press, 1963).

[14] Reprinted in Ishii, *Japanese Legislation*, p. 720.

The tradition continued in the postwar democratic era.[15] The Japanese judicial system was organized hierarchically, with effective control at the top, and developed an internalized institutional emphasis on providing like solutions to like cases, helping to render their decision making predictable and contributing to a reasonably sound business environment. Courts had a capacity to handle civil and commercial disputes, but the number of judges was kept low in comparative terms. This in turn helped keep litigation rates low in Japan relative to other advanced industrial democracies.

Some scholars have focused on the ability of the Secretariat of the Supreme Court to manipulate judicial career incentives by making assignments to different parts of the country.[16] There seems to be some evidence that judges who decided against the ruling party in a series of cases in the early 1970s suffered some career penalties. However, the judiciary as a whole is structurally independent, and no one has asserted any overt interference with the Secretariat of the Supreme Court. Whatever else their faults, the Japanese judges are generally seen as free from corruption so prevalent elsewhere in the region. No judge has ever been found to be corrupt, quite different from the bureaucrats or politicians in Japan.[17] Judges have a strong sense of corporate identity and have internalized an ideology of following the law. The Japanese situation can be characterized as one in which collective independence is secure, even if individual judges are subject to pressures to conform.

It is worth restating how remarkable the Japanese story is from a comparative perspective. Billions of dollars have been spent in judicial reform and institutional development programs globally, yet we have virtually no evidence of any judiciary shifting from being characterized as dependent to one that is independent. The Meiji Japan story, like that of contemporary China, really involves institutional creation rather than institutional transformation. Thus the issue was not replacing an institutional culture but creating one from scratch, which is perhaps surprisingly an easier task. The case suggests that genuine judicial independence is at least one possible outcome of the current reform programs in China.

Taiwan and Korea

Taiwan and Korea were colonized by Japan in 1895 and 1910 respectively, and the basic institutional structures of government were transferred, including the legal

---

[15] See generally John Haley, *Authority without Power: Law and the Japanese Paradox* (New York: Oxford University Press, 1990).

[16] J. Mark Ramseyer and Eric B. Rasmusen, *Measuring Judicial Independence: The Political Economy of Judging in Japan* (Chicago: University of Chicago Press, 2003); Setsuo Miyazawa, "Administrative Control of Japanese Judges," *Kobe University Law Review*, vol. 25 (1991).

[17] See John Haley, "The Japanese Judiciary: Maintaining Integrity, Autonomy, and the Public Trust." Lectures and Occasional Papers, Whitney R. Harris Institute for Global Legal Studies, no. 3. Washington University School of Law. http:// law.wustl.edu/igls/lecturespapers/2003–3Haley-JapaneseJudiciary.html; see discussion in Frank K. Upham, "Political Lackeys or Faithful Public Servants: Two Views of the Japanese Judiciary," *Law and Social Inquiry* vol. 30, pp. 421–455 (2005).

system. Within two decades a Japanese-style colonial government structure was in place, including cabinet government, courts, police, and legislation.[18] From early on, though, law was adopted not as an instrument to maintain independence in the face of Western colonialism, as it had been in Japan, but as a tool to deprive Korea and Taiwan of independence in the interests of Japanese colonialism. Judges were primarily Japanese, although Koreans and to a lesser extent Taiwanese could become judges. As the colonial period went on, more qualified local candidates appeared because of the creation of the imperial universities that became Seoul National University and National Taiwan University. These trained local talent who increasingly joined the various legal professions, including the judiciary.

After independence, the basic structure of the Japanese judiciary as a discrete bureaucracy survived in Korea. Judges were trained with lawyers and prosecutors in a special program at Seoul National University and later at a training school run by the Supreme Court. This ensured that the courts themselves played the central role in socializing the legal profession and allowed judges to internalize the positivist ideology that characterizes Japanese courts today. Judges saw themselves as servants of the law, charged with deciding cases consistently.

In the early 1960s, Korea experienced a brief period of democracy, and the courts became increasingly willing to decide cases against the government. But the scope of independence was limited and eventually constrained under the military regime of Park Chung Hee. When the Supreme Court decided cases against the perceived interest of Park, he reappointed members of the court, excluding those who had voted against him. He also passed a new constitution, the so-called Yushin Constitution of 1972, without provision for judicial review. During the 1970s, judges were relatively quiescent in deciding cases against the government. Still, ideals of independence were present.

The story in Taiwan is different. The island had a longer and more positive experience of Japanese colonialism, and those Taiwanese who had become lawyers and judges were familiar with the Japanese tradition of judicial independence, such as it was. Taiwan was integrated into the Republic of China with the Japanese defeat and soon became the last bastion of Chiang Kai-shek's regime. Like other aspects of the government structure, the judiciary was then dominated by "mainlanders" who had retreated with Chiang during the loss of the mainland. Some of these judges were of high quality, but they were unable to exercise independence in cases of importance to the regime. In the 1950s, the Kuomintang (KMT) passed a law making it harder for the Taiwanese constitutional court to exercise judicial review, but the KMT never had to take the power away from the courts. As time went on, however, Taiwanese judges began to rise in the judicial hierarchy, and they tended to internalize the Japanese rather than the Republican Chinese tradition. The seeds of judicial independence were cultivated by these judges.

---

[18] James Palais, *Politics and Policy in Traditional Korea* (Cambridge: Harvard University Press, 1976).

One can think of the East Asian configuration as having independent courts with a fairly small scope of activity. In both Korea and Taiwan, in the economic sphere, the judiciary retained autonomy. It had a distinct professional ideology and norms of neutrality in most cases. Both regimes had at least a nominal commitment to the rule of law and legality, which prevented them from, say, jailing judges wholesale.[19] Independence, however, did not extend to control of politically sensitive matters. Both the KMT and the Korean strongmen developed means of monitoring and disciplining judges, particularly in politically sensitive disputes. These mechanisms of discipline were easier for a Leninist party like the KMT to implement than, say, Park Chung Hee in Korea, whose interference with judicial independence was clumsier.

The scope of judicial activity increased dramatically in Korea and Taiwan beginning with democratization in the late 1980s.[20] The courts helped resolve several crucial cases in the democratization process in the early 1990s. In particular, newly emboldened constitutional courts became more active, striking legislation of the old regime and seeking to provide a more solid legal basis for governance. Many decisions had to do with administrative law and criminal procedure, two areas where the courts could play a constructive role in ensuring responsiveness of low-level government actors to new elites. As political competition increased, the courts began to play an even more important role. When divided government emerged in Taiwan in 2000, for example, the constitutional court became the locus of a major dispute around the country's fourth nuclear plant. The court played an important role in encouraging the parties to come to a political compromise. In Korea, the constitutional court was called on to decide whether the elected president should be removed in an impeachment. It allowed him to remain in office but also reaffirmed that the court would be the decision maker in this and other highly sensitive matters in the future. In both countries, the courts enjoy a good reputation for quality and independence. The story of Korea and Taiwan after democratization is one of expanding both the scope and level of independence at the same time.

In Japan, which has remained a democracy continuously since 1946, the courts have expanded authority in the last decade as part of an overall reform of the legal system. These reforms have not focused on independence per se; indeed, some reforms such as introducing a jury system and the involvement of the public in judicial appointment processes seem designed to enhance transparency and accountability rather than independence. But the scope of judicial activity seems to be increasing

---

[19] Weitseng Chen, "Cross the Bridge When There? China-Taiwan Comparison of Rule-of-Law-Without-Democracy Strategy for Transition," *Yale Law School Student Scholarship Series* #55 (2007), available at http://lsr.nellco.org/yale/student/papers/55.

[20] See generally Tom Ginsburg, *Judicial Review in New Democracies: Constitutional Courts in Asian Cases* (New York: Cambridge University Press, 2003).

with nascent signs of more judicialization.[21] The focus on independence has been less clear than those in Korea or Taiwan, however, in part because the judges had such a high baseline of autonomy.

LESSONS FOR JUDICIAL INDEPENDENCE IN CHINA

What lessons can be drawn for China from these cases? An initial point is that more attention should be placed on the best historical antecedent for China's reform program, the experience of Meiji Japan. Like China's leaders today, the Meiji reformers sought to enhance national power and independence through legal reform. Their focus was largely instrumental: judicial independence was part of a package of modernizations that included industrial and military modernization as well. Similarly, the system was an oligarchy of sorts, although China's Communist Party is far more institutionalized than the personalized Meiji system.[22]

It is also worth recalling China's early twentieth-century attempts to develop the legal system were directly influenced by Meiji developments, because Japan was the sole example of a non-Western power that had voluntarily integrated Western law. Japanese served as legal advisers, drafting statutes and sharing experiences.[23] In addition, Japan adopted the Western colonial rhetoric about law that had itself prompted Japan's own reform. Thus Korea's legal system was deemed uncivilized and unable to protect the rights of Japanese nationals there. China's own republican reformers sought security from Japan through modernization, including modernization of law.[24] The first attempts to reform the punishment system, set up the judiciary as a distinct branch of government, and establish independence in adjudication were developed both in reaction to, and informed by, the Japanese experience. These attempts were ultimately unsuccessful, but not because of the actions of judges, who at times exhibited great courage in defending independence.[25] Rather, the politicization of the judiciary under the Kuomintang and the escalating civil war doomed the first attempts at developing judicial independence.[26]

---

[21] C. Neal Tate and Thorsten Vallinder, *The Global Expansion of Judicial Power* (New York: NYU Press, 1995).

[22] Peter R. Moody, Jr., "Genro Rule in China and Japan: A Comparative Perspective," *Journal of Chinese Political Science* vol. 12, no. 1 (April 2007), pp. 29–48.

[23] Xiaoqun Xu, *Trial of Modernity: Judicial Reform in Early Twentieth Century China 1901–37* (Stanford: Stanford University Press, 2008), p. 52 reports on leading scholar Ogawa Shigejiro advising on the Prison Law of the Great Qing.

[24] Xu, *Trial of Modernity*, p. 1. Xu quotes Shi Lianfang, writing in the *Falu pinglun*: "The so-called modern state is defined not only by whether it is independent and unified, capable of protecting its own people and fulfilling international obligations, but also, as one of the main conditions, by whether it is a state of 'the rule of law.' If we destroy the rule of law ourselves, that would be no less than to provide evidence for Japan's international propaganda!"

[25] Xu gives the example of Lu Xingyuan, Chief Justice of Jiangsu Provincial Court, removed because he refused to hand over a communist suspect arrested in the International Settlement to Chinese authorities.

[26] Arguably, one can see earlier antecedent notions of judicial independence in some of the Chinese imperial institutions. Xu, *Trial of Modernity*, p. 17.

One of the most important lessons to be drawn from the East Asian countries is the collective nature of judicial independence in civil law systems. The judiciaries in all three countries functioned as unified national bureaucracies. In contrast with China (and the United States) where most courts are responsive to local governments that select and (until recently) funded them, the East Asian cases saw the judiciary as another branch of national government. In Japan, judges spend their careers rotating in two- to four-year stints in various regions around the country, helping to reinforce a sense of corporate identity in the judiciary and preventing judges from becoming too embedded in local matters. In Korea and Taiwan, judges can also rotate to different positions and undergo collective training and socialization.

The East Asian countries also instituted severe tests to ensure that only the best and brightest could enter the judiciary. In Japan and Korea, the test is a generalized bar exam that prospective judges, prosecutors, and lawyers must all pass, and the pass rates fluctuated between 2 and 4 percent for most of the postwar period. Taiwan's judicial exam did not include practicing lawyers and had a slightly higher although still miniscule passage rate. This ensured that judicial service was relatively high status, what Dezalay and Garth characterize as an "ornamental Confucianism."[27] No doubt it also helped dampen judicial corruption that has plagued so many other countries.

Both of these conditions lack in contemporary China. Although China has done a good job of improving the qualifications of judges so that a majority now have higher education, that process must continue. The key issue is not just education but status, and that is far harder to engineer. If status is entirely identified with money, it will be difficult to draw the most talented jurists into the judiciary. South Korea confronts this problem today because of patterns of retirement by judges into the legal profession once they reach a certain age. This practice has caused concerns about the erosion of judicial independence because it is feared that judges are capitalizing on their connections in arguing cases before the courts they used to serve.

By far the greatest threat to judicial independence in China comes from the fact that judges are dependent on local governments for appointment, promotion, and, until recently, funding and material security. This has been widely remarked upon and even identified as a priority for the national government to some degree.[28] There is seen to be a severe risk of local favoritism, the antithesis of independence. The issue also goes to status: when funded and managed by local governments, judges are likely to be viewed as one more government agency rather than being independent actors who can hold government accountable.

---

[27] Yves Dezalay and Bryant Garth, "International Strategies and Local Transformations: Preliminary Observations of the Position of Law in the Field of State Power in Asia: South Korea," in William Alford and Setsuo Miyzazawa eds., *Raising the Bar: The Emerging Legal Profession in East Asia* (Cambridge: Harvard University Press, 2007), pp. 92–94.

[28] Opinion of the Central Political-Legal Commission on Several Issues in the Deepening of Reform in the Judicial System and the Work Mechanism, covered in http://news.sina.com.cn/c/2008–12–05/ 01571678500o.shtml.

Greater centralization – and professionalization – is now a priority for the Supreme People's Court, which has improved its own status at the national level and has contributed to the resolution of a number of high-profile policy matters. Supervision and management of local courts by superior courts will, of course, burden those at higher levels. Yet it seems essential for the collective independence of the judiciary as a whole.

Another point is that independence limited to routine cases, a la Singapore, is hardly the ultimate ideal. Judicial independence is most tested in high-profile national cases and has been demonstrated clearly by constitutional courts in Korea and Taiwan in recent years. Although a system of judicial review of legislative action has been called for in China, it is likely some years away. Such a power effectively exercised, however, is the hallmark of judicial independence and the rule of law, for government will then be responsive to the law in matters great and small.

It is worth noting that the features I have emphasized in the Northeast Asian cases, namely a meritocratically selected national bureaucracy with a rotation system, parallel features of governance in imperial China. Certainly there was no judicial independence in the structural sense in imperial China: magistrates were all-purpose officials who combined executive and judicial functions. Nevertheless, the overarching concern with the risk of corruption informed all aspects of institutional design. The ancient "rule of avoidance" involved sending magistrates far from their home regions and was employed to ensure that magistrates did not become overly involved in local politics, enhancing impartial adjudication and independence.[29] Judges in China today enjoy no such institutional insulation from the governments that pay them.

CONCLUSION

The east Asian countries provide a viable and convenient model of developing judicial independence that holds important lessons for China. The cases illustrate that unpacking judicial independence, and viewing it not as a unitary quality but one that varies across time, space, and area of law, has payoffs. Two points in particular stand out: the possibility of independence in an authoritarian setting and the importance of collective independence.

First, it is certainly possible to speak of independence even in an authoritarian political system like contemporary China. Like democracies, authoritarian governments have some incentive to empower judiciaries and grant them genuine independence, as do democratic governments. The difference is that the scope

---

[29] Ironically, this rendered the magistrate more dependent on sometimes corrupt local county functionaries, undermining official goals to some degree. Another imperial antecedent for collective independence was the extensive system of appeal, designed to ensure some modicum of independence in adjudication as errors would be corrected by higher level officials.

of judicial independence in authoritarian regimes is less wide than in democracies, even if courts enjoy high levels of independence in particular areas. Typically authoritarians will empower courts to help provide predictability in the economic sphere without hindering core regime policies or interfering in the political sphere. Sometimes authoritarians also use courts to discipline lower-level bureaucrats and provide legitimacy. For all of these reasons, we can be optimistic of the continued trajectory of judicial independence in China, at least for the vast majority of cases that do not have major political overtones.

Second, one can distinguish independence of the judiciary from independence of judges. The countries under consideration have tended to utilize mechanisms that emphasize collective independence of the judiciary as a whole rather than the independence of individual judges. The Japanese model features a hierarchically organized judiciary, with strong internal controls and a strong sense of corporate identity among the judges. The judiciary as a whole, because it can act with relative uniformity, can compete for resources in competition with other government agencies. It also involves a difficult examination, ensuring both high quality and high status for judges. Judges serving in a bureaucratic hierarchy, under central national control, can develop a consciousness of their role and internalize norms of professional behavior. In turn this makes them more effective judges, more likely to be trusted with important issues by the state and by private parties. They are not, however, independent of other judges in making decisions.

Becoming more like Japan in terms of judicial independence actually involves a return to China's not-so-distant past. The reforms suggested are in fact consistent with aspects of China's ancient legal tradition, even if they are best exemplified today by China's neighbors. A unified, hierarchically organized judiciary is the best route to achieving China's goals for legal reform, whatever they may be.

Index